"...a tender and moving biography of this highly improper Philadelphian. Chippy Patterson emerges from these pages as a blend of St. Francis of Assisi and François Villon, of the Good Samaritan and Huck Finn...a fascinating character."

—*The New York Times Book Review*

"A fine book of an interesting life."

—*Chicago* (Sunday) *Tribune*

"Mr. Lewis is a fine writer with a mastery of the concrete and particular. He has done an important and interesting biography of a curious and strangely charming personality."

—*Saturday Review*

THE WORLDS OF CHIPPY PATTERSON
was originally published by Harcourt, Brace and Company.

Books by Arthur Lewis

The Aaronsburg Story
*Carnival
*Children's Party
*Copper Beeches
The Day They Shook the Plum Tree
*La Belle Otero
*Lament for the Molly Maguires
*The Worlds of Chippy Patterson

*Published by POCKET BOOKS

ARTHUR H. LEWIS

The Worlds of CHIPPY PATTERSON

PUBLISHED BY POCKET BOOKS NEW YORK

THE WORLDS OF CHIPPY PATTERSON

Harcourt, Brace edition published 1960

POCKET BOOK edition published November, 1973

This POCKET BOOK edition includes every word contained in the original, higher-priced edition. It is printed from brand-new plates made from completely reset, clear, easy-to-read type. POCKET BOOK editions are published by POCKET BOOKS, a division of Simon & Schuster, Inc., 630 Fifth Avenue, New York, N.Y. 10020. Trademarks registered in the United States and other countries.

L

Standard Book Number: 671-78336-X.
Library of Congress Catalog Card Number: 60-10928.

This POCKET BOOK edition is published by arrangement with the author.

Printed in the U.S.A.

FOR *Juliet* WITH LOVE

TO BEGIN WITH

Christopher Stuart Patterson, Junior, lived in three worlds.

The first is a wonderful world of privilege and wealth. Here you meet proper gentlemen and attractive ladies. They keep their appointments, they dress sedately and in clean linen, and they tell the truth as a general social rule. (Now and then they may practice harmless deceptions. One lady, for example, poured tea for me while she, herself, drank straight gin from a crystal water goblet.)

It would be unfair to call them snobs because then you imply a desire to emulate superiors. Obviously a society that once refused to accept an Emperor's brother because he wasn't "well-born" and is currently cool to a lovely young Princess because it claims her husband is a promoter for a gambling house admits to no superiors.

Protected by inherited wealth from the economic struggle that coarsens most men's lives, sheltered by an insurmountable barrier that blocks out undesirables, surrounded by friends unruffled by ambition that might make them better men but poorer company, small wonder the people in the world to which Chippy Patterson was born rarely leave it vertically or willingly. Yet Chippy voluntarily ejected himself from it almost as soon as he was able to stagger into another and totally different one.

His second world? Its hard core is City Hall, the Courts of Oyer and Terminer and General Jail Delivery. Close by are Chinatown, Skid Row, and the Gold Coast. While there are in it some ordinary workaday citizens (lawyers, waiters, policemen, priests, judges, reporters, and bartenders, for example), it's filled mainly with scoundrels. Some of these are funny, some are vicious, and some are merely pathetic. Their offenses range from murder to the delicate nuances of crime only a student of Krafft-Ebing would appreciate. They, too, have an ineffable attraction for the curious.

The third world of Chippy Patterson is that of the inner man. What possessed him, or obsessed him, to follow so extraordinary a path? Was he to blame, or his parents, or his surroundings? Was he paying subconsciously for the omissions of his forefathers? Or had he been tempered by brimstone to enjoy the havoc he created by making a sorry spectacle of justice? Was he a character actor who basked in courtroom drama or did he have a genuine desire to help those whom others shunned? Or was he simply the kind of man who didn't give a damn about anything?

Everyone who knew Chippy Patterson has a theory—and no two are quite alike. Each attempt at a conclusion arrives at a different answer. It is possible that his third world can be seen by fitting together the pieces of the first two. That task, however, I must leave to the reader.

In gathering material about these worlds for this book I have had the help and co-operation of many people, and I wish to express my gratitude to Norris S. Barratt, Jean Barrett, Andy Christolas, William "Bill" Connelly, John M. "Cap" Cummings, Jimmy Day, Tom Finney, Dorothy Ann Harrison, Nick Hayes, Father Francis Hoey, Sam King, James Lambert, Bernard L. Lemisch, Ada Hetherington Patterson Lucas, James V. Magee, Thomas D. McBride, Louis F. McCabe, Roy L. McCardell, Harry Ogden, Thomas P. "Tip" O'Neill, George Wharton Pepper, Charlie Phillips, Agnes Allen Curry Regan, Maxwell Rosenblum, Frank Toughill, Mary Sims Tyson, Ralph B. Umsted, Bill Whittem, John Wickas, George W. Wilkins, Morton Witkin, Edward Wood, Jr., and Ben Zion.

My special thanks are extended to Florence Collis, Herb Davis, and other staff members of the Free Library of Philadelphia; to the men on the city desks and the librarians of the Philadelphia *Inquirer* and the Philadelphia *Evening Bulletin;* and to the guards at the Death House, Western State Penitentiary.

I am particularly indebted to Marie Rodell for her editorial acumen and skills, which she gave so generously.

Several newspapers and periodicals have graciously

permitted me to quote from their publications; for these courtesies I am grateful to the Philadelphia *Inquirer*, the Philadelphia *Evening Bulletin*, and the *Shingle*, official publication of the Bar Association of Philadelphia.

Reported conversations included herein have been examined, whenever possible, by the actual participants and are as accurate as individual memory and the passage of time allow.

ARTHUR H. LEWIS
Philadelphia, Pennsylvania

The Worlds of
CHIPPY PATTERSON

CHAPTER 1

THE FIRST TIME I saw Chippy Patterson was on my first day with the Philadelphia *Inquirer*, back in the mid-twenties. I was standing in front of 619, the reporters' room at City Hall, with Frank Toughill, the *Record* man, waiting for a boy from Horn and Hardart's to bring us coffee, when down the corridor walked a strange-looking character.

He was about six feet two or three. Unkempt iron-gray hair jutted from beneath a tight-fitting, dirty, checkered cap; his feet were encased in high fishing boots; papers bulged from his pockets. His progress along the hall was impeded by a swarm of noisy little men clamoring for attention. Some screamed at him, while others tugged at the sleeves of his tattered coat. Every few moments his fingers dipped into his right-hand pocket to dig out a coin that he pressed into the outstretched palm of a petitioner. The latter would then shuffle off, his place filled at once from an apparently endless reservoir of humanity which seemed to ooze out of cracks in the floor.

As he came abreast of us he looked in our direction and touched the brim of his cap with a forefinger that, even at a distance of three or four feet, I could see was carefully manicured. With a soft, but obviously cultured, "Sh. . . . Gentlemen, please," he stilled the babble and then, pausing momentarily, smiled at my companion and called out, "Good morning, Mr. Toughill." He glanced at me with the bluest, saddest eyes I ever saw, gave me a friendly nod and a "Good morning, Sir."

"Good morning, Mr. Patterson," said Frank.

The crowd and its central figure resumed their slow progress down the corridor.

I turned to my colleague with raised eyebrows.

"Who's the ill-clad patrician?"

Toughill grinned.

"That's 'Chippy' Patterson. 'Chiffy' Patterson if you wear the old school tie," he said. "Just a minute."

The *Record* man raised his voice and shouted above the din which had begun again.

"Anything special today, counselor?"

The tall, gaunt gentleman paused and raised his hand for the silence which followed at once.

"Nothing of interest for you today, Mr. Toughill, I'm afraid. But thank you for asking."

I looked at Frank.

"Who's Chippy Patterson?"

He smiled tolerantly at my ignorance and excused it with a "That's right. You're not from Philly." He continued. "Chippy's the best goddamn criminal lawyer in the city and maybe even in the country!"

Our coffee arrived. Frank made no move, so I paid the boy. We stood there, leaning against the tile wall, drinking the coffee hot and black.

"I could tell you a hundred stories," the *Record* man went on. "Look!"

Toughill pointed toward the end of the long hall.

"He's gone into six ninety-six. That's Oyer and Terminer. Probably got a murder trial in McDevitt's court right now. And I wouldn't be a bit surprised if he had another one before Gordon in four ninety-three this afternoon."

"How come we don't cover them?" I questioned.

Frank shook his head at this naïveté.

"Hell, the *Record* couldn't use a line. Neither would your paper. These are Negro killings. That's what Chippy meant when he said there was 'nothing of interest.' He knows we won't print a stick about them unless a white man's involved."

"Doesn't he have any white clients?"

"Good Lord, yes! Hundreds of them. He'll represent anybody who asks him: white, black, yellow, or red, even if they don't have a dime. Rapists, abortionists, safecrackers, perverts, madams, whores, pimps, and even some big-time bootleggers and con men, particularly if they happen to be broke. Besides all this, he's got about thirty or forty homicides a year. But no matter how much money he takes in, he gives it all away or spends it by the time he goes to bed."

I looked skeptically at my companion.

"Don't believe it, if you don't want to. But it's the truth. And what a dream in front of a jury. They eat out of his hands. So do some judges."

"Frank," I said, "what about the leeches hanging around him? And his clothes! Does he have to dress like a scarecrow? What about his accent? He didn't acquire that in Frankford. I don't get it."

"Nobody else does, either. You're right about the accent. That's pure Chestnut Hill, boy; nothing phony there. Delancey School, then Penn Charter or Germantown Academy. I forget which. After that, Penn Law. His old man was president of the same bank *his* father founded, dean of the University Law School, and chief counsel for the Pennsylvania Railroad. Died a couple of years ago and left millions, but not a dime for Chippy. Chippy's mother used to run Society."

I saw Chippy Patterson just twice more. The first time was in Camden Police Court, where he defended a Negro prostitute and made an ass out of a vice-squad detective. How Chippy got in the picture I don't know, but there he was, representing a gigantic woman. Muldoon, the policeman, fat and red-cheeked, testified he had placed the defendant under arrest when she accepted the proffered $2 fee in the room to which she had taken him. That was all.

Chippy, in dulcet tones, asked the officer to repeat his testimony. Then, raising his voice sharply, he startled the policeman with, "You're certain that's all that happened in the lady's room, Mr. Muldoon? You know you're under oath."

"That's all that happened, counselor," answered Muldoon. "I handed this whore her dough and made the pinch. Don't you believe me, counselor?"

"No, I don't, Mr. Muldoon," replied Chippy. Then he placed his client on the stand. He asked her only one question.

"Can you tell us anything about Mr. Muldoon which

we can't observe here in court—anything that maybe his wife or somebody close to him might know about?"

"Yes, sir!" she answered looking directly at Muldoon, who by now was growing beet red and was covered with sweat. "The gentleman's got a big, jagged scar right across his belly, pretty near as big . . ." She groped for a comparison. "Well, as big as his . . ." At a loss for words she demonstrated its size by standing up and running her hand across her huge abdomen.

Everybody roared with laughter.

"Get the hell out of here, Muldoon!" blasted Magistrate Pancoast, "unless you want us to verify the witness's testimony. The prisoner is discharged!"

The last time I saw Chippy was at Corson's Inlet, where I went fishing on a day off some years ago. I remember the sun was coming up when I got there, and I scarcely recognized the old man in a checkered cap and high fishing boots, all by himself, casting from one of the piers. It was Chippy all right, and he looked very bad. I was going to speak to him, but we had a boat rented by the hour and the men I was with were in a hurry to get on the water, drink beer, and do some fishing. I did wave, though, and I think he waved back. Now I'm sorry I didn't stop to talk.

A couple of weeks after that Chippy was dead. Some said he died of a heart attack, and others said it was tuberculosis he'd contracted from the girl he was living with at the time.

Years later I came across a copy of the *Shingle,* official publication of the staid Philadelphia Bar Association. I opened it at random. An italicized quotation from the Talmud headed a page: "Slay the sin rather than the sinner."

This was the first paragraph:

"On February 17, 1933, the Philadelphia Bar lost a member who was, in some respects, so incredibly unique that it may well be doubted whether the legal world has ever seen his like."

Pretty strong, I reflected, for members of a most conservative bar that prides itself on a nearly three-century-old tradition of legal titans from Andrew Hamilton to Supreme Court Justice Owen J. Roberts. The term "Philadelphia lawyer," used either in praise or opprobrium, has international significance.

I read on.

"In boyhood, Patterson, Jr. attended the finest private schools in the country and was something of a Beau Brummell. Later, he began to dress carelessly and to shun his well-to-do-companions, seeking more and more the lower strata of life. Without a telephone, a secretary, a law book or even an office, he practiced over a score of years. For fees he took whatever was offered, however insignificant. He was not a mere 'mouthpiece' to the accused, but their champion as well as father confessor. He owned a cemetery lot with two requirements for 'admission'—death and a prison record. . . . Many a Sunday he spent among the graves, laying flowers and straightening crosses.

"Despite the almost complete transformation which had estranged him to his loved ones, he remained to the last unchanged in one respect—his taste for the classics. He read them avidly at every opportunity and could recite from memory page after page of verse.

"He was more than a public defender. His attitude was almost that of co-defendant. As he stood at the bar of the court, pleading for some victim of fortune's scourge, he seemed to acknowledge at least part of the guilt in being a member of a society which permitted children to grow up in sordid slums, amid ugliness, vice and crime, only to die in loneliness and despair."

Except for newspaper stories nothing else was ever written about Chippy, and the vast majority of those who knew him have long since vanished from the scene. But here and there, if you search far enough, you can still find men and women who recall with love, pride, and often with gentle laughter, their friendship with C. Stuart Patterson, Jr. First of all there is Chippy's ex-widow, if that's the proper title for the woman to whom he was married for a short while before she divorced him. Her name is Ada Hetherington Lucas Patterson Latham, and she lives in a penthouse just off Rittenhouse Square. She's a Caldwell, and her lineage is as ancient and distinguished as the Pattersons'. Not only was she Chippy's law clerk and investigator; since she attempted to handle his fiscal affairs, she must have been the world's most frustrated bookkeeper. They were together in that brief period when Christopher Stuart Patterson, Jr. unsuccessfully attempted to become a conventional, commuting father and husband.

At the other end of the social ladder there's a retired madam who at one time operated the most exclusive "house" in Philadelphia on Diamond Street west of Eighteenth, but who now lives by herself in a three-story brick dwelling facing Franklin Square. C. Stuart Patterson, Jr. was her lawyer for many years. As a matter of fact she probably paid him one of his earliest retainers. "At first," she said, "Mr. Patterson was my client. Then I was his."

There's a parish priest in Ashland, up in the dying hard-coal regions of Pennsylvania, who knew another side of C. Stuart Patterson, Jr. He is Father Francis Hoey, who, prior to his "exile" for the performance of a marriage which pleased Chippy but not Cardinal Dougherty, was chaplain at Eastern Penitentiary.

There is Bill Whittem, the druggist's son, last of Chippy's boyhood companions. Bill runs the pharmacy at 105 Bethlehem Pike; it hasn't changed much since his father opened it right after the Civil War to serve society folk who were just beginning to move out of Rittenhouse Square to Chestnut Hill. At eighty-seven, "Doc" Whittem has 20/20 vision without glasses, and his hearing and his memory are as keen as they ever were. There isn't much about Chippy's childhood and early youth "Doc" doesn't remember.

There is Lou McCabe, Ben Lemisch, and Tom McBride. All three are practicing members of the bar and were casual, infrequent associates of Chippy's in many a well-remembered courtroom victory. There is Ben Zion, who used to be Chippy's clerk. There's a guard in the death house at Western Penitentiary who shared Chippy's vigil with the four Olney bank bandits the night before they were electrocuted. There is Mary Tyson, for Chippy the little girl next door, now a lovely, gracious old woman whose chalet adjoins that of Charlie Chaplin in Vevey, Switzerland.

There are a couple of Chippy's cousins, whose eyes light up with pleasure when they recall their rebellious relative. Other Patterson kin, even a quarter of a century after Chippy's death, still shudder at the mere mention of his name.

There was Ruth Draper, whom I met in Chicago after a performance of *An Evening with Ruth Draper*.

"From Philadelphia, are you?" she said, looking interested. When I told her I used to work on a newspaper there, I sensed her next question. It came, inevitably.

"Did you know Chiffy Patterson?"

Regretfully I told her how tenuous was our acquaintance.

"He was my favorite cousin. A lovely, lovely man," she sighed.

She asked me if I liked her "Children's Party," which I always thought was her funniest reading. I told her so.

"Thank you." She went on, "When I was very young, I used to visit the Pattersons at Gracehill, named after a great aunt of ours. My mother was a Dana, and Chiffy's mother, Ellen Stuart, was her cousin. Aunt Ellen used to gather all the neighborhood boys and girls together on warm, early-summer afternoons, before their parents took them to Newport or Narragansett or Europe. There were Biddles and Peppers and Whartons and Cadwalladers and Simses, and we'd have ice-cream parties in the little summerhouse, shaped like a Japanese pagoda, on a corner of the lawn. I remember the tall, beautiful boxwoods which seemed to enclose us in a world all our own—and the brook where Aunt Ellen let us dip our feet if the weather was hot enough and if Uncle Christopher wasn't around.

"Sometimes, when the party was almost over, Chiffy would stroll in, dressed in his cricketing uniform, looking so handsome. He played very well, you know. Not in his brother George's class—George was the best player in the United States. But even so he was quite good. Chiffy was older than I and so very sweet. He'd pile all the children in the dog cart and ride us everywhere in Chestnut Hill and buy us peppermint sticks at Whittem's drug store. We teased him mercilessly, but he never became angry. . . . My 'Children's Party' is based on recollections of Gracehill."

Years ago I went out to Eastern Penitentiary to do a story on a kidnapper who'd spent some 30 years there. Warden Tees asked me to return in a day or two; my man was in the prison hospital. But, as a sort of consolation prize, if I had nothing better to do, and if the prisoner didn't mind, would I like to talk with another con to be released that afternoon? This one was a "lifer," in prison since 1932 for killing a South Philadelphia grocer during a hold-up.

The warden took me into his own office. A few minutes later he brought in a slight, middle-aged man and said, "Shake hands with Pete Valenti."

Pete was shy and diffident to the point of timidity, and afterward, when I looked up his trial in the newspaper room of the Free Library, it was hard for me to reconcile him with the tough, sneering young thug who 20 years before had shot his unresisting victim to death. If anyone deserved the death penalty, the press of that era pointed out, it was Valenti. But Pete was fortunate enough to retain C. Stuart Patterson, Jr., and the jury, to the utter disgust of the judge, recommended mercy.

Valenti has the distinction of being the last of the Patterson clients to be released from the penitentiary. If Chippy had been alive, Valenti said sadly, but without bitterness, "he'da got me out on parole in maybe six, eight years."

Several members of the working press who covered City Hall during Chippy's era and are still operating out of 619 will tell you that Pete was not exaggerating Patterson's ability to keep his homicidal clients out of jail. If he couldn't win jury acquittals, and he certainly didn't win them all, he was highly successful in his appeals before the Pardon Board in Harrisburg. As a matter of fact, his "box score" for defense of murderers should establish some sort of record.

From 1907 until his death in 1933, Chippy defended 401 men and women charged with homicide. Even with "cop killers," regarded by all living policemen as blood stains on their shields to be erased only by homeopathy, he did rather well. Of the 25 he defended, five were found not guilty and 15 were given jail sentences; only five went to the chair. His record for the remaining 376 defendants is almost unbelievable. Of these, 166 were acquitted; 207 went to prison for an average of six years each; while three paid the supreme penalty.

Although Chippy used audacious arguments, quips, and quotations to win his innumerable victories, he never was the courtroom orator. He never flailed and he never ranted. Even though, on occasion, he could, with bitter invective, utterly destroy a witness for the prosecution, most of the time his irony was gentle. Although his courtroom achievements were greater than Clarence Darrow's, quantitatively if not qualitatively, he did not employ Darrow's technique of didactic treatises, couched in highly literate prose, which appealed to the reason of judge and jury. I doubt very much if Chippy was capable of the intellectual approach. In any event he wouldn't have had the time for planned openings or summations.

His attraction for juries lay in his obvious sincerity and his simultaneous, contradictory identification with both Philadelphia's ruling classes and the humble prisoner he was defending, so that the twelve felt they were imposing sentence not only upon the accused but upon counsel as well.

It's questionable whether Chippy could have functioned as well today as he did in his time. That measure of his success due to identification with the aristocracy of the community would be almost totally lost in the present era. Except for the rare, and probably elderly, juryman, still awed by the presence of a "Philadelphia gentleman," the average citizen of William Penn's "greene towne" pays little heed to an erstwhile ruling class which long ago retired from its golden throne. The mores of Philadelphia, merely strained by a World War and a major depression, could not survive the cataclysmic destruction of the Republican Party. A 250-year-old oligarchy of benevolent despotism crumbled into dust in the three or four seconds it took Jack Kelly, leader of a howling, triumphant Democratic victory parade, to leap up fifteen brownstone steps to the Union League.

Unless you are a third- or fourth-generation Philadelphian, steeped in the city's traditions, or a student of her ancient history, you may find it difficult, if not impossible, to visualize the enormous power once wielded by a comparatively few descendants of the several dozen families who reached the Delaware on William Penn's sailing barque, "Welcome," in 1682.

While many differed from the Proprietor and chose Protestant denominations other than Quaker, nearly all, with the exception of bonded servants, craftsmen, and laborers especially chosen for the tasks ahead, were men and women of wealth, breeding, political position, and prestige in their native England, Scotland, and Wales. They were accustomed to rule (a few even held hereditary titles) and, despite their tolerance of other faiths, kept themselves socially aloof from the common herd.

For approximately 175 years, this little group of aristocrats and their progeny, augmented slightly by several kindred French and Dutch families, provided the city, state, and nation with leaders in every field. Then suddenly the fountainhead ran dry. Rulers ceased to rule and surrendered their power to a band of political opportunists who raped and looted a great city and turned it into a huge bawdy house.

The gay, wicked, irresponsible era in which Chippy lived was perhaps the most fascinating in Philadelphia's long and generally respectable history. Much, if not all, of its color has faded.

Gone is Chinatown, in its heyday populated by 7,000 Orientals who erected against other Philadelphians a barrier as effective as it was invisible. Here Chippy roamed, greeted as friend and counselor by warring On Leongs,

Hip Sings, and Five Brothers, and by the few white women who frequented its narrow streets and alleys.

Gone, too, is the Tenderloin, Eighth to Sixth, Race to Vine. This was Skid Row, where every doorway was occupied by a drunk sleep-it off, and a score of chronic alcoholics could be found in the gutters of a single block; where two cheap burlesque theaters, a dime museum, three all-night movies, 30 or 40 fifteen-cent flop houses, and countless saloons flourished. From this blighted area and the six city "squares" of adjacent Callowhill, where prostitutes plied their trade by soliciting from first-floor cribs which lined both sides of the street, came the bulk of Chippy's clients.

Nor is there much left of the "Gold Coast," where Chippy recruited his few better-paying clients from among the con men, burglars, bootleggers, hired assassins, assorted racketeers, and kept women who maintained plush homes and apartments in the vicinity of Broad Street and Columbia Avenue, two miles north of City Hall.

Even the pattern of downtown Philadelphia has changed. City Hall remains the same, outwardly at least, and the Bellevue-Stratford Hotel still caters to the haute monde. The Union League, with the pride of a retired, arthritic board chairman, stays fiercely independent of times that have moved on since the Golden Age of McKinley, when C. Stuart Patterson, Sr. was its president, and stands in splendid isolation, continuing to bar Negroes, Jews, and Democrats and to serve the best food in Pennsylvania. Both the Philadelphia Club and the State in Schuylkill Club to this day have waiting lists that could not possibly be accommodated in two centuries, and ambitious mothers artfully contrive to secure for their debutante daughters coveted invitations to the Tuesday Afternoon Dancing Class at the Merion Cricket Club, prelude to a bid to the Assembly itself.

But Broad Street Station has been razed. Skyscrapers, apartment houses, and a multi-million-dollar hotel have risen on the site of the old Chinese Wall—the one-mile, 25-foot-high road bed of the Pennsylvania Railroad which once bisected the city. New streets and boulevards stretch from the heart of the city to the Turnpike beyond.

Saddest, perhaps, of all the sacrifices to progress occurred in 1942 with the mechanization of the First City Troop, military unit of the gentlemen of Philadelphia and the oldest regiment of United States Army Regulars. This was General Washington's Honor Guard, whose proud battle flags bear the scars of every war, except the Mexican, since the Revolution. You do not join the Troop as you do the Army, Navy or Marine Corps. You have to be asked. Until jeeps, tanks, armored battle, and command cars replaced horses, no young Philadelphian was likely to forget the vision of nearly a hundred tall, handsome, self-assured gentlemen, in bright, silver-faced blue coats, white skin-tight pants, shining high black boots, high bearskin helmets, and gleaming sabres, astride magnificent mares and stallions, thundering hoofs flying down Chestnut Street, on the thrice yearly Troop parades.

I think today Chippy would have been lost in his own Philadelphia. Most of his friends, colleagues, and clients are dead, and the Chestnut Hill families he renounced have fled to well-prepared suburban retreats. The only club Chippy might have joined eagerly would be the Diners', because it would have enabled him to distribute his largesse almost completely at government expense. No doubt the Diners' would have blackballed him, since he had neither a fixed place of business nor computable income.

CHAPTER 2

CHRISTOPHER STUART PATTERSON, Jr., like the rest of us, came from a long line of ancestors. The difference between Chippy, though, and most of the rest of us is that his family line is easy to trace, a kind of genealogist's delight.

His ancestors were largely men of affairs, rich enough or important enough to have left their mark wherever they chose to live and so to become part of the public record. The first of Chippy's forefathers to come to America was a native of The Netherlands. He was the Reverend Hendric Cuyler, who landed in New Amsterdam about 1649, settled in what is now Albany, New York, accumulated a considerable portion of worldly goods, and begat 14 children.

The distinguished minister's children in turn married the offspring of other important citizens; and after a few generations, the Reverend Mr. Cuyler's progeny were spread out all over New York, Pennsylvania, New Jersey, and Virginia, taking active parts in the early development of the nation and fighting in all her wars. There were Danas, Astors, Delanos, Biddles, Cadwalladers, Pattersons, Stuarts (on the paternal and maternal sides of Chippy's family), and Lees and Carters of Virginia.

One of Reverend Cuyler's descendants, another pastor, the Reverend Cornelius Cuyler, a chaplain in the Revolutionary War and a Philadelphian by adoption, married Eleanor deGraeff of Schenectady, New York. Their youngest son, Theodore, a graduate *cum laude* of the University of Pennsylvania, class of 1838, became one of Philadelphia's great trial lawyers and a director of the Pennsylvania Railroad. He married Elizabeth DeWitt, of New York City; their daughter Jane married Joseph Patterson, thereby becoming Chippy's grandmother.

Joseph Patterson was the descendant of a well-to-do English and Scotch-Irish family. John Patterson, his father, opened a warehouse at Second and Walnut Streets shortly after the Revolutionary War. He prospered, and in his town house, on the east side of Third Street below Chestnut, entertained many titled English and Irish visitors. In 1791 he married Martha Stuart, daughter of Colonel Christopher Stuart, aide-de-camp of General Washington, a first cousin of Gilbert Stuart, the colonial artist.

John and Martha Patterson had seven sons. Joseph, the third son, born in 1808, was, according to Edward Patterson, Justice of the Supreme Court of the State of New York and Joseph's grandson, "a man of great intellectual power and a splendid specimen of the American gentleman." Joseph chose banking as a career. Although he never ran for nor held public office, he was active in Philadelphia's civic affairs.

Joseph's generation was about the last in which the great founding fathers of Philadelphia who arrived with or before William Penn—Bringhursts, Brintons, Biddles, Longstreths, Shippens, Morrises, Tysons, etc.—furnished the city, state, and nation with dynamic leadership, politically, morally, and intellectually. From this score of families came signers of the Declaration, governors, philosophers, statesmen, philanthropists, and scientists, who used their prestige and power to develop the Republic.

Jane Cuyler and Joseph Patterson had three sons and two daughters. The second son, Christopher Stuart, who was to become Chippy's father, was born June 24, 1842.

Christopher, with a half-dozen young sons of Philadelphia gentlemen, was coached by a private tutor, and when he was old enough was sent to Lawrenceville Academy. Later he matriculated at the University of Pennsylvania, where he graduated, *magna cum laude,* at the age of eighteen.

Although elected to Phi Beta Kappa, he still found time for cricket, which he played brilliantly, and for lawn tennis, at which he was exceptionally good. Other sports—rugby, boxing, soccer—requiring physical contact with his opponents, he detested. He was a member of the First City Troop, and during the Civil War served with his regiment as a sergeant in Captain Landis' Battery. He was severely wounded at Carlisle in July, 1863, was decorated for bravery, and discharged.

He returned to Philadelphia to resume his education and began reading law in the office of Judge William A. Porter. Two years later he was admitted to the Bar. He was just twenty-three years old when he opened his suite of offices in the new Bullitt Building on South Fourth Street. The twin problems which bedeviled most fledgling members of the Bar, money and clients, did not exist for Christopher Stuart Patterson, Esq. He had an inheritance of $100,000 from an uncle who had died in 1854, and family connections assured him a steady flow of clients. Even without backing he probably would have succeeded, although it might have taken longer. He was handsome, self-possessed, and brilliant, and the lack of a sense of humor never was a handicap for a corporation lawyer.

He joined the Philadelphia Club, Sons of the Revolution, the American Philosophical Society, and the Union League, and continued his interest in cricket. With the famous Newhall brothers he formed an eleven, later to be known as "The Gentlemen of Philadelphia," which met and defeated the best England could offer.

At the Assembly of 1866, Ellen Stuart, whom Christopher had known from childhood, made her debut. Less than a year later, June 16, 1867, she and Christopher were married. Although many "Stuarts" and "Stewarts" appear in the Patterson genealogy, Ellen was only distantly related to Christopher. Her branch of the Stuart family was English and Scottish and claimed kinship with royalty. The first of the clan to arrive in the New World was John, a merchant of Leeds and Edinburgh, who left England to settle in Philadelphia about 1697. Most of his descendants remained there and were active in the affairs of the city and the commonwealth.

When the Christopher Stuart Pattersons returned from a "grand tour" of Europe, where they spent their honeymoon, they moved into 2003 Delancey Place, Joseph Patterson's wedding gift to his son and daughter-in-law. This was a comfortable four-story, seventeen-room brick house completed shortly after the Civil War.

The house was built to last. Its six-inch walls kept the Pattersons cool in that short portion of Philadelphia's hot summers before they went to Newport and provided another advantage by offering a protective layer of silence from outside noises.

The Christopher Stuart Pattersons had five children in fairly rapid succession. The first born was George, on October 10, 1868. He was followed by Joseph in 1870, Eleanor in 1872, and Francis in 1873. The next, Christopher Stuart Patterson, Jr., called "Chiffy" by two-year-old

Francis, who couldn't pronounce "Christopher," was the last of the children born in the Delancey Place house. There was a gap of ten years before Ellen gave birth to her sixth and final child, Jane Cuyler Patterson, whose history was to be tragic.

CHAPTER 3

THE LITTLE MORE than half-century between the moment John B. Biddle, M.D. slapped breath into an eight-pound infant, and N. B. Groton, D.D. tossed the first shovel of dirt into Chippy's grave, might be called the Age of Pomposity. It started some time before 1875 and for all but a comparatively few it ended on a bleak October day in 1929. Nowhere was this Age of the Stuffed Shirt, this Era of Smugness, this Period of Chauvinism (anything you can do, we can do better) more evident than in Philadelphia, although it certainly was in full flower at Boston, New York, Baltimore, and probably Scranton, Pennsylvania.

The tariff was high; Grant was in the White House; and all the rest, from Hayes to Hoover, were yet to come. True, in the years following, the nation's capital was due for two temporary upsets, Cleveland and Wilson—three, if you care to include the slightly distasteful administration of Teddy Roosevelt—but not one of these achieved the cataclysmic results of F.D.R. America was in the safest of all possible hands. It was the Union League forever!

God never shed His grace more generously than He did over Mr. Ward McAllister and Mrs. William Astor, Mrs. Fiske Warren and Mrs. Sarah Drexel Fell Van Rensselaer. For those who sat securely within the sacred, well-guarded gates of the Meadow Brook Hunt, the Porcellian and the Philadelphia Clubs, it was not a question of being too well bred to look disdainfully upon outsiders who raised polite but persistent clamors for admission. To the dePeysters, Stuyvesant Fishes, Cabots, Lowells,

Lawrences, Cadwalladers, Biddles, Wistars (and Wisters), Norrises, Morrises, Cuylers, and Pattersons, there was no outside world. It was as simple as that.

Chippy was born on a Sunday. In 1875 Philadelphia's blue laws were rigidly enforced. There were no sporting events, and theatres, saloons, and stores were shut tight. Once morning church bells stopped ringing, only an infrequent horsecar clattering along the cobblestones or the mournful moo of a lost cow wandering through the streets broke the silence. Obviously, for the vast majority of the city's 794,000 residents, the Day of Rest meant what that title says. Church, replete with an interminable sermon spouting fire and brimstone until noon; then the big indigestible meal of the week, followed by a long afternoon siesta; a light supper of leftovers; and so to bed to gather strength for the 60-hour work week ahead. This was the pattern in thousands upon thousands of narrow two- and three-story brick row houses which lined street after sunless street.

Except for servants living in rear mews, this was not the pattern for residents of the Rittenhouse Square area or Society Hill, near Fourth and Walnut Streets, where a few dozen families still occupied ancestral homes. Services at Christ Church, Second and Market Streets (oldest Anglican Church in the United States), or at Holy Trinity, Walnut Street near Nineteenth, were soothing, the brief sermons in excellent taste, and the music supplied by skilled, well-paid professionals.

After a meal, better prepared, more varied, and considerably less starchy than those eaten by most Philadelphians, the upper classes were not confined to their homes for recreation. The long, cheerful bar at the Philadelphia Club, only eight or nine squares down tree-lined Walnut Street, was open seven days a week. So were those at the Rittenhouse, Markham, and Racquet, the latter founded by Chippy's great-grandfather, Theodore Cuyler. There was horseback riding along Fairmount Park's winding bridle paths or on the huge estates of friends in Chestnut Hill and Jenkintown. While golf was a decade away, lawn tennis courts were available, and, weather permitting, many a Sunday cricket match was played on the greens of the Manheim or Germantown Cricket Clubs.

For sporting gentlemen who liked more robust fun, there was usually a cock main at Fortside Inn or in the mews of Rittenhouse Square. For amorous gentlemen, discreet madams operated parlors on Poplar Street open six days a week to anyone with the price but on Sundays closed to all but the aristocracy.

In none of the eight daily newspapers printed in Philadelphia on Monday, September 20, 1875, will you find mention of Chippy's birth—Christopher Stuart Patterson abhorred publicity in any form, either for himself or his family. There was plenty of other news, however.

Philadelphia's crime of the century, the kidnapping of five-year-old Charles Brewster Ross, came to an inconclusive end (the little boy was never seen alive) with the conviction of William Westervelt in Quarter Sessions Court.

In the *North American* of the same day, sandwiched between an announcement of the opening of Germantown Academy for its 128th season, and the proclamation of Mr. B. Percival, who "begs to inform the public he will open a store for the French Pork Trade," comes casual word of a giant of his generation.

"Walt Whitman, the poet," wrote some observant reporter in the manner of O. O. McIntyre, "was in Philadelphia yesterday. He wore the usual broad Spanish sombrero, his long white silver-gray hair streaming underneath; and although his step was feeble, his conversation was as buoyant and genial as before his recent severe illness."

The *Record* reported, "Brigham Young, the Mormon, is seriously ill and much consternation was felt by his 17 wives and 44 children."

Indians still roamed the plains. Under a Fort Laramie, Wyoming Territory, dateline, the Philadelphia *Item* reported that "three redskins were the object of an intense search by U.S. Cavalry for scalping John Little and five members of his family on the Little ranche (the *Item*'s spelling) near the mouth of the North Fork."

But it was a single paragraph in the *Inquirer* which announced in a most casual and belittling manner the end of a boyhood hero whose exploits filled a hundred surreptitiously read paperbacks and whose adventures were an inspiration to millions of his abject admirers.

"A dispatch from Pine Hill, Ky. reports the death of Jesse James. . . . James used to be well-known throughout the country as a notorious Mississippi outlaw whose depredations produced much excitement some time ago."

Mr. George W. Child's newspaper, the *Public Ledger,* observed without editorial comment that of the 323 Philadelphians who died the week preceding the day of Chippy's birth, 99 were under one year of age. "Marasmus," the medical term for starvation, was the killer.

Other ailments plagued the city fathers. "The Board of Health," said the *Inquirer*, "is worried about the return of the Epizooty which prevailed so seriously a few years ago when The Great Epizootic killed thousands of horses and paralyzed the horsecar industry in the United States."

What concerned Philadelphians most in 1875 was the approaching Centennial Exhibition in Fairmount Park. Everything about the coming attraction, scheduled to open May 10, 1876, was big news. Even newspaper advertisements were influenced by the event. "Centennial hoop skirts, especially adopted to the present style of dresses," were offered at 50 cents by William T. Hopkins of 1115 Chestnut Street. "Exhibition bustles, made of the best French Hair Cloth," sold for from 81 cents to $10, according to the *Evening Star.*

"Delegates from the Territory of Colorado," said the *Star,* "big men astride big horses, responded with whoops of delight to wildly cheering Philadelphians eager to get a look at cowboys from what would soon enter the Union as the Centennial State."

The visit of a delegation of Proper Bostonians, headed by the Honorable Leverett Saltonstall, Hamilton Alonzo Hill, Joseph V. Meigs, and Charles Francis Adams, Jr., was given ample coverage in every daily. Following a lunch at the Philadelphia Club and a tour of the grounds, the gentlemen were entertained in "The Yellow Mansion," Dundas Lippincott's town house at Broad and Walnut Streets. Among the guests was Mr. Christopher Stuart Patterson, Sr.

Whatever effort Philadelphians put forth to be certain the Centennial would be a success was amply justified by a comment the departing Mr. Saltonstall made.

"I am pleased," the Bostonian declared unequivocally, "with progress at the Exhibit."

Further Centennial information was revealed in the *Evening Bulletin,* which reported, "The Centennial Commission had its feet firmly on the ground in rejecting an offer from a physician (unnamed) of Talladego County, Alabama, who requested permission to display his invention of a flying ship."

"No!" answered the Commission, "Man was not meant to fly." The Federal government, however, had more faith and granted the Alabama scientist a 17-year patent.

While the Centennial offered future pleasures, present ones could be had by theatrical-minded Philadelphians, who, in the fall and winter season of 1875, were given their choice of no less than 15 simultaneous attractions, ranging from Mrs. Scott Siddon's Shakespearean readings at the Academy to *East Lynne* at Fox's Mammouth Theatre on Chestnut Street above Tenth.

For Philadelphians who liked to dance and never expected to be invited to the Assembly, a score of "professors" offered to teach "the art of Terpsichore, including the Boston and the Glide to limited groups at reasonable rates."

Lusty males seeking illicit pleasures could read between the lines of the many paid notices which appeared under the heading of "Personals." "Woman of refinement with many abilities seeks companionship from a member of the opposite sex with a similar nature," read one, while another declared that "Attractive young lady would like to earn extra money instructing (it did not state what was to be taught) young or middle-aged gentlemen."

For those who sought alcoholic escape from the world's cares, plenty of opportunities were offered on almost every page of all newspapers. "Y.P.M. Whiskey, best in the world," could be bought for $4 a gallon. Messrs. Carstairs and McCall delivered "pure rye in bond" for 60 cents the full quart.

It was whiskey, not working conditions, which the press blamed for recurring labor and other riots in the hard- and soft-coal regions of Pennsylvania and elsewhere in the United States.

"Whiskey inflamed mobs," said the *Sunday Dispatch* of September 26, 1875, "caused rioting in Pottsville and Shenandoah and the burning of two churches in Mahanoy City." Under a heading THE MOLLY MAGUIRES, the *Telegraph,* next evening, deplored "The murderous jealousy between the Irish and the Welsh and the English caused a Welshman to be bludgeoned to death near Broad Mountain and six fires set in the farming district of Mahanoy Valley by drunken mobs."

With the Knights of Labor founded less than six years before and John Mitchell still in knee breeches, organized labor as such did not yet exist. Even Philadelphia's liberal newspaper, the *North American* (oldest in the United States), had "no use for any man, woman, or child who attempted revolt against the hands that fed them."

Job scarcity was no cause for labor unrest in 1875. Although hours were long and wages low, work was available for every able-bodied man, woman, or child over ten who wanted employment. Opportunities for the latter were particularly good, and classified columns were replete with inviting appeals for "a half-grown girl, strong, sleep in, $2.50 per week."

For Philadelphians, held in the toils of what the press of its day called "Demon Rum," Chippy's grandfather Stuart and John Wanamaker, the merchant prince, offered hope. Together, the two men, working against the combined efforts of the more conservative ministerium, brought to the city those great evangelists, Moody and Sankey, spiritual ancestors of the Billys Sunday and Graham.

There was little interest in spectator sports, either amateur or professional, unless "gentlemen" were involved, and the press of the day gave mere passing mention to baseball—"Chicago beat the Hartfords, 14–3," or "the Athletics lost to the Mutuals, 4–6. The general play of the home club was very fine." Cricket, on the other hand, was well covered, and during the week of September 19, 1875, when the International Cricket Tournament was held at the Germantown Cricket Club, from two to two and one-half columns were devoted to descriptions of every game in each of the metropolitan dailies. The final game was won by The Gentlemen of Philadelphia, who triumphed over The British Officers.

Before the last decade of the nineteenth century, newspapers didn't hire society editors or columnists to report on social activities. Until about 1890, when members of the Social Register themselves furnished complete guest lists to the press (to make sure everybody got in), it was not quite *de rigueur* to appear in the newspapers except upon the occasion of a return to Rittenhouse Square from summer "cottages" at Cape May, Bar Harbor, or Newport, or from completion of the "Grand Tour."

Typical was the arrival of the ocean liner *Ohio*, which steamed up the Delaware, then filled with sidewheelers and sails, to dock at the foot of Christian Street on a late September day in 1875. Down the gangplank walked cabin passengers (the only ones reported) Mr. and Mrs. John Fields, Mr. and Mrs. John Hood and Miss Ellen Gowen Hood, Mr. and Mrs. George Biddle, Mr. and Mrs. Robert Cadwallader, etc., etc., and several Pattersons, including the Reverend Mr. H. M. Patterson and Mrs. H. M. Patterson (Chippy's granduncle and aunt) and Mr. Franklin Stuart Patterson (his cousin once removed).

The *Ohio* also carried 385 steerage passengers, who had cleared quarantine at The Lazaretto on Tinicum, Philadelphia's Ellis Island. These men, women, and children were promptly whisked away to the coal mines of Schuylkill, Luzerne, Lackawanna, and Carbon Counties, some 100 miles away, on the Pennsylvania Railroad's new "Immigrant Express."

Even as early as 1875, when it was only in its twenty-ninth year, the P.R.R. had achieved a position of unbelievable importance in the life of the city, state, and nation. Its president and directors occupied magnificent offices in a large marble building on Fourth Street below Walnut. From here they operated 2,000 miles of track and owned rolling stock consisting of 1,000 locomotives, 25,000 freight and 500 passenger cars, not including the baroque private car of President "Tom" Scott, built at a cost of $100,000 and more elegant than anything possessed by Europe's kings.

There was scarcely a page, from the first through editorial, social, and financial, in every one of Philadelphia's newspapers which did not carry some news relating to this railroad's activities. Despite publishers' understandable temptation to go easy on items unpleasant to such a profitable, newsworthy, and influential corporation, most Philadelphia papers pulled no punches in reporting the railroad's many accidents, and if there were any attempts to muzzle the press, they were unsuccessful.

But accidents, though frequent and often serious, did little to prevent the tremendous expansion of U. S. railroads in general and the Pennsylvania Railroad in particular. Fortunes were being amassed by those who felt the nation's future lay in this form of transportation. Unlike the New York Central, the Union Pacific, or the Wabash, which became the possessions, in fact almost the playthings, of single individuals, control of the P.R.R. never passed into the hands of a strong man. Its voting stock was held by interlocking boards of directors of Philadelphia's banks, brokerage houses, and lawyers, most of whom were members of the city's upper classes and belonged to the same clubs, attended the same social functions, and lived in Rittenhouse Square and later in Chestnut Hill. While these men only rarely entered the political arena directly (preferring to accept nothing less than membership in the U. S. Senate), through their awesome prestige and their heavy financial contributions they exercised complete control of the Republican Party and made puppets out of city councilmen, state legislators, and governors.

The Pattersons, Stuarts, and Cuylers were among those whose lives were closely linked to the destiny of the

P.R.R. William C. Patterson was a charter member of the Pennsylvania Railroad Company, incorporated in April, 1847, and when the *North American,* 25 years after Chippy's birth, published the names of Philadelphia's 140 millionaires and the origins of their wealth, Christopher Stuart Patterson, Sr. was on the list. Railroad investments were given as the source of his wealth. Money was hardly a problem in the smoothly operated household at 2003 Delancey Place where the newborn Christopher Stuart Patterson, Jr. uttered his first protest to the world.

CHAPTER 4

THE ONLY ONE around today who can report on Chippy's first years is Mr. George Wharton Pepper—former U. S. Senator, distinguished member of the bar, and frequently referred to as the Brahmin's Brahmin—and his recollections of Chippy during this period are vague (*he* claims).

"As a lad of ten or twelve," Mr. Pepper said, "I remember visiting the Pattersons on Walnut Street and playing tag and hide-and-go-seek with George and his sister Eleanor. There were two smaller children and a very little one who must have been Chiffy. Mrs. Patterson used to serve all of us cookies from a triangular container. I can recall to this day that it was dark blue with a red top and came from Finley Acker's.

"Mr. Patterson was most kind but a bit aloof, 'stuffy' I suppose you'd say today. It was not until years later, after Jane Cuyler died and Chiffy gave him so much trouble, that I knew him better—not that anyone knew him too well. He was a very proud man, and I got the impression he was fearful people might be pitying him or even laughing at him. But at the time we're talking about it seemed to be a very jolly household."

Mr. Pepper paused and stroked his chin.

"If we played until dark, George and I would walk to the West End Livery Stables at Twentieth and Wilcox

Streets and bring back the carriage so that Mr. Patterson could take me home. Most of the people in the neighborhood kept their horses there. When it wasn't too late Chiffy would come along and sit between Eleanor and me in the back of the carriage while George rode up front with his father. Often Mr. Patterson would stop in and chat for a moment with my parents. We lived on lower Walnut Street then, and I was always hoping we'd move up to the Square so I could be near my playmates."

The Pepper family was among the last to hold out against the flow to Rittenhouse Square and adjacent Walnut and Spruce Streets. When the Christopher Stuart Pattersons moved there, those wooded acres were beginning to be recognized as almost the only decent place a Proper Philadelphian might live. The one possible exception was Society Hill, which was being rapidly absorbed by banks and insurance companies whose directors did not care to be so close to their offices.

The Square was named in honor of David Rittenhouse, the Philadelphia astronomer, and enclosed completely, first with a high wooden fence and later with an iron one. The only way anyone could get in and out of it was through a gate, shut every night by a private watchman who sounded a bell of warning before he clamped the lock. Gradually Philadelphia's first families began to leave their large, old-fashioned pre-Revolutionary houses two miles to the east and build up-to-date homes in this attractive, convenient location, either on the Square itself or in the pleasant, quiet, shady streets adjacent to it.

Commerce and industry were banned permanently, and an unspoken but reasonably well-kept restrictive covenant barred undesirables, although no strong objections were voiced when a sort of "pet Jew," Henry Cohen (a friend of Governor Curtin and one of the few Jews admitted to the Union League), moved into a home on the Square sometime in the 1850's. Nor did anyone try to stop Fanny Kemble, an actress and a divorced one at that, from becoming a neighbor, even though she was not accepted socially. By the end of the Civil War all four sides of the Square were built up with imposing town houses, and the quiet streets surrounding it were being filled with other members of the upper upper class.

During the five years the Pattersons lived on Walnut Street, C. Stuart Patterson, Sr. was moving ahead financially. His practice had grown tremendously. Having a grandfather who was once chief counsel for the P.R.R. and an uncle who was its present legal head, made it a foregone conclusion he would become a member of the P.R.R. legal staff, as he did in 1875.

While he engaged in little trial work, his briefs were thorough and he had a way with litigants. No doubt that same self-possession, that ineffable aura of a "Philadelphia gentleman" which clung to him (and later to Chippy), was responsible for the ease with which he handled plaintiffs with claims against the railroad. Since he was on a retainer basis, he was able to devote time to his private practice and to the affairs of the Western National Bank, the one his father, Joseph Patterson, founded. Its board of directors chose him as chief counsel in 1875 and four years later elected him president, a title he held for 45 years.

It was inevitable that the Republican Party would ask him to run for office, but Patterson refused, although he was active behind the scenes. When young Bill McKinley came east in 1876 to campaign on behalf of Rutherford B. Hayes, the two men, McKinley and Patterson, became friends. Years later the hospitality McKinley received at 2003 Delancey Place was returned, and Mr. and Mrs. Christopher Stuart Patterson, Sr. were frequent White House guests.

While he steered clear of actual participation in politics, C. Stuart Patterson, Sr. took a leading role in many civic affairs and was at least "among those present" where his interest was merely tangential. At the opening of the long awaited Centennial in Fairmount Park, he was in the first carriage to follow that of President Grant. When the new building of the Academy of Fine Arts was dedicated, Christopher Stuart Patterson, Sr. sat on the dais. Later that evening he and Ellen were hosts to distinguished figures in the art world at a reception given in the ballroom of the Hotel Continental.

Patterson was on the first run of the new P.R.R. express, later christened the Broadway Limited, which made the 911½ mile trip from Philadelphia to Chicago in 23 hours, 40 minutes, on July 11, 1877. A few days afterward, when the Brotherhood of Locomotive Engineers struck the entire P.R.R. system, Patterson accompanied Major General Brinton, in command of the First Division, National Guard, dispatched by Governor Hartranft to dispel the rioters (casualties: 43 dead—5 troopers, 38 strikers; 61 wounded—14 troopers, 47 strikers). Patterson went with the Guard to quell violence in Scranton, and when police were unable to handle disorders in Philadelphia, he was one of management's emissaries to the White House to persuade President Hayes to call out the Marines.

Busy with affairs of the day, Christopher Stuart Patterson, Sr. had few hours to spare for his family, and as his importance and wealth increased, the evenings he spent at home became less and less frequent. The responsibility of raising the children was left to Ellen and Nurse Margaret Johnson, who came to the Patterson household as a young girl in 1869 and remained there until her death 50 years later. Almost from his birth, Chippy became Nurse Johnson's favorite. It was to his beloved "Peggity," rather than to his parents, that Chippy turned for help through childhood and troubled adolescence.

C. Stuart Patterson, Sr. was never able to establish easy communication with his children. There was little, if any, of the camaraderie that exists between most parents and their offspring—family jokes shared, secret nicknames, games invented, and all the rest of those things that forge strong bonds between parents and children.

Ellen, on the other hand, was a deeply devoted mother, and, as if to compensate for her husband's aloofness, became what today would be termed "overpermissive." Except upon rare occasions, Christopher was not told of his children's misbehavior, and then only when Mrs. Patterson felt that neither she nor Peg Johnson could handle the situation. Normal scrapes went unpunished, and when a few sharp slaps on the rear end, delivered by a firm but loving father, were essential to prevent future and larger transgressions, they were never delivered. Christopher simply wasn't home enough to know what was going on in his own household.

Ellen, like most of the women of her generation, belonged to the school which believed implicitly in the old Roman law of pater-familias—the husband was in every sense the head of the household. She taught the children obedience and respect for their father, and when they addressed him they said "Sir," and they didn't slouch when they said it. No matter how much any of them may have disagreed with him in later years, their differences were not public property.

CHAPTER 5

ELLEN'S GREAT LOVE, second only to her children, was gardening, and it was this, as much as anything else, which caused the Pattersons' move from the heart of the city to Chestnut Hill. During the years they lived on Delancey Place their home was filled with plants and flowers, grown in pots scattered everywhere the sun could be caught and in a minuscule patch of green at the rear of the house. Ellen was even able to raise a lovely variety of yellow roses in a tiny rooftop greenhouse that Christopher had built for her shortly after their marriage.

The family bank recently had acquired 30 acres of unimproved land in Chestnut Hill just west of Stenton Avenue, running north almost to the Bethlehem Pike. It was available to the right buyer, and C. Stuart Patterson, Sr. was the right buyer. About five acres was wooded, and a clear stream, abounding with trout, ran through the north end of the tract. The ground was high (old Joe claimed it was the highest point in Philadelphia) and the neighbors desirable (Biddles to the north, Whartons to the south, Vauxes to the east, and Drexels to the west).

Transportation was good. By 1854 the Reading Railroad had completed a spur line with a passenger stop at Willow Grove Avenue, about a half mile away, and Christopher knew his own railroad planned to build the Chestnut Hill Station within a few hundred yards of Stenton Avenue, a three-minute walk to the Patterson property.

In the Free Library of Philadelphia there is a large map of Chestnut Hill drawn in 1929 by Joseph Patterson Sims, the architect, Chippy's favorite cousin. If you follow it carefully and read all the fine print you see a good slice of American history, beginning with William Penn's visit in 1683. Penn came there then to inspect some of the land granted to him that year by the Leni Lenape Indians, who gathered annually at Council Rock, about three-quarters of a mile south of the plot bought by Christopher Stuart Patterson, Sr.

Construction of Gracehill was begun early in the spring of 1879, and the Pattersons moved there from Walnut Street about six months later. In the meanwhile Christopher sold slightly less than half of his original 30 acres to his older brother Theodore, another member of the bar, and to his cousin Grace Sims, Joe's mother.

Joe had a picture of Gracehill taken, he thought, around 1890.

"It's a kind of bastard architecture," he explained, "Victorian, American, and Teutonic. But it was a damned comfortable house, and solid too. Fieldstone, probably quarried within twenty miles. This wasn't a particularly good period, and some of the houses built then were gruesome. But I always thought Gracehill had a pleasing quality about it."

It must have been a summer day when the photograph was taken. The foliage is full and rich, and a half dozen chairs are scattered along a wide verandah covered with vines which creep all along the side of the house right up to its gabled rooftops. From the center of the front porch, four steps lead to a narrow dirt walk splitting a lawn so beautifully kept you can almost sense its velvet softness.

In the extreme foreground there's a huge oak and an old-fashioned horse chestnut tree with a limb that barely touches the outside of an attic window, no doubt providing a challenge to Chippy and his brothers, and moments of terror to their mother and Peg Johnson.

Unless you count a bird caught in flight, there's not a sign of life about. Where were the Pattersons when the photographer snapped his shutter?

"Maybe Newport," Joe Sims said. "That's where they went nearly every July and August. Or could be they were all standing right in back of the camera watching. You can be sure of one thing, though, Uncle Christopher wasn't around. He never would have permitted anyone to take a picture of *his* house."

Of course you can't see into the house, and neither the east side nor the rear of Gracehill is visible in the picture. Beyond the rear porch is a huge, gnarled old English beech, the kind of tree completely irresistible to every boy with a penknife. The initials are there, faded but clearly visible, GSP, FP, JP, and the rest. Chippy's is halfway up the trunk, below the first thick limb, and carved in the center of a circle. Linked to it is another circle with WW inside—for William Whittem.

There are other initials, carved by the Pattersons' playmates. All manner of B's for Biddle and Buckley; V's for Vaux, C's for Cadwallader, S's for Sims, and a D or two, which could have been for Drexel.

Thirty years ago, when the present occupants of Gracehill moved in (they don't call it that any longer), a high iron fence surrounded what was left of the original acreage.

"My father told me," Edward F. R. Wood, Jr., who lived there, explained, "that when Eleanor sold off parcels of the estate from time to time she kept getting rid of the iron fence extending into property she no longer owned but making sure to join the ends together to enclose what still remained. May be something symbolic there. I don't know. We bought about an acre and a half from her with the house, so there must have been a hell of a lot of fence to dispose of—whatever amount it took to completely encircle twenty acres.

"Eleanor was a fine equestrienne. When I was a child, I used to see her riding through the park with her friends. Her brother Joe, the one who was a newspaperman, was a fraternity brother of mine (Zeta Psi) at Penn. He died long before I was born, but out at the House we've a few cups he won for horsemanship. I've a feeling she and Joe took many a jump over the fence, probably scaring Mrs. Patterson half to death. It's just about the right height for a thrill, although I wouldn't want to try it."

It was easy to picture the two of them, Joe and Eleanor, long before arthritis crippled her, astride their horses, followed by C. Stuart, Francis, and George, the cautious one (Chippy didn't care for the sport, and Jane couldn't mount a horse), riding through their grounds out to the park."

Ed went on.

"I never saw the fence (my father had it torn down as soon as we moved in), but I'm told it was over four feet high and not the least bit ornamental. The kind used in English deer parks to keep the animals from wandering in front of driveways. Could be there still were a few deer foraging through Chestnut Hill when Gracehill was built."

A three-car garage has replaced the two pony sheds and the carriage house that had stalls for four horses and quarters for a stable man and boy. Toward the rear of the garden are remains of two lawn-tennis courts, abandoned 30 or 40 years ago. Beyond a low stile there is a slight incline from the top of which you can see several houses, each one surrounded by a sizable lawn bordered with shade trees.

"All this used to be part of the Pattersons' grounds," Ed explained. "It didn't compare to the Vaux or Houston estates, but it was just about the choicest spot on the Hill."

On the opposite side of the garage, almost impossible to see from any other part of Gracehill, is a square of magnificent boxwood, each side of which is probably 40 feet long and 10 feet high. This was Ellen Patterson's pride and joy. Surrounded by the towering boxwood is a garden so lovely it takes your breath away. To be seen all but a few months of the year are dozens of varieties of flowers of every conceivable color, beginning to bud or already in bloom, arranged in geometric patterns, with smooth grass footpaths between.

"This is hallowed ground for female flower enthusiasts," Ed said. "Mrs. Patterson and her friends founded the Garden Clubs of America here. There used to be a Japanese summerhouse right in the center, where Ellen Patterson entertained guests at tea."

The main house, in C. Stuart Patterson's day, had 24 rooms and five baths. Four of the baths were on the second floor; the fifth, for use of the servants, was in the basement. On the first floor were a large, formal dining room, a breakfast room overlooking the garden, a huge old-fashioned kitchen and butler's pantry, a good-sized library, and a spacious drawing room opening into a music salon, where, in later years, C. Stuart installed a pipe organ no one ever learned to play. A circular stairway led to the second floor. Here were the family and guest bedrooms, Peg Johnson's two-rooms-and-bath suite, a bright sewing room facing north, and a game room with a dart board, poker table, and a 14.2 billiard table, where Chippy learned to play a highly skillful game—he could beat everyone except brother George.

Through the windows of the master bedroom on the second floor you can still see the horse chestnut (although it is old and feeble-looking) visible in Joe Sims' photograph. But the oak is gone ("lightning, twenty years ago," Ed Wood said). Bill Whittem once showed the Woods where Chippy's room had been. It faced the garden, and from the windows you could look out upon the ancient beech, the boxwood, the tennis courts, and the dry path where the brook once flowed. All about the house are the gentle wooded rises and green slopes which make Chestnut Hill such a delightful place to live in. It was as lovely a view as you're likely to find in Philadelphia, and you wonder why a boy could find no peace and little happiness here and what dark forces compelled this troubled adolescent to pour his security from a whiskey bottle.

CHAPTER 6

LIFE at Gracehill those first six years must have been pleasant. Although Patterson, Sr. was busy with his practice and the P.R.R., he managed to spend more time with his family than he ever had before, or would again. Ellen had her garden and the children everything to make them happy—ponies, tennis courts, a playhouse, a brook to fish in or dam up, and their own miniature cricket field.

What family life there was centered outdoors, where Christopher encouraged competitive sports despite the fact that there never was much question about the outcome of any game in which George was a participant. He usually came in first, and while he bent over backward to be scrupulously fair and never played to the galleries, he played to win. There was a fierce drive in George which somehow found expression the moment he grasped a bat or a racket.

All the youngsters from neighboring estates joined the Pattersons, and Gracehill, almost from the moment the family moved there, became the most popular place on the Hill. Each child had his own circle of playmates, and friendships which lasted a lifetime were begun there. Ellen entertained extensively, and her Japanese teahouse in the boxwood garden was a quiet retreat for herself and other young Chestnut Hill matrons, an escape from shouting children at play on the courts or in the fields.

These were happy days for Chippy. He had his friends, all classmates at Germantown Academy, where he joined George, Joe, and Francis after two terms at Delancey. There was Ed Buckley; Jack Cadwallader; Chuck Biddle; Chippy's cousin, Johnny Sims (the architect's older brother); and of course, Bill Whittem. For boys of nine or ten there wasn't nearly enough time to do all the things they wanted to do. Besides the fun to be had at Gracehill, there was a blacksmith shop near the Chestnut Hill Station on Bethlehem Pike where the boys stood for hours fascinated by the forge, the clang of the anvil, the sparks, the bellows, and particularly the smith, Bert Osbourne, who once was a circus strongman.

They even had their own swimming hole.

"It was the most dangerous place you ever heard of," Bill Whittem said, "and it's a wonder any of us lived to grow up. An old abandoned quarry out in Whitemarsh, about fifty feet wide and filled with black, cold water. It seemed bottomless. Not even the divers they sent down once, when there was a report that kidnappers had tossed Charlie Ross's body there, touched bottom.

"A tree grew near the one side of the quarry with a limb that stuck out over the water like it was just made for it. We got hold of a thick rope about thirty feet long, knotted one end, and tied the other to the limb. Then we used to climb the tree, sit on the knot, jump out, swing over the water, then drop off. The sides near the top of the quarry were smooth, but about ten feet below they were filled with jagged rocks. We were all pretty good swimmers, but that wouldn't have done us much good if we'd struck a sharp stone with our heads."

He paused for a bit at the recollection, then went on.

"Once Chiffy pulled a joke that scared us out of ten years' growth. I get goose pimples even now when I think about it.

"Chiffy, you know, loved practical jokes all his life, particularly if they knocked the wind out of stuffed shirts and as long as they didn't physically injure anyone. Late one afternoon—I guess it must have been September, because all the kids had come back from Bar Harbor, or Europe, or wherever they were—we wanted to take one last swim before school started.

"The air was cold, but the water was wonderful. We had our usual gang, and there were a dozen other kids from Whitemarsh and Germantown. But gradually they all left after the sun went down, and finally there was only

Chiffy, Ed Buckley, Davey Smythe, Chuck Cadwallader, and me. We knew our parents would be worrying about us and that we'd catch hell and maybe the woodshed after we got home, but we stayed anyway. Finally it got so late the only light we had was the reflection of the moon on the black water.

"We were taking turns on the rope swing and shivering with cold when we sailed through the air. Naturally we were bare-assed, and when we climbed out of the water we had no towels to dry ourselves. We didn't dare to take them from home because we were all strictly forbidden to swim in the quarry. Chiffy's turn was last, and we were going to go then. While he shinnied up the tree, we were trying to get our clothes over our wet bodies. Our teeth were chattering so much we could hardly talk. The quarry looked mighty gloomy.

"We heard Chiffy's splash and waited for him to come over the side and pick up his clothes. We didn't think anything of it for a few minutes because we'd been there for hours and jumping in and climbing out was sort of automatic. We were almost dressed when Davey spoke up.

" 'Where's Chiffy?' he asked.

"Somebody said, 'I heard him jump in, but I didn't see him get out.'

"We stopped what we were doing and looked around. There was no sign of him, and we ran to the water and stared down. Not a ripple. By this time it could have been five minutes after we heard the last splash, and we didn't know what to do. A million problems and horrible thoughts came to our minds. Should we jump in and try to find him? Ought we to run for the police and let them know we'd been swimming where it was against the law? Who'd tell Chiffy's mother he was drowned?

"I don't know how long we stood there paralyzed with fear. Then all of a sudden, right in the middle of the quarry where the moonlight was reflected in a straight line, up comes Chiffy, treading water and holding a good-sized object in his hands. It looked like a pink torso.

" 'It's Charlie Ross,' he said very quietly. 'I found him on the bottom.'

"This was a moment I'll carry with me to my grave," said Bill. "We could have killed Chiffy. Of course it wasn't Charlie Ross. It was one of Nora's old dolls he'd hidden. While we were dressing he came out of the water, got the pink doll, and stood in the shadows. When he saw us looking for him, he swam underwater to the center of the quarry and surfaced at exactly the right time."

All the Patterson children did well in school. Joe without effort attained one of the highest averages in the history of the Academy. George led his form, although he was somewhat of a grind. (He was also the only one of his brothers to receive a good mark in what today is called "citizenship" but then was labeled "deportment.") Francis, too, was near the top, and Chippy, who depended solely upon memory and rarely cracked a book except for the two subjects he loved, English and Latin, was an honor student. Eleanor had no difficulty in taking many prizes at Agnes Irwin and Bryn Mawr.

Except for summers spent at Cape May or Newport, life for the children was centered in Chestnut Hill. Here were their home, school, and companions. They were able to achieve the insularity of royalty, only rarely coming in direct contact with children or grown-ups of a lower social and economic status.

Once in a while they played hookey and sneaked into a matinee at Keith's new theater on Eighth Street below Vine or to the Eden Musee, on Arch Street near the Reading Terminal, where an assembly of assorted freaks was on display. Like most Philadelphia children the Pattersons, too, were taken to view the famous annual Mummers' Parade held on New Year's Eve.

Talk about the parade to any Philadelphia father and he *may* recall the gorgeous costumes, clowns, string bands, and magnificent floats. But it's more likely he'll remember the exquisite, endless agony of shoulder pains brought on by holding aloft a couple of screaming six- or eight-year-olds, one at a time, their weight increasing geometrically by the minute, for five hours while he stood on a wintry sidewalk, shoved by crowds and battered by wind and snow.

This was not for C. Stuart Patterson, Sr. The Pattersons and their friends viewed the parade from a box set high up in front of the Dundas Lippincott mansion at Broad and Chestnut Streets, sheltered from the elements and warmed by iron containers filled with live coals that the servants renewed frequently.

Over the years there were many other occasions when the children left Gracehill openly or surreptitiously to go into town. Once, Chippy recalled, when he was no more than eight, Eleanor and her friend Bessie Altemus sneaked him into center city (under pain of tremendous punishment if he talked) to see a marathon dance at Carpenter Hall, Thirteenth and Chestnut Streets.

Infrequently, after a few weeks of carefully budgeting their allowances (Christopher believed in teaching his children the value of a dollar) or by wheedling an extra 50 cents from their mother who was not told how it was to be spent, Francis and Chippy, in the custody of Joe, would spend Saturday afternoons at Forepaugh's Dime Museum, next to Keith's on Eighth Street.

Once in a while Christopher and Ellen would take the children in town for some special event. One such occasion was the visit of David Kalakaua I, King of the Hawaiian Islands, who was given a reception at the Hotel Continental, September 25, 1881.

Another event Chippy remembered all his life was the funeral of his great-great-uncle, Major General Robert Patterson.

"I was about eight or nine," Chippy once told Tom McBride, "and I sat upright between my parents in the carriage in back of the hearse, awed by everything and a bit frightened to be so close to my father, and too scared to fidget. I had never seen my Uncle Robert, but his picture hung over the mantel in our library, and I knew he was a West Pointer and a hero of the Mexican War.

"There must have been a hundred carriages, all draped in black, the horses with black tassels. An army band, playing the Funeral March, led the cortege. The governor was there, and he helped my mother from the carriage, then lifted me down. I'll never forget all the army officers, their swords dangling from their sides, standing at attention while the pallbearers carried the coffin up the stairs at Broad Street Station and placed it in a railroad car, draped with American flags and with the shades down."

Another occasion which impressed Chippy, perhaps because it was one of the few times he spent many hours alone with his father, was a trip the two of them made to Baltimore. C. Stuart was asked to give his opinion on some litigation involving a home there owned by a cousin, Betsy Patterson Bonaparte, widow of Jerome and consequently a grand-niece of Napoleon.

Chippy had been in bed for a week with some childhood ailment. His father, to Chippy's joy, suggested it might do the boy good to get out in the air and come to Baltimore with him. The two, father and son, left for Maryland early in the morning. This was a hundred-mile ride, and a briefcase, filled with work Christopher planned to do while they were traveling, was left unopened. Instead, as the train sped along, he marked the points of interest along the P.R.R.'s right of way. Whatever Christopher had to do in Baltimore was accomplished in a short while, and the pair boarded the train that afternoon. A porter locked a table in place between their two Pullman chairs, and served them a memorable dinner. Christopher unbent completely, asked questions about the things he thought would please his son, and listened carefully to Chippy's answers.

It was a notable day for Chippy, one he was to recall vividly all his life.

Chippy spent his tenth birthday in London. In June of 1885 the P.R.R. sent Christopher and several other administrative officers and engineers to an international conference of railroad men. Patterson felt this was an excellent opportunity for his children to broaden their education and decided they would go along with Ellen and him. There was some question of Ellen taking the trip because she was pregnant again. Since she wasn't expecting the baby until late January or February of the following year and was in fine physical condition, her doctor permitted her to make the voyage providing she returned by mid-August.

It was quite an entourage which sailed down the Delaware River on the S.S. *Ohio:* Christopher and Ellen, their five children, Peg Johnson, a young handmaid, and Christopher's oldest brother, Theodore. In addition, Patterson had engaged a well-traveled Englishwoman who hired out to Chestnut Hill families making the "grand" or lesser tours. Problems of dealing with Europeans, thought by most Americans of that era to be decadent, dishonest and quite stupid, were left to Miss Vinnie Patch, a name which surely should have inspired confidence.

The trip was without incident except for a summary dismissal of the maid, who had to be replaced with an English-born substitute. Uncle "Theo," acting on a theory he maintained throughout a busy lifetime—"If they're big enough, they're old enough"—had discovered the girl's charms and was himself discovered in the act of this discovery by Ellen. Ellen and Christopher sailed for Philadelphia in early August, but the children stayed on in the custody of Peg Johnson, Miss Patch, and George, who was past seventeen and a very sobering influence on anybody.

Toward the last week of September they left Liverpool and landed in Philadelphia October 2. Ellen and her doctor had either miscalculated or her youngest infant was a month premature. Jane Cuyler Patterson was born December 23, 1885.

CHAPTER 7

OUTWARDLY, at least, Jane's birth changed the pattern at Gracehill very little. For the first few years Jane was slow but apparently normal. She walked at eighteen months and talked four months later. Ellen was unable to breast-feed her, and a wet-nurse was hired. The house was large enough to accommodate baby and nurse without infringing on the other children's established rights, and one of the guest rooms was turned into a nursery.

If anyone felt the difference Jane's presence made, it was Chippy. He'd been the baby, and overnight this position of importance and privilege in a household of five children came to an abrupt conclusion. The squeeze was at the other end, too. George, past seventeen, six feet two, 185 pounds, hero of the Academy's football, tennis, and cricket teams, and now starring as end on the Haverford College varsity football eleven, was the apple of his father's eye.

Francis, called "Dike" (no one remembers why), closest to Chippy in age if not in temperament, was of no help to his younger brother. He was completely self-centered, and at thirteen had already informed his father, who hoped all his sons would follow the law, that he had no intention of being anything but a physician. He was so set on this profession that when he was in the eleventh form, only two semesters from graduation, he left his brothers and friends at Germantown and transferred to Episcopal Academy because he believed that school offered better courses in science.

Eleanor, thrilled with the presence of a new infant to take the place of dolls only recently cast aside, had no time for her little brother. The long morning walks they took together through Chestnut Hill (both were early risers and used to meet at breakfast before the rest of the household got up) were ended, and secret hideaways both discovered and shared near the stream and in the woods at Gracehill were deserted or visited by a lonely little boy.

Joe, nearly sixteen when Jane was born, and almost as tall as George, was quiet, shy, and perceptive. He sensed Chippy's mounting difficulties and tried to befriend his younger brother, but he was having his own troubles. He wanted more than anything else to be a newspaperman (pretty low on his father's scale unless you were a publisher), and he didn't have Dike's stolid, unswerving resistance and imperviousness to pressure. Gentle and unhappy about hurting his father, it grieved him to say "no" to the law.

The Pattersons, normally unsentimental, made much of their children's birthdays. The night before the event, presents from Ellen and Christopher and each brother, from Nora and Nurse Johnson, were carefully wrapped and put on the billiard table in the game room, which was officially out-of-bounds for the birthday child until the following morning. Later in the day there was a party with cake and candles when the children were young, or a dinner dance when they grew older. No matter how busy Ellen and Christopher were, they made it a point to be on hand.

But Chippy's eleventh birthday was a failure. On his tenth, the one spent in London, there were a gift and a cablegram from his mother and father, the wire almost as impressive as if its senders were there. But in September of 1886, Society had its biggest event in many years, the marriage of Miss Rita Armstrong and Anthony J. Drexel, Sr., at Long Beach. The P.R.R. ran a special train to accommodate the scores of Philadelphians who attended the wedding. Christopher and Ellen were guests at Villa Elberon, the Drexel mansion, where they remained for several days. Then they went to Pittsburgh, where friends entertained Ellen while Christopher and two or three of his railroad colleagues watched John L. Sullivan knock out Frank Herald.

They completely forgot their youngest son's birthday, and although the others placed gifts on the billiard table and Peg Johnson did her best to comfort the weeping eleven-year-old, Chippy's feelings were hurt and the children's party held that evening without Christopher and Ellen was not a success. A present his parents hurriedly bought and gave Chippy the next day had little value.

A few days later Christopher made sure to be on hand to watch George play his first international cricket match at the Germantown Cricket Club. George, whom the

North American dubbed "The Little Wonder," was the star of the game. The 32 runs he scored helped The Gentlemen of Philadelphia defeat The Gentlemen of England. A great victory celebration was held that night at the club, and the following evening Christopher and Ellen gave a dinner dance at Gracehill for members of both teams.

Chippy was probably no more sensitive than most eleven-year-olds, and in a family of six brothers and sisters he must have learned that none could be the favorite and parents' love had to be shared equally. Unfortunately for his youngest son and for the other children as well, Christopher was unable to establish the impartiality of his affections. George was always first.

C. Stuart again began to spend less and less time at home. The P.R.R. was expanding in every direction. Through stock manipulation, rate reductions, and politics it became the largest transportation system in the world. The battle with forces trying to prevent this was constant. The Goulds and the Vanderbilts had no love for the P.R.R. and used every means, legal if possible, to try to prevent the growth of the Philadelphia giant. Then, too, labor was starting to flex its weak muscles; like Antaeus, every time it was slapped down to earth, it arose stronger.

An important legal strategist, Christopher Stuart Patterson, Sr. was appreciated more and more by directors of the railroad, who rewarded him with salary increases and stock bonuses.

This was the age of Dreiser's *Titan,* and the P.R.R. was not the only utility gobbling up weaker competitors and fattening directors and stockholders at the expense of the public. Philadelphia's upper classes, whose ancestors would have raised holy hell, turned their heads away (and worse still, shared in the gains) while Charles T. Yerkes, a Quaker at that, and his colleagues, Peter A. B. Widener and William L. Elkins, systematically looted the city's transportation system. By bribe and coercion these unholy three (Widener, the erstwhile butcher boy, furnishing his share of the cash from huge profits made by supplying Union troops with mutton) manipulated city councils into granting them low-cost franchises guaranteeing them a complete monopoly of Philadelphia's streetcar lines for 30 years.

Yerkes, deserted by his partners when the going got rough, went to jail. But his colleagues rose to glory by gaining an almost complete monopoly of the nation's gas-lighting system. They accomplished this in little more than a decade by one of the most ruthless, cynical, and destructive strategies in the history of American finance. One of the few Philadelphians to protest publicly was John Wanamaker, the merchant, scorned by the *haute monde* as a mere peddler. But his loud and persistent cries of "Stop, thieves!" were drowned out by the roar of fat dividends pouring into the coffers of Philadelphia's aristocrats, who supplied Elkins and Widener with cash through their purchases of United Gas Improvement stock.

Although the upper classes stretched out open palms to grasp these increasingly larger dividends that the Messrs. Widener and Elkins offered them, Proper Philadelphians turned thumbs down on social acceptance of their business partners.

In 1887 Christopher was invited to join the faculty of the University of Pennsylvania Law School. For any Philadelphia member of the bar, no matter how great his prestige, this was an honor equivalent to knighthood and one awarded to only comparatively few. Those tapped were at the peak of their profession, financially independent, morally above reproach, and socially acceptable. Despite the fact that it would cost him what few hours remained from his other duties, Patterson accepted with alacrity. He was at once well liked by his colleagues, who dubbed him "C. Stuart" (the name stuck), and respected by the student body, although it took a rather whimsical view of his subject, "Constitutional Law," or perhaps of the way he taught it.

George, after two years at Haverford and two more at Wharton, entered Penn Law, Class of '91. It must have been a proud moment indeed for C. Stuart when he welcomed his favorite son to the class and realized that the day when the two would share offices and practice was no longer distant.

CHAPTER 8

THE CHILDREN were growing up. By the time George was in his second year at law school, both Joe and Francis had joined him at the University. Eleanor was a freshman at Bryn Mawr, and Chippy was in the eleventh form at the Academy. About this time C. Stuart and Ellen were making the unhappy discovery that their youngest child was "different." She was slow to learn and physically sluggish. Had she been born into a family of less distinction, she might have made a better go of life. But the competition was much too keen for a child with a mentality which Dr. John McCloskey, later the Patterson family physician, classified as "dull normal."

"If Jane Patterson had belonged to an average household she might have done all right," he explained. "She could even have married and led a useful life. She wasn't pretty, but her features weren't bad—she had the straight Patterson nose I always thought was like the Barrymores'—and if she hadn't stuffed herself and got so obese, she might have done better. But she had five brilliant, handsome siblings. When they discussed books, politics, the theater, law, or almost anything, I'm sure she didn't know what was going on. No wonder she felt rejected."

For Jane, food, eaten furtively because her diet at meals was closely supervised, became the means to achieve a sense of security and fulfullment she could get no other way. When she thought no one was looking, she would snatch an extra piece of bread from the plate, or, escaping from Nurse Johnson, sneak into the pantry and gorge herself hurriedly with little thought of what she was gobbling.

She must have been about seven or eight before she

began to steal anything else. Gradually, loose change, as well as various articles which could be of little value to anyone except their owners, and certainly none to Jane, began to disappear. There was a book of Keats' poems given to Eleanor (called "Nora") by her favorite teacher, a pair of Francis' cuff links, a loving cup George had won at the Academy, and a fancy belt buckle of Chippy's.

Since it was inconceivable to C. Stuart or his wife that any member of the family could be involved, the servants were questioned and a housemaid, under suspicion, was fired (and later rehired with apologies when the truth was known). Still the petty thievery continued. Sometimes Ellen's guests returned to their homes puzzled over the disappearance of coins they were sure were in their purses when they entered Gracehill. None dreamed of mentioning it to Ellen until, one day, four of her guests, following an afternoon at Gracehill, decided to shop together in Germantown.

One of the ladies was Emily Pepper Vaux, Ellen's cousin, whose son, Norris Wistar Vaux, later became a physician and remained one of Chippy's few faithful Chestnut Hill friends. Many years afterward she told the story to her son.

"Grace Buckley was with me," Mrs. Vaux recalled, "but I can't remember who else except that there were four of us. We were in Jones', and I bought a trifle which cost a few cents more than a dollar. Your father never liked me to charge anything under two dollars. I took a bill from my wallet, then searched through my purse for the pennies. I was sure I'd had a lot of small change, but I thought little of it when I couldn't find a cent. Grace laughed and said, 'Oh, here, let me lend you the two cents,' and she looked in her pocketbook, only to make the same discovery.

"Then the others did the same thing. There wasn't a dime's worth of small change among us. We stared at each other quizzically, and someone asked, 'Did this ever happen to any of you before?' We were all shocked and kept completely quiet for a moment or two before each of us admitted this wasn't the first time we'd found money missing after we left Gracehill.

"It was summer, and we'd spent that afternoon in the garden with Ellen. Of course our handbags were lying around, but we couldn't recall anyone being near them or us except Jane, who was playing nearby most of the time. Ellen served lemonade, but the maid who brought it placed the pitcher on the table and left immediately. There could be no doubt whatsoever in our minds. We recalled a number of similar occasions with like results.

" 'Someone,' said Grace, 'has to tell Ellen,' and since I was her cousin, I was elected. You can't imagine how it feels to tell one of your closest friends you suspect her daughter of being a thief. It was the most difficult task I ever had to face, but it had to be done and I did it."

Ellen and Nurse Johnson made a complete search of the house. In the corner of a closet on the back stairway between the second and third floors they found poor Jane's loot—a pile of coins, inexpensive jewelry, and other trifles which had been missing and thought mislaid. There was nothing of real value, and with the exception of the money, which couldn't possibly be identified, everything else in the heap belonged to a member of the family.

Ellen was frantic. She was afraid to tell her husband because she didn't know how he would react. She would have liked to handle the problem herself, but it was beyond her.

C. Stuart was told. His reaction, for one so remote from the affairs of his own household, was surprising. Completely in control of his emotions, he took Jane into the library, shut the door, and spoke to her quietly. Then he sent the child to bed and told Ellen that even though Jane had promised never again to steal and appeared penitent, he was sure that unless she were watched carefully at all times she would probably continue her thievery. The other children were informed, with admonitions to keep their eyes on their sister as much as they could.

This was the point at which Jane's life, and possibly Chippy's, might have changed if psychiatry had been available. But there was no one to whom the Pattersons could turn for help. The understanding of neuroses, or their diagnosis, prognosis, and treatment, was far beyond the scope of even the best psychiatrists of the day.

At that time there was nothing Christopher and Ellen could do except keep a close watch on Jane and hope she'd grow out of it. Despite the fact that she was not permitted to enter a store unattended, the child frequently managed to sneak away by herself into many a Germantown shop. Storekeepers knew who the little girl was and soon became alerted to her petty pilfering. They let her take what she wanted, then sent a bill to her parents.

As long as Jane stole nothing but articles of small value, there wasn't much talk. Store owners were discreet (and besides they were paid), so that comparatively few people knew about the child's kleptomania until she was sixteen. Then, at some gathering in the Stotesbury town house, an expensive brooch belonging to Mrs. Stotesbury was missed after everyone had gone home.

Insurance investigators, quietly checking the guest list, soon ran down Jane's name. By the time they were ready to call on C. Stuart, Ellen, who had heard of the theft, which could not be kept quiet because of the value of the stones, suspected the worst. She and Nurse Johnson confronted Jane, who readily confessed and handed them the brooch. Christopher and Ellen were unable to face their friends, and George returned the jewelry to its owner. The Stotesburys were most understanding, and prosecution was of course unthinkable. But Christopher's proud name had been harmed, and even though his associates were completely sympathetic, he was shaken.

By this time Chippy, too, had given him many a heartache, beginning, perhaps, during the boy's last term at the Academy, the year Eleanor made her debut. Chippy had been doing well at school both scholastically and athletically, and his behavior wasn't too bad. His marks, particularly in English, history, and Latin were excellent, and even in subjects he disliked, algebra, chemistry and biology, he did far better than average. He had little understanding of mathematics or science and depended entirely upon memory to get him by. He had begun to read omnivorously, and as soon as he came home from school he would shut himself up in his room for hours, poring over the latest book by Robert Louis Stevenson or re-reading Plutarch and Dickens.

He was tall for his age, and before he was sixteen had attained his full height of six feet two, although he weighed only 160 pounds. He was a fine batsman and bowler and played on the first cricket eleven. He was also a good half-miler, and had been on the varsity tennis team for three seasons. If you didn't probe into his home life, it would be difficult to understand why he wasn't happy. The fourth and last of the Patterson brothers at the Academy, he was probably the best liked by both faculty and student body. His humor was droll, rather mature for his age, and what was important was that he could laugh as heartily when the joke was on himself as he could when it was on someone else. He was beginning to attract girls (and vice versa) and was much sought after as an escort at Chestnut Hill teenage affairs.

His first love was Mary Sims (now Mary Tyson) with whom he had grown up. She was tall, full-bodied, lively, and pretty, with fair skin and long black hair. All through childhood they were in and out of each other's homes, and Chippy took Mary to most of the Chestnut Hill parties they both attended. He was her escort at Nora's debut. It was the kind of youthful romance which could easily have developed into marriage if Chippy had been more stable and Mary more understanding. Before mature love could develop they drifted apart. There may have been a reason for their final break. It could have been Chippy's drinking, which was becoming a serious problem even before he reached seventeen.

Throughout his life Chippy often thought about and spoke of Mary, and so many of the women he loved resembled her—tall, handsome, dark-haired, and vivacious. Mary married Richard Tyson at eighteen and after that lived most of her days along the Riviera and in Paris.

"I was very intimate with my cousins, the Pattersons, and frequently was at their home," she wrote. "Chiffy was a beautiful boy, and he had the most equable disposition of anyone I have ever known. He was never anything but perfectly good-humored, but with a capacity to tease—he himself keeping in perfect good temper—that had the result of quite infuriating Dike. With all this he was far and away the funniest person I have ever known.

"Of all the family, he was my pet and my darling. I wish I could remember all his remarks and absurdities. Only some—and they perhaps the least absurd—happen to stand out. As he matured, he was the first person I knew who appreciated Kipling, and he bred in me a like admiration. He had a keen appreciation of good literature and could read a page, close the book, and recite it to me verbatim.

"One day I was driving in the country in a dog cart with two young men. A dog kept following us. I was worried for fear he was a stray and begged the young men to stop to take him in. This they would not do, but Chiffy saw us and took the dog in and fed it until it wandered off somewhere else. Afterwards, we sat on the lawn at tea, and one of the young men, a bird fancier, was most interested in a bird in the tree above us. "Better not do that, Buck,' said Chiffy, 'or Mary'll make you adopt it.'

"Then he started to drink. The first time I was so shocked I could hardly believe it. He couldn't have been over fifteen. Sometimes he would be so unsteady he could barely stand up straight, but as soon as he'd call for me and greet my mother he seemed to be able to pull himself together, for the moment at least. I knew she never suspected anything. He was never loud, always a perfect gentleman.

"It's a wonder Aunt Ellen didn't find out sooner. I've often thought she knew all along and didn't make a fuss because she was afraid Uncle Stuart would discover it. After Nora's coming-out party, where I almost had to hold him up, I told him I would never go out with him again if he drank. I wish now I had tried to understand him better.

"Oh, yes, one more thing. When Gracehill was broken up, Nora took an apartment in Chestnut Hill, and when I went to see her I noticed Chiffy's professional card nailed on the front door. I demanded 'Why?' and her answer was, 'No better burglar insurance in the world!' "

Chippy's first escapade, which could have resulted in serious trouble but didn't simply because neither he nor his friends were suspected, occurred shortly after the famous blizzard of March, 1888. Philadelphia, as well as the rest of the East Coast, was hit hard by snow and high wind. Schools were closed for two weeks.

During the preceding few seasons the raising of chickens had become a fad for Academy and Penn Charter students. Many a mother, torn between delight at finding her son evincing an interest in animal husbandry and bewilderment at his sudden, widespread enthusiasm, would have been horrified to learn the boy's true motivation. The chickens were bought, bred, and traded for the sole purpose of training them to be killers. Their value was directly proportionate to their savagery. Cock fighting was the most popular sport of the hour. It was strictly illegal, yet it flourished like a nurtured weed, and not a day passed without a bloody battle fought in some stable on a Germantown or Chestnut Hill estate. There, scores of youngsters muffled their screams of joy while two game-cocks fought to the death.

Chippy, Bill Whittem, and Chuck Cadwallader each owned a third share in a very small but fearless bantam they christened Caligula.

"What this rooster lacked in size," Bill said, "it made up in courage. We'd had it almost two years, and it was so tiny you could put it in your overcoat pocket. We raised it in Chiffy's barn and spent more time training it than we did at our school work. We read every book we could get about feeding and trimming fighting birds. Caligula got plenty of workouts and never lost a main.

"Part of his valor was congenital, but I admit the rest was artificial. Shortly before each fight we used to give our bird a few drops of Colafra, an old-time patent medicine my father sold. It was very popular, probably because it was forty per cent alcohol. Most of the time we'd feed Caligula a couple of drops orally, but once in a while, when he rebelled, we'd inject a dose rectally with a syringe I'd borrow from the store.

"Right after the big blizzard, all of us were so pent up we couldn't stand it a minute longer. The roads were still pretty bad, but late one afternoon I worked my way over to Gracehill and picked up Chuck on the way. We found Chiffy in the barn exercising Caligula and decided we'd take the bird with us and try to find a match for him. Chiffy hitched his pony to the dog sled, and we started out in the direction of Fortside Inn, but there was nobody there so we kept going. When we got to Gwynedd, somebody told us there was going to be a main in an unused barn opposite the Penn Lynn Country Club that night.

"We found the place and stuck around. It was a new dairy barn, owned by Mr. E. B. Smith, President of the Germantown Saving Fund Society and a good friend of Chiffy's father.

"Pretty soon lots of men began to come around and enter the barn. There was a fellow at the door who tried to keep us out, but Chiffy walked in as though he owned the place, and the man let us get by.

"The floors were covered with fresh straw and the mow filled with hay, which must have been put there just before the storm broke. There were thirty stalls, but fortunately they were empty because the cattle hadn't been brought in yet. Word had gotten around, and within an hour there were a hundred men and boys surrounding the pit in the center of the barn. By the time we got started it was dark outside, and the barn was lighted by kerosene lamps, hung pretty low.

"Caligula won his first three fights easily without Colafra, but he looked awfully tired for the final. You're not supposed to pick up your bird after he's once in the pit except to fix his spurs if they come loose. We were using 'short heels,' spurs about an inch and a half long, and one of them came undone. Chiffy reached down to pick up the bird. The place was a mess, full of blood and feathers. There was a lot of money changing hands, and everyone was excited.

"The three of us were standing over Caligula. I knew

what Chiff wanted to do, so I passed him the syringe. We were bent down close to our cock, and I didn't think anyone saw us, but when Chiffy pulled back the plunger and shot it into Caligula some big guy who'd been losing money all evening saw us and jumped up.

" 'What the hell are you doing?' he screamed and leaped forward. As he did, he knocked a lamp down into the straw. In about half a minute the barn was ablaze. There was a wild scramble for the doors. We ran ahead a couple hundred feet to where we had the pony hitched and looked back. The building was a mass of flames. Chiffy was almost the last out, and he had Caligula tucked under his arm. But the bird was dead before we even got back to Chestnut Hill.

"There was an awful stink about the fire; the barn was a total loss. Somebody from the Club reported they saw a pony sled, and police tried to trace it. We were scared to death and laid low and behaved ourselves for a long time afterward. Chiffy said one night his father looked at him kind of funny and said he'd had lunch with Mr. Smith that day. But if he suspected Chiffy he never said anything, and that was the end of it.

"The next day Chiffy bought another bird which looked pretty much like Caligula, and we kept it around for a while, then got rid of it. It wasn't a fighter, and we had no more heart to try to train it. Besides, that was the end of chicken mains as far as we were concerned."

CHAPTER 9

BEFORE Chippy finished his first year at Penn, he had three experiences which in that era moved him to the head of the class. He got drunk; he was seduced; and he spent a night in jail. These three events, as Chippy or other members of the profession would have said, were consecutive and not concurrent actions.

Alcohol was no stranger to the Patterson household. It was an accepted part of their culture, and none of the family, their guests, or servants gave it any more thought than they would have given to another course of a well-served meal. Their cellar was a modest one, and since C. Stuart, who liked a highball before dinner and a glass of light wine with his food, did not regard himself as a gourmet or connoisseur, it contained few vintage labels.

None of the Pattersons' friends considered ability to hold liquor a social asset. A hollow leg was placed in the same category as a hollow head. A drink was an aperitif or an adjunct to a meal, not the meal itself. No lady or gentleman drank his dinner. Except in orthodox Quaker households, the European custom of wines served with dinner was followed. Drunkenness was regarded with utter disgust, and eventually the sot who overindulged frequently found himself sitting on the outside looking in.

With rare exceptions the social functions of Philadelphia's upper classes (the Assemblies, for example) were, and still are, conducted with decorum and dignity. Café society never did exist in Philadelphia.

It's hard to believe Chippy's drinking could have gone unnoticed as long as it did. A possible explanation is that a true family life did not exist at Gracehill. The structure was there, but it was a mere shell without substance.

Nurse Johnson, warm and sympathetic, into whose comforting arms Chippy would run when he was small, was now devoting much of her time to her youngest charge. The head of the family, who could find leisure to speak at nearly every important civic affair, to cruise on J. P. Morgan's yacht Corsair, to represent the City of Philadelphia in Berne at the 600th anniversary of the Swiss Republic, and to head a P.R.R. relief train sent to aid survivors of the Johnstown flood, was apparently too busy to pay attention to the serious needs of his own children.

Ellen, far less involved with social affairs than a woman of her position might be, and almost completely uninterested in Philadelphia's growing social problems, was, nevertheless, because of her beauty and charm, in great demand as a hostess. She was able to find time to join Mrs. Grover Cleveland and Mr. William Platt Pepper in sponsoring a Charity Ball at the Academy, to receive Robert Todd Lincoln at the Acorn Club, and to open the Wissahickon Horse Show.

Chippy began to take secret nips when he was no more than fourteen years old. By the time he was a freshman at Penn he was a moderately heavy drinker. Morning and evening doubles weren't enough, and he began to hide a bottle in his bedroom for afternoon shots. Discovery was inevitable, but it was not until the evidence was incontrovertible that C. Stuart, Ellen, and the rest of the family realized what had been going on for several years right under their noses.

It happened on a June day in 1891. This should have been the start of a particularly fine summer for the Pattersons. The trustees of the University had just asked C. Stuart to become dean of the law school. Nora was ready to announce her engagement to a young Boston banker, and she and her mother were happily shopping for the trousseau. The Sunday *Item* published Joe's first signed article and he and Dike were planning to go to England to watch George play cricket. Although George was the youngest member of The Gentlemen of Philadelphia's Eleven, the nation's press had just hailed him as "the greatest cricketer the United States has produced since Bart King."

It had been an exciting day. There was a shipside party for George and the rest of the team, and the Pattersons, including Jane, participated. Champagne flowed freely, but Chippy quite ostentatiously didn't touch a drop when toasts were drunk, even though his father poured him a glass and said, "Here boy, drink up. This won't hurt you a bit." Afterward Chippy wandered off and wasn't seen again that day. The family had dinner in town and returned late in the evening, assuming Chippy had been with his friends and was by then in bed.

During the night a noise awakened C. Stuart. He came downstairs to investigate and found his youngest son sprawled out on the library floor, an empty whiskey bottle by his side. Patterson was livid with rage. He pulled Chippy to his feet, dragged him along the room and down the steps into the cellar, pushed him into the coal storeroom, locked the door, and left.

Although there was little sleep for C. Stuart, he controlled his anger and told no one that night, not even Ellen, who hadn't awakened. Early the following morning he broke the news to the family. Ellen was horrified and unbelieving. Her first impulse was to rush to the basement and see for herself, but her husband would not permit it. He sent Dike and Joe down with the key and told them to remove Chippy and use the backstairs to take him out of his mother's sight.

When his brothers opened the storeroom door, Chippy was sitting up in a corner, a filthy mess. Not knowing where he was when he woke up in total darkness, he had staggered into the coal pile and struck his head against an iron shovel. The Tenderloin couldn't have produced a better example of a stumblebum. He had vomited, his clothes stank, and his eyes were glazed.

Holding him at arm's length, Joe and Dike took him upstairs, undressed him, and put him in a warm tub. When they'd scrubbed him clean, Dike dressed the cut on his brother's head, and he and Joe carried him to his own room to sleep it off. Through all this Chippy remained in an alcoholic stupor, from which he did not recover until late that afternoon.

An abashed, penitent, and hungover Chippy sat down to a family conference called to decide his immediate fate. He readily admitted the extent of his drinking, thereby clearing up a long-standing mystery of missing whiskey. But despite threats to take him out of college, stop his allowance, and put him to work, he refused to state categorically that he would never take another drink. All he'd say was, "I'll try my best," and with this his father and mother had to be content.

For the next few months Christopher felt the best plan for Chippy would be a summer of hard labor under a hot sun so that he'd be too tired at night to go anywhere but bed. Joe offered to give up his European trip and stay with his youngest brother, since C. Stuart, Ellen, Nora, and Jane would be in Newport and George and Dike in

Europe. Christopher said "No" and that if Chiffy, at almost sixteen, couldn't handle himself, he never would. If the boy behaved he'd return to Penn in September. If not, something less pleasant would be offered.

This was a year of depression, with thousands of unemployed roaming the streets of Philadelphia looking for work, but there was no trouble finding a job for Chippy. He was put in a navvy gang building a spur to a colliery on top of Broad Mountain in Schuylkill County. Only the foreman, Llewelyn Davies, an old-time railroader, was told who his new hand was. He also received instructions to keep his eye on Chippy but to show him no favors.

The work gang lived in two ancient converted freight cars shunted to a siding. They slept on straw bunks, 32 men to a car. The cook, water boy, and foreman occupied an old caboose, which, compared to the other accommodations, was sheer luxury. Davies, whose lilting Welsh voice made him sound as though he was singing even when he called out commands, and Chippy were the only English-speaking members of the crew. The cook and his fourteen-year-old son who served as water boy were Greek, and the rest were Poles, Czechs, Russians, Lithuanians, Slavs, and Hungarians, immigrants from the farms and villages of every central European nation. Orders were acknowledged with universally understood grunts of assent.

The hard-coal regions' day began at 5 A.M. Then, the first throaty growl of a colliery whistle, ascending arpeggio-like from basso profundo to shrieking soprano, filled the morning air and was hurled across the blackened valleys. Hardly had the sound reversed the scale and with a prodigious sigh been sucked inside the iron belly of its creator when an answer came from another breaker on top of an adjoining mountain. Before the original offender had a chance to reply, blasts from scores of collieries, stretched out a mile or two apart for one hundred miles from Lykens to Carbondale, joined the wild serenade.

This was the weird choir which sent Chippy leaping out of his bunk the morning after his arrival at Vulcan work camp. Later, like a faithful, well-trained dog who answers only his master's call, Chippy would be able to sleep through all the whistles until his subconscious responded to a sound peculiar to the voice of New Boston Colliery.

The preceding day, some 48 hours after Chippy had sobered up completely, Davies had met him at nearby Morea, where the P.R.R.'s Pottsville Express made an unscheduled stop to discharge this one important passenger. During their brief walk, with Chippy towering over the five-foot-two Welshman, Davies explained the setup to his polite charge. Breakfast, he said, was at 5:15 and would be served, rain or shine, from an open flat car. Work, at the sound of another whistle, began at 5:30 and continued until the 11:30 blast, which announced a half-hour dinner break. Then it went on until the whistles sounded again at 4 P.M. Supper, the third hot meal of the day, was at 5. For the next month or two Chippy would work with a crew unloading stone, sand, and rails from 60-ton gondolas moved in each day on the siding.

Just as they reached the car containing Chippy's bunk and before Chippy realized what was happening, Davies bent down, opened young Patterson's Gladstone bag, reached in, and pulled out two quart bottles of whiskey.

It was twilight when Chippy climbed into the car which was to be his home for the next three months. Most of the men were sound asleep, and a weird symphony of assorted snores assailed his ears, and an overpowering odor of sweat, tobacco, and garlic penetrated his nostrils.

Morning ablutions were perfunctory, and Chippy was probably the only member of his crew with a toothbrush. Washing was speedy—a head dipped under the spout of a small tank filled by the water boy every day from a cold clear stream, faces sloshed and rubbed vigorously to drive away last vestiges of sleep, and hands washed with a bar of yellow soap and dried on communal towels.

A bright orange sun, signifying the hot June day to follow, was just beginning to peer from the east end of the valley below as Chippy stepped down from the car.

"It was a wonderful morning," Chippy recalled to Bill Whittem. "I'd slept better than I had in months. When I hopped down from the car, the most appetizing odor of bacon I had ever smelled in my life seemed to fill the whole mountain top. I was ravenously hungry. We lined up in front of the cook car and were handed the biggest bowls of hot oatmeal I ever saw with as much milk and sugar as you wanted. When this was finished, you got large chunks of bacon (pretty fat, but it tasted wonderful) and thick slices of rye bread. I had to hand it to the old man's railroad. Maybe they paid only a dollar a day, but there was plenty to eat."

CHAPTER 10

ABOUT the simplest job workers in a navvy gang perform is shoveling stone or sand from a gondola. When the 5:30 whistles blew there were two loaded cars on the siding, and Davies sent Chippy, with three others, on top of one of them. Each man seized a shovel from a stack before he climbed up. For anyone who'd never done a day's work in his life the job was brutally hard, and after an hour, when a hot sun beat down on the sweating laborers, Chippy was almost ready to collapse.

"I don't know how I got through that first day," Chippy used to tell Bill Whittem. "I think I ate my evening meal—I'm not sure—and when I woke up the next morning I was so stiff and sore I could hardly move. A hot bath and nice soft bed would have been heaven. Muscles I didn't even know existed were aching so badly I could hardly move. I made up my mind about one thing: When this summer was over I'd never do a stroke of physical work again as long as I lived. This is one of the few resolutions I've kept."

Saturday was payday. Almost from the moment the men arose there was an air of restlessness throughout the camp. Shortly after noon two sharp blasts from an engine in the distance announced the approach of the paymaster. Work stopped automatically. When the heavily guarded car pulled up and came to a stop, Davies blew his own whistle. The men lined up in front of the paycar. Forty years later Chippy could repeat the names Davies called out alphabetically as each man stepped out of line to make his "X" on the time sheet and collect his pay.

"Adamaitis, Blazejewski, Cheracovage, Damulewicz," all the way down to "Zinchak." There was no envelope for Chippy the first week.

The moment closing whistles blew on payday there was an immediate exodus of most of the men in the direction of Morea. Chippy, who'd been told by the foreman this was his one chance for a weekly bath, went along and took a change of linen and a clean suit with him. In the tiny "patch" men split up into groups of five or six, and Chippy followed one into a house. There, for five cents, a towel, soap, and enough water for a shave and a bath (the latter taken in a washtub in the kitchen) were supplied.

As soon as the last man finished his bath, shaved, and dressed, his group hurried back to camp and ate supper, served a half hour later on Saturdays. Davies, who spent Saturday night and Sunday with his brother in Pottsville, invited Chippy to join him, but Chippy, despite the refreshing bath and clean linen, was so tired he couldn't think of anything but sleep.

An air of heavy-handed levity permeated the camp the moment Davies was out of sight. There was backslapping, loud laughter, and a general air of relaxation. A dozen bottles appeared from nowhere, and somebody handed one to Chippy, who automatically raised it to his lips and took a long pull.

"I felt as though someone had jammed a red-hot poker down my throat," he once told Norrie Barrett. "My head snapped back so far I could feel my spine crack. It was the most potent stuff I'd ever tasted, and that first time all I did was taste it. Later I found it quite palatable. The others drank it like orange juice. It was potato whiskey, distilled by the cook in his spare time, and it must have been at least one hundred twenty proof."

Before the sun set, a farm wagon drawn by two horses came up the mountain road and pulled into a clearing about 50 yards from the tracks. Aboard was the driver; four girls, big, buxom, and heavily rouged; four cots; and four army pup tents. Shop was set up in about ten minutes, and a brisk business began immediately thereafter. Each man lined up before the lady of his choice, paid the driver-procurer 25 cents, and took his turn.

"It was quite an efficient operation," Chippy recalled years afterward to one of his clients, Mrs. London, who ran quite a few efficient operations herself, "but I found it singularly unappealing. I determined I'd rather hang on to my virtue than lose it this way."

There were no whistles on Sunday, and Chippy slept. He, the cook, and a few others were the only ones who remained at camp. The rest got up as usual and walked three miles down the mountain to Mahanoy City or the same distance across the mountain to Frackville to attend early Mass and spend the rest of the day visiting cousins or friends from the Old Country.

By the end of the following week Chippy's routine was established. His muscles were hardening; he was acquiring a deep tan; and with the exception of the few drops of potato whiskey which had escaped down his throat in that first attempt to drink it, he hadn't touched alcohol since he left home. His appetite, which had been very bad for the preceding six months, returned, and he ate enormously. On the second Saturday he got his first pay, a letter from his mother, and a brief note from his father. Both wished him well and hoped he'd behave himself.

Next day, distant church bells woke Chippy. He persuaded the cook to heat enough water for a bath, which he took in a large basin used for washing dishes. Then he shaved, dressed himself carefully, and began to walk down the mountain to Mahanoy City. A farm wagon loaded with a family on its way to church picked him up and took him to town. Chippy wandered up Mahanoy Street, passing church after church until he came to the First Episcopal, which he entered. When services had ended and he was about to walk down the steps to the street, someone tapped him on the shoulder.

He turned to face a well-dressed, attractive woman who

was probably in her late thirties, although to Chippy she could have been anywhere between twenty-five and fifty.

"You wouldn't be Nora Patterson's brother, would you?" she asked.

Chippy answered, "Yes," and the woman went on.

"This is a funny coincidence. I'm Eileen Winters, and my daughter, Helen, is in your sister's class at Bryn Mawr. Just yesterday Helen had a note from Nora saying you were working nearby learning railroading and she hoped Helen would have a chance to meet her handsome young brother. I saw you during services, and I kept thinking you didn't look as though you were from the coal regions. Then I put two and two together and guessed who you were."

Chippy, anxious for female company—as a matter of fact for that of anyone who spoke English—was interested and said he would be delighted to meet Helen.

"I'm so sorry," Mrs. Winters said. "My husband took her to Cape May yesterday where she's going to spend the summer with her grandparents. But please come home to dinner with me. I'm alone and I'd be delighted to have you."

The scene was set quite simply. Chippy, in describing life in a navvy gang to the lady, mentioned the hazards of bathing.

"Oh, my! You poor boy," his hostess commiserated. "As soon as we've had dinner you go right upstairs and get into a nice warm tub. Everyone's away and you won't be disturbed."

When Chippy emerged from a steaming hot bath, the absent George Winters' robe thrown over his shoulders, and stepped into the adjacent bedroom, Eileen Winters was waiting.

George Winters, who was a homosexual, made it a point to be away each weekend, coming home Sunday evening after young Patterson had left. But toward the end of the summer Chippy began to get restless. In late August Eileen Winters joined her daughter at Cape May. Chippy never saw her again. He stayed in camp Saturday nights and found potato whiskey more and more palatable. On Sundays he slept late, read the books Nora and Joe sent him, and drank steadily. He never missed a day's work or shirked on the job. Whatever reports were sent to C. Stuart must have been good. When Chippy returned to Gracehill in September for his birthday, he was greeted as the prodigal and treated with kindness.

CHAPTER 11

THE PATTERSONS were together for the first time that summer, and C. Stuart, in an expansive mood, decided to celebrate this occasion and Chippy's birthday with a family dinner at La Pierre (it was actually called *The* La Pierre) Hotel. The only outsiders were Dick Buckley and Bill Whittem, invited to please Chippy. Even George, back from Europe with a trunkful of new cricket trophies and the kudos of royalty, was most affable and made no reference to his youngest brother's previous indiscretions. Had it not been for two unfortunate mistakes in timing C. Stuart made that evening, the modest affair might have been as pleasant as Chippy had expected. C. Stuart made his first tactical error immediately after coffee was served. He arose to say he had a happy announcement to make. Everyone, including Chippy, since it was his birthday which was being honored, expected that whatever was said would have some reference to him—perhaps a discreet compliment (undeserved, only Chippy knew) announcing a gift to his youngest son, as a reward for the boy's rehabilitation.

Instead, Patterson walked toward George, put his arm around his eldest son's shoulder in an unprecedented display of affection, and proposed a toast to the new firm of "Patterson and Patterson," which would open for the general practice of law the following morning in the Bullitt Building.

The second mistake was using champagne for the toast.

This time Chippy didn't spurn it. He had only one drink and refused a refill, but that was enough to set him off. After dinner Chippy asked for and was granted permission to spend the night at the Buckleys'. Dick, to cover himself, had already informed his own family he was sleeping at Gracehill. Instead of taking the Chestnut Hill local out of Broad Street Station, the pair walked from the hotel to pay their first (and last) visit to Applegate's Carousel. Bill Whittem, whose classes at Philadelphia College of Pharmacy had begun the week before and whose life was more restricted than those of his wealthier companions, went home to study.

"It was one of the smartest things I ever did," Bill said, "because that night turned out to be a wild one for Chiffy and Dick. Before it was over they both landed in jail. I found out about seven the next morning. I opened the door, and there was a boy waiting for me with a note. It was from Chiffy, and he asked me to get in touch with Uncle Theo right away and get him down to City Hall as soon as he could make it. He was to be sure not to tell C. Stuart anything at all and to ask for Albert Kerkopski, of Frackville, when he got to the Hall.

"I pedaled over to Uncle Theo's, woke him up, and handed him the message. I told him I hadn't the slightest idea of what it was all about except that they, Chiff and Dick, had planned to go to Applegate's Merry-Go-Round, which was a low-class bawdy house. You could tell Uncle Theo anything."

Applegate's Palace of Flying Animals, called the "Merry-Go-Round" or "Carousel" or "Flying Circus" by sporting gentlemen of the day, was the largest and most unusual house of prostitution in the Quaker City. Until Clayton McMichael, editor and publisher of the *North American,* and John Wanamaker hounded city councils into action, Applegate's, like all the other lesser-known resorts, concert dens, and massage parlors, operated with the full knowledge and consent of the police department.

At that time almost all of Philadelphia's emporiums of vice were contained in two small islands, one north and one south. The theory was that by imposing boundaries beyond which organized vice was not permitted, all evil would be concentrated in areas easily controlled and thus the possibilities of contamination would be limited. There was only one bad feature about the theory. It didn't work.

Near Applegate's corner, a plain-clothes man was assigned to steer strangers in the right direction. Inside, several uniformed patrolmen maintained order while the captain's man kept close to Mr. Applegate for the dual purposes of seeing that nobody got ideas about armed robbery and that the proper payoff was made promptly after the 5 A.M. closing. Applegate's had a bar almost a hundred feet long, in front of which thirsty men and women, two and three deep, would line up screaming for service from the eight bartenders. Breughel would have found Applegate's a wonderful subject for his brush.

Of the 150 or more prostitutes who plied their trade nightly at the Carousel, less than a score were on the house payroll. The remainder—professionals, semi-pros, and "amateurs"—used Applegate's merely as a place to drum up business which was finished elsewhere.

Applegate's was a huge barn of a place, originally built as a public livery stable. What gave it its colorful name of The Flying Circus was the décor and the attire of waiters, waitresses, and bartenders. The waiters were dressed as clowns, the waitresses in tights, and bartenders were made up to resemble circus strongmen. The last idea sounded as though it were applied psychology. A large canvas canopy, painted in bright circus colors, was suspended from the ceiling and hung over most of the center of the floor.

All along the sides of the place were dimly lighted padded booths for two. In front of each was a large wooden animal—horse, lion, tiger, leopard, etc.—similar to those found on a merry-go-round. Waiters served their customers by passing trays over the tops of the animals, but if occupants wanted to enter or leave they had to climb over or crawl under. This was supposed to be funny, and perhaps it was. A reasonable amount of privacy was insured, although Applegate's hired help came around too often for guests to use booths for beds.

Those not deeply concerned with privacy seated themselves in one of the carousel "carriages" placed side by side all over the floor between the booths and the bar. In the center of each of these was a table, and it was the duty of the scantily clad waitresses to see that drinks were replenished as soon as glasses were emptied.

On a busy night Applegate's Flying Circus must have been quite a place. Even after nearly three quarters of a century it's not hard to imagine the bare-armed, mustachioed bartenders deftly sliding glasses along the polished bar to their screaming customers; the swish of beer gushing from taps; the clang of a gong each time a new barrel was bunged; the waiters, loaded trays held high over their heads, scurrying between carriages across the crowded floor; the guests, in various stages of undress and intoxication, climbing in and out of booths to head for the "ladies," the "gents," or the outside; the violent retch of one who'd had too much; the frequent shriek of a waitress, pinched too hard even for her toughened skin; the constant trek of amorous gentlemen up and down the stairs; and the dull clop of a bouncer's billy striking the skull of a quarrelsome drunk.

Chippy and Dick aimed at Applegate's but their route was devious. Philadelphia young men on the town for a night usually made it a point to stop at one of the dozens of massage parlors and steam baths which dotted Cherry, Arch, and Race Streets.

After a few drinks in a Race Street saloon, Chippy and Dick spent a pleasant hour at the famous Mlle. Burgon's Vapor Baths, on Cherry Street. Relieved and refreshed, they pushed open the swinging doors leading to Applegate's bar at about 11 o'clock. A half hour later they were in jail. They hadn't been served their first drink when police holding riot sticks burst through every entrance in a surprise raid led by the superintendent of police.

The uproar was tremendous as scores of uniformed patrolmen lined up every customer and employee and eased them into waiting patrol wagons. Even policemen working for the house, who probably had no previous knowledge of the raid, joined brothers-in-arms and turned against the hand which a few moments before had fed them. The raid, rare in Philadelphia police history, was made at the insistence of the Messrs. McMichael and Wanamaker. Women and girls screamed and fainted. Others attempted to escape by smashing basement windows and crawling to safety through an alley in back of The Flying Circus. Few escaped, and according to the *North American,* three hundred men, women, and young girls were arrested and taken to City Hall.

Chippy and Dick had the presence of mind not to give their right names or addresses. It was five o'clock before Chippy got a message smuggled out to his understanding uncle. Theodore Cuyler Patterson arrived shortly before eight and effected the immediate release of his clients. A temporarily chastened C. Stuart Patterson, Jr. reached Gracehill about 10 A.M. in time to be driven to town to register at the University for the coming semester.

All in all it was a rough night for The Flying Circus and the beginning of the end of Mr. Applegate, although he was acquitted of the crime with which he was charged that morning. On May 7, 1892, a fire of unknown origin burned Applegate's to the ground.

CHAPTER 12

"To THE mysterious process of osmosis," said Ira Jewell Williams, Esq. (Philadelphia Club, St. Anthony's, First City Troop, and Fish House), "we must give credit for much of what Chiffy Patterson learned at the University. I ought to know. For seven years we sat near each other in most of our classes at college and law school. When Chiffy was present, which could not have been more than three-quarters of the time, he slept. Usually a heavy aroma of alcohol, mingled with the pungent smell of peppermint oil, preceded his entrance and hung over him like a cloud wherever he went.

"Yet, amazingly enough, whenever he was called upon by one of his instructors, he managed to hear his name and to awake, fully alert even if only for the moment, able to give the correct answer to whatever question he was asked. His term papers were sheer delights and probably accounted for his teachers' willingness to excuse his odd conduct."

Fortunately for the dignity of C. Stuart and George, who joined the faculty in 1892 as a quondam fellow, several miles separated the law school from the main campus of the university. Even so, reports trickled in to this highly respectable pair and no doubt caused them great embarrassment.

To Francis, the only other Patterson at Penn after Joe quit to become a newspaperman, every one of Chippy's misadventures was reported promptly. Dike's own campus life was exemplary. Together the two youngest Pattersons, except for height and weight, did not look alike. But they shared a strong family resemblance, and when they were apart, Dike, to his utter disgust, was frequently mistaken for Chippy and greeted with great familiarity by characters, campus misfits, he couldn't possibly have known, obviously intimates of his youngest brother.

Eleanor was having her own problems. While her fiancé's background was the best (Beacon Hill, Groton, Harvard and the Porcellian), he was turning out to be a heavy drinker, and Nora felt one alcoholic per Patterson family was enough.

That spring Eleanor broke the engagement and left Gracehill temporarily to share an apartment on Walnut Street, east of the Square, with her friend Bessie Dobson. In those days unmarried young ladies needed a good reason to live away from home, and attendance at the Academy of Fine Arts provided them with an acceptable excuse. Chippy was given a key to the apartment, and when he was too drunk or hung over to get to Chestnut Hill he stayed with Nora and Bessie until he sobered up and felt well enough to go home. He came and went as he pleased, although there were certain provisos. He was not permitted to bring any of his drinking companions with him, and the only whiskey he was allowed to have on the premises (and that was kept under lock and key) was the "hair of the dog" a most understanding sister provided.

That same year brought trouble to the Reading Railroad and many Philadelphia banking institutions and presaged the panic of 1893.

Minor depressions used to be called "hard times," and big ones were aptly labeled "panics." It was obvious to the alert breadwinner of 1892 that a panic was on the way. The message came early that year. Two banks, the Keystone and the Spring Garden Street, closed their doors forever shortly after January 1. On February 10, Congress ordered an investigation, which revealed the cause of the failures was over-speculation. But Congress could do nothing to help the thousands of depositors, including hundreds of small businessmen, who were wiped out. Unemployment started in a minor way in a few isolated sections of Philadelphia, but a major catastrophe was in the making.

The main worry of the majority of Philadelphians, working for $14 a week, out of which they fed and clothed large families, sent as many of their children as they could through grammar school, and bought their own homes, was usually the inability to put aside a few dollars for those rainy days of unemployment which were inevitable every decade.

So far there was no real cause for alarm. The Keystone and the Spring Garden Street had comparatively few liabilities (and unfortunately fewer assets), and the business failures and resultant unemployment their closing caused were absorbed in the economy of a city with a population of over one million.

But when in 1892 the P.R.R. began to manipulate Reading Railroad stock as part of a giant pincer movement to control all Eastern railroads, it was gambling with the lives and destinies of thousands of citizens, and was one of the major causes of the depression which followed. There was nothing illegal about the P.R.R.'s operations in the market. C. Stuart Patterson, Sr., the expert on corporate law and a director of the Philadelphia Bourse; his son

George, who by then was retained by the railroad; and the rest of their staff made certain every move made was within the law.

The Reading was organized about 1830 to haul coal from Mauch Chunk and the surrounding Pennsylvania anthracite fields to Philadelphia's rich markets. By the time the P.R.R. decided to compete, the Reading and another medium-sized operator, the Lehigh Valley, had developed tidy businesses. Then the war of the railroads began.

The theoretical chip which ostensibly caused the fight was knocked off the shoulder of President Archibald A. McCleod of the Reading by no less a scrapper than Commodore Vanderbilt, but as in later events at Sarajevo this was the excuse, not the reason. Mr. George B. Roberts, president of the P.R.R. and a very correct sixth-generation Philadelphian, stood on the sidelines and egged on both contestants.

In the meanwhile Mr. Roberts and a pool of wealthy P.R.R. directors and carefully selected Proper Philadelphia stockholders (by no means the smallest of whom was C. Stuart Patterson, Sr.) were playing the market by ear and were, as the occasion required, bullish or bearish with Reading Railroad stock.

How well they succeeded was evident by February 17, 1893, when nearly half a million Reading shares were unloaded in a falling market. Work ceased, trains stopped running and pay cars on their way to distribution points were recalled. On Tuesday, February 21, the Reading went into receivership and the P.R.R.'s combine was ready to buy it for a song. Unfortunately for the Pennsylvania's well-laid plans, J. Pierpont Morgan stepped into the picture and called the tune, a duet, not a solo, to be sung by the New York Central and the P.R.R. There was an amicable division of the loot, railroad territories were reassigned, and again everybody was happy, with the possible exception of Reading employees, all of whom missed several pay periods and many of whom were fired, and stockholders not in on the deal.

To celebrate the occasion Mr. and Mrs. Roberts, Mr.

and Mrs. C. Stuart Patterson, Sr., and several other directors and members of the legal staff of the P.R.R. and their New York Central counterparts, including Commodore Vanderbilt, enjoyed a brief Carribean cruise on the *Corsair,* with Mr. Morgan the host.

Nobody could ever justly accuse the P.R.R.'s directors and legal staff of creating the devastating panic which followed the Reading debacle, but it was part of a snowball which gained momentum and size and developed into the avalanche of 1893.

CHAPTER 13

DURING Chippy's years at Penn his devotion to alcohol allowed him little time to make new friends or spend many hours with old ones. Partly through choice and partly because few of his classmates could keep up with him even if they had wanted to, he went through college much on his own. He was actually pledged to Psi Upsilon, but instead of turning over the check his father gave him for the initiation fee, Chippy forged an endorsement, got an unsuspecting merchant to cash it, and never showed up at the ceremonies.

One of the very few friendships Chippy developed during his college years was with a Jew, the first he had ever talked to socially in his entire life, and with whom he spent many hours during their years together at Penn. This boy didn't look Jewish, didn't "act" Jewish, had no Jewish inflection, and his name, Rosengarten, could have been of Germanic origin. There are Chestnut Hill Rosengartens listed in the social register, and the scion of that family, Adolph G. Rosengarten, was actually at Penn during Chippy's time there. A case of mistaken identity was responsible for Chippy's friendship with David Rosengarten, who was in no way related to his prominent Gentile namesakes.

"Shortly after Psi U. asked me to turn in my pledge pin (and quite justifiably I ought to add)," Chippy once told

Ben Zion, his law clerk for eleven years, "I walked in to Philosophy completely sober and aware of my classmates, perhaps for the first time that semester. To my left was Ira Jewell Williams, and to my right was a sophomore I didn't know at all. I'd heard the professor address him as 'Rosengarten,' and I assumed he was one of the Rosengartens we knew.

"That morning I was quite the bright young man, wide awake, alert, and hell-bent to join in every debate. They'd been talking about Spinoza, probably for several days, although I hadn't been aware of it. I don't recall much of what was said, except that from Spinoza's philosophy we began to probe into his religion, and before long we were discussing Jews in general, discrimination, fraternities, etc., which I suppose was what the teacher wanted us to do. Lord knows I didn't know much about Jews—never even thought about them—and I certainly wasn't conscious of the fact that there'd been a campaign of anti-Semitism going on in Philadelphia. Our professor told us that several of the city's most respectable newspapers had been printing derogatory remarks about Jews.

"I must have been shocked, probably showed it, and made some vague statements in defense of Jews. To my surprise Rosengarten backed me with some pertinent facts, and I rather think we improved our position.

" 'How come you know so much about Jews?' I asked him on the way out. He shook his head quickly from side to side as though to clear it, raised a quizzical eyebrow, and looked at me to make sure I wasn't kidding. Then he grinned.

" 'Why not?' he asked. 'I'm a Jew.'

" 'You're crazy, Rosengarten. I've seen your family in Holy Trinity!'

" 'You haven't seen mine,' he answered. 'Our synagogue is on New Market Street.'

"One Friday after class," Chippy recalled, "Rosengarten invited me to his house for supper and to meet his family. I hated to accept his invitation because I knew I'd never be able to ask him to Gracehill. At school, except for the ten- or fifteen-minute periods between classes, we hadn't much of a chance to talk together—David was always rushing away from the campus to work somewhere—but on Friday evenings he told me he relaxed and stayed home with his family. I remember stopping at Finley Acker's for a box of fancy cakes to take with me for David's mother, not realizing it was a kosher house and that my gift, accepted graciously, would of course never be eaten."

If Chippy's first knowledge of Jewish life had been gained from a visit to the Rosenbach, the Wolf, the Snellenburg, or the Gratz home, it's doubtful he would have noticed any difference between life inside a North Broad, Sixteenth or Seventeenth Street mansion and that at Gracehill. But his initial entrance into a Jewish household was at the Rosengartens', where the differences were enormous. This was a large family of poor people who lived simply but with dignity. The Rosengartens, mother, father, an octogenarian grandmother, and seven children ranging in age from David to his baby sister Rebecca, had emigrated from Russia shortly after the pogrom of 1882.

The older Rosengarten was a tailor employed in a sweat shop on Washington Avenue. Near-illiterates themselves, the parents were fanatical about their children's education, which to them was as important as food and shelter. Almost inconceivable efforts were made to put David through college. He was on a full scholarship, which he won in a competitive examination; he worked before and after his classes and studied between midnight and 5 A.M.

From the Rosengartens Chippy received far more than he gave. All through his undergraduate years at Penn he spent at least every other Friday evening in their home. A place was always set for him at the supper table, and no unkind comment was ever uttered about his condition, whether he was so drunk he could hardly hold up his head or arrived cold sober. He experienced and witnessed kindness, love, and understanding, and he was singularly stirred.

"I used to look forward to those Friday nights," Chippy

recollected to Zion, "even though I felt it must have been a real imposition for me to eat the food of which I'm sure they had none to spare. God knows they never made me feel as though I was depriving them of anything. I felt like the very devil every time I sat there enjoying myself and realized I could never ask any of them to have dinner with me at my home.

"Theirs was a very happy household, and the contrast between Bainbridge Street and Gracehill wasn't pleasant to contemplate. David got sick toward the end of his senior year, although he managed to graduate. He died of t.b. the following summer, and I didn't even go to his funeral. I meant to, but I guess I was drunk. I never bothered to call on his parents. The Rosengartens moved away afterward, to Arizona I think, because two more of the children got t.b., and I lost track of them."

The Nineties, gay only for some, moved on and the Pattersons and others with them. C. Stuart Patterson, Sr. became a director of the P.R.R. Abe Buzzard, the famous horse thief and "Outlaw of Welsh Mountain," was converted to Christianity. Eleanor Willing (who was to become Mrs. George Stuart Patterson) made her triumphant debut at the Natatorium. Trolley fares went up to five cents a ride, free transfers were eliminated, and John Wanamaker said "I told you so!" Francis Patterson began a one-year internship at Jefferson Hospital. Lillian Russell played to capacity houses in the Opera Comique at the Broad Street Theatre, and Chippy, Dick Buckley, and Bill Whittem took three of the chorus girls to the Hotel Brighton in Atlantic City after the Saturday-night performance.

Joseph S. Patterson became financial editor of the *Evening Star*. Eleanor Patterson gave up her Walnut Street apartment to return to Gracehill. Rosanna Jackson, aged four, of 1137 South Seventh Street, died of scarlet fever, and her grief-stricken mother paid for the printing of the following poem, which she herself wrote, in the obituary column of the *Public Ledger*:

"Precious Little Rose
We lay thee down to rest.
But thye spirit's gone to God.
To mingle with the blest."

William McKinley became President of the United States, and Mr. and Mrs. C. Stuart Patterson, Sr. and Mr. George Stuart Patterson paid their first visit to the White House. The *North American* bitterly assailed Kensington soup kitchens for the poor. Mrs. C. Stuart Patterson, Sr. won honorable mention at the International Flower Show for a rose developed at Gracehill. Drexel and Company took over the reorganization of the Reading Railroad. Mr. C. Stuart Patterson, Sr. was the principal speaker at the dedication of the Philadelphia Bourse.

Jane Cuyler Patterson entered Friends Hospital for the Treatment of Mental Diseases. Boies Penrose was approved for membership in the Union League. Bill Whittem became a Ph.G. and a full partner in his father's drug store. George Stuart Patterson took a year's leave of absence from the P.R.R. legal staff to accept a temporary appointment as first assistant district attorney.

Fighting Bob Fitzsimmons k.o.'d Jack Hall at New Orleans. The Democrats didn't even bother to nominate a candidate for district attorney, and the post went to the Republicans by default. Ira Jewell Williams, William A. Gray, John R. K. Scott, Isabelle Darlington, and 33 others graduated from the University of Pennsylvania Law School, class of '97. One of the 33 was Christopher Stuart Patterson, Jr., ready, his long-suffering parents believed, to give up his youthful indiscretions, settle down, and begin the serious business of practicing law in the City and County of Philadelphia.

CHAPTER 14

"THE MORNING after I finished law school," Chippy once reminisced to Jim Lambert, who used to cover City Hall for the *Evening Ledger,* "my father and I sat drinking coffee together on the verandah at Gracehill. My father's cup contained nothing but coffee, but mine included a double shot of rum, which I poured, surreptitiously I hoped, from a bottle concealed under a cushion for just such an occasion.

" 'You're almost twenty-two years old,' my father said, 'and for the past seven or eight of these you've given your mother and me many a sleepless night. We don't know where you are. We don't know what you're doing. We don't know whom you're with. You bear my name, Christopher, and this gives me grave concern. I think you will admit you have not brought us much happiness, and I'm not going to tell you how many times I've wanted to resign as dean when rumors of your extracurricular activities reached me. But the point now is that you *have* graduated from the best law school in the country. I don't know how you did it, but the fact remains you did. You have a chance to redeem yourself in your own eyes and in ours.'

"I nodded my head in agreement and took another sip of coffee.

" 'Your mother, Eleanor, and I,' my father went on, 'would like to go to England this summer to see George captain our team in the Internationals. You know Joe isn't well, and we want to take him with us; the change might do him good. Francis will be spending his nights at Jeff, and you'll be alone at Gracehill. Frankly, I'm fearful of what you might do. I don't want to have to be afraid every time I open a cablegram.'

"I looked at my father. It was the longest speech he'd ever made to me. I drank some more coffee, and he went on.

" 'You take your bars August tenth. If you pass, you'll be admitted to the finest profession a man can have. In September you may either join George and me—there'll be room for you in the firm—or if that has no appeal, we can always find a place for you with the railroad. Or, I'm inclined to believe, there isn't a bank in this city which would not be pleased to have you join its legal staff. Or if you'd like to try public office for a few years I'm sure the district attorney or the city solicitor would be glad to place you. Think it over.'

" 'What do you want me to do now, father?' I asked him.

" 'Pour out what's left of that Coffee Royale and give me your word of honor as a gentleman you will not take a drink until we come home. You owe us that much.' "

"What about the rest of that Coffee Royale, Mr. Patterson?" Jim Lambert asked.

Chippy smiled.

"Well, by that time there was only a quarter of a cup left, so I tossed it out on the grass, shook my father's hand, and said, 'All right. You have my word.' "

For the next two and a half months Chippy stayed close to Gracehill, leaving only to see Jane on visiting days at Friends and taking her for shirt rides in a new Haynes roadster, the first automobile the Pattersons owned. Francis was busy day and night at the hospital, and these two Pattersons got together only once that summer. Chippy spent most of his time stretched out on a hammock in the garden preparing for his bar examinations or re-reading his favorite books. He did not take a drink.

C. Stuart, Ellen, Eleanor, and Joe spent an enjoyable summer traveling throughout England and following the matches, their pleasure marred only by Joe's obviously failing health.

The Pattersons returned to Philadelphia August 9. On August 10 Chippy took his bar examinations. They ended the afternoon of August 11. He spent that night at Gracehill and the following morning left home "to look around downtown," he said. He had about $5,000 in cash with him, graduation gifts from uncles, aunts, and cousins. This was the last his family heard from him for more than eight months.

Boies Penrose found him sleeping on a Washington park bench the following April. Chippy didn't have a dime, and only the vaguest recollections of where he'd been much of the time. He did remember that he had headed directly from Gracehill to McGillen's Ale House on Drury Street, where he drank steadily all day.

He recalled spending Christmas week in a Youngstown, Ohio, bawdy house and New Year's Day in the Morgantown, West Virginia, jail. He was living with a saloonkeeper's widow in Salamanca, New York, when news of the sinking of the Maine (February 15) reached him.

During this prolonged spree he could account for only a few high spots and never did have any clear idea how he happened to wake up one rainy spring morning, covered with newspapers, wet, cold, hungry, and broke, to find a huge man bending over him saying, very gently, "Wake up, Chiffy." It was Penrose, and Chippy couldn't have fallen into better hands. The enormous, 300-pound Philadelphia aristocrat lifted him to his feet, hailed a hansom, and took him to the Penrose Washington apartment. There, after a hot bath, a shave by Penrose's valet, a change into clean linen, Chippy, wearing his old suit, freshly pressed, greeted his host, who'd been waiting patiently. No lectures. No questions. Instead, he was given a shot of bourbon (of which Penrose consumed more than a quart daily) and as much food as he could manage to hold down. Then the two returned to Philadelphia, where Mr. Penrose delivered his charge to the doors of Gracehill.

After his parents' first wave of relief at seeing their son alive, his presence at Gracehill, at least as far as C. Stuart was concerned, was just about tolerated. The United States was at war with Spain, and Chippy applied for a commission in the army. He was accepted, commissioned a second lieutenant, May 15, 1898, and assigned to Battery D, Sixth Artillery Regiment, U.S. Volunteers.

The Sixth, 42 officers and 1,540 enlisted men, Major General E. O. Otis in command, sailed from Boston for the Philippines August 1, and landed at Manila three weeks later. With the exception of frequent and bloody clashes with Aguinaldo's natives, Chippy's tour of duty on the island was not unpleasant. In Manila he drank at the English Club and slept with any number of officers' wives. In the mountains of the interior and at Mindanao, Sergeant Henry Skelly, whom he had successfully defended in a court martial and who later became his self-appointed valet, supplied him with a native beverage that reminded Chippy of the potato whiskey he had drunk on the navvy gang. He was stationed at Lake Lanao when he received word his brother Joe had died of pneumonia.

Chippy remained in the Philippines for over three and a half years, drinking as much as he could, fornicating whenever the opportunity presented itself, and fighting as little as possible. He never rose above the rank of second lieutenant. He liked what he saw of the easy island life and determined that when the war was over this was where he would spent the rest of his days as a civilian. He felt sure his father would be so relieved at this decision that he would be willing to support him as a remittance man.

Malaria altered Chippy's plans. At Lake Lanao he succumbed to a comparatively mild attack of the disease and was sent to the U.S. Army Hospital at Manila, where he spent the following three months. He was discharged from the hospital and from the service at about the same time. The last week of his stay on the islands he was a guest of Governor William H. Taft, a friend of C. Stuart, who'd been notified of his son's illness and who had cabled the governor a request "to do everything possible to make my son comfortable."

Chippy sailed from the Philippines early in December and arrived at Gracehill Christmas morning. The year was 1902.

CHAPTER 15

THIS WAS the last Christmas Chippy spent at Gracehill, and if it was not the happiest it was at least one of the most peaceful. The family was together, and there was a semblance of unity, brought on, perhaps, by Joe's death and the subsequent realization of their own individual vulnerability. In addition to Chippy's return, Francis had come back to Philadelphia only a few weeks before from a world tour as ship's surgeon on the S.S. *Ohio,* and Jane had been given a temporary release from Friends. George, living at Gracehill now, was shortly to announce his engagement to Eleanor Willing and soon would be setting up his own household.

Chippy was able to enjoy Christmas dinner with the family and to greet friends and relatives who called at Gracehill and regale them with stories of his stay on the islands. But the next day he collapsed and had to be carried upstairs to his bedroom, where he remained for almost a month. The combination of heavy drinking, malaria, and irregular eating had wasted his body, and he weighed less than 140 pounds, 50 pounds under his normal 190.

For four or five weeks Chippy rested. Francis prescribed plenty of milk, eggs, and other fattening foods. Nurse Johnson and Eleanor, who had little else to do but stay with her brother, brought Chippy up to date on all the events which had taken place in Philadelphia during the three and a half years he had been away. Ellen, who was doing practically no entertaining since Joe's death, dropped in at least twice a day to see if Chippy was comfortable, and George, on his way in or out of the house, usually found a moment to spare the convalescent. His father made an effort to develop some rapport between himself and his son, but unfortunately this came a little late. The subject of C. Stuart Patterson, Jr.'s future was not discussed.

By the end of February Chippy had regained much of his strength, most of his weight, and all of his craving for whiskey. Since his return to Gracehill he hadn't touched a drop. Even the milk punches he drank in great quantities were flavored with some non-alcoholic extract. Bill Whittem used to stop in whenever he had the time, and Chippy tried to persuade the young druggist to bring him a bottle of medicinal whiskey. But Bill, warned by every member of the Patterson household each time he arrived at Gracehill, was adamant.

"I think at this stage in Chiffy's life," Bill recalled, "he would have welcomed a shot of Colafra. Every bottle of anything containing alcohol was removed from any place Chiffy could possibly get at. I'm sure the old man put new padlocks on the wine cellar. They all felt this was as good a time as any to try to get him to break the habit.

"When Chiff got well enough to leave the house, C. Stuart got him a job with the Girard Trust, writing briefs or something. I don't believe he lasted there more than a couple of weeks. One night after we closed the store, I walked over to Gracehill. As soon as the butler led me in, I knew right away I'd made a mistake coming. I could see into the library where the family—Aunt Ellen, C. Stuart, George, and Nora—were having some kind of conference, and they all looked pretty grim.

"Nora glanced up, saw me, and turned questionably to her father. I heard him say, 'Ask him to come in, Nora, maybe he knows something.'

"Nora explained that Chiffy had left home the day before and they hadn't the slightest idea where he was. I hadn't either. Chiff hadn't said a word to me about going away, although I knew he was drinking again and I suppose they did, too.

"They were all very much upset. This time I think he lit out with some of the Girard Trust's money. I never did learn the truth about that part, but if money was missing, C. Stuart made good."

A few days after Bill had been told of Chippy's most recent disappearance, rumors began to seep into Whittem's Pharmacy, which for almost a century has been a repository for gossip about the ladies and gentlemen of Chestnut Hill. Fortunately for these gentlefolk, Bill, like his father before him, is discreet, and nothing he sees or hears reaches the world beyond his doors.

"All the participants are dead now, so I can tell you," Bill said, "but I better not mention names because the children are still very much alive and around. Well, one of the most beautiful debs I ever saw—we used to call them buds, then—had come out about the time Nora did, or possibly a year or two sooner. I think she was a little older than Nora and about three or four years older than Chiff.

"I always believed she was partial to Chiffy, and I never could understand why he never had much time for her. She was just his type. She was lovely. Tall, maybe five seven or eight, dark hair, and very full-busted. Quiet, too. Chiffy danced with her at parties and at the Assembly, I guess, but as far as I know that was all. She married a very attractive chap. They had three children, and I always thought they were happy. Never a whisper of scandal.

"Then, all of a sudden! It just doesn't figure. She left her husband and family and took off with Chiff. I don't think it was planned. They must have met accidentally in town or at the bank and made their decision on the spur of the moment. Chiffy used to be like that. They went directly to the Astor. Somehow or other the husband found out. Perhaps they were seen in the dining room. They couldn't stay in bed all the time, you know.

"The husband was a good friend of George's, and he must have known Chiff. You'd imagine he'd have felt like dashing over to New York and shooting Chiff, but he was a pretty decent guy, and he wanted to avoid a scandal. He, George, and C. Stuart had a conference, the upshot of which was that George went to New York alone and brought his brother back with him. A couple of weeks after that the wife returned to Chestnut Hill and her family. The marriage broke up soon after, and she left Philadelphia. As far as I know, she never came back."

There wasn't much of a welcome for Chippy when he

returned to Gracehill. He was drinking heavily, and his conduct was completely unpredictable. He might appear at dinner or stay in his room for an entire day and eat nothing. Some nights he would wander through the house as though he were lost, and Nora once discovered him sitting in the billiard room in the middle of the night staring out of the window. She was the only member of the family who had a kind word for him. The rest avoided him whenever they could. This was easy. C. Stuart, who had been appointed a member of the President's Monetary Commission, was in Washington much of the time, and frequently took Ellen with him. George, by then assistant chief solicitor for the P.R.R. and a full professor at the law school, was spending more and more time away from home. Francis, while living at Gracehill, had opened an office in downtown Philadelphia. It was Dike who took a hand this time in Chippy's affairs and persuaded his younger brother to try a new alcoholic "cure" a classmate of his at medical school had developed and which was meeting with some success. Chippy had little faith in cures—he'd tried so many of them—but he readily agreed to Francis' suggestion, and the pair went off to Connecticut, where Dike signed his brother into the retreat for the full treatment.

Chippy remained at Hartford for nearly two months and came back to Chestnut Hill with little confidence in his ability to stay away from whiskey. Always willing to believe in his son's eventual rehabilitation, C. Stuart approached Chippy with the idea of establishing a separate office, completely independent of George and himself. Chippy wasn't overjoyed, but he readily acquiesced, realizing, perhaps, that while it was almost six years since he'd passed the bar exams, he had never practiced law. He was twenty-seven years old.

On the morning of April 10, 1903, Chippy opened his own law offices in Suite 701-703 Pennsylvania Building, 1500 Chestnut Street (telephone S2841D). Within one hour he had his first client, Aline Mason, charged with murder in the first degree.

CHAPTER 16

ABOUT eight months before C. Stuart Patterson, Jr., elegantly attired in a new frock coat, gray striped morning trousers, black patent-leather shoes, and bowler drifted aimlessly into Room 453 City Hall, four men were playing a friendly game of scat in a South Philadelphia home. The host was Caesar Hines, destined, before the afternoon ended, to be the fatal victim of his own anger and frustration at a run of poor cards. His partner was Aline Mason, who shared Caesar's bad luck and, in a sense, his misfortune.

August 17, 1902, fell on a Sunday and a particularly dull one at that. The biggest news was the trek of 50,000 masochistic Philadelphians to Atlantic City, where they stood patiently along the sandy beaches awaiting the end of the world. The *deus ex machina* invoked and promoted by the Reverend Smart Alexander Jones, "Prophet of the Blue Mountain," was to be a giant tidal wave, which would wash away humanity's sins with salt water. The P.R.R., happy to cooperate, ran special excursion trains from Camden to Atlantic City, carefully noting in their advertisements that "all tickets are good for a return trip." What could they lose?

That day, leg men from Philadelphia's seven daily papers covering the morgue, hospitals, and police stations, desperately seeking news in a hot, somnolent city, walked into 33rd District Headquarters at Seventh and Carpenter Streets and hopefully thumbed the docket. There, on a desk in front of the drowsy perspiring house sergeant, was a scrawled entry, "Aline Mason, 48, colored, held on a charge of homicide in connection with the death of Caesar Hines, colored, 52. Bullet wound in heart. D.O.A. Jefferson Hospital. Detectives McGlinchey and Barratt."

Reporters, even though news was a scarce commodity that day, scorned this item and quickly turned to the next page.

The months went by, and at almost the same moment deputy sheriffs were leading Mason out of his cell at Moyamensing Prison, where he'd been held without bail since the shooting, Chippy was pushing open the swinging doors of the Bellevue Bar, where he'd had his first drink since before he left for Hartford. The destination of this oddly assorted pair was the same, although they reached it by different paths.

Mason arrived at City Hall in a prison van and, with a deputy on each side, climbed three flights up the broad stone stairway leading to the prisoner's foyer of the Court of Oyer and Terminer and General Jail Delivery. Christopher Stuart Patterson, Jr., an empty day looming ahead, strolled north on Broad Street. Rigged out in the only clothing elite members of his profession considered fitting, he entered an elevator in the south corridor of the Hall. Simply because most of the occupants of the car got off at the fourth floor, so did Chippy. The crowd walked east to 453, and Chippy followed it inside, entering the courtroom just as Mason stood in the prisoner's cage, pleaded "Not Guilty," and took the pauper's oath.

At that moment Judge Craig Biddle happened to glance from the prisoner to Chippy, who had slipped, unobtrusively he hoped, into a chair in the rear of the huge, high-ceilinged courtroom, where he could remain onobserved and catch a wink or two until his thirst became irresistible.

He had no sooner slouched down on the hard seat than he was aroused by the loud harsh voice of the crier bawling, "Mr. C. Stuart Patterson! Mr. C. Stuart Patterson! Come to the bench, please!" At first Chippy was sure his father was being paged, and he turned around to see if C. Stuart was there. Then, still puzzled, he stood erect and looked up at the front of the room. A slight, tight smile broke the usually sober mien of Judge Biddle, who nodded to Chippy and beckoned him to the bench.

"Good morning, Mr. Patterson. Welcome to my court."

"Good morning, Sir," Chippy replied. "I'm honored to be here."

The Court's eyes moved from Chippy to the prisoner in the dock and the smile vanished. Then Judge Biddle addressed Chippy again.

"Will you represent the defendant, Mr. Patterson? He is without funds."

"Of course, Your Honor, if the Court wishes," Chippy answered.

"Thank you, Mr. Patterson. The Commonwealth of Pennsylvania versus Aline Mason will be heard tomorrow morning at ten o'clock. Crier, call the next case!"

Even the most experienced criminal lawyer ought to have more than 24 hours to prepare a case properly, particularly if his client is charged with a capital offense. But when Judge Biddle turned over Aline Mason's defense to Chippy and gave him one day to get ready for the jury, he was not breaking precedent. This was long before the Voluntary Defenders, Legal Aid Society, or Civil Liberties Union, and penniless defendants, guilty or innocent, considered themselves fortunate to get anyone to represent them. Usually their fate lay in the hands of court-appointed political hangers-on and legal misfits eager to earn the small fee the Commonwealth paid for defense of a pauper.

Although counsel for Mason had yet to try his first case and this indigent Negro's life depended upon the unproven skill of a novice, the prisoner got a better break than he could have expected. The Patterson name (and it's likely that, in the beginning at least, Christopher Stuart Patterson, Jr. was unaware of its power in City Hall) got counsel his first dispensation, one which his client shared by reflected glory. From the very moment young Patterson stood before the bench and agreed to represent Mason, the wheels of privilege began to turn.

While Chippy knew little or nothing about court procedure, he surely realized that in order to prepare a defense he would have to spend some time with his client. Normally the prisoner would have been placed in the sheriff's van and returned to Moyamensing, there to be held until the following morning. His attorney would have had to consult with him in jail. But bailiffs who held

Mason in custody would hardly dream of asking this handsome young member of the bar, who bore such a distinguished name and appeared to be a personal friend of Judge Biddle, to ride all the way down to Tenth and Reed Streets to talk to his client in the grimy cells of "Moko."

Instead Mason was taken to a bright clean cell on the seventh floor of the Hall, one usually reserved for Commonwealth witnesses held in protective custody. Even before Chippy was guided there by an obsequious deputy, Mason was given soap, hot water (his first in eight months), and a towel so that he could make himself presentable. A bailiff unlocked the prisoner's cell, held the door open for Chippy, and with his pocket handkerchief ostentatiously brushed off the lone chair inside. Then he discreetly withdrew to a corner of the room, where he stood, arms akimbo.

"I'm right here, Mr. Patterson," he said, "if this nigger gives you any trouble."

Mason, who looked as though he hadn't enough strength to crush another one of the bedbugs which infested Moko, stood abjectly by his cot, one hand nervously clutching the other, and said nothing. Chippy turned to the deputy.

"It's all right, Sheriff," he said, "*Mr.* Mason and I will get along fine. You may leave."

The deputy, baffled at the unpredictable actions of gentlefolk and almost unable to believe his own ears, looked questioningly at counsel. Then he withdrew reluctantly, but to be certain of re-establishing his superiority over the prisoner, couldn't resist a parting shot.

"Mason," he warned, "don't give this gentleman no trouble."

There wasn't much dignity left in Mason, but what little remained after his stay at Moko, rose to the surface.

"Sir," he said after the guard was out of earshot, "I ain't got no money at all to pay you with, and I did kill Caesar. Now if you still want to be my lawyer, I'd like it fine; but if you don't, that's okay, too."

"I still want to be your lawyer," Chippy answered. "Go ahead and tell me how it happened."

The story Mason told was simple. Somehow a peaceable game of scat, played by four old friends over a few bottles of cold beer, turned into a homicide.

"I wasn't drinking like the cops said. We had only enough cash to buy three bottles between the four of us, and that had to last all afternoon. I don't know exactly what happened. One minute everything was good, and the next, Caesar, he gets mad and bangs his cards down on the table. Then he rushes out and comes back with a revolver.

"He ain't mad at me. I'm his partner. But he points that gun at Joe, one of the other players. I jumped up to knock it out of Caesar's hand, and it goes off and shoots Caesar. That's all there was to it."

Chippy believed the story and the following morning told it to the jury. The trial didn't last more than a couple of hours, and much of this time was taken by the assistant district attorney, Samuel W. Salus, in probing prospective jurors. Chippy, on the other hand, used a device he later employed only occasionally to build up confidence in a hostile courtroom. This was to accept, without challenge, every panelist passed by the prosecution. The dangers of such a grandstand play are obvious, and most criminal lawyers employed it sparingly and only when some highly developed sixth sense told them the odds were with the gamble. But in the case of the Commonwealth of Pennsylvania vs. Aline Mason, Chippy's ready acceptance of all jurymen was without guile.

"They all looked honest to me," he said afterward.

Dressed in resplendent garments, completely at ease, he sat quietly and let Sam Salus make all the noise. Some of the confidence he radiated brushed off on his client, and Mason and the two defense witnesses, the other scat players, held up well under severe cross-examination. Chippy's plea to the jury was brief and his manner earnest, but when he stood in front of the box and held himself erect, pausing for a moment before speaking, there was an ineffable feeling, almost electric in intensity, which passed between the panel and counsel for the defense.

On the stage this immediate rapport between actor and audience is seen rarely in the lifetime of a critic; its occurrence in a courtroom is even less frequent. Judge Biddle, on the bench for 30 years, sensed the quick unspoken exchange of sympathy between C. Stuart Patterson, Jr. and the 12 jurors, and he leaned back, a slight smile on his patrician face, and listened.

All the stenographic notes of that unimportant trial have crumbled into dust, and there's no one around City Hall today who remembers what Chippy said to his first jury. But some years afterward, one of the 12, in need of a lawyer, almost instinctively sought out C. Stuart Patterson, Jr. He reminded Chippy about the Mason case and told him how the panel had arrived at a verdict of involuntary manslaughter instead of murder in the first degree which the district attorney demanded.

"We all felt this way, Mr. Patterson," he explained. "If a man like you believed this poor colored man's story, what right had we to question it?"

Judge Biddle sentenced Mason to a term of from two to five years at Eastern Penitentiary, but since the prisoner had already spent eight months in Moyamensing, he was out on parole within five months. Nobody knows what Chippy did with the fee he received from the clerk of court as soon as the jury was discharged, but it wouldn't be unreasonable to assume he turned it over to Mason's family and used his own money to get drunk that evening. He picked a bad night for it.

Perhaps if Chippy had gone directly to Gracehill from City Hall, he might have been greeted with newly won respect from his father and George, who, by the end of the day, surely were told of Chippy's courtroom victory. Even though Christopher Stuart Patterson, Jr. had handled the kind of case neither of them would have touched under any circumstances, the fact remained that he won it, and this would have impressed them.

Chippy didn't go home. He returned to his office, Judge Biddle's praise ringing in his ears. He hadn't had a drink in more than 24 hours, and he was thirsty. There was an unopened bottle of rye he had been able to hide from his secretary, who had been carefully hand-picked by George with orders to notify him (George), C. Stuart, or Dr. Francis, if, as she was told, "Young Mr. Patterson does anything he shouldn't do." The inference was clear. This arrangement was not kept from Chippy.

As soon as he entered Room 703, Pennsylvania Building, he walked into his private office, shut and locked the door, and pulled a bottle from behind the false fireplace. While his secretary kept rapping and calling out "Mr. Patterson, please!" Chippy finished more than half the bottle. Then, with a cheerful wave of his hand, he said goodbye and left the building, only to reappear that evening at a reception where George's engagement to Miss Eleanor Willing was announced.

By that time he was in poor shape. He'd been drinking steadily for four or five hours at the Racquet Club. Someone may have said, "Hey, Chiff, aren't you going to George's engagement party?" or perhaps he recalled the event himself. At any rate he left the bar, hailed a hansom on Walnut Street, and leaning on the driver's shoulder for support, entered the Bellevue. He was obviously intoxicated, he needed a shave, and he was still wearing court attire. Even though this happened nearly 60 years ago and with one exception all the principals are dead, Mrs. George Stuart Patterson (nee Eleanor Willing) still winces when she recalls the unexpected arrival of her brother-in-law-to-be on this important occasion.

The widow of George Stuart Patterson is not only a Willing but also among her ancestors were Shippens. This puts her on a par with those few, rarefied Philadelphians able to claim both Whartons and Peppers or Biddles and Cadwalladers among their forefathers. The only other American city which can do as well is Boston, where any combination of Cabot, Lowell, Lawrence, or Lodge would produce the same effect.

It wasn't that Chippy was noisy or obnoxious at the Willing-Patterson party. It was mainly that he was there at all and that no one could predict what he might do. He weaved in and out of the ballroom; danced with one or two of the prettiest girls; congratulated George with drunken stateliness; and wished Miss Hoy, Eleanor Willing's aunt, the best of luck, then wandered out of the hotel. He was not seen for three days, and the only one who really looked for him was S. Morris Waln, a wily old criminal lawyer who happened to be in 453 during the Mason trial and caught Chippy's plea to the jury.

CHAPTER 17

S. Morris Waln was a descendant of an old family of Friends. He was shrewd, honest, an excellent judge of human nature, and his fees were high. He knew the law and had a reputation for securing acquittals where convictions seemed certain. Unlike many of his contemporaries, who frequently "orated" before judge and jury, Waln's summations were delivered with quiet simplicity.

What had begun as a general practice when Waln first hung out his shingle in 1870 had developed into one of the most profitable criminal law practices in Philadelphia. He had no partners or associates, and clerks prepared his briefs and did routine office and City Hall chores. Despite the type of client he represented, Waln maintained a high standard of legal ethics and professional conduct. He did not swear, smoke, or drink, although he readily forgave these weaknesses in others. For the career which lay ahead of him, Chippy could not have found a better mentor than this clever Quaker.

The afternoon of the Mason trial, Waln was in 453 waiting to file a motion with Judge Biddle. He had never met Chippy, but he knew both Theodore Cuyler and Theodore Patterson well and had a nodding acquaintance with C. Stuart. Despite the face that Waln was busy with a case which was to develop shortly, he remained in court to listen to Chippy's summation. He was impressed with young Patterson's ease, sincerity, and the quick rapport he was able to establish with the jury. When Chippy left the courtroom, Waln walked to the bench, where he and Judge Biddle exchanged a word or two in praise of Christopher Stuart Patterson, Jr. and predicted a glowing future for the lawyer who'd handled his first case so well.

Waln was tired; he was getting old; and he felt it was time he found someone to share the work load, particularly jury appearances, which he always believed were a lawyer's most important function. On the surface Chippy seemed to meet all the requirements and he thought that if he could interest this young man in some sort of association it would be to their mutual advantage. At the time he had no idea of the extent of Chippy's drinking.

Among Waln's many clients were three abortionists who'd been under police scrutiny ever since they set up their establishment on South Twelfth Street. Although the trio had been questioned many times, not one of them had ever been arrested. However, in the mature opinion of the leader of this trio, Mrs. Elizabeth Ashmead, a nurse, that time was fast approaching. "Evil-minded detectives," she told her attorney, had been delving into the facts surrounding the death of one Annie Spencer, who died a few hours after her arrival at the "Twelfth Street Rest Home." The cause, according to Dr. Matthew McVicars, house physician, was pneumonia. Police thought otherwise and said so.

"Prove it!" demanded Mrs. Ashmead.

"We will!" was the detectives' retort.

It took Waln nearly a week to reach Chippy, who had not returned to his office or to Gracehill after leaving the Willing engagement party in disgrace. He was beginning to have blackouts and had no clear recollection of where he spent the time between his departure from the Bellevue and his appearance in Dr. Francis Patterson's office on Walnut Street, leaning on the arm of his secretary, five days later. Waln had telephoned many times and left messages at 703 Pennsylvania Building and at Gracehill, but they were unanswered. It took Dike a day to dry out his brother, and Chippy, deeply apologetic, finally met with Waln.

The older lawyer's proposition, offered only on a temporary basis, appealed to Chippy. He liked Waln at once and felt this association could benefit him professionally and perhaps even help him to do something about his personal life, which, for the first time, was causing him grave concern. Chippy was to maintain his own office for a while. If the experiment proved satisfactory to both lawyers, the younger would then move into Waln's office and become a partner.

The first case they discussed was Mrs. Ashmead's. In the light of further developments, Chippy's reluctance to represent this "nurse," her twenty-one-year-old son, Howland DeWitt Ashmead, and their colleague, Dr. McVicars, and his repugnance at the kind of crimes he thought it more than likely they were committing were understandable. Chippy could barely conceal his disgust with the Ashmeads and their medical colleague, and after his first session with them intimated to Waln that he'd like "to sit this one out." Waln's answer was right to the point.

"Patterson," he said, "when you practice criminal law you take everything that comes along. If you're going to choose only the 'nice' ones you might as well go back to work for the Girard Trust. I don't like the Ashmeads either, but I'm their lawyer. It's up to you to decide to stay with them or get out now. Make up your mind."

Chippy's decision was to stay with them.

Mrs. Ashmead was about forty-five. She was a tall, thin, raw-boned woman with a harsh manner of speech, and if she had any endearing qualities they were buried deep inside her flat torso. Mother and son each had a long narrow face and a pinched nose tipped with a perpetual bead of moisture which fascinated Chippy.

Sometime later, an eighteen-year-old girl swore she was Mrs. Ashmead's daughter, Grace, although no one could understand why anybody would want to claim Elizabeth Ashmead for a mother. As a matter of fact Grace didn't appear to be overly bright. Or perhaps it was only an odd sense of humor that caused this pimply-faced adolescent to burst into gay peals of laughter every time the district attorney produced evidence detectives had dug up (quite literally) to prove the nurse an infanticidal monster many times over. Grace's hilarity was shared by her mother, and both, according to the *Press*, "indulged in audible titters and gazed with smiling faces into the horrified countenances of the spectators."

Philadelphians in general at the turn of the century apparently possessed a rather tolerant attitude about abortion. Mrs. Ashmead's neighbors on both sides of her darkened, gloomy, four-story brick house must have been most understanding. Actually some of the daily papers printed advertisements so thinly veiled that a harassed male was given his choice of a dozen or more practicing physicians who claimed they would "discreetly and successfully handle problems vexing young men or women at reasonable rates."

Even though he did no advertising, such an obliging Hippocratian was Dr. McVicars, whose shingle hung from the front of his home and office on Wharton Street. His connection with the "Twelfth Street Rest Home" and association with Mrs. Ashmead, to whom he frequently referred as "my colleague, Dr. Conde," came as a surprise to his South Philadelphia patients, whose usual ailments he treated at modest fees and who gave him the respect due a kindly, able family physician.

When Chippy entered the case, Mrs. Ashmead's immediate problem was Annie Spencer's untimely death. Annie was a pretty, twenty-three-year-old housemaid employed by a prominent West Philadelphia family. According to police the girl became pregnant and named not one but three putative fathers for her unborn child. While none of the trio would admit paternity, all were eager to contribute sufficient cash to enable Annie to dispose of the object of their mutual embarrassment.

Both the Ashmead-McVicars team and police agreed upon certain basic facts: that Annie was a patient of Dr. McVicars; that she registered at the rest home shortly before midnight, March 3, 1903 and was signed in by Mrs. Ashmead herself; that she was subsequently treated by Dr. McVicars; and that she died about three A.M.,

March 4. Beyond this point defendants and authorities were in utter disagreement.

The death certificate to which Dr. McVicars affixed his signature listed *"croupous pneumonia"* on the line marked "cause." "Her lungs were filled when I first examined her," Dr. McVicars testified. "It wasn't her lungs which were filled," replied the district attorney. "This girl died of an illegal abortion."

Somebody cared enough about Annie to write an anonymous letter to the police, who even then were investigating Mrs. Ashmead's activities. The nurse was interrogated constantly, her house was placed under close surveillance, and for a time most of the 14 beds in the nursing home were unoccupied. This situation was intolerable for the proprietress and her associates. "We're being harassed," Mrs. Ashmead told Mr. Waln and later his assistant, Christopher Stuart Patterson, Jr., "and police are preventing us from running a legitimate nursing home."

"This is an infringement of our clients' constitutional rights," said Chippy. "Let's demand an immediate indictment."

His older colleague agreed, and police, aghast at counsel's audacious request, hastened to oblige. On June 5, 1903, Elizabeth Ashmead, Dr. Matthew McVicars, and Howland DeWitt Ashmead were brought before a grand jury, which listened to evidence presented by the district attorney and decided a prima facie case had been established. Each defendant was held in $5,000 bail, charged with abortion. All three were tried jointly before Judge Martin and a jury on August 7, 1903. William A. Gray represented the Commonwealth.

If the newspapers expected a sensational trial, they were disappointed. The only defendant Chippy permitted to take the stand was Dr. McVicars, who made an excellent impression. Another physician, this one with a spotless reputation, testified that as recently as one month prior to Annie's death, he had treated her for a severe head cold, which, in reply to a question asked by Chippy, he said might easily have developed into pneumonia. The physician further stated that he had observed no signs of pregnancy. Under cross-examination, however, he did admit he had not made a complete physical check of his patient, and in answer to a hypothetical question propounded by Mr. Gray, said it was possible the girl was then carrying a child.

Since Chippy did not put either of the Ashmeads on the stand and produced no character witnesses, he was thus able to block Mr. Gray's constant attempts to introduce evidence which tended to blacken the past reputations of his clients. And because the district attorney was unable to show a previous pattern of behavior which might have led the Ashmead-McVicars combine to commit the crime with which they were presently charged, the jury had to base its decision solely upon whatever evidence was established in the matter of Annie Spencer's death.

Police work was shoddy, and incredibly enough there had been neither post mortem nor exhumation. To counteract this defect, which easily could have won or lost his case, Mr. Gray was able to show that the victim was sexually promiscuous and might well have been pregnant. That line was a mistake, which Chippy seized upon at once by vigorously defending the dead girl's honor and castigating the district attorney for staining the purity of one unable to defend herself. He thereby won the jury's sympathy, if not for his clients at least for their alleged victim. Should they convict the prisoners, the conclusion was that Annie was a bad girl. The opposite decision restored her tarnished honor. The jury was out less than one hour, and all three corporeal defendants, led by a ghostly virgin, were acquitted.

Had the team of Ashmead and McVicars disbanded right then and there, in all likelihood their past sins would have remained uncovered. But theirs was an evil partnership with an unholy lust for money. Within eight months their names and deeds shocked an unbelieving Philadelphia; made headlines in every newspaper in the country; and disgusted their counsel, Christopher Stuart Patterson, Jr., so much that he almost gave up the practice of law when he had scarcely begun.

Chippy's share of the fee in the Spencer case was $2,000, an enormous amount in those days, even for the defense of alleged abortionists. Chippy hung on to it for less than a week. He bought expensive gifts for every member of the family and spent the rest at the Brighton Hotel in Atlantic City with a girl from the chorus of *The Black Crook,* then playing at the Broad Street Theatre.

When Chippy returned to Philadelphia a week later, he was broke, sober, and frightened over a blackout lasting several days. He discussed this with his cousin, Dr. Vaux, who had just started to practice medicine. The physician's advice was succinct and clear. "Quit drinking." But Chippy wasn't ready to give up alcohol.

For the next few months, when he was sober enough to get to City Hall, he appeared for many of Waln's clients. The old Quaker was glad to have Chippy try some of his difficult cases but had abandoned the idea of accepting young Patterson as a junior partner. Other lawyers, including several of his classmates whose practices were strictly commercial, were handing C. S. Patterson, Jr. the occasional criminal case which finds its way into the office of every attorney.

CHAPTER 18

MRS. ASHMEAD and her colleagues hit page one the morning of March 30, 1904, when the *Press* broke a story exclusive for only one edition.

"FIFTY INFANTS BURNED ALIVE IN HEATER," the *Press* screamed in a 48-point streamer, booting complacent Philadelphians right out of their chairs. The story followed:

"Revolting tales of how as many as 50 living babies were packed together in aprons and then thrown into a red hot furnace were told by Coroner Dugan at the inquest into the deaths of Mary B. Sloan and Sarah Hughes who died last year from criminal operations and whose bodies were recently exhumed.

"The sensation of the day came toward the end of the testimony from Dr. L. Moser, of North 3rd Street. Moser, who is known as the 'King of Malpractitioners' is at present under indictment for death in a criminal abortion and believing that members of the syndicate 'betrayed' him, he was willing to give the most damaging evidence against the accused woman and her companion.

"The Coroner asked [Moser]: 'Did you ever see any newborn children there?' [at the Ashmead house].

" 'Yes. Many of them.'

" 'How were the children disposed of?'

" 'There was a big heater there in which they were cremated.'

" 'How were the babies carried into the heater?'

" 'In aprons. Mrs. Ashmead carried them and put them in the furnace.'

" 'Do you know if any of these babies Mrs. Ashmead put into the furnace were alive?'

" 'Oh, yes. Some of them were alive. They were crying, but I don't know if all of them were.'

"When Moser took the stand Mrs. Ashmead smiled and laughed the whole time."

During the seemingly endless day of sensational testimony a bit of grisly humor was unconsciously injected by a Dr. Joseph H. King, who claimed to be a "specialist." He admitted wanting to cash in on the lucrative trade. He persuaded Mrs. Ashmead to rent him an office in the South Twelfth Street home, but after three weeks there he was advised to leave by a "certain Dr. Moore who told me [King], 'You might as well get out, Doc. Whatever happens you'll get the blame and Mrs. Ashmead all the credit.' "

Chippy was not at the inquest. It may be that he was busy elsewhere in court, although he was drunk so much of the time that he had become too irresponsible to be of value to his associates. Waln was present, but he felt this was not the time to ask questions or raise objections. He was probably happy to see his clients behind the strong, safe walls of Moyamensing. Tempers of Philadelphians reached a fever pitch when other newspapers picked up the story.

Each day for a week more and more revolting stories of the Ashmead-McVicars combination were revealed in the press. A "baby farm" was uncovered on the outskirts of Camden, New Jersey. There, those of the infants born on South Twelfth Street whom their midwife, by some strange process of selectivity, had decided should live, were kept and later sold for adoption or used by unscrupulous women to blackmail paramours. Coroner Dugan estimated Mrs. Ashmead's share of the take from her branch operation on the other side of the Delaware at $900 a week. The press hinted at a long, secret dossier of male victims. This, they said, her lawyers would use to "blow the lid off" Philadelphia society. But Waln and Chippy were able to assure many an anxious gentleman that if the nurse ever owned a "little black book" (considered standard equipment for all abortionists and blackmailers) she had never shown it to them and chances were it did not exist.

For months the prisoners languished at Moko and Chippy went his own way. He was rarely sober now, and attorneys who had been referring cases to him were fast losing confidence, not in young Patterson's ability, which he proved every time he went before a jury, but in his reliability. He was getting careless about his person and attire. While he never failed to bathe daily, he often had a two- or three-day beard, his hair grew long and unkempt, his suits were unpressed, his shoes unshined, and his shirts dirty and frayed at the cuffs. He hardly ever went to his office, and messages left there were unanswered. Either he disregarded appointments or arrived so late for them that clients refused to wait and sought legal advice elsewhere. They felt it was better to have a less able lawyer who showed up in court on time than a brilliant attorney who was never there when needed. Chippy was spending only occasional nights at Gracehill, where he entered and left like a wraith, appearing unexpectedly, hardly speaking to anyone, and then disappearing almost before the family was aware of his presence.

George and Eleanor Willing were married May 26, 1904, at the home of the bride's aunt, Miss Ellen Hoy, on Delancey Place. Except for the unscheduled appearance of Chippy, who weaved in and out of the potted palms in a rare mood of hilarity, the wedding went smoothly enough.

No public mention was made of Chippy's appearance at the ceremony. Those who were present must have sucked in their breaths with apprehension at the sight of this unwanted brother, his clothes disheveled and his breath reeking of alcohol, swaying unsteadily on his feet, and merrily edging his way through the shrubbery to the front of the room.

(More than half a century later, ask George Stuart Patterson's proud, still handsome widow if she remembers her brother-in-law Chippy's arrival at the wedding and she answers, with a momentary pause and a visible shudder, "No comment!")

In the meantime the public, its thirst quenched by blood-letting in the Sino-Japanese War or diverted to other scandals, had nearly forgotten all about the Ashmead case, which was, of course, what Chippy wanted. Then, on August 4, he exploded a bombshell. With no notice to the district attorney's office or anyone else, he appeared before Judge Audenreid in Quarter Sessions Court with a petition demanding the immediate release of both prisoners.

"Seeking freedom from their cells in Moyamensing, in which they have languished since March 30, last, when they were committed by the Coroner to answer to the awful accusations developed by the infanticide and malpractice charges, Elizabeth Ashmead and Dr. McVicars," said the *Press* of August 5, "through their attorney, C. Stuart Patterson, Jr., yesterday invoked the aid of an old and almost forgotten law under whose technical provision they claim the right to be discharged.

"They claim that because they were not indicted until three months after they were committed and have not yet had the opportunity to be tried, they can no longer be legally held in prison. Mr. Patterson first found the law hid away in the musty volume of Pennsylvania Statutes of the year 1785 and extended in 1860. He brought his petition to Judge Audenreid in Quarter Sessions Court yesterday and had the law with him, claiming that under it his client was entitled to be discharged as it 'provides that where there is a failure to indict or try a prisoner within two terms of the time he had been committed to prison, he shall upon application be entitled to be discharged.' Under the then existing law a term in Quarter Sessions Court covered a period of two months, while under the present system every month constitutes a term in itself."

After his first gasp of astonishment Judge Audenreid, an intelligent, impartial jurist was inclined to laugh the petition out of court, but Chippy had with him the volume containing the statute in question and had deliberately let some of the dust which had accumulated on its covers remain. With a grin, Chippy brushed it away and passed the book to the bench. His Honor glanced at it quickly and turning to an attaché, said, "Get Mr. Gray in here at once!"

A few minutes later a breathless assistant district attorney entered Quarter Sessions. Without a word Judge Audenreid gave Chippy's petition to him. Mr. Gray read through it once quickly, and the Judge, a smile on his lips, watched the young assistant read it again, this time more slowly, his lips shaping the words silently. Judge Audenreid handed the opened volume down from the bench. He waited until this, too, was read.

"Well, Mr. Gray," he said quietly, "you've seen Mr. Patterson's petition. Shall I release the prisoners cr have you an answer?"

"Your Honor," the assistant district attorney protested loudly, "you can't possibly release these prisoners. Their crimes are unspeakable. We *know* they are in prison. They haven't been tried because three key witnesses are missing."

He looked over at his classmate suspiciously.

"Perhaps Mr. Patterson knows where they are."

Chippy refused to become annoyed or angry and said nothing.

"Mr. Gray," admonished the Judge, "you owe Mr. Patterson an apology. I'm certain counsel would never dream of concealing evidence. I'll give you four days to file an answer. In the meanwhile the prisoners will remain where they are."

The Court turned to Chippy.

"You have the right of habeas corpus, you know, Mr. Patterson?"

Chippy wisely ignored the Court's suggestion, but the following morning Mr. Gray filed his answer, averring that any delay was caused by absence of Grace Ashmead, Jennie Harshaw, and DeWitt Ashmead, witnesses badly needed and, by the connivance of the prisoners, not available. Judge Audenreid then dismissed both the district attorney's and defense counsel's petitions without delivering an opinion. This Chippy noted in his exceptions and advised his clients not to plead. The Judge then ordered "not guilty" pleas entered for them.

On August 6, DeWitt Ashmead, who'd been hiding out as a prisoner in the Montgomery County Prison at Norristown, under an assumed name, suddenly appeared and was promptly taken into "protective custody" by the police.

On September 16, Chippy appealed Judge Audenried's decision and secured a writ on the district attorney, signed by the presiding judge of the Superior Court, requiring the Commonwealth's office "to show cause why a writ of habeas corpus should not be issued against the keeper of the county prison to establish legal ground for the prisoners' detention." In his petition Chippy contended that the coroner's inquests into the cases of two young women, alleged to have died as a result of criminal operation, were illegal because neither the coroner nor the jury viewed either of the bodies and the defendants were unable to secure trial within two terms. The rule was made returnable in the Superior Court on Monday, October 3.

On October 3, the district attorney himself, Mr. John

C. Bell, appeared before the Superior Court with an answer. He contended that "a writ of habeas corpus cannot be used as a writ of error to determine the correctness of the rulings of the Court of Oyer and Terminer and that Judge Audenreid's decision on the question was a final determination of the petitioner's rights."

The Superior Court, on October 27, dismissed Chippy's petition and ordered the defendants to trial. Even though he had lost his appeal to the higher court, young Patterson had accomplished his purposes. He had placed the district attorney's office on the defensive; deflected the press's anger at the prisoners into interest in a legal sparring match; and delayed the trial until the public was indifferent and bored.

Minus most of the furor the original arrests had caused, Mrs. Ashmead and Dr. McVicars went on trial Thursday, January 26, 1905. Mr. Patterson was not available. Dr. McVicars was acquitted of all charges, but his colleague was found guilty of criminal abortion and sentenced to three years at Eastern State Penitentiary, her commitment dating from the time of her incarceration. The doctor, his lesson learned, dropped out of sight forever. But Mrs. Ashmead, upon her release from prison, took to the hills of New England. She was last heard of August 14, 1909, when she was charged with operating a "baby farm" on the outskirts of Greenville, New Hampshire.

Not long after Chippy appeared before Judge Audenreid, he collapsed in the dining room of the Bellevue. His favorite waiter, John Wickas, called Dr. Francis, who took his brother to Gracehill and put him to bed. His weight was down again under 150 pounds, and Dr. Vaux told Chippy that continued drinking would shortly bring about a complete physical and mental collapse. Chippy remained in bed, sleeping badly and eating little. On December 24, Dr. Vaux stopped at Gracehill for a daily call on his patient. When he got there, he was told that Chippy, after reading a telegram, had left home some time during the night. Except for Nora, neither family nor friends saw him again for ten days.

CHAPTER 19

THE PHILADELPHIA of Chippy's era was much the same politically as most American cities of the time, better than a few and worse than most. Its peculiar tragedy lay in the fact that it might have been the best. As long as Society Hill and Rittenhouse Square stayed in control, good government was the rule. The ability, intelligence, integrity and experience that characterized this small group of aristocrats resulted in the honest and efficient performance of public duties. A Proper Philadelphian accepted a responsible position in municipal government, elective or appointive, not because he needed the job but because of his sense of noblesse oblige.

When the city's natural leaders abdicated and left a huge gap, the rascals moved in to fill the vacuum. They took over the Republican Party and through it ran the city like an absolute monarchy, responsible to no one, least of all God, levying tribute or dispensing largesse as they chose.

Jim McManes, earliest of these freebooters, was known by his many followers as "James the First." If a mixed metaphor may be used, it could be stated that James the First milked the gas works for a million dollars a year. For every ton of coal supplied to make artificial gas for Philadelphia users, Jim McManes levied $1 in tribute. To be certain he was not cheated, his trusted followers checked off each delivery at a central point. Nobody bothered to weigh the coal, so it would not be unreasonable to assume that suppliers short-weighted the city enough to pass on James the First's levy to the public.

He was finally ousted by a group of reformers who came from within the confines of the Union League and were led by a devout Philadelphia Quaker, Philip S. Garrett. With Anthony J. Drexel and others, including Theodore Cuyler but not Christopher Stuart Patterson, Sr., he headed a Citizens' ticket which nominated and elected Samuel G. King, a reformer, as mayor. King went the way of all reformers. He lasted one term and the Machine was back again until it was smashed by the Bullitt Bill (named after William C. Bullitt, of Chestnut Hill) which gave the city a new charter and a measure of temporary self-rule.

The Gas Works Gang was succeeded by the Hog Combine, led by a master of the old school, the distinguished Senator from Pennsylvania, the Honorable Matthew S. Quay. Quay, through his lieutenant Dave Martin, took over the Philadelphia Republican City Committee and with it the city. He ousted all the Gas Gang ward leaders and substituted his own. Anybody who resisted Quay's commandos was promptly beaten up and tossed in jail by those members of the Philadelphia Police Department who had sworn fealty to the Senator. Quay then created fake companies to bid on city contracts for jobs he never expected to be done. Since Quay owned city councils, members of which were also stockholders in these corporations, it was not surprising that their bids were always the lowest. As a matter of fact, they were the only ones. All others were tossed, unopened, into the wastebasket.

Quay could afford to be low bidder. His companies had no overhead, no construction, labor, or material costs. They existed only in Quay's imagination. The huge sums they were paid for work they didn't do were deposited in one of the several banks the Senator owned and distributed to his fiefs after he took the lord's share.

The Hog Combine, which dealt in people, not pigs, and was so named by a newspaperman of the day to illustrate the gluttony of its members, used the People's Bank (a misnomer if there ever was one) for a clearing house where loot could be divided in private. In 1895 Quay broke with his lieutenant, Martin. "When thieves fall out . . ." reasoned John Wanamaker, it was time to give the Senator a battle. Backed by a few other honest citizens, the merchant investigated the People's Bank. They uncovered a mess so sorry that even Mr. Wanamaker, who suspected the worst, was shocked by the frightening depredations, the extent of graft, and the widespread moral corruption.

John Hopkins, the bank's cashier, shot himself to death with a hunting rifle. On his desk Wanamaker's sleuths found Mr. Quay's telegraphed advice: "If you buy and carry a thousand net [indicating stock] I will shake the plum tree." (This was interpreted by the press of the day to mean that Quay would manipulate the chosen stock so that the "fruit" or dividends would fall whenever he wanted it to.) From then on he became known as Matthew "Shake the Plum Tree" Quay.

In 1904, the *Public Ledger* decided to get into the fight and help Mayor John Weaver and merchant Wanamaker beat the organization.

Weaver had come into office as a result of a combination of circumstances which included a latent revival of interest in good government, a feud between the Old Guard and the New (both thoroughly dishonest), and public disgust at the incredibly blatant thievery of Samuel Ashbridge, Weaver's predecessor.

"I have four years to serve," said His Honor upon taking his oath of office in a brief message which even *Mein Kampf* does not exceed in candor. "I want no further office when I am out of this one, and I shall get out of this office all there is for Samuel H. Ashbridge."

The *Ledger* chose an exposé of white slavery as its contribution to the re-establishment of law and order. It did not attack prostitution, per se, then regarded as an excusable social error.

Chippy was roused from his bed at Gracehill shortly before Christmas, 1904, by a message from a client, Celia Stone. Mrs. Stone operated three "legitimate" houses all within two blocks of each other. She had a staff of 20 girls, not including two attractive colored maids in each establishment who combined household chores with an occasional break in the monotony when some gentleman wanted to "change his luck."

The institution Mrs. Stone and her Philadelphia colleagues operated was a kind of club where a man might linger for a few gay hours in the company of kindred male and pleasant female companions. Many of the girls were beautiful, and all were accomplished. The décor may have been rococo, but you can be sure it was expensive. Madam could well afford the best. And to top it off there actually was an artiste of sorts who could truthfully say he earned his living playing the piano in a whorehouse.

While there were a few foreign imports, the majority of prostitutes came from the small towns and farms of Pennsylvania and neighboring New Jersey. The drab up-state hard-coal regions were particularly productive to the trade. Girls employed by Mrs. Stone and the other "respectable" madams entered the life of sin on a purely voluntary basis.

Obviously this kind of establishment could cater to a relatively small percentage of Philadelphia's lusty male population. Even in its heyday, from about 1890 until World War One, there were never more than 40 or 50 "parlor houses" in the entire city. None employed more than 20 girls and a few only a dozen. Besides, an evening at Mrs. Stone's, or in a similar place, was not inexpensive. The standard minimum fee was $10, but what sporting gentleman would be cheap enough to leave only the *couvert?*

The madam would not tolerate boisterous drunkenness, although no small part of her profits came from the sale of intoxicants. Whiskey, 100-proof bourbon or rye bottled in bond and taken neat, was the standard beverage. No patron would dream of leaving without buying a bottle or a round for the assembled guests. Quite frequently a bon vivant, celebrating his birthday, wedding anniversary, or another noteworthy occasion, would order a couple of magnums of champagne for the house.

Madam sold no food, not even an occasional breakfast *à deux* served free to particularly special guests, but patrons did not have to go hungry. Within easy reach were huge platters filled with pickled hard-boiled eggs; Lynnhavens on the half shell and pungent, fresh horseradish to go with them; chunks of biting Cheddar or aged, imported Swiss; fat Yarmouth *Matjes;* thick slices of spicy baked Virginia ham; and loaves of black, heavy, German pumpernickel.

What with the large initial investment, including outright purchase of a three- or four-story building, decorating costs, the police captain's cut, operating expenses, legal fees, etc., there was good reason for the fact that only a comparatively few such places were in existence, even though profits were high. Men had their favorite institutions and girls to whom they returned. Trouble with duly elected authorities or their police representatives was rare, and life for Mrs. Stone, her colleagues, and employees should have been serene, and much of the time it was.

Mrs. Stone's headquarters was on Franklin Street, and it was here that Chippy arrived on a cold and snowy winter night.

Except for the sound of his own footfalls on the front steps and a dim light coming from a second-story window, the house, to Chippy's astonishment, was quiet and dark. Normally at 3 A.M. the place would be brightly lit, and gay sounds of laughter, song, and the tinkling of piano keys would have filled the night.

It was a most disturbed madam who cautiously opened the door to admit her attorney. Mrs. Stone's perturbation, she explained, arose, as it had on previous occasions, from the operation of what were known then as "slave pens," despised by the owners of all legitimate houses like Mrs. Stone's.

Since the total number of girls employed in Philadelphia parlor houses never exceeded 1,000 and clients were limited to gentlemen who could afford to pay well, it was obvious that the great masses of men had to seek illicit pleasure elsewhere. As a result, scores of unspeakably wretched brothels sprang up all over the slum areas of Philadelphia during the first few years of the century. With only infrequent interruptions they continued their existence for more than a decade, a large share of their profits helping to support the Organization and their exorbitant rentals swelling the dividends of the banks or trust funds owning properties where they were located. They were called "pens," and their inmates were correctly labeled "slaves."

The majority of girls, most of whom were unwilling victims of the white slave traffic of that era, were under the age of eighteen. Many were less than sixteen, and children of thirteen and fourteen were no rarity. They were forced into prostitution by criminals who had no compunctions about kidnapping unwilling victims, raping them, and then, under threats of violence carried out unhesitatingly on all those who attempted to escape, holding them as actual peons. Without a penny for themselves, they took care of as many as 50 men in a single night.

"I was tipped off," Mrs. Stone told Chippy. "The cops are going to close up every pen in the city. That's all right with me. They ought to be closed up, but how do we know they'll stop there once they get started? They might turn on us. I run a decent house. I pay the captain regularly, and I've never had any trouble. I hated to bother you in the middle of the night, Mr. Patterson, and I'll make it worth your while. For the first time in my life I'm scared. As soon as I got word I shut up right away, but now I don't know what to do. I can't afford a raid."

"You did the right thing by closing, Mrs. Stone," Chippy assured his client. "Let me try to find out what's going on. It may be only a rumor. Stay where you are until I get back, and tell your friends to do the same. Don't admit any customers."

Within a few hours Chippy had learned the truth. Newspaper Row knew a vice story or a crusade was imminent, but just when and where it would break no one was sure.

Even though John Weaver, a quasi-reformer, was in power, his predecessor had corrupted the city's police so badly that no one, particularly cynics of the working press, believed anyone in authority could afford to stage raids. However, they underestimated the power of the *Public Ledger*, then looking for a point from which to launch an attack on the Organization.

Many honest detectives and policemen who had never

succumbed to bribery or corruption, although transferred to remote police districts in the northeast, remained in the Philadelphia Police Department. John Wanamaker had their names. Mayor Weaver, working with the merchant and the *Public Ledger,* promised these men there would be no reprisals from their superior officers if they would cooperate. They agreed, and an undercover investigation was begun almost at once. Since everything was wide open it required little sleuthing skill to develop all the evidence needed by The Watch and Ward Society, a private "do-good" organization of churchmen, and to swear out warrants for the arrest of known white-slave operators.

The *Ledger*'s goal was to show the tie-in between the Republican Party, which had its headquarters in the Betz Building, on South Penn Square opposite City Hall, and organized vice. "Legitimate" houses, such as the one Mrs. Stone operated, would not be touched. Of this Chippy was assured, and with that encouraging information he returned to North Franklin Street, there to await developments. It was too late to go home to Gracehill. Besides, Chippy was hardly the one to pass up the opportunity of spending several days and nights in the company of a grateful madam and 20 beautiful women, with plenty of liquor, fine food, and the phenomenally good fortune of being the only male present.

The *Ledger* broke its story the next morning, December 25, 1904. It pulled no punches.

"WHITE SLAVE PENS OF PHILADELPHIA AND THEIR PLACE IN THE ORGANIZATION," was the streamer. The subheads were equally disturbing. "PROTECTED BY THE CORRUPT MACHINE OF WHICH THEY ARE THE MOST USEFUL SERVANTS, TRADERS IN VICE MAINTAIN IN THIS CITY A HUNDRED INFAMOUS RESORTS WHERE YOUTHFUL VICTIMS ARE BOUGHT, HELD IN BONDAGE AND SACRIFICED!"

"Radiating from the Betz Building," the story went on, "like wires from a telephone station are the lines controlled by the Organization. By direct contact these lines lead to strange places and hold strong men as if in the grip of steel. All channels of official authority can be reached by these lines; the Magistrates are ever in direct touch; the police force responds to the slightest signal and the men in high stations outside the place of politics bow low upon command from the head center of the Organization.

"At the very bottom of the well of iniquity is the White Slave Syndicate in its awful business for and in consideration of thousands of fraudulent votes. Every white slave house in the city is well known to the police. A correct roster of these places is on file at City Hall and the lieutenants of police who permit them to exist know the places and proprietors as well as they know their own homes.

"White Slave houses differ from the ordinary brothel in that the inmates have been sold to a life of shame and that they personally receive nothing for their sacrifices. The prices paid for a white slave range from $250 to $2500, the latter being the export price.

"The White Slave Syndicate operates about 100 houses in the city and in each house there are from four to twenty girls. The syndicate sells no liquor. To gain admittance to a white slave house it is only necessary to open the door and walk in. In addition to the political services rendered, the proprietors of these resorts pay from $25 a month to $50 a week for police protection."

The *Ledger*'s sordid story continued for column after column. Organization politicians were named and payoffs properly labeled. The city was shocked, and within a few hours after the newspaper hit the streets, ministers discarded the Christmas-day sermons they had prepared and called for action from their pulpits. Weaver's picked squad of police went to work at once, and raids, which could hardly have been in the nature of a surprise, were staged in all the blighted areas. In the meanwhile most of the corral owners had shut down and transported their slaves across the Delaware into New Jersey hideouts.

However, a few operators had so much faith in the protection they had been buying they did not bother to close. Raiders, smashing down front doors, found eight owners still doing business, hours after the tip-off. They and 107 of their partially clad child slaves, not one of the latter over seventeen years old, were taken into custody and brought before Magistrate Williams in City Hall.

One hundred and six of the slaves were sent to the House of Correction to be treated for the diseases they had acquired and to be salvaged for whatever doubtful future awaited them. The one hundred and seventh, whom witnesses testified had been beaten savagely into a state of hysteria and who was described as a "frail child of fifteen" became Chippy's problem.

Her name was Maryla. She had been removed to Philadelphia General Hospital when word of her condition, together with all the gossip produced by the raids, reached Mrs. Stone. Like so many of her colleagues, she was sentimental. She begged Chippy to see if he could help the little girl.

Together he and Mrs. Stone went to the hospital, where they were told the child was sleeping under heavy sedation, but despite the hell to which she had been subjected the prognosis was good. Maryla needed only rest and kindness. Chippy got in touch with Nora, who was happy to hear from her brother and agreed to do what she could to assist Maryla. A few hours later Eleanor Patterson, looking quite regal, descended upon the charity ward of Philadelphia General Hospital, a private nurse in tow, and removed Maryla to Lying-In Hospital. There she met Chippy and placed Maryla under the care of Dr. Vaux, whose comment was that Chippy looked worse than the child.

Chippy and Mrs. Stone left $1,000 with Nora to provide for Maryla (when the girl recovered, Nora sent her back to her family in Poland), and Chippy returned to North Franklin Street. He had been drinking steadily now for more than a week.

The next time any of his relatives saw him, he appeared at the Benedict's Ball in Horticultural Hall, with a beautiful woman on each arm, both as attractive as any of the matrons or debutantes present, although they seemed to have a different air about them.

At the head of the foyer stairway was the receiving line

headed by Mrs. Alexander Brinton Coxe, dressed, according to the Philadelphia *Item,* in "an elaborate imported gown of white duchess point lace over a foundation of white satin and trimmed with spangled net and pearls while at her throat and in her hair glistened diamond ornaments." With drunken dignity Chippy proceeded to introduce his ladies to Mrs. Coxe, to the other patronesses, and to the distinguished guests.

George S. Patterson and his bride (who herself headed the Benedict's receiving line a half century later), Dr. Francis and his fiancée, Miss Edith Adams, and Nora left the moment Chippy entered.

Chippy's ladies joined in the dance, but word soon got around that they were two of Mrs. Stone's beauties.

Fortunately for Patterson a blackout prevented him from recalling most of that evening.

When he recovered consciousness, he was in a private room at Lying-In Hospital. He had no idea how he had got there. The date was January 5, 1905, exactly two weeks since he had left Gracehill. Dr. Vaux was standing by his side. Chippy looked up at his cousin, managed a weak smile, and said, "Okay, Norrie, I've had it!"

That afternoon, accompanied by Dr. Vaux, Chippy voluntarily committed himself to Pennsylvania Hospital for Mental Diseases at 49th and Market Streets. Here, in the institution made famous by Dr. Thomas S. Kirkbride, he hoped to be able to learn to face life without the bottle.

At the time of Chippy's stay at "Kirkbride's," the more progressive mental institutions, of which this was one, had a well-established routine for the treatment of alcoholics. There was no abrupt withdrawal of whiskey; during the first five days of confinement Chippy was given bonded bourbon in gradually decreasing quantities all the while his non-alcoholic liquid intake was being increased. By the beginning of the sixth day whiskey rations ended, hydro-therapeutic baths were begun, and Chippy was urged to take as much exercise as he could stand.

When he had been there for several months, Chippy organized cricket teams among the inmates and brother

George refereed several intramural matches. C. Stuart, who was footing his son's hospital bill, had forgiven Chippy for his transgressions, and he, Chippy's mother, Nora, and Peg Johnson were regular visitors. Francis, who had married Edith Adams and was practicing medicine, came to see his brother when he had the time.

There were other callers. Mrs. Stone and one or two of Chippy's grateful clients never failed to spend a few hours each week with their counselor Joe Sims and Uncle Theo came whenever they had the opportunity. But most of his long hours at the mental institution Chippy spent in his attractively furnished private room on the second floor whose two barred windows overlooked a wide sweep of lawn and a high stone fence beyond. He read omnivorously—the classics; his old favorites, Stevenson, Cooper, Milton; and others—but he never so much as glanced at a law book, legal journal, or newspaper. It was as though he was attempting to purge himself completely of his profession and the present era. He seemed perfectly content to remain where he was.

At the end of his second year Chippy earned weekend privileges and could have gone to Gracehill from Friday noon until Sunday evening in the custody of his parents. But apparently he preferred the seclusion and security of the hospital and chose to spend all his time there. He left Kirkbride's only once, and that was to attend Jane's funeral. His sister's condition, both physical and mental, had been deteriorating rapidly since adolescence, and her short unhappy life ended on her twenty-first birthday.

After Chippy had been at Kirkbride's for nearly 33 months, he grew restless and asked to be discharged. He was released October 7, 1907. He never took another drink.

CHAPTER 20

A MONTH after Chippy walked out of Kirkbride's he reopened his offices on the second floor of 1523 Chestnut Street. He knew exactly what he intended to do with what was left of his life. From that day until an afternoon about 25 years later when he collapsed shortly after defending a penniless Negro charged with homicide, he did not deviate from the course he set. The road he took led him further and further away from his family and the world of Chestnut Hill, until, at the end, the days of his childhood and youth seemed like a strange and unbelievable dream.

Yet, despite his own conscious desires, Chippy never gave himself completely to any one of the thousands upon thousands of clients whose lives he affected in varying degrees. He could laugh with them, rejoice with them when they "beat the rap," or comfort them when they stood in the shadow of the chair, but he could never be one of them. Some wafer-thin but indestructible barrier stood between him and them, and no matter how much he tried he never could break it. Even with the women he loved and who in turn loved him he always held some small portion of himself in reserve.

The Pattersons made one last abortive attempt to influence Chippy to return to Chestnut Hill and the career they still had faint hopes he might choose. Norris Vaux, who was to be married shortly, was giving a small dinner party at the Racquet Club for his ushers and a few other friends and relatives. Francis was an usher, and he asked his cousin to invite George and Chippy. Norrie, interested in the prospect of observing his ex-patient's reaction to the sight of freely flowing alcohol, was delighted to oblige. With apparent ease Chippy refused to drink anything except Perrier water.

After the party George and Francis walked back with Chippy to the Bellevue Stratford Hotel, where he had gone directly from Kirkbride's. George had a proposal. As a debt of gratitude to C. Stuart, and this was exactly how it was phrased, would Chippy spend the next few weeks fishing and hunting with his father and George at Jekyl Island before making any decisions affecting his future? There would be no pressure, George assured his youngest brother, and Chippy would be free to leave any time he wanted to.

Although his mind was already made up and he realized the utter pointlessness of the trip, Chippy agreed, but he was adamant in his refusal to return to Gracehill. The following evening Mr. and Mrs. C. Stuart Patterson, Sr., Mr. and Mrs. George Stuart Patterson, Dr. and Mrs. Francis Patterson, Nora, and Chippy went to the Broad Street Theatre, where they saw George M. Cohan and Edna Wallace Hopper in *Fifty Miles from Boston*. After the performance they all walked two blocks north to the Broad Street Station, where P.R.R. President Alexander J. Cassatt and his wife were their hosts in the president's private car. Then, when everyone but C. Stuart, George, and Chippy had left, "Balmoral" was coupled to #89, the A.C.L. Express, and at two A.M. pulled out of the giant train shed bound for Savannah.

At Savannah they were met by a friend of C. Stuart's, and in a few hours a launch took them to Georgia's "Golden Isle" and installed them in a magnificent clubhouse, ready for the excellent hunting and fishing the island offered. The trio of Pattersons remained on Jekyl less than three weeks. They fished or hunted for small game every morning and afternoon and played whist with club members in the evening.

Almost from the start it was obvious to C. Stuart that his mission would fail. He and his son acted toward each other like polite strangers. Chippy, who loved fishing enough to endure the boredom he felt otherwise, would have been willing to stay longer, but George made the break. A wire to President Cassatt sent "Balmoral" back to Savannah for the return journey.

At Nora's request Chippy agreed to give up his room at the Bellevue and live in a small furnished flat she rented for him on Germantown Avenue, within walking distance of Gracehill.

It was a simple matter for Chippy to pick up the kind of practice he had left, and the paint on his office door was hardly dry before clients began to pour in. Word got around City Hall and magistrates' courts that the lawyer who not only didn't give a damn whether he collected a fee but could actually be counted upon for a small handout was back in business. Within a few weeks his two-room suite was jammed to overflowing with clients of all sexes and colors: men, women, homosexuals, whites, and every shade of black and yellow—the latter compliments of Norrie Vaux, whose hospital, Lying-In, was adjacent to Chinatown.

They waited outside the corridor, some from dawn, until Mr. Patterson arrived each morning, and they tugged at his sleeves for attention even before he could insert the key in the lock. They shoved themselves inside as the door swung open, and in a few moments there was standing room only. Most of the ladies and gentlemen had two things in common: lack of funds and lack of distance from the approaching forces of law. As a matter of fact, quite a number of clients were not even a few jumps ahead of the police, and it was not unusual for a member of the Detective Bureau to interrupt, politely, of course, a consultation between Chippy and a client and place the latter under arrest.

The din started as a kind of low rumble, which began when Chippy reached his office at about 7 A.M. By 9:55, when he left for the Hall, it had mounted to a desperate roar, which funneled down the long corridor, hit a rear wall, and richocheted into another hallway. The chaos was unbelievable, and none of Chippy's secretaries could stand it for more than a week until one morning Master Sergeant Henry Skelly, his thirty years of Army life ended, walked in and took over the management of office, secretary, clients, and his ex-lieutenant.

Skelly was regular Army and made no attempt to hide this fact even out of uniform. He was short, perhaps an eighth of an inch over the five feet six minimum, and he couldn't have weighed 130 pounds. But people, including several professional fighters, who thought his manner was only an act, found out to their astonishment that the sarge was as tough as he looked. The rules of the Marquis of Queensberry meant absolutely nothing to him, and since he always fought to win quickly he never fought fair. What gutter fighting he hadn't learned in the slums of Buffalo, where he was born, he picked up during a tour of duty at the U. S. Embassy in Tokyo, where a friendly Japanese jiu-jitsu instructor taught him every trick in the book and added a few of his own.

Skelly's voice was surprisingly deep for a man of his stature, and except when he spoke to Chippy, whom he worshipped, to Ada Hetherington, whom he adored, or to any "real" lady or gentleman, he sounded like a drill sergeant barking orders to a particularly stupid squad of enlistees. It took him no time at all to reduce the frenzy at the office into a kind of controlled madness.

To begin with, the sergeant fired whatever timid young secretary was there at the time of his arrival and hired a nasty, ill-tempered, middle-aged, reformed circus shill who distrusted every representative of mankind regardless of race, creed, color, or national origin, not excluding her husband (currently winding up a long sentence at Eastern Penitentiary), Sergeant Skelly, and even Mr. Patterson whose apparent decency she was certain was only a mask for a mind and soul steeped in duplicity.

She was tall, angular, and lantern-jawed and wore her smooth gray hair pulled straight back and tied into a large knot, making her look not unlike a representative of the Home Missionary Society of the Evangelical Lutheran Church. She and the sarge were grammar-school classmates in Buffalo. Before running away with the operator of a crooked gambling wheel in a circus, she had taught school and regarded the motley gang that assembled daily in Chippy's office as just so many annoying and dirty little boys and girls whom frequently she would reduce to complete silence with a glance of utter contempt. She bore the unbelievably romantic name of Elaine DuBarry, but Chippy was the only one who used that title. With complete unconcern and without any apparent disrespect, Skelly called her by her childhood nickname, which for some unaccountable reason was "Pigshit."

The first time Bob Hoffard, who used to cover City Hall for the *Bulletin,* heard this dignified, aloof female addressed in such a cavalier fashion he said he was sure his ears had tricked him.

" 'For God's sakes, Chip,' I said, 'what's with this pig-shit deal?'

"He grinned. 'If you think that's funny, you ought to be around when one of my colored clients, trying to be respectful, calls her Miss Pigshit.' "

Chippy plunged into work with almost unrestrained energy and set a pace few could follow. Sleep meant little to him, and he could exist with only a few hours a day. Although the city directory listed the apartment on Germantown Avenue as his residence through 1908, 1909, and 1910, Chippy spent most of his nights at the Bellevue, getting to bed sometimes as late as 4 A.M. and then not going to sleep until he had read a few pages from one of his favorite books. He arose promptly at six, ate a large breakfast in the hotel dining room, and then took a cab to his office less than three blocks' distance. He even took a taxi from there to City Hall, and that was only a few hundred yards away.

By then he had established a system of tipping he maintained throughout his life, raising gratuities when prices went up. Breakfast at the time was 40 cents. For this he left a dollar and accepted no change. The same was true for the taxi ride, but if either was more than fifty cents Chippy left an extra dollar.

He was usually at the office no later than 7 A.M., but no matter how early he arrived, Skelly was there before him. At first the sergeant had a furnished room on Fifteenth Street above Arch, but later, wherever the lieutenant lived, this self-appointed valet and bodyguard had a room close by.

Clients in need of a handout in addition to legal services were not the only ones who entered the office. There were plenty of others, including the "easy money" boys, who began to drift in. Mayor Weaver had tried to make life difficult for pimps, gamblers, burglars, con men, pickpockets, and other assorted racketeers of the day, and they were happy to retain a seemingly infallible counselor. Unlike the bulk of the people who sat in Mr. Patterson's waiting room, these clients' pocketbooks were lined, and, what's more, they had no objections to paying a stiff fee or retainer.

Chippy gave no preferential treatment to these aristocrats, who had to wait their turn beside absolute paupers. Regardless of his position in the hierarchy of crime, each client was given a number by Skelly, based solely upon the time of his arrival. When the sergeant called that number, then and only then was a client permitted to see Mr. Patterson. The exceptions to this strictly enforced rule were men and women whose immediate freedom was at stake, as, for example, a murderer with, you might say figuratively or even literally, "fresh blood" on his hands. Those in such desperate straits had precedence. This system was maddening to clients with money to spend.

The line moved in and out of Chippy's office faster than one would have suspected. Many a "client" wanted only a kind word, and some needed "two bits, Mr. Patterson, please," for the morning drink they had to have to get through their wretched day and who went to the one man they were sure would understand this pressing need. Obviously, in the three hours Chippy spent interviewing scores of men and women each morning, he couldn't possibly probe for details and had to depend upon fast courtroom thinking for the successes that were piling up. Those accused of major felonies returned for afternoon interviews after court adjourned or for evening conferences, with Skelly on hand to give an assist in locating friendly witnesses and in general helping to build up a case for the defense.

Except for legal holidays, when he went fishing, Chippy spent an average of five hours a day on trial in Oyer and Terminer. Besides this grueling schedule he attended night police-court sessions held four evenings a week from 7 until 10 at City Hall or in the various magistrates' offices scattered all over Philadelphia. In these upper and lower courts he represented an average of no less than 25 clients a day. This gave him little time to keep up with new law or prepare his cases the way his colleagues, accustomed to handling two or three court cases a day at the most, could do. During the first two years out of Kirkbride's he represented 11 defendants charged with homicide. He won five acquittals, while not one of the other six was convicted of a crime more serious than involuntary manslaughter.

Because trial records have long since been destroyed and since none of these cases required an appeal to a higher court which would have resulted in the printing of a paper book that might have survived, the only way these early successes of Chippy can be measured is by newspaper accounts of the crimes. If we are to believe the press, then certainly at least two of the 11 defendants deserved hanging, and you wonder by what legerdemain Chippy was able to convince a jury to return with ridiculous findings. George Riccuitti and Albert Pasquale were arrested a few minutes after shooting to death a South Philadelphia storekeeper who caught them in the act of robbing his place of business. There were three adult witnesses, including an off-duty detective; the defendants admitted firing five shots into the victim's body. Yet they were convicted only of *involuntary* manslaughter. They served less than three years each at Eastern Penitentiary. It's difficult to understand how Chippy could have convinced any 12 citizens that the storekeeper's death was an accident.

Not until 1911 did Chippy handle any "page one" homicide where trial records and evidence are on file.

The most satisfactory analysis of Chippy's unique courtroom abilities was once given by Louis F. McCabe, a brilliant lawyer who in later years was associated with Chippy in many of his major successes as well as his most depressing failure.

"Chippy's greatest asset," said McCabe, "was a profound working knowledge of human nature, and the ability to utilize this knowledge with almost instinctive reactions. He was able to sense the attitudes of the judge, prosecuting attorney, jurors, and witnesses, to sift and to shift them around in kaleidoscopic fashion so as to effect the result most favorable to his client. Among numerous and diverse possibilities, he seemed to select the one to which he must cater, or the one that he might risk offending with the least damage to his client. Thus in approaching the problems of cross-examination of a child witness, before a judge who was known to look with disfavor upon an aggressive cross-examination, Chippy was able to size up the relative advantages and disadvantages of an aggressive cross-examination and a complaisant approach.

"A great deal of the skill of brilliant trial lawyers is devoted towards protecting their record. They must do this, particularly in a bad case, so that on appeal they will not be held to have waived any objections. Every lawyer knows these tactics sometimes irritate a jury and usually give the jury the impression that the testimony objected to is particularly feared by the defendant. Chippy, however, represented in a very large number of cases persons who were not in a position financially to appeal. Therefore, protecting the record was not of too much interest. Chippy was a master at 'rolling with the punch.' He could meet the most devastating volunteered remark of a hostile witness with a benign smile, a triumphant side glance at the jury, as though he had actually trapped the witness. He might even say, 'Why didn't you say that on direct examination?' or 'Yes, indeed, that's just what I'm driving at, that's just what I'm trying to get from you.'

"Chip had no great knowledge of the whys and wherefores of the rules of evidence. What he did have, however, was a wonderful working knowledge, a good rule-of-thumb knowledge, and a remarkable memory. As he was in court every day, Chip was able to catch the moods, habits, and proper reactions of both judges and juries in various other rooms. When he sensed what he used to call an atmosphere of guilt around the courtroom, he became very, very hard to find. Repeated calls from that room would find Patterson trying a relatively unimportant case in another room and stringing that out so that the case he was trying to duck would have to be continued.

"Generally, his manner in court was gracious. However, when he felt the occasion demanded it, he would go hammer and tongs after judge, district attorney, or witness. He was afraid of no one."

CHAPTER 21

THE strenuous schedule Chippy set for himself obviously left little time for romance. This is not to imply there were no women in his life. Adjacent to Chippy's suite at the Bellevue-Stratford, where he was a permanent guest after giving up his rarely used Germantown Avenue apartment, there was a connecting room, seldom vacant. The hotel had strict house rules, enforced by clerks who sat behind desks in front of the elevator banks on each of the Bellevue's 15 floors, and Chippy was careful never to affront the clerk on his floor, the eleventh, by escorting any unattached female to his suite. He simply rented the room adjoining his and gave a key to the current woman of his choice.

Chippy always had a predilection for tall, big-bosomed women, and in the latter part of 1908 whatever hours he had to spare he was spending with Lucia Cooper, a featured performer at the Casino Burlesque on Walnut Street, where she was billed as "The Girl from Venus." If Lucia was typical, that planet was populated by women of generous proportions. Miss Cooper, according to contemporary advertisements, was "Six Feet of Golden Dynamite——44 x 30 x 36."

About this time a Chinese chauffeur-houseboy who worked for the John Hunter Lucas family got into trouble with the law. Lucas was a friend of Norrie Vaux, and the latter asked Chippy to represent Wong Loo. Wong was a normally trustworthy employee with a weakness for occasional sprees usually indulged in on his own time.

One day Loo "borrowed" the Lucas's Stanley Steamer

and instead of driving to Broad Street Station, where he was supposed to pick up Lucas's father-in-law, A. G. Hetherington, president of the Philadelphia Civil Service Commission, took off on his own and headed for Chinatown, where he had a few drinks too many. Driving back, unquestionably under the influence of Barbados rum, he smashed the Steamer into a car parked in front of the Union League. The noise of the crash was far worse than the slight damage, but fate was stacked against him. The owner of the car was Henry Winston Chesley, III, who disliked all Orientals. The police surgeon, Dr. Elias Hoover, who examined Loo when he was placed under arrest at Chesley's insistence, hated alcohol in every form.

Wong was pronounced drunk at the 19th District Police Station and thrown into a basement cell. By the time he sobered up he was afraid to call his employers, who, in the meantime, had reported him and the car missing. The following day, when they learned what had happened, they got in touch with Dr. Vaux, who they knew was Chesley's physician.

Dr. Vaux asked Chesley to drop charges against Loo and assured him that he would guarantee payment of all damages to the Chesley car if neither Wong nor the Lucases would pay. But Chesley was adamant, and the committing magistrate could do nothing except hold the chauffeur under $500 bail on a charge of drunken driving. Dr. Vaux posted the bond himself and called Chippy. By the time the case came to trial before Judge Barratt a few months later the Lucases had forgiven Loo completely and were in court as character witnesses.

Until scientific blood tests were developed, a man's sobriety, in Philadelphia at any rate, was determined by his ability to walk a straight line in the presence of a qualified physician. There was a white stripe, about two inches wide, painted on the floor of every police station, and Wong, put to the test, apparently had failed completely. Dr. Hoover, bristling with importance, was eager to testify to that effect. He was seated next to Patterson behind a long table to the left of the jury box when Chippy leaned over and whispered into his ear.

"You know, Doctor," he said complainingly, "it's not at all fair of you to expect a man with a wooden leg to walk a line as straight as a man who has full use of both his limbs."

Dr. Hoover looked scornfully at Wong's lawyer and replied, "Don't you believe I've thought of that?"

When he was called to the stand, the physician, who was the sole witness for the prosecution, testified that Loo was unable to walk a straight line.

"Naturally," he added pompously and with a triumphant smirk at Chippy, "I've taken into consideration the fact that the defendant had a wooden leg."

John C. Bell, the assistant district attorney prosecuting the case, looked puzzled, and, knowing Chippy, a bit disturbed by this unsolicited bit of information. But obviously, since he knew nothing about Wong's physical handicap, his place was to say nothing.

Chippy did not cross-examine and simply called his client to the stand.

"Will you lift your right trouser, please, Mr. Wong?" he asked. Wong obliged and displayed a thin, hairy, yellow leg. Chippy pretended to examine it closely and then turned to the Bench.

"Your Honor," he said, "would you please request Dr. Hoover to check my findings? This feels like a perfectly sound limb to me."

Judge Barrett was no teetotaler. He had had previous dealings with Dr. Hoover, whose fanaticism about alcohol invariably annoyed him. Beginning to anticipate Chippy's strategy, he nodded his head.

"Certainly, Mr. Patterson. Dr. Hoover, please let the Court and jury know if the defendant's leg is his own."

The physician, quite vexed, strode up to the stand and pinched Wong's leg so sharply that he winced with pain. The jury tittered.

"Well, Dr. Hoover?" asked His Honor.

"It's his own, Judge," he answered and remained in front of Wong expectantly.

"Thank you, Doctor," Chippy said. "That will be all."

"What about the other leg?" the physician shouted, rising to Chippy's bait.

"The other leg?" Chippy said softly, and then closed in for the kill. "But of course, Doctor. You don't think I'd attempt to conceal evidence from a physician as learned as you. Wong! Pull up your left trouser."

Wong obliged and displayed the other leg, equally thin and hairy. By this time the jury, with scarcely concealed laughter, was hanging over the side of the box.

"Pinch it, Doctor!" taunted Chippy. "Let's put science to work."

The physician didn't budge. He stood there, a deep red suffusing his face.

"Go ahead, Dr. Hoover," ordered Judge Barratt. "You're the one who led us to believe the man had a wooden leg."

The doctor, by now realizing he'd been the victim of his own pomposity and with his dignity torn to shreds, nipped Wong's leg gently, although he must have felt more like using a scalpel. Then, to the sound of laughter, he hurried down the aisle and stalked furiously out of the courtroom. When Judge Barratt had regained his composure, he turned to the jury and directed an acquittal.

"This," he concluded, "was obviously a case of mistaken identity."

It wouldn't be fair to say that the case of the Commonwealth vs. Wong might have taken a different turn if Lucas's wife, Ada, hadn't been seated in the front row during the trial. But it's more than likely that her presence, of which Chippy was acutely conscious, stimulated young Patterson into performing with an extra dash of enthusiasm. Although Ada was the mother of three children, she looked like a debutante. She was tall, slender, and restless, and Chippy appeared on the scene at the proper moment.

"Father and I were sitting up in front of the courtroom listening to other cases," Ada recalled, "when Wong walked in with his lawyer, the one Norrie had gotten for him. I knew it had to be Chiffy Patterson. I'd heard about him all my life. He was completely poised and so absolutely handsome. He made me think of the way John Drew used to walk on stage and electrify the audience the moment he appeared. That's the way it was with Chiffy. He said 'Good morning!' to the Judge, smiled in the friendliest way at the jury, and glanced over and nodded to my father. Then he looked at me, and his eyes held mine for a few seconds. I knew right then and there I simply *had* to meet him.

"I didn't know how he was going to get a jury to acquit Wong, but I was sure he'd win."

A few days later Ada asked Dr. Vaux to introduce her to young Patterson. The meeting took place in Chippy's office. If ever the right time and place combined to create the perfect setting needed to inform this sheltered young woman that there could be a life more exciting than the one she'd lived for some 20 odd years, they were there the moment Dr. Vaux led Ada into Chippy's suite. The waiting room was jammed with the usual assortment of characters barely held at bay by the sergeant, whose growls at his charges subsided into dulcet tones when this delicately scented, elegantly attired lady removed a long black kid glove to shake his hand. In the corner, seated haughtily behind her desk, was Chippy's secretary, pounding away madly at her typewriter and trying to accept as calmly as she could the presence of this lovely woman whose picture appeared so frequently on the society pages she read.

Even the client speaking to Chippy when Skelly opened the lawyer's door to announce Mrs. Lucas and Dr. Vaux was above the usual cut. It could have been anyone of the dozen dull assorted criminals or wretched panhandlers who had already been interviewed that morning. Instead it was George Flatico, a debonair young confidence man, whom Chippy represented and continued to represent for a quarter of a century. George's crimes ranged in variety, time, and place from inducing eager pre-World War One bettors to place their money on horses long after the races had been run to selling property he did not own to Miss Miriam Hopkins of Hollywood and New York.

At the time Flatico made Ada's acquaintance he was

about twenty-three or twenty-four. He looked, she said, exactly like Adolphe Menjou and had all of his suavity. Born in Italy, he came to the United States as a child of seven, and almost before he could speak English he was milking his classmates of their pennies by selling them "lucky" soil from the gardens of the Vatican. The soil, of course, came from the back yard of the Flatico home on Fitzwater Street. His policy concerning the "games" that enabled him to live in luxury—when he wasn't living in jail—was to "keep 'em simple."

In his youth, department stores fascinated him. He regarded them with love, and was deeply offended when this affection was not returned. "They have so much in them," he used to point out to Ada and Chippy with awe, "who could ever tell what was missing in a thousand years?" The fact that stores took precise annual inventories meant nothing to Flatico. He was only fifteen years old when he developed a technique by which, except for an unfortunate coincidence, he might have shared the profits of Wanamaker's, Gimbel's, and Strawbridge's for years.

Donning a well-fitting Western Union boy's uniform and looking spruce, alert, and intelligent, he would deliver a fake message to a department store requesting the bearer be given some expensive, easily selected article, to be charged to the "sender's" account. The signer of the telegram was always one whose name was in the Blue Book and who would naturally have an account at all the better stores. The inference was that the article was to be a gift for someone whose anniversary or birthday was suddenly remembered.

The trick was neat, and it worked for quite a while, until the long arm of coincidence stretched out. George arrived one morning at Strawbridge's jewelry counter on the first floor with a telegraphic request for a "lady's wrist watch to cost no more than $200" and to be "gift wrapped, given to bearer, and charged to sender's name." The clerk, who had just finished reading his daily newspaper, did a double take when he saw the signature on the telegram. It was the same as that of a banker who had just absconded with a large sum of depositors' money and whose picture appeared on page one that very day. While the clerk pretended to make a selection of watches, he tapped the "security" button with his foot, and a few moments later a store detective appeared.

George was questioned at length by the chief of customer security, who thought for a fleeting moment the banker actually had been stupid enough to send the telegram. But when he was convinced Flatico knew nothing of the sender's address and the boy had chosen a name at random, he sent George on his way with, as Flatico later told Chippy, "a solid boot in the rear end."

This time George was charged with defrauding Wanamaker's of several thousand dollars' worth of rare perfume. Flatico, umhampered or perhaps even inspired by Ada, who sat listening with starry eyes, was completely frank. He had had his eye (or nose), he said, on the swank perfume and cosmetic shop, then located near the store's Juniper Street entrance, for some time.

Arriving a moment or two after Wanamaker's opened, wearing a loosely fitting linen duster, George stepped behind the counter and introduced himself to the young lady already there as the new perfume salesman. He looked the part, played it well, and unquestionably delighted the girl, pleased to have the company of such a charming colleague. He appeared to be completely familiar with the stock and had no difficulty in selling much of the expensive French perfume for which the store was famous.

George made sure to ring up the correct amount of the sale or make out the proper charge slips. Business was unusually brisk that morning, and the temptation to short-change customers must have tried Flatico's patience sorely. What no one except George knew was that his duster was lined with padded pockets ready to receive quarts of perfume retailing for as high as $20 a gram.

Within an hour or so George was ready to take off. Nonchalantly, he stepped from behind the counter and told his fellow clerk he was going to smoke a cigarette, expecting to walk out of the Juniper Street entrance and fade from her life forever. As luck would have it, a shoplifter, observed by a store detective, chose that moment to hurry by the perfume counter on her way to the same exit. She ran into George so hard she knocked him to the ground. He fell with a crash, and the air of Wanamaker's was suddenly heady with expensive scents. Only the padding of the duster saved George from injury. In the melee which followed, Flatico was apprehended, turned over to city police, and released in $1,000 bail, charged with theft.

Flatico, hardly a stranger at City Hall, admitted nothing to the bunco squad. It took no more time for the prisoner to raise bail than the seconds required to unclip a fat bankroll and peel off ten 100-dollar bills. Five minutes later he was at Chippy's office awaiting his turn.

By the time Flatico's case reached trial, Ada, completely bowled over by Chippy, had given up most of her social activities and was spending nearly all her spare time at the office on Chestnut Street. As Ada later remembered, she never had more fun in her whole life. Beauty, Skelly soon found out, was not all Mrs. Lucas possessed. She had a sharp mind, and before long, under the sergeant's guidance, Ada was a better sleuth than her mentor. Completely sure of herself, Mrs. Lucas had no fear of any person or place, and in pursuit of information for a Patterson client, entered dives most prostitutes would have shunned. Dressed in the height of fashion and with absolute aplomb she talked to hardened criminals, who invariably removed their caps or hats when she addressed them and attached "ma'am" to their replies.

Chippy turned Flatico's trial into a farce. Everyone who entered the courtroom that morning was liberally sprayed with perfume by an attractive "demonstrator" who stood in the corridor passing out "samples." By the time Judge Finletter took his place on the bench, the courtroom reeked to the top of its 40-foot ceiling. His Honor, accustomed to the acrid odor of formaldehyde, which usually managed to surmount, for part of the day at least, the normal smell of the unwashed bodies and alcoholic breaths of courtroom attachés, prisoners, witnesses, and audience, wrinkled his nose at the rather pleasant change and gave a puzzled glance at his crier. But when the case of the Commonwealth vs. George Flatico was called and the charge read, His Honor understood. Barely suppressing a smile, he looked expectantly at counsel for the defense, whom he greeted with raised eyebrows. Then he sat back to await what he was certain would be a cheerful break in the tedium of presiding over a courtroom invariably filled with unimaginative lawyers defending commonplace clients accused of committing banal crimes.

Members of the jury, quick to sense the mood of the judge, were grinning with anticipation. Chippy, even before the trail began, had achieved his goal, and Wanamaker's very real loss of some $13,000 in perfumes would be regarded as some sort of huge practical joke played on the store by a completely harmless, if mischievous, happy-go-lucky prankster.

On the stand, Mr. Flatico admitted everything but intent. The impression counsel attempted to create in the minds of the 12 was that the fun-loving George simply could not resist those wholesome American practical jokes which surely the jury, men of the world with great senses of humor themselves, would appreciate. Why, the very thought of a pratfall on a couple of quarts of liquid costing a thousand times as much as the best bottled-in bond whiskey was enough to make a citizen double up with laughter.

Judge Finletter would not have permitted many attorneys to get away with this kind of defense and turn the dignity of his courtroom into a shambles. But, in a sense, C. Stuart Patterson, Jr. was teacher's pet and given liberties denied his colleagues. And you may be sure Chippy never hesitated to take advantage of any situation which might benefit a client. This case was no exception. He chuckled with the talesmen; he quoted the obvious (and anticipated) Shakespearean "rose by any other name," probably one of the few fragments of literature members of the jury recalled from school days, thus allowing them to share counsel's erudition; and then, over the valid objections of the district attorney, he laughed the Commonwealth vs. George Flatico right out of court.

Demanding that the Commonwealth produce visible proof of Flatico's crimes, he turned to his client's peers, and, with heavy-handed humor, he asked, "Where is the corpus delicti?"

The district attorney's brief rebuttal was heard with ill-concealed amusement. The jury was Mr. Patterson's all the way. His Honor had had enough. It was time to get back to work. Almost with a sigh he delivered a charge utterly demolishing defense counsel's point of a "corpus delicti." Then, audibly sniffing the heavy air he concluded with:

" 'You may break, you may shatter the vase if you will,

" 'But the scent of the roses will hang around it still.' "

The jury squealed with delight and could hardly wait to acquit Mr. Flatico, who thus acquired a nickname he was to carry proudly the rest of his life. As "The Corpus Delicti Kid" he roamed the earth, making his livelihood by following the con man's credo and "taking" every man with larceny in his heart. Ada last heard from "The Kid" in 1950, when he was spending his sixty-fifth birthday serving a 215-day sentence in Boston's Deer Island prison for operating a variation of "the badger game."

CHAPTER 22

ALTHOUGH he saw little connection between love and matrimony, Chippy realized soon after their meeting that if he wanted Ada he'd have to marry her. His clients kept him far too busy for routine courtship, but since Mrs. Lucas appeared content, even anxious, to spend her time at the office, he knew he could dispense with the normal social amenities leading to wedlock. Ada had her own marital problems, including a husband who was reluctant to give her up. She was in the office much of the day or out investigating cases under Skelly's tutelage, while her two older children were at school and Gally, the youngest, at home in the care of a maid.

Nora, who dropped into Chippy's office at least two or three times a month and occasionally brought the aging Peg Johnson with her, was the first of the family to know about Ada. The two women got along well together, and Nora, who had never given up hope her brother would finally settle down, encouraged the romance. While C. Stuart and Ada's father were casual acquaintances and Ellen Patterson knew John Hunter Lucas's mother slightly through the Garden Clubs, neither of Chippy's parents had ever met Ada. The one time Chippy good-naturedly deviated from his course and agreed to attend the debut of one of Ada's younger friends, C. Stuart and Ellen were introduced to the woman their son was to marry.

It was not a particularly happy meeting. Both C. Stuart and Ellen were conventional, and it embarrassed them to find Chippy openly squiring somebody else's wife in front of several hundred of their friends. The only thing to be said in favor of the match, as far as they were concerned, was the fact that Chippy looked well, was dressed immaculately in formal attire, and seemed happier than he had ever been.

Actually Chippy had as much reason to attend the debut as Ada, since the young lady to be launched into Society that evening was Mary Paul, daughter of Mr. and Mrs. James W. Paul, distant cousins of the Pattersons. The affair, which left a sour taste in the public's mouth and gave the evening's "bud" a nickname she had difficulty living down, more than ever convinced Chippy he had made no mistake in turning his back on the world in which he was born. This debut was one of the most lavish events of a season in which every affair had to be a bit more spectacular than its predecessor.

The scheduled highlight of the evening was the simultaneous release of 5,000 captive South American butterflies, which were to flit through the air before settling on the magnificent array of orchids filling the hall on every side. Unfortunately, when the lights were dimmed and dancing ceased while colored spotlights dramatically swept the huge room, the butterflies were unable to fulfill their part in the performance for which they had traveled 3,000 miles. All of them were dead.

It took a long while for Madame Mary Astor Paul Munn Allez to live down the unpleasant label of "Butterfly Girl" given to her the following morning by scornful reporters. But when she died in France, July 29, 1950, the old nickname was forgotten, and the two new ones she had acquired in the meanwhile were far more flattering. As "The Angel of Paris" she had stayed on when most expatriate Americans fled. During the Nazi invasion she fed, clothed, and sheltered thousands of refugees. Then, when her adopted nation organized the Maquis, she joined their ranks and with complete Chestnut Hill disregard for social inferiors, carried important messages to Switzerland right under the noses of the Gestapo. For these later services she was known simply as "Pauline."

"After this one," Ada recalled, "Chiffy was through. I knew that, and I never asked him to attend another social function as long as we were together. Don't think for a minute I missed all those affairs I thought I couldn't live without until I'd met Christopher Stuart Patterson, Jr. In a couple of weeks after I walked into his office, I didn't give a damn if I never went to another 'at home,' theatre party, Assembly, or dinner dance."

The new life Mrs. Lucas was leading proved more and more fascinating, and an estrangement from her husband was inevitable. Within six months after meeting Chippy, Ada and her husband began a legal separation that finally culminated in divorce. In the meanwhile, however, Ada and Chippy were together constantly when Chippy was not in court. As soon as he shut up shop for the night, the pair, sometimes with Skelly and more often alone, entered a world Ada had never dreamed existed within a scant two miles of her home.

There was Skid Row, with its male and female derelicts sleeping in gutters and doorways; street missions trumpeting salvation; flop houses, their lobbies filled with beaten men smoking corncobs while reading last week's newspapers under naked electric bulbs hung from the ceiling; barber schools, their students trimming the beautiful hair of winos (you rarely see a baldheaded one); basement tattoo shops, where sailors sat patiently waiting their turn; all-night movies, their torn plush-covered seats infested with bedbugs; burlesque houses, with sweaty Amazons grinding and bumping only inches away from the quivering nostrils of degenerates crowding the aisle runways; drugstores, with live leeches and prophylactics on view between huge red and green jars; restaurants, with printed menus pasted behind fly-specked windows offering complete meals for a dime; "medical" offices displaying shudderingly realistic wax models of ravaged victims of venereal disease; pawn shops, with violins, typewriters, diamonds, fraternity pins, barely visible in back of wire-meshed windows; second-hand clothing stores, with barkers outside summoning the passing trade; and saloons, dozens and dozens of saloons, filled 24 hours a day with the world's castoffs.

Through the crowded, noisy, dimly lit streets Ada and her escort wandered night after night on their way to or from Chinatown and the Gold Coast, not only unmolested but treated with respect by everyone, including thugs who'd smash a sober man's skull or roll a drunk for the price of a bottle of sherry.

"We'd pass some besotted brute who seemed ready to cut a throat," Ada recalled, "and as soon as he'd recognize Chiffy, he'd straighten out, pull himself together, remove his cap, and say, 'Hello, counselor' and Chiff would reply, 'Good evening, Mr. Redstone' or 'Smith' or whatever the man's name was. Then maybe a ghastly beat-up old prostitute would sidle by, look up shyly at Chiff, and whisper, 'Hello, Mr. Patterson' and he'd answer very politely, 'Good evening, Miss Smith' or 'Jones.' I don't think there was a bum on Skid Row who didn't know C. Stuart Patterson, Jr. His fingers were in and out of his pockets all the time, and they didn't have to ask him for a handout. Chiffy would say he didn't want to 'embarrass them.' As if they could ever be embarrassed!

But you had to love him for it. He made them all feel good."

Their last stop in Skid Row was at the Galilee Mission, on Vine Street, source of many a non-paying Patterson client and recipient of whatever money Chippy had left in his pockets by that time of night. Now in its sixth decade, the Mission has been operated by George W. Wilkins ever since he opened it shortly after the turn of the century. Wilkins, a former All-American guard, had much in common with his friend C. Stuart Patterson, Jr. Scion of a wealthy Utica, New York, family, he suddenly and for no apparent reason gave up a brilliant future to spend his life among the down-and-outers.

In Chippy's day, the Mission was in the dead center of a teeming human cesspool. Despite Skid Row's physical changes, the business of feeding, clothing, sheltering, and saving the souls heaped on society's junkpile goes on just the same for Wilkins. He's past seventy now, looks no more than fifty, and he doesn't have much time to relax. But if you catch him in an off moment and mention Chippy Patterson's name, he'll stop what he's doing to reminisce briefly:

"When I first opened the Mission, Chiffy and Ada used to stop in every night, and he dressed pretty well, looked good, and had plenty of money. He'd come in, raise his hands over his head, and say, 'O.K. George, clean me out.' Since I was always short of money, I always did. Then, while I'd talk with Ada, he'd talk to some of my customers who thought they needed a lawyer, maybe to draw up a will, although the Lord knows they had nothing to leave or they wouldn't be with me.

"He'd take them in one corner of the room and speak to them very seriously, making notes of what they said. Sometimes they'd come down to his office the next day for a 'consultation.' Once in a while they actually did have a legitimate case in court, which he'd handle for them. He never charged them anything. Sometimes he'd bring me a dozen Lynnhavens on the half shell, packed in ice at the Bellevue where he'd eaten his dinner. He'd lugged the package around with him all evening, just because he knew I liked them and wouldn't get them otherwise.

"While I'd be eating the oysters he'd pretend to taste the soup we always have on the stove, to see if our 'clients' were getting their money's worth and that I hadn't watered it too much. We'd fool around and go through the same act of him raising his hands over his head and me emptying his pockets as though I was covering him with a revolver. There'd be times when my 'take' was as high as two hundred dollars, but he made me keep it all. The funny part is that later on he didn't dress any better than my customers. In fact he looked worse than most of them."

Only the width of narrow Mildred Street separated McShea's Lucky Dollar Saloon on the edge of Skid Row from Shim Loo's Shanghai Tea Gardens, at the tip of Chinatown, but few men or women crossed in either direction once night had fallen. Skid Row was noisy, obvious, and it sinned openly, but Chinatown was quiet, devious, and its evil subtle. The Chinatown of Chippy's era embraced a mere few city blocks from Cherry to Vine and from Eighth to Tenth Streets. Nobody knows exactly how many lived in this area of less than two square miles. Estimates range from a conservative 2,000 to a prideful 7,000. Whichever figure you choose to accept, you can be sure that the vast majority of the population was Chinese, that only a minute percentage of the total was female, and that of this percentage a mere handful, including Mission girls, were white. The community was almost completely self-sufficient. It even had its own theater, the Lyceum, on Vine Street below Eighth, where as early as 1889 the Soon Lin Lock, or Imperial Chinese Dramatic Company, presented ancient dramas of the Celestial Kingdom.

In daylight, visitors entered Chinatown at their own risk and were usually unmolested. Even though they may have been fascinated by alien smells, exotic window displays, closed doors concealing all manner of imagined vice, and the sight of oddly garbed Orientals gently bouncing along Race Street on soft, padded feet, long queues beating time on slightly hunched backs, the cold stares and silence that greeted rubbernecks were unendurable. Sightseers, after a few minutes' exposure to contempt and thinly repressed violence, were eager to hurry their steps north to a more understandable Tenderloin, or south to historic old Arch Street, determined never to cross the border again.

At night the picture changed. It was then that unscrupulous Chinese who grew rich on opium, gambling, smuggling, and murder emerged from heavily barred doors of their houses and took over this dimly lit Oriental island. There were many who said Philadelphia's Chinatown at the turn of the century contained as much wickedness as Port Said. Both Moy Soong, "mayor" of Chinatown for half a century, and Lieutenant John Barry, commander of the 6th Police District, did their best to discourage intermingling of the races during daylight hours and positively forbade it the moment the sun set.

Chippy was one of the few exceptions. He could walk into Chinatown any time of the day or night and enter any house as a welcome guest. Very early in his career he had proved his ability and established himself as one who would never betray a confidence. Just what he did to merit this no one ever knew, but Norrie Vaux thought it was a matter involving Soong's nephew, accused of some violation of the Immigration Act and threatened with deportation. Chippy's position with Moy Soong was secured, and through this polished gentleman, who was above internecine politics, Chippy, as the occasion required, represented each of the three tongs, Hip Sings, On Leongs, and Five Brothers, as well as their individual members.

Center of Chinatown's illicit night life, neutral grounds for warring tongs, and suspected headquarters for a ring of opium smugglers was a sprawling, four-story frame building, known by members of the working press who had never been inside as the "House of a Hundred Rooms." This grim, unpainted structure mushroomed over half a city block on a site now occupied by a prosaic Bell Telephone Building.

The House had only one entrance, a narrow door no

more than 20 inches wide, which opened on a dark alley five feet from curb to curb. On the third floor, facing Race Street, were three pinched windows, always tightly shuttered. There were no other entrances or exits unless you included a well of unknown depth, leading from the basement, via a convolution of subterranean streams, into the Delaware River. At least this was the presumption of police, whose deductions were based on the fact that often men last seen entering the House were later found floating underneath a Dock Street pier.

Chippy was inside the House many times. He never discussed what he saw there with anyone, not even Ada. But Dr. Vaux, who was occasionally summoned from Lying-In to treat very sick Chinese male patients and, once, a white woman who could not be removed to the Hospital, described what little he was permitted to view.

"From the outside," Dr. Vaux said, "the House looked like a four-story building. When you got inside it was subdivided into twice as many floors. There were dozens of narrow passageways leading God knows where. You'd never see a soul walking along one of them, and yet I knew there were probably as many as several hundred people there most of the time. Sometimes a door would open and a glimmer of light shining from oil lamps would reveal a group of Chinese gambling quietly around a table. I knew the corridors were filled with tiny cubicles each with only a narrow cot and just about enough room for one man to squeeze inside and smoke his pipe. A heavy scent, which I recognized as opium or a derivative, saturated the place.

"A number of the rooms were beautiful. They took up two of the subdivided floors or one of the regular ones, but the effect, after you stepped down into one of them from the low halls, was startling, and the ceiling seemed very high. I was in these once in a while to treat some of Chinatown's hierarchy who lived there permanently, I guess. All I saw had enormous beds, thick Oriental rugs, and plush furnishings. There'd be signs of a woman's presence, but except once when I took care of a mighty sick white girl, I never saw a female there."

The House of a Hundred Rooms was the largest but by no means the only place of its kind in Chinatown. All along Cherry, Race, Ninth, and Eighth Streets were similar smaller establishments, the interiors of which were seen only rarely by a male Occidental, although at least one and sometimes two white women, kept by wealthy Chinese, lived in each of these.

There are a few retired Philadelphia policemen who recall the old Chinatown. One of these is Jack Stein, who spent 31 years attached to the 6th District, from 1896 until 1927. Jack knew Chippy, Ada, and the Chinatown that existed long before the combined efforts of the Delaware River Bridge Commission and the Bell Telephone Company destroyed it almost completely and left only a handful of neon-lighted "chop suey joints" which obviously seek white patronage.

"I remember one of the first times Chippy Patterson brought his lady friend into Chinatown," Stein recollected. "This was about nineteen hundred and eight or so, and I didn't know who she was then, but I met her afterward. She was some big-shot society woman, but she wasn't a bit high hat, and we got friendly afterward. Well, it must have been some time after midnight when my partner Big Hugh Riley and I saw them under a street light crossing over from McShea's.

"We often used to see Chippy walking into Chinatown late at night, but we had never before seen him bring a girl friend along. We didn't patrol Chinatown, you know. All Lieutenant Barry did was put enough men at the edges to keep out white rubbernecks who might get hurt. We didn't give a damn about what went on inside unless it got too rough in a tong war or something, and then a whole squad of maybe thirty, forty cops would go in together.

"I said, 'Good evening, Mr. Patterson, everything okay?' And he said, 'Good evening, officers,' and introduced us to Ada. Big Hughie, who was six feet seven inches tall, weighed three hundred pounds, and wasn't afraid of anybody, didn't like the idea of Chippy and this lady going into Chinatown alone at that hour and asked Chip if he'd like an escort, but Chippy smiled and said, 'No, thank you, gentlemen. We'll be all right.'

"It was pretty dark, and on a foggy or rainy night you couldn't see more than a couple of feet ahead of you. We watched him and Ada going up Race Street for as long as we could until they were out of sight. It was quiet as the grave, and the only thing you could hear was their footsteps. It was hard to believe thousands of Chinks were all around them and us. I know I wouldn't have wanted to walk through that place at night alone with a lady. I'd a hell of a lot rather have Hughie and a .38 for company. But Chippy! Nobody touched him, and the next night we saw him do the same thing again. He never said where he went, but I'll bet there wasn't a place in Chinatown he hadn't been in."

Chinatown abounded in "characters" that police of the day divided into three categories—useful, evil, and harmless. Included in the group classified "useful" was a stool pigeon called, by reason of a speech impediment, "Whispering Willie." Ada says that to her dying day she will never forget the first time she met him.

"Thank God," she recalled with a shudder, "the sarge wasn't far away when this oddball walked into the office. He'd been there before, but I didn't know it. It was late afternoon, and I was alone in the office. Chiff was down at Moko taking testimony, Miss DuBarry had gone for the day, all the clients had left, and Skelly was out having a drink. I was sitting in the private office when I heard the door open and I looked up to see a tall, fat, pock-marked half-caste staring at me. His neck was twisted down almost to his shoulder and bent over to one side, and he had huge hands which dangled out from sleeves that were about four inches too short for the arms.

" 'Where's Mr. Patterson?' he asked in a voice so soft I could barely hear him. I was absolutely petrified, and I think I might have fainted right then and there if the sarge hadn't come in that minute. After this character went away, Skelly told me that many years before Willie somehow or other had managed to survive a hatchetman who had nearly decapitated him. From then on he never could straighten up his head, and his vocal cords were permanently injured so he couldn't raise his voice above a sound like a cross between a whisper and a croak.

"The fact that he lived after his death was ordered gave him immunity from further tong discipline, Skelly told me. He eked out a living as a police informer, and Chiff used him occasionally to dig up information."

In the second category was "Chinatown Flossie," the only white woman not called "Sister," a title given to all Occidental females—prostitutes, addicts, missionaries, etc.—who lived in Chinatown and temporarily or permanently had forsaken their own kind. "Flossie," police said, was all bad. Her record showed she was the estranged wife of a Newark, New Jersey, rabbi. She was procurer, fixer, corrupter, fence, executioner, and Judas. A gaunt, stringy, sexless woman replete with vanity, she liked to be considered Chinatown's queen and strutted about the streets in what she imagined was a regal manner. Flossie consulted Chippy once, and that meeting was set by the "mayor" at the House of a Hundred Rooms. Flossie had been left a few hundred dollars by her mother, who after 40 years of estrangement had remembered her oldest daughter in her will. While the "Queen" had no desire to return to her childhood home, she wanted every cent coming to her. It was a simple matter for Chippy to arrange for a power of attorney and send Ada to Freehold, New Jersey, where Flossie's mother had lived, collect the funds, and bring them to Philadelphia.

A few hours after Flossie died in the Chinatown where she had lived since 1874, an envelope was delivered to Chippy. Inside was a note, signed by the "Queen," requesting that C. Stuart Patterson, Jr. ship her body back to Newark and bury it in a Jewish cemetery next to her husband. Whether this was a deathbed conversion or an assignment in assassination, Chippy never knew. When Charlie Phillips, who took over Skelly's duties in 1915, checked Newark records, he found the rabbi very much alive, a fact, Sam was sure, the "Queen" most certainly knew.

In the last group of Chinatown's "characters" were the missionaries, well-meaning women, ignored by the police and tolerated by most of the Chinese, who respected their sincerity and not their judgment. They staffed these outposts to Christian civilization and tried, by means of kindness if not understanding, to convert the Chinese from the worship of their ancestors. Infrequently the process was reversed.

CHAPTER 23

NOT FAR from Grant's Tomb on Riverside Drive is a statue of General Sigel, one of Grant's line officers. He served his native Germany brilliantly, then headed an unsuccessful revolt against the army and fled to Switzerland for his life, finally escaping to the United States in 1852. When the Civil War broke out, he offered his services to the Union, was commissioned a brigadier, and later raised to the rank of major general.

The general was a proud man. He was lucky to have died in 1902. Had he lived only a few years longer, his heart would have been broken by his favorite grandchild, Elizabeth, called Elsie.

As a little girl, Elsie, daughter of Franz Sigel's eldest son Paul, often kept her grandfather company when the general was called upon to make speeches outside of New York. Whenever the old man and Elsie came to Philadelphia, where the general spoke several times at the Academy of Political Science, they were guests of the Pattersons. Chippy vividly recalled C. Stuart and the aging German fighting the Civil War over again in the drawing room at Gracehill. He also remembered taking the general's small, blonde, curly-haired grandchild for rides in the dogcart with Chestnut Hill children.

When Elsie was about sixteen years old, her mother, active in church work, took her to a Lutheran mission on

Mott Street in New York's Chinatown. Elsie was impressed, not by the mission, but by a handsome English-speaking young Chinese "convert" named Leo Loo Lim. Lim, while purportedly engaged in proselytizing his countrymen, was actually using the mission and Sunday school as fronts for a profitable trade in opium.

For several years afterward, without her parents' knowledge, Elsie returned to Chinatown but not to the mission. Lim had two other covers for his illegal activities. One was a restaurant on New York's Pell Street and the other a grocery store on Race Street, in Philadelphia. Above the Pell Street place Lim maintained living quarters, and here the general's granddaughter spent nights when she was supposed to be visiting classmates. Like many other parents, the Sigels were both unsuspicious and overpermissive, and it came as a frightful shock when Elsie brought Lim home one day and introduced him as her fiancé. There was little the girl's parents could do at that stage except, perhaps, resort to violence, an idea which certainly must have crossed Paul Sigel's mind many times.

During one of Elsie's temporary returns to her family—it might have been when her lover was away on a "buying" trip—the girl attended one of the Philadelphia Assemblies. Her escort was Philip Van Ryn of Ardmore, whose younger sister, Harriet, was a former schoolmate of Elsie's. The two girls had not seen each other for more than a year, and this reunion at the Bellevue was to have an unhappy effect on the suburban Philadelphia debutante and her family. Harriet, like Elsie, was blonde, attractive, and bored with the social life into which she was born. A few months after the general's grandchild and Harriet renewed their friendship, the Van Ryns moved to Detroit. The day of their departure Harriet disappeared. Police were notified, and when they could find no trace of the girl, Van Ryn hired private detectives, who were equally unsuccessful.

One afternoon in the spring of 1909 Skelly knocked on Chippy's door to announce that C. Stuart Patterson, Sr. and another gentleman, a Mr. George H. Van Ryn, were in the outside waiting room. They were admitted at once. It was the first time Chippy had seen C. Stuart in almost a year. They shook hands cordially, and from appearances this might have been one of a number of weekly father-and-son conferences. C. Stuart quickly explained that his friend needed help he hoped Chippy could supply. While the younger Patterson listened attentively, Van Ryn, broken by worry, told the story of Harriet's disappearance and the futile efforts to trace her.

"It was as though the earth swallowed her," Van Ryn said. "Even if she were dead and we knew it, this would be better than what her mother and I have gone through. Until two weeks ago we hadn't the slightest idea where she might have gone or if she was still alive. Then my wife received an anonymous letter which gives us a little hope."

Van Ryn reached into his pocket and pulled out a thin sheet of paper on which was written in an almost illegible scrawl, "Your daughter is living with a Chink on Race Street." The envelope had been sent to the Van Ryns' old Ardmore address and forwarded to Detroit; there was a delay of more than ten days between the date of the postmark and delivery of the letter.

"I came to Philadelphia immediately," Van Ryn continued. "I had a note from the Detroit chief of police to your superintendent. He sent me to talk to a Lieutenant Barry, who was helpful but said I was too late. The lieutenant told me he was able to learn that two white girls and two Chinese men came over from New York about three weeks ago. One couple returned and the other remained until a few days before I arrived. Barry said he had reason to believe one of the girls was Elsie Sigel. I suspect the other girl was my daughter.

"The officer admitted he had come to a dead end and suggested I get in touch with C. Stuart Patterson. I was sure he was talking about your father, whom I've known for many years, although I couldn't understand how he could assist me in this situation. At any rate I called on him, and he told me that Lieutenant Barry should have added 'Jr.' to the Patterson and that's why I'm here. The strange part of it is that it all ties in. Your father, and perhaps you, too, knew the general, and he and Elsie were actually in your home. Harriet and Elsie went to school together and met again through my son Philip at last year's Assembly.

"That's my story, Mr. Patterson," Van Ryn concluded with a sad smile. "I'm getting used to telling it these days."

"Of course I'll do what I can," Chippy promised. "Get in touch with me in a couple of days."

That evening young Patterson pored over police reports and learned one fact not given to Van Ryn. The girl who'd been with Elsie was pregnant and while in Chinatown had talked with a young Chinese medical student about a possible abortion. When her request was refused, the girl and her male Chinese companion had left Philadelphia. Chippy turned over this information to Dr. Vaux, who said the only medical student fitting Lieutenant Barry's description was a friend of his, a young Americanized Chinese named Shue Hoe, who at the time was a senior at the University of Pennsylvania Medical School. Hoe would be on duty at Lying-In the following night, and Norrie Vaux arranged to be present when his cousin talked to the young man.

Hoe was more than co-operative. A glance at the picture of Harriet which her father had left with Patterson was enough.

"This is the young lady," Shue told Chippy. "There is no doubt about it. When I examined her a few weeks ago, she was about two months pregnant. She was very frightened and wanted an abortion. I turned her down and advised her to have her baby."

"Do you know where she went?" Chippy asked.

"No, I don't," Shue answered, "but I think perhaps Miss Sigel may, or you might get in touch with 'Sister' Seeley. She's a white girl who has been living with my people in New York. Her mother lives in this city somewhere. If you don't have any luck, come back to me, and perhaps my father, who is a leader of the Five Brothers, may help. We have connections everywhere. I know the man who was with Miss Van Ryn. His name is Woo Gah. He's a gambler, and I think he sells opium."

Mrs. Anna Ziegler, of Philadelphia, whose daughter, Betty, was known as "Sister Seeley," told Chippy he should have no trouble speaking with the girl, who was in New York. Chippy visited Betty the following day, after court closed. She knew about Harriet, although she had never met her, and was able to give Chippy Elsie's address.

"It was a cold-water flat on the fourth floor of a tenement," Chippy recalled to Benny Lemisch. "Nobody answered when I knocked, so I walked in. It was a wretched-looking place and murderously hot. No rugs on the floor and a couple of battered chairs in what was supposed to be the living room. The window faced a blank wall and was covered with soot. An old Chinese was fast asleep, curled up in a corner, with a pipe by his side, and the smell was absolutely awful. There were three more rooms in back of this like a chain—we used to call them railroad flats—but no sign of Elsie or anyone in them.

"There were several beds, all without covers, with bare, torn mattresses, and the kitchen was really a mess. Dirty dishes, bits of food lying around, the faucets dripping into a rusty sink, and an overpowering stench everywhere. I wasn't sure what to do, whether to wait or come back. Then Elsie, at least I assumed it was Elsie, walked in. She was a far cry from the curly-headed little girl who used to visit us. This one opened the conversation with, 'What the hell do you want?'

"She was a sorry-looking woman who might have been forty, even though I knew she couldn't have been more than twenty-two. Her physical deterioration over the past few months must have been rapid. Her face was drawn and dirty, and she was as skinny as a rail. Her hair was straggly, and you couldn't tell what color it really was. Despite the fierce heat she had a black shawl thrown over her shoulders. I wasn't at all sure I would be able to reach her.

"It was easier than I expected. She was willing to go downstairs with me, and we walked into a little restaurant on the corner. I told her who I was and what I wanted. Either she was too far gone to remember me or didn't want to. I didn't try to stir up memories. She had no objections to talking about Harriet and told me she had had a letter from her as recently as a few weeks ago and that Harriet was on her way to the West Coast with Woo Gah but she did not know exactly where. She actually agreed to help and promised me the next time she heard from Harriet she would forward the girl's address to me. I gave her my card, a few dollars, and left. There was nothing else I could do."

Chippy returned to Philadelphia and stopped in to see Van Ryn. He told the older man about his conversation with Elsie and that it was quite possible he would soon learn Harriet's address, although he cautioned Van Ryn not to be too optimistic. Chippy had all he could do to dissuade Van Ryn from rushing to New York to visit Elsie. This was early in May of 1909.

Chippy heard nothing from Elsie. Van Ryn, who had returned to Detroit, kept writing frantic letters and telegraphing for news, but there was nothing to report. Then on June 19, less than a month after Chippy visited her, the Philadelphia *Press,* on page one, under a New York dateline, carried the following story:

"Elizabeth, daughter of Paul Sigel and granddaughter of General Franz Sigel, the German warrior who enlisted with the Union Army in the Civil War, was a victim of one of the most sordid murders in the history of New York. Taken from a trunk in the room of a Chinaman . . . in the Tenderloin, the body was in such a condition as to make identification nearly impossible. A peculiar white-headed pin, given to Miss Sigel by her grandfather was helpful. Sun Leon, owner of a restaurant on Pell Street, where the white girl was a frequent visitor, is under arrest.

"According to Mr. and Mrs. Paul Sigel . . . their daughter had been missing since June 10. They had been expecting her any day on one of her rare visits to their Wadsworth Street home. Mr. Sigel said it was not unusual for Elsie to wire them about her arrival so that their home would be free of any guests who might be embarrassed by their daughter's presence.

" 'Elsie did whatever she liked,' Sigel said bitterly. 'But she also kept her promises. If she said she'd be home, she would have been there if she hadn't met with foul play.'

"The former occupant of the place where the body was found is an English speaking Celestial called Leo Loo Lim. He is thought to be from Philadelphia, where he assumed the name of William H. Lion. Police are searching for Lion, who is believed to be quite wealthy and who has not been seen in his usual haunts for at least ten days. Elsie's entry into the mysterious ways of the Chinese came through her now grief-crazed mother, who was long identified with Sunday Schools and mission work in Chinatown."

As soon as Chippy learned of Elsie's death, he called Lieutenant Barry. The pair went to New York, where the Philadelphia police officer asked the detective inspector in charge of the case if he would permit Chippy to go through Elsie's effects to try to find a clue to Harriet Van Ryn's whereabouts. The New York policeman agreed, providing Chippy waited until after the post mortem. This took place the following day, according to the *Evening World*.

"An autopsy was performed on the body [of Elsie Sigel] yesterday by Dr. Philip O'Hanlon, Coroner's Physician, which showed the girl was not strangled as first believed but took poison or was given it. 'There are only two drugs which would have such an extraordinary and immediate effect on a body as to cause instant asphyxiation. They are cyanide of potassium and prussic acid,' said Dr. O'Hanlon.

" 'Both,' the physician declared, 'are inaccessible to the ordinary person, but the hidden secret movements of Chinamen and their undoubted facilities for procuring such drugs without difficulty lend further belief to the theory that Elsie Sigel was the victim of a depraved band of Chinamen, masquerading as Christian converts in order to win their way into the confidence of unsuspecting women.' "

Before police turned over Elsie's meager possessions to her father, the inspector told Chippy he was at liberty to sift them as carefully as he cared to, but he assured the lawyer that police had already done so and that there were no clues. However, the detective said, in Leo Lim's quarters on Mott Street, the missing Chinese had left more than 500 letters from women all over the United States, including two he felt could be of interest to Mr. Patterson. The ones which the New York *World* published the following morning were from Elsie to her lover and established a motive for the death.

"You seem to be growing cold to me. Just think of the sacrifice I made for you of my family, my friends. For God's sake don't forsake me. Elsie."

The other letter the inspector showed Chippy but did not release to the press was written on stationery of the Adelphia Hotel in Philadelphia, where the detective said the writer had checked out several days before Elsie's murder. Her home address was fictitious, and police were not able to locate her. Her letter to Lim was a dozen pages long, filled with erotic passages. There was one comment about a girl who might have been Harriet. "When I'm in Frisco," she wrote, "I'll show Gah you've got a better girl than the deb he's been—"

Chippy felt the reference was to Harriet, and he passed this information to the Chinese medical student, who said he'd ask his father for help.

About three months later, Dr. Vaux asked Chippy to come to Lying-In Hospital to see Hoe, who told Patterson the Five Brothers had located Harriet in San Francisco. The tong had kidnapped her from Gah, and in the ensuing scuffle Gah and two other members of his tong, the On Leongs, were shot to death.

Pressed for details, Hoe told Chippy Harriet and her lover had been forcibly removed from a train bound for Southern California from San Francisco. Gah, fearful of being questioned by police looking for his friend Leo Lim, had been in hiding ever since he had learned of

Elsie's murder. During the kidnapping Gah was fatally wounded. Harriet knew nothing of her lover's death and was in a state of shock. At the moment she was being cared for by an important member of the Five Brothers within the shadow of the Mormon Tabernacle in Salt Lake City. Hoe assured Chippy the girl was well protected by members of his tong, who pledged her safekeeping despite the fact they were sure the On Leongs would attempt a "rescue party" and seek revenge.

Afraid Van Ryn might jeopardize not only his daughter's safety but that of the family holding her and upset the delicate position of everyone involved, Chippy told him only that his daughter's whereabouts was known and that he might expect to see her in Philadelphia, where the Five Brothers insisted she be delivered within two weeks. Then Chippy explained to his own father exactly what had happened and suggested arrangements be made to bring Harriet in from Salt Lake City in a private car, with railroad police to furnish protection. Chippy agreed to go to Salt Lake City himself and take Skelly and Lieutenant Barry with him. The girl would be brought to Lying-In, where Norrie Vaux could take care of her.

"My father was wonderfully co-operative and most efficient," Chippy said. "Skelly, Lieutenant Barry, who brought Big Hugh Riley with him, and I left for Chicago the following day. When we got there the next morning, railroad security police met us and we were transferred to a P.R.R. private car and taken to Salt Lake City on the D. and R.G. Hoe's father handled all the plans out there. We were shunted to a railroad siding late at night. It was silent except for occasional train whistles in the distance or the hiss of steam coming from a switching engine. The four of us sat around smoking, hardly exchanging a word. Shortly after midnight there was a rap on our car door and the Lieutenant and Big Hugh, revolvers drawn, called out, 'Who's there?' There was a pre-arranged signal, and Barry opened the door and flashed a light into the darkness.

"Harriet was asleep, under sedatives I imagine. She was brought in on a stretcher and guarded by four Salt

Lake City policemen accompanied by a highly cultured elderly Chinese gentleman who spoke to me for a few minutes and said the girl was as well as could be expected. He advised us to watch her carefully. A bit later he left, and our car was coupled to an east-bound express and we pulled out for Chicago and Philadelphia."

Harriet was still in a stupor when the train arrived at Broad Street Station. Lieutenant Barry had telegraphed to his district from Chicago, and a Lying-In ambulance with a police escort met the party and took the girl to the hospital, where she was installed in a private room. A uniformed policeman was placed at her door, and no one was admitted without permission from Dr. Vaux.

Harriet regained full consciousness in about 24 hours. Despite the ordeal her physical condition was good, and she seemed resigned to her situation. Although she was not told of her lover's death until some time later, she surmised as much immediately when he did not appear at the hospital, and even seemed reconciled to life without him. She displayed little emotion. It was as if she had lost her capacity to care about anything, including the coming baby.

In the meantime Chippy was being deluged with telegrams from both Van Ryn and his wife. But Dr. Vaux advised Chippy not to allow them to see Harriet until the girl herself had given consent to such a meeting. The physician felt Harriet might be bitterly resentful toward everyone, including her parents, who had changed the course of a life she had chosen for herself. He was afraid any reunion highly charged with emotion could well lead to suicide.

Dr. Vaux and Chippy had dinner with the Van Ryns shortly afterward. The physician carefully explained Harriet's condition and broke the news to them that their daughter was pregnant; that the putative father was probably the dead Gah; and that they could expect to be grandparents of a half-caste sometime in mid-February.

"Your daughter's been through a frightening experience," Dr. Vaux warned. "Nobody knows why she did what she did and you may never find out. To blame yourselves or Harriet for what's happened would be pointless. Probably you've all been at fault somewhere along the line. Be grateful she's alive and is *not* an addict. You must resign yourselves to the fact that it's more than likely Harriet will not want to go home with you, at least for the present. You should not try to force her."

Chippy told Ben Zion that evening was one of the most difficult he had ever had.

"It was a frightful jolt to the Van Ryns," he said. "After Norrie told them all he felt they should both know, I had to break it to her father, when I got him alone, that his daughter's life was in grave danger if she were to leave Lying-In. I did assure him Harriet was completely protected while she was there and that no one could possibly molest her. The old boy had real courage and took it like a man."

The first meeting between Harriet and her parents went well. Dr. Vaux made sure Van Ryn knew that the uniformed policeman who normally sat outside his daughter's door was close at hand and that Mrs. Van Ryn was not conscious of his presence.

Van Ryn and his wife spent an hour at their daughter's bedside. When they met Chippy in his office later in the day, they told him Harriet seemed glad to see them and added that they were determined to accept the situation, difficult as it was. So grateful were they to have their daughter alive and well they said they could face the problem of the grandchild with equanimity. Chippy refused to accept any fee or expenses and brushed off the Van Ryns' profuse offers of thanks.

Dr. Vaux urged both parents to return to Detroit until Harriet herself expressed a desire to see them. The physician reassured Van Ryn that his daughter would be protected in every way. He said C. Stuart Patterson, Sr. had already taken care of this problem with the police department. He suggested that Mrs. Van Ryn plan on spending the last ten days of Harriet's pregnancy in Philadelphia. The Van Ryns' grandchild, he said, would be born about the middle of February, and indications were that delivery would be normal.

Chippy called on Harriet once to ask her if he could do anything for her. She did not recognize him and had no recollection of the kidnapping, the stabbing of Wah, or the trip from the West Coast. Her child, a boy, was born February 20, 1909. Dr. Vaux had to hand the Van Ryns their final blow.

"The baby's father," Dr. Vaux told Chippy, "couldn't have been Gah; if I hadn't done the delivery myself I'd have sworn there was a hospital mix-up. Its features were definitely not Chinese."

The last time Dr. Vaux saw the Van Ryns was late one evening, two weeks after the baby's birth, when parents, daughter, and grandchild left the hospital in a chauffeur-driven car. A month later Lying-In was the recipient of an anonymous gift of cash, which Dr. Vaux concluded was a parting gesture from the Detroiters. Sometime the following summer Chippy received a touching letter of gratitude signed by Harriet and one from her parents. The envelopes were postmarked "Melbourne, Australia."

The On Leongs had no intention of forgetting the deaths of Elsie and Gah or Harriet's kidnapping. Because the tong had lost face, it could have lost control of the illegal trade between China and the United States. Its subsequent attempts to regain prestige, which bear a striking similarity to the internecine gang wars of a generation later, were reported in the *Bulletin* of April 18, 1910.

"That the murder of Elsie Sigel last fall was the cause of the double murder here and in New York is the belief of police after the reign of terror in the Chinatowns of both cities last night when five men were killed and others wounded in this city and New York.

"Trouble started yesterday afternoon in New York when members of the Five Brothers killed Hung Fook, an On Leong, and Ing Mon, a gambling hanger-on. Prevented by police, the On Leongs moved on to Philadelphia. At the grocery store of San Do and Company, 927 Cherry Street, two Chinese, dressed in American clothes, walked in and handed Chu Nong, the manager, a letter, which was his death warrant. Then they killed him. Immediately Shue Hoe, his son, a former student of the

University of Pennsylvania, Temple University and Central High School, an Americanized Chinese, now a student at the University of Pennsylvania Medical School, rushed forward and himself was shot.

"City Hall detectives and Lieutenant Barry of the 11th and Winter Street District said the feud grew out of the kidnapping of a white girl who had been living with a member of the On Leongs. The kidnapping occurred, according to Barry, when the white girl was removed from a train after first being drugged.

"Shue Hoe was first held as a material witness. He was later released in the custody of his counsel, C. Stuart Patterson, Jr."

Police made a number of arrests in the shootings although no one was ever convicted of these crimes. Chippy represented several of the defendants, both On Leongs and Five Brothers, but the district attorney was not able to present prima facie cases to the grand jury and no indictments were drawn. Until she died in 1932, Harriet Van Ryn's connection with the case was known only to C. Stuart Patterson, Lieutenant Barry, and a few others, all of whom kept their secret well.

CHAPTER 24

FINAL PAPERS for Ada's uncontested divorce from John Lucas were granted May 28, 1910. The following day the society columns of all Philadelphia newspapers carried brief notices to the effect that Ada and Chippy would be married June 1. Announcement of the wedding came as no surprise to most members of society and the friends of both prospective bride and groom.

There was little enthusiasm for the marriage on the part of either family. While Chippy had been faithful to Ada, the quantity of his former well-publicized amours was discouraging to the bride's friends and relatives, who were sure he never would take his marriage vows seriously. His previous alcoholism and past escapades, along with his continued scorn for Philadelphia's sacred cows, did not presage the kind of secure marriage Ada's widowed father had hoped she would make. Hetherington was extremely fond of his ex-son-in-law, with whom he frequently hunted, fished, and golfed, and was bitterly disappointed by the divorce.

C. Stuart and Ellen were opposed to the match. High-church Episcopalians, they did not believe in marriage after divorce. While neither dared make any attempt to discuss the subject with their son, C. Stuart and George met with Ada's father. They presented what they thought were valid objections to the romance and asked him to use whatever influence he had to prevent a marriage they were sure could end only in unhappiness. While he agreed in principle and said he appreciated their concern for his daughter's welfare, he could do nothing.

Nora was the only one who endorsed the romance wholeheartedly. She was fond of Ada and believed the marriage would be a stabilizing influence on her favorite brother.

They were married at the home of Ada's grandmother, Mrs. Seth Caldwell, Jr., with only relatives present.

Ada is a gracious old lady now, too busy with her great-grandchildren and grandchildren to bother with the Society she gave up to marry Chippy, and totally uninterested in competing with her ex-sister-in-law, Mrs. George Stuart Patterson, for the leadership of Philadelphia's 400. You can see traces of Ada's beauty in her patrician features, and she carries herself like a woman of thirty. Her penthouse apartment, high above Rittenhouse Square, where she has lived most of her life, is filled with flowers and plants she raises in a tiny hothouse.

"It was a beautiful wedding," Ada recalled. "Chiffy looked handsome and seemed far more mature than all the others—'sophisticated' is the word, I guess. He'd seen and done more than any of them, and his life was full of so many different kinds of people. Everyone was happy; even Dike came over, shook hands with his brother, kissed me, and wished us the best. I don't believe Eleanor

Willing was pleased with either of us. She never could stand Chiff.

"But all the rest were gay, and everything looked wonderful, and our future together bright. If I'd ever had any doubts about Chiff, they were dissolved. I was sure we'd be happy. We left for New York right after the ceremony. Nora's wedding gift was our honeymoon, a few days at the Waldorf and two weeks in Bermuda. That was all the time Chiff could spare, and I didn't want to be away from the children any longer than that.

"Chiff promised me faithfully there would be no interruptions to our honeymoon. He'd been working like a dog and needed a vacation. I don't believe he'd had one full day off for more than two years. He'd wound up most of the important cases on his calendar. I had spent so many hours helping Skelly prepare them I hardly had time to get my trousseau together. Chiff made arrangements with John R. K. Scott (*there* was a brilliant lawyer even if he couldn't touch Chiff)and 'Foghorn' Fow to handle all the cases which couldn't be continued. He'd also left enough money with the sarge to take care of the morning handouts so he wouldn't have them on his mind."

She paused, arose from her chair, walked to the window, and looked down on the Square below for a few moments, then came back and continued.

"Our first two days were wonderful. We arrived at the Waldorf on a Tuesday, and our ship wasn't sailing until Thursday evening. We walked up and down Fifth Avenue and looked in all the shops. After a while I was afraid to say I admired anything in the windows, because the moment I mentioned something appealed to me, Chiff would walk into the story and buy it. The first evening we had dinner at Delmonico's, and Chiff bought me champagne, but he wouldn't touch it himself. I was so proud of my husband. He was the handsomest man I ever saw. I think I must have paraded him up and down Peacock Alley a hundred times so that everyone could see us.

"Our second evening, after the theatre, we had supper on the Waldorf Roof. It was a magnificent night, not too warm, and the stars never looked brighter or New York gayer. I'd made Chiff bring his tails with him, and I had a long, white evening gown and was wearing a tiara which had belonged to my great-grandmother Caldwell. . . ."

But the newlyweds never got to Bermuda. On Thursday morning Chippy received a telegram from Dimner Beeber, a Philadelphia lawyer who had been working with Chippy on the defense of a Beeber client charged with homicide. Beeber was an excellent and highly successful lawyer. His practice, however, was restricted to negligence and other civil suits. When he had consulted Chippy originally, it was Beeber's plan (and this was the way most lawyers operated with Chippy) that Patterson would handle the jury trial while Beeber would take care of the paper work.

In the meanwhile Chippy and Ada were married and Chippy was forced to withdraw from the case. Beeber was most reluctant to release him from his obligation, but there was little he could do about it. He would either have to appear himself or engage another colleague.

Beeber decided to go it alone. The trial began on Wednesday, the day after Chippy's wedding. By late afternoon a jury had been selected and locked up for the night and the case continued until the following morning. Beeber, deeply concerned about his client's welfare and badly shaken by the enormous difference between representing a client with nothing to lose but money and one whose life was at stake, panicked. His telegram to Chippy was strong, and in it he told Patterson he was dissatisfied with his co-counsel's ethics and would ask for Bar Association censorship. Chippy was not disturbed by Beeber's threats, although he had to admit the lawyer was correct in his statement that Patterson's retirement from the case placed the client in jeopardy. With no hesitation, as Ada recalled, Chippy told her they would have to cancel the Bermuda trip and return to Philadelphia at once.

"I'll make it up later," Chippy promised his bride of less than three days, but Ada said, "He never did. When we got back to Philadelphia he got so involved in cases that were waiting and clients were so happy to see him I was sure then I'd had all the honeymoon I was ever going to have. I knew for certain then what I'd always feared, that to Chiff the client came first, before me, before the children, and even before his own life. I'd either have to adjust to this or give him up. I decided to try to make the adjustment."

You wonder if Charles Wilson, the client for whom Chippy disrupted his wedding trip, ever realized how lucky he was that the Monarch sailed Thursday instead of Wednesday. When Chippy reviewed the file with Beeber it looked as though the Commonwealth had an excellent chance of proving murder in the first degree. With Chippy in the courtroom, the prisoner, instead of being sentenced to hang, was convicted of the lesser charge of voluntary manslaughter.

CHAPTER 25

ADA's wedding gift from her father was the deed to a 14-room "cottage" surrounded by three acres of wooded lands near Newtown Square on the West Chester Pike, 15 miles from City Hall. The P.R.R. offered excellent commuter service from a station only a few hundred yards from the Pattersons' driveway.

What little entertaining there was centered about West Chester, some 12 miles away. The limited opportunities for social life suited Ada. She was determined this marriage would be a success and was willing to make every sacrifice to keep her husband and children happy.

They called their home "Hollyeva" because it reminded Chippy of a similarly named site he knew and liked in Honolulu. At first everything went well, and Chippy made an effort to disassociate his office life from his home. He was very much in love with Ada and extremely fond of the children, who, in turn, adored him. Each had a Shetland pony, and on Saturdays when their new father did not go into the city, he rode with them all through the countryside, a huge collie at their heels. Occasionally he would take them in to Wanamaker's tearoom for lunch, then to Keith's for three hours of vaudeville. While he often did not return from the office until late evening, at least he did come home, and for a few months he spent most of his weekends at Hollyeva.

He stayed away from Chinatown, the Bowery, and the Gold Coast, and restricted contacts with his clients to City Hall, his office, and Eastern Penitentiary or Moyamensing. He even gave up the infrequent fishing trips to Corson's Inlet, where he, Bob Comber of the *Bulletin,* and a few others used to spend all day Saturday when there were no cases to prepare for Monday morning.

"I could hardly believe my eyes," Bob once said, "when I saw Chippy, three small children in tow, walking down Chestnut Street on Saturday afternoon. He looked happy, and I guess he was. I took them all in to Whitman's and bought them sodas. Chippy sat up there on a stool eating ice cream just like a kid. I asked him how life was treating him, and he answered, 'Wonderful! I never had it so good.'

"A couple of months after that I met Chip in court one Friday and he asked me if I wanted to go fishing the next day. I said 'sure' and asked him if he was going to take one or two of the kids with him, or maybe Ada, but he shook his head and said, 'No. Just pick me up at the Bellevue, if you will, at the usual time,' which was 5 A.M. Chippy didn't talk about Ada on the trip. I had a feeling it was all over."

The first but not the final break in their marriage came six months after the honeymoon. Ada and the children returned to the Hetherington home on Chestnut Street ("for a visit" she told everyone, although nobody was fooled). The fact that the servants at Hollyeva were retained and the house kept open indicated Ada's reluctance to consider the separation final. Chippy moved back to the Bellevue.

"There was no single cause for the dissolution of our marriage," Ada said. "It was just one incident after another. Chiffy was sweet, and he'll always have a place in my heart, but he did the damnedest things! Maybe in themselves they weren't bad, but when they accumulated he was impossible to live with.

"For example, on a Saturday afternoon he'd take the children in town to have lunch at their grandfather's. Then they were supposed to go to Keith's and come home in time for dinner. He'd never show up at my father's, and he'd take them all to lunch some other place. They could eat anything they wanted, three portions of ice cream or pie or anything else, and naturally they'd be sick. Then, if they liked the show, they'd stay to see it twice or three times and come back home around midnight. I'd try to reason with Chiff, but he'd shrug his shoulders and laugh. He never grew angry no matter how much I scolded him. Now you don't break up a marriage for that, but there were many other things.

"And he never had any money. He was making plenty when we were married. I know, because I tried to set up some sort of bookkeeping system right before I quit going to the office. He'd collect a fee, and before I could enter it in the ledger and make a deposit in the bank, he would have lent the money to somebody or given it away, which was the same thing. His income, even with all the free work he did, must have come to more than twenty-five thousand dollars a year, and in those days that was a lot. Chiffy hadn't a dime. It's true he spent precious little on himself, but a man ought to feel some responsibility for the future of his wife and children. I paid every household expense with my own money, and I was always 'lending' Chiff a few hundred dollars, which I know he gave away."

The first separation lasted for about two months. It was the "Corpus Delicti Kid" who unwittingly brought them together again. One day the housekeeper at Hollyeva telephoned her mistress at the Hetherington home that a large crated package marked "Fragile. Handle with Care" had arrived. Almost too big to get through the doorway, it was postmarked "Chicago."

Ada had been looking for an excuse to call Chippy, and this was it. "It sounds like a belated wedding present," she said. "Let's open it together." They rode the

West Chester local to Newtown Square that evening and the children were with them. The package was a wedding present from George Flatico. Inside was a colorful painting signed only "Vincent." There was a note from the sender which read, as well as Ada can recall it, "From the best private art collection in Chicago. It was hidden in a dreary corner where it will never be missed."

"I didn't know what to do," Ada said. "It had to have been stolen. It was absolutely magnificent, a landscape. I'd never seen anything like it before. I was afraid to hang it, so we rewrapped it and put it up in the attic. I don't know what happened to it when our marriage finally broke up. Maybe we gave it away. I wish now I could have kept it, stolen or otherwise. It was a Van Gogh, of course, long before he was famous, but old George Flatico, he recognized a good thing when he saw it."

During this second period of reconciliation Chippy engaged in one of the most incomprehensible acts of his life. With a heavy roster of clients, including four men and one woman awaiting trial on homicide charges, Chippy accepted an appointment as assistant district attorney. This meant he would no longer be able to represent clients in criminal court and had the immediate effect of restricting his practice to civil suits, about which he knew little and cared less. Fortunately for one more generation of murderers, felons, and misdemeanants, Chippy's term of office lasted less than 20 hours and the number of cases in which he represented the prosecution totaled one. His handling of this lone case, from the standpoint of the Commonwealth of Pennsylvania, was a miserable failure. The episode began this way.

One early spring afternoon, a few days following Ada's return to her husband, the couple were strolling south on Broad Street. This was part of Chippy's agreement to stay away from clients two hours a day and spend them with his wife. Just as they passed the Union League at Broad and Sansom Streets, Samuel P. Rotan, the district attorney, Judge Audenreid, and Mayor Rudolph Blankenburg emerged from the street-level door of the Club. They had been attending a meeting during which the generally low caliber of Rotan's assistants was discussed.

As the press had been pointing out, the district attorney's staff, many of whom were incompetents left over from the previous administration, was finding it increasingly difficult to get convictions against skilled criminal lawyers. Blankenburg, a sincere reformer, urged Rotan to hire better-equipped assistants regardless of their political value. Chippy happened to pass by at the propitious moment.

"Speak of the devil," said Rotan as he smiled at Chippy, shook his hand, and said "hello" to Ada. "Want to be a district attorney, Chip?" Rotan asked casually.

"Okay, Sam," Chippy answered just as offhandedly.

"You're hired!" he said, and before Chippy had a chance to change his mind or call Rotan's bluff (if it really was a bluff), he was sworn in as an assistant district attorney by Judge Audenreid in chambers. Rotan assigned him to the case of the Commonwealth vs. William Diefenderfer. The charge was homicide.

The *Evening Times* thought the switchover of sufficient importance to run the following story on page one.

"Judge Norris Barratt, members of the Fourth Estate, and all with business in room 653 City Hall, today received a shock from which many have not yet recovered. It all happened when C. Stuart Patterson, Jr., prominent criminal lawyer and the bane of the District Attorney's office these past years, arose in Court to announce he represented the prosecution. The defendant was William Diefenderfer, 37 years old, of Main Street below Roxboro Avenue, accused of stabbing to death William Miller, 29 years old, of Hartranft Street. Sam Salus, who used to be an assistant district attorney himself, represented the prisoner.

"The hubbub which followed Mr. Patterson's announcement was so great His Honor had to call for order twice and threaten to clear the Court. The jury was sworn in with a speed that must have established a record in Oyer and Terminer and General Jail Delivery. Neither Mr. Patterson nor Mr. Salus, opponents in many a courtroom battle although previously in reversed positions, issued a single challenge.

"It was with an obvious effort that Mr. Patterson stayed on his own unfamiliar side of the fence. He seemed to want to help Mr. Salus. Frequently, during the brief trial, Mr. Patterson caught himself just in time before he sat down near the prisoner's box and it appeared to us that he restrained himself with great difficulty from putting his arm about the prisoner's shoulders. Something in the new Assistant District Attorney's mind must have warned him at the last moment that this just was not done.

"The trial was all over by one o'clock recess. Mr. Patterson's attacks, if such weak sorties could be called attacks, were pitiful and Mr. Salus had no trouble establishing the fact that his client acted in self-defense against a younger, stronger and more aggressive antagonist. Obviously Judge Barratt concurred, and His Honor's charge was in the nature of a directed acquittal. The jury was out of the box less than a half hour before it turned Mr. Diefenderfer free.

"Apparently Mr. Patterson, known as 'Chippy' to a large portion of this city's population which has to do with our courts, decided he would lend his superior talents to the District Attorney's Office as a sort of balance. It may be stated categorically that our Prosecutor for the past year has not been as successful with juries as he might be if he had assistants of the caliber of Mr. Patterson or some of this gentleman's associates of the criminal bar.

"While we await with eagerness Mr. Patterson's next appearance as Mr. Rotan's assistant we think it only fair to call your attention to the masthead of this newspaper so that readers may note, if they have not already done so, today's date."

That issue of the *Evening Times* was dated April 1, 1911.

Whether Chippy's resignation was formal, informal, or involuntary is not a matter of record. However, he never again appeared in court as anything but counsel for the defense. Dr. William Drayton, Chippy's cousin, a guest at the Patterson-Lucas wedding and a psychiatrist of note, believed Chippy's willingness to serve on the district attorney's staff had far deeper significance than the playing of a mere practical joke.

"I think this was strong evidence of Chiff's schizophrenic tendencies. He was always torn between his desire to lead a 'normal' life in the world to which he was born, as exemplified by his marriage to Ada rather than to some of the women I used to see him with, and his feelings of guilt which forced him to share the lot of the decidedly lower half. By accepting a position of assistant district attorney, in one swift stroke he severed the ties which bound him to those strange people with whom he could have had little or nothing in common. I'm sure he had a constant awareness that their hold on him was getting increasingly powerful and that one day they would destroy him. The fact that he remained in the district attorney's office for only a day and that he made a farce out of the single case he handled in no way changes my opinion."

Although they remained together, more or less, for another year, about this time Ada became convinced that there was nothing she could do to save the marriage.

"I don't know what happened to Chiff. Suddenly he got dreadfully sloppy about his clothes. Nora told me he was a sort of Beau Brummell when he was younger, and when I married him, even if he wasn't a fashion model, he still dressed well and made a fine appearance. On those rare occasions we went out together he certainly was nothing to be ashamed of. But something got into him. He wouldn't let me have his suits pressed, or if I had them pressed, he'd continue to wear the one he had on even if it didn't have a crease and looked as though he'd slept in it.

"When his clothes were torn, he wouldn't bother to have them mended. Just wore them that way. Some gangster named Murphy gave him an old cap with a bullet hole in it, and he started to wear that instead of a hat. And his boots! He must have had two dozen pairs of shoes in his closet, but he wouldn't put any of them on. He stuck on old fishing boots in the morning, kept them on all day, and wore them when he came home at night. I'll say this for him, though, he used to shave and bathe a couple of times a day and change his underclothing each time.

"Then he got on a case which kept him away for weeks. The children rarely saw him any more, and we didn't have a real home. All they ever knew about their father was what they could read in the papers. He could have handled the case, I think, without staying away, but that wouldn't have been Chiff. He had to live it to the exclusion of everything else until the verdict was in."

CHAPTER 26

ABOUT a hundred yards and a hundred years separated the old West Indies Trading Company, operated by Chippy's great-grandfather, John Patterson, and the New Dublin Saloon, kept by Frank W. McMahon, on the southwest corner of Second and Spruce Streets. Although they were not on the same social level, John Patterson and Frank McMahon would have had much in common. Each man was wealthy, dignified, a Latin scholar, a lover of the classics, an Irish patriot, and inordinately proud of his family. And each possessed a normally equable disposition which, in a single moment, could flare into an anger terrible to watch.

The front of the Indies Company warehouse was filled with barrels of Barbados rum, black-strap molasses, spices, sugar, and tobacco from Cuba and the rest of the Antilles. In the rear of the building Patterson had his offices and private sitting room. The latter became a sort of private club, where, according to Chippy's cousin, Justice Edward Patterson of the New York judiciary, "very grave old gentlemen, friends of Lord Edward Fitzgerald, 'Napper Tandy' Wolfe Tone, and the rest of the Young Ireland Party, with the love of Ireland still strong in their veins, gathered to drink hot toddies, smoke their meerschaums, and discuss the tyranny of England."

Nearly half of the first floor of McMahon's three-story house was taken up by the bar, which had an entrance on the corner. Patrons were big, tough, ignorant, hard-drinking, noisy, unruly, violent dock workers—quick to respond to quiet, meaningful authority, the latter supplied by McMahon. Although he was less than five feet six inches and weighed no more than 150 pounds, he ruled his domain with an air of complete sovereignty. His bright blue eyes, darting up and down the long bar, missed little, and he sensed approaching trouble instinctively and stopped it, usually with a quick smile or a soft word, before it developed.

It was only when his patrons became abusive and threatened to brawl that this diminutive Irishman's pleasant smile faded, his eyes turned cold, and, without raising his voice, he silenced or dismissed the troublemakers with sharp words. Rarely did McMahon lose his temper, but when he did, his fury was almost uncontrollable. On one occasion, a huge longshoreman McMahon refused to serve because he felt the man had had too much already called the proprietor a "cheap shanty Irish bastard." Before anyone realized what was happening, McMahon leaped over the bar, knocked the offender to the ground, and beat his face into a bloody, shapeless pulp. After which, McMahon wept all night and refused to be comforted.

On the Second Street side of the saloon was the "Ladies Entrance." The sign above this door was a misnomer. McMahon frowned upon women who drank, and the occasional female who wandered in accidentally was neither made welcome nor served anything alcoholic. Three steps led up from the sidewalk to a cozy, cheerful parlor in the center of which was a large round table surrounded by a dozen or more comfortable, runged wooden armchairs with a shining brass spittoon beside each. On cold winter nights, when the wind blew up from the frozen Delaware River, a stone's throw away, and howled outside the windy corner, men seated about the table were kept warm by a log-burning fireplace which also heated buttered rum the little saloonkeeper served his guests in large, earthen mugs. While some of the conversation was devoted to literature, much of it was about "Dev," the "Black and Tans," and the freedom of Ireland.

McMahon's family occupied the second and third floors above the saloon, which they rarely entered. Mrs. McMahon, an attractive woman with jet black hair, blue eyes, and a fair skin, was a cut above her husband socially if not intellectually. She was a graduate of St. Mary's Academy and used to tease her self-educated husband by telling him how lucky he was to have married into "the lace-curtain set." It was a happy, closely knit family, deeply religious but without false prudery. All five daughters were attractive, modest, and well-behaved children. Annie, the oldest, was a real beauty and her father's favorite. She was tall, had her mother's hair and complexion, and, if the many pictures which later appeared in the nation's press were good likenesses, bore a striking resemblance to Miss Maureen O'Hara of Hollywood. Between Annie and her father there developed the sad, sweet relationship fathers and daughters sometimes share.

Often when her mother or sisters teased Annie about a current "beau" and asked her when she was going to get married, the girl would reply, perhaps more revealingly than anyone realized, "Only when I find a man like my father." Annie was physically well developed and mentally mature for her age when she graduated at sixteen from high school. Her marks were excellent, and her father wanted her to go to college, but instead she chose to work. Her parents, sure she would be engaged within a few years, thought the choice a wise one. All her current admirers, and there were many, were clean-cut, decently raised Irish Catholic youths who not only respected Annie's virtue but also appreciated her father's reputation.

Annie got a job as a secretary-receptionist with a real-estate operator. She was warm, friendly, and well-liked by her employer and his clients.

Shortly after Annie's seventeenth birthday, February 10, 1910, the desk adjoining hers was occupied by George A. Leary, a successful real-estate promoter who usually worked out of his home but who had agreed to come in to help for one month. Leary was a bachelor. He lived with his father, a widower, and an unmarried older sister. He was tall, well-built, had short-cropped iron-gray hair, and carried himself with an air of aloofness some women found attractive. He was fifty-five years old when he began a torrid romance with a girl whose father was 15 years his junior. His character was unblemished; he was a good son and brother, a devout Catholic, and had heretofore led a decent life.

It's hard to understand what Leary had to arouse such undreamed-of passion in Annie McMahon, but whatever the aging bachelor possessed it was enough to make her surrender her virtue less than two weeks after they met.

Thanks to the excellent quality of the stationery and black ink John Wanamaker provided free of charge in his store's mezzanine writing room, it's possible, half a century later, to pinpoint the exact night of Annie's seduction. In the district attorney's office there is a piece of yellowed paper upon which Annie, in the careful Spencerian script of a diligent schoolgirl, wrote her lover to thank him for accepting *her* gift of love. You can picture her now, skin flushed with recent memories, shielding the letter she was writing from the eyes of housewives on either side who smiled at the pretty, innocent picture she presented. The date, written boldly below the embossed "JOHN WANAMAKER READING ROOM," is May 9, 1910.

"My Darling Sweetheart," Annie wrote to the man she had met for the first time three weeks before.

"No doubt you will be very much surprised to receive this hastily written note but I could not rest until I had written to ask you to forgive me for being so disgruntled this morning.

"What an ungrateful little beast I must seem to you when you have done anything and everything to make me happy and contented. I do not want you to think I am ungrateful because I am not . . . Just because I love you I seem to think that I must unburden all my woes on you.

"Do you know that I owe a very big debt to you. Well I do. Last night you opened the gates to a very delightful though sometimes a very sad world to me, so therefore I owe you the entrance fee which shall be just what you want to make it. . . .

"I am, your Annie, a repentant sinner."

The course of their romance can be followed easily in Annie's letters (and there are dozens of them) to her aging Romeo. Whatever he said in return, we have the word of Mr. John Kent Kane, his attorney, that his client made no marital promises.

"I have examined each of the *carbon* copies of your letters to Miss McMahon," wrote Mr. Kane to his client, October 10, 1910, "and in them I find nothing which would lead me to believe you encouraged the lady with offers of matrimony."

Annie, on the other hand, was completely ingenuous.

"Last night was wonderful again," she wrote George on May 16. "I never knew love could be so divine and at the same time so terrifying. . . ."

When the letters were made public, it was this quality of frankness that divided Philadelphia's citizenry and press into two camps, one supporting Annie as a wronged innocent and the other denouncing her as a young Jezebel. Whatever side you support, you must be impressed by Annie's speed in learning the facts of life and George's facility as a teacher.

The lover's first quarrel was on May 20, brought about, apparently, as subsequent letters reveal, by the fact that George chose to spend the weekend of his birthday (his fifty-sixth) with his family instead of with Annie.

"All day long," wrote the penitent Annie, "I have been reproaching myself for the rudeness with which I treated you yesterday afternoon; sweetheart, you cannot imagine how miserably unhappy I have been; and then to have you come in just when I was as blue as indigo seemed to me to have been the most wonderful and delightful pleasure I ever had.

". . . But heart o'mine, you will think this a very doleful letter, no doubt, but I am far from feeling doleful. Indeed I think I am more genuinely happy than I ever was. With many hopes that you will enjoy these few days, knowing that I shall if you do, I can safely sign myself,

Your loving,
Annie."

P.S. I hope you have a *very very* happy birthday and while you are adding one to your years I know that you are subtracting ten from your heart."

It must have been difficult for Annie to keep the affair from her mother and father. You wonder what excuses she gave to explain absences from home every Wednesday evening until midnight and a good number of weekends as well. The only possible explanation was that her parents trusted Annie implicitly and didn't dream their daughter would deceive them deliberately. The first hint of their suspicions came in a letter Annie wrote June 29.

"Dear Heart," she said. "Of course I was pleased you wanted me but dearie, I am afraid that I may go out there too often. You know the old story of the pitcher and the well. Then, too, I do not know what mother will say. When I got home she was just coming in. She did not *say* much, you know what looks mean.

"I do not know how I am going to post this as I am supposed to be getting ready for bed (it's only 10 P.M.), but I'll find some excuse I hope. Don't forget the Trysting place and even if it is impossible for me to go out anywhere I can come and see you at 45th and Walnut.

Your only,
Annie."

There's a macabre touch in her note of July 1. "Be careful, sweetheart, of those dangerous firecrackers," she warned George, "so that you don't get hurt, for then what would I do?"

Until her letter of July 12, obviously referring to a weekend at the Learys' Atlantic City cottage, was revealed to the press, most Americans who avidly followed Annie's brief biography were of the opinion that the beautiful young Irish girl was a wronged innocent. This brief note, written with an air of near abandon, even wantonness, however, revealed a hitherto unsuspected sophistication and cast serious doubts about Annie's morals.

"Sweetheart of Mine," went the letter. "I felt pretty bad on Monday, though. I have two large stripes on my wings.

"Hope your arm is not giving you much trouble though of course I am not very sorry. You did not think I was a modern Sandow, did you? Even Samson did not do much more than that. I don't know what your sister must think of me but she certainly was angry, wasn't she? I really could not blame her either. I am writing to her tonight. I found that I came home with both of your sister's prayer books.

Yours, with all my curves,
"Snake."

"The poetry of motion is all right but hard on the muscles of the legs."

Annie continued in the same vein on July 26, following another weekend at the shore. "Did you arrive home dreadfully tired as I know you must have after all *we did?*" she asked. (The emphasis is Annie's.) "I think now of what we were doing at this exact moment yesterday and I am filled with ecstasy. If only it could go on and on. . . ."

At about the same time that Annie's parents grew suspicious, Leary's ardor either cooled or else he decided the pace set by Annie, some 39 years his junior, was too much.

"Father received your telephone message," Annie wrote August 1, "and he was *very* curious. He looked at me kind of strangely and wanted to know who it was. He doesn't *really* suspect but it's hard for me to lie to him. I always used to tell him the truth."

"I wanted so badly to see you yesterday, dearie," wrote Annie, August 4. "It was the first time you failed to meet me at the Trysting place. I walked up and down Walnut Street for an hour and felt so lonely. Are you ill, dear heart? I am worried. Mother is beginning to ask me a lot of questions and I don't know how to answer her."

Then, on August 11, Annie complained, "It's been ten days since we've been together. I miss you so.

"Mother has ceased asking questions. I suppose she is waiting for me to confess so she can say, 'Bless you, my children.' Little does she dream of what is in store for her. Mother remarked without any intents I know, that she was thankful every day of her life that none of her daughters had ever given her the slightest cause for worry. I tell you, dearie, I felt pretty small then. I haven't the slightest idea how she will take this blow."

The "blow" to which Annie referred was her pregnancy. How she was able to keep this from her mother for as long as she did can be explained only by the fact that between the two there had always been complete understanding and trust.

Annie had been carrying her child for about two months when George sent her to an abortionist with admonitions not to pay him the price he first asked.

"Now as to his 'Nibs,' " Annie wrote on September 16, "you were certainly right when you said he was an old thief. The idea, $300, for five days and he wouldn't take a cent less. And even then at that he has no assurance that it might not be dangerous. Just a chance, that's all."

Less than a week later Annie had a change of heart. Conscience, or the remote hope that George would yet marry her despite his very firm statements to the contrary, made her decide against an abortion. With intelligence and courage but without a trace of bitterness she outlined her position, leaving the final decision to George. It's hard to believe that her tragic letter of September 21, the last she ever wrote to her lover, was penned by a seventeen-year-old girl whose protective parents, only five months before, would have been shocked to believe their daughter could have listened to a slightly off-color story.

"Dearest George," she wrote, still using the stationery John Wanamaker provided. "I want to give you my views on the subject which at present lies heaviest on our minds. There are only three things to do. The first is for me to have medicine and treatment to kill this being, but this is so heartless and cruel, dearie, that I am sure you will not blame me for shrinking from this and it cannot be right for us to call this being into existence and then, because it does not suit our convenience, to destroy it this way.

"The second is that I shall go away and have 'It.' This, I think is the most serious, involving, as it does, not only you and I, but also this creature that is to come. You and I have never had any question raised about our people and we do not realize the terrible thing it must be for a man or woman to be ashamed of its parents. Oh, sweetheart, I could not stand that.

"Then we come to the third refuge, marrying. This, you will admit is rather a delicate subject for me to discuss with you. I have always understood that you would not marry anyone but I do wish, my darling, you would reconsider. But, my darling, if you do not think you would be happy with me, or that I would not be a satisfactory wife, do not hesitate to say so, because surely I deserve that much consideration, that you will be at least quite frank with me.

"So, goodbye, sweetheart, till I hear from you.

Lovingly yours,
Annie."

P.S. "I suppose I do not have to ask you to be careful of this letter. Please, please, do not let it out of your hands for one instant and when you understand its message, then destroy it. Meet me, if you can, at the Trysting place."

George did not destroy Annie's letter. The last communication between the lovers remains in an excellent state of preservation in the files of the district attorney's office. And the meticulous George's neatly penciled marginal comments, "J.K. (his lawyer), please note. The girl (no longer 'sweetheart' or 'snake') knew I would not marry her," are as clear as they were in 1910 when they were written.

On October 6 Annie first confessed to her mother, who in turn broke the news to her unbelieving husband. McMahon's reaction was utter fury. He hit Annie across the face for the only time in his life and drove the bitterly weeping child to her room. Then he pulled a revolver from the bottom of a bureau drawer and dashed out of the house before he realized he didn't even know the name of his daughter's betrayer. By the time he turned around and reached his own home his mood had changed to one of bitter self-condemnation. He wept openly in front of his wife, who was comforting Annie, and begged his daughter's forgiveness.

In the meanwhile Annie had told her mother everything about the affair, including George's name and the fact that she was probably, by her own calculations, about three months pregnant. Mrs. McMahon was overwhelmed not only by her daughter's incredible conduct but by her own naïveté. She was a strong woman, however, and succeeded in reconciling father and daughter and breaking the additional news to her husband that Leary was fifty-six years old. The only hope Annie offered was that George was single, that she was in love with him, and that she wanted to get married.

When she had managed to calm both husband and daughter, Mrs. McMahon suggested they talk to Mr. Patterson.

Early the following morning, the trio drove to Hollyeva, where Chippy had agreed to see them. Chippy, who during the past year alone had probably represented a hundred unwed mothers and reluctant fathers, could have predicted, with accuracy, Leary's reaction to the suggestion of a wedding.

"Don't hold out too much hope for marriage, Annie," Chippy said. "Since he hasn't been in touch with you for several weeks I'm inclined to think he will already have gotten his own lawyer. However, I'll try to talk to him tomorrow, and after that we'll consider what's to be done next. In the meanwhile, I must caution all of you—you, in particular, Frank—not to communicate with George Leary in any way."

Then he smiled down at Annie, put his arm around her, and said, far more prophetically than he or the others could imagine, "Don't worry, child. This isn't the worst thing that could happen."

Chippy was right about Leary. When he attempted to make an appointment with him, he was referred to John Kent Kane, a reputable member of the bar. Chippy always felt that if McMahon hadn't grown impatient, some sort of arrangement, perhaps even matrimony, might have been worked out between the two lawyers.

Without discussing his intentions with anyone, the saloonkeeper took the first of a series of misdirected steps. He called on Leary, October 8.

"I went out to where Leary lived," McMahon later told the district attorney in Chippy's presence, "and got there a little past seven o'clock in the morning. I rang the bell and Leary opened the door. I was shocked. The man looked almost old enough to be my own father.

"I said, 'I suppose you know who I am,' and he said, 'Yes, I do.' I then said, 'What do you propose to do in this matter?' and he said, 'I haven't given it much thought.'

"I answered him, 'It should not take a man long to make up his mind what to do,' and he replied, 'I won't say what I will do until I have a talk with your daughter again. Can I see her tonight?' I told him yes.

"I came home and told my wife. She asked me if Mr. Patterson had been consulted, and I lied to her and said he told me it was all right. That evening my wife and daughter went out to see him. When they came back my wife told me that Leary had insulted her. I went over to Magistrate Carey and got a warrant for his arrest and the constable and I went out to Leary's house, but when we got there everybody was in bed and we waited outside the house until the next morning. I rang the bell and Mr. Leary's sister came to the door and I asked if Mr. Leary was in.

"She said 'No' and tried to close the door, but I put my foot in the doorway and walked in back through the kitchen and found him hiding under the table. The constable placed him under arrest and brought him down to the magistrate's office."

Only when McMahon, Leary, and the constable reached Carey's office was an attempt made to notify

Chippy. But the time Skelly located him the hearing was over. Leary pleaded guilty to charges of fornication and bastardy and was held for the grand jury with bail set at $300.

Whatever slight hopes Chippy had for a marriage which would legitimize Annie's baby were smashed by the saloonkeeper's impetuous actions. Patterson assured Kane that McMahon had acted without advice of counsel, but Leary's lawyer, who had been willing to talk to his client about the possibility of a wedding to be followed by a legal separation immediately after the baby was born, told Chippy this would be impossible now.

His arrest, the first in George Leary's respectable life, was a fearful shock. Bitterness was his first reaction. "I won't care," he wrote Kane on October 12, with considerably more truth than he imagined, "if they print my name on the first page of every newspaper in the country." He reiterated his decision not to marry the girl ("at my age it would be ridiculous") although he continued his offer of a cash settlement and volunteered to pay all hospital costs and doctor bills when the child was delivered.

On January 13, all the principals met at a reputable doctor's office; Kane had requested an examination of Annie to determine when the baby would be born. McMahon, unable to control himself at the sight of Leary, shouted, "You dog!" leaped at Leary and knocked him to the floor. Chippy and Kane, both present, had to restrain him.

Immediately after the assault, Leary instructed Kane to withdraw all offers. "I will pay nothing," he wrote. "McMahon called me a contemptible cur and said threateningly, 'You wait until this is over!' He threw me down and hit me. Patterson pulled him away and then they all had the nerve to sit down to a conference. I took my hat and umbrella (and for this gesture Leary must have summoned up what little dignity he had left) and walked out of the office. I never want to see any McMahon ever again except in a court of law."

McMahon, who only on rare occasions touched the stuff he sold over the bar, began to drink. He never smiled and spoke only in answer to direct questions. He rarely entered the downstairs backroom, and gradually his friends drifted away to another place with a more congenial host. He still ate with his wife and daughters, but he hardly ever looked at Annie and as soon as the meal was eaten he retired to his bedroom to read.

Annie's baby was born April 2. She nursed her child, a boy, for ten days, then released him forever to St. Vincent's Home, where it is presumed he was given out for adoption.

There's an odd note in the files of the district attorney's office dated May 1, 1911 and addressed to no one in particular. It was signed "Sister Superior" and evidently referred to an inquiry made by an unknown person.

"In reply to your request," the brief letter said, "a tall, middle-aged gentleman who told us his name was George Thompson appeared at the Home April 28 and asked permission to see a male child delivered to Annie McMahon April 2. We had to refuse the gentleman in accordance with our regulations. He seemed upset, then asked us if he would be permitted to pay whatever costs there had been. I told him the bill had already been paid. Then he handed me a sealed envelope which he said contained money and told me he would be deeply obligated if it could be given to the McMahon baby wherever it was. I told him I would see that it was done. He left and to the best of my knowledge he never returned."

CHAPTER 27

THERE was little sleep for Frank McMahon any night. On the night of May 3, 1911, there was none at all. Shortly after six o'clock in the morning, he went downstairs and opened the bar for a couple of dockworkers waiting outside and shivering a bit in the brisk spring air. He swallowed a double shot of whiskey and stayed in back of the bar serving customers without a break throughout the day. He served them mechanically and answered their questions tersely. Most of the time he stared into space. Customers seemed relieved when John McDermott, McMahon's bartender, arrived about 4 P.M. to take over.

As soon as McMahon had checked the cash, he went upstairs. His wife heard him enter their bedroom and open and shut a bureau drawer. He came out, paused for a moment in the doorway of the sewing room where Mrs. McMahon was seated. He kissed her lightly on the forehead and gently squeezed her arm. She'd been crying and was afraid she'd break down if she attempted to speak. She tried to smile, but by that time her husband had turned away and was walking out of the room toward the back stairs.

Frank turned the corner and walked up Spruce Street, through Rittenhouse Square where dozens of children, their chattering nursemaids hovering nearby, were playing in the warm sun by the fountain. Ed Reilly, a former habitué of McMahon's backroom, out in the Square with his grandniece, saw the saloonkeeper and waved. The salutation was not returned. McMahon crossed the Schuylkill over the South Street bridge, then turned north to Spruce once more and continued west. He reached 55th Street just as the Westminster chimes in the belfry of the Bethany Temple Church at 54th and Pine Streets sounded the hour of seven.

It was still bright, and a dozen boys and girls were playing Red Rover in the middle of Spruce Street. There wasn't much traffic along this quiet, shady West Philadelphia street, except for an occasional streetcar, a horse-drawn dray returning to the stable, or a Ford, Krit, or Saxon noisily chugging its way to Cobbs Creek. Most housewives were inside "redding up" so they could either join their husbands tending tiny back gardens or go out to the front porch, there to sit on rocking chairs and gossip with the neighbors for an hour before putting the children to bed.

George Bushman was standing on the northwest corner of 55th and Spruce Streets outside of Appel's Drug Store, waiting for Clarence Frick Muir, a registered pharmacist, to fill a prescription for Mrs. Bushman's lumbago. Inside the pharmacy, in addition to Muir, who was in the rear, were two other men. One was the owner, Albert A. Appel, who stood behind the cigar counter gazing idly through the front window, hardly hearing the prattle of Alexander H. Besore, a salesman. On the southwest corner, impatiently waiting for a trolley, was Edna M. Shultz.

John C. McElwee was approaching the corner and proceeding south on 56th Street on his way to his Pine Street home. Mrs. Mary L. Hess was inside her home, two doors south of Delancey Street, fluffing the pillows of the parlor couch from which her husband, James E., had just arisen to step to the front porch where he could smoke his after-supper cigar. This was a privilege not granted within the house. Behind the box of his trolley car, Walter S. Kunkle, the motorman, was traveling west on Spruce Street near 55th, stamping his foot heavily on the pedal which sounded a warning bell.

Not one of these men and women, or as a matter of fact, any number of others, paid more than scant attention to a little man who seemed to walk aimlessly along Spruce Street before turning the corner of 55th. At the precise moment the last note of the Westminster chimes struck, a pistol shot rang out. George Muir and others first thought it was backfire. It was followed by two similar sounds at intervals of perhaps five seconds. There was a fourth and final shot a quarter of a minute later.

By that time George Leary, mortally wounded, was sitting, head bent down, on Mrs. Hess' freshly scrubbed front porch steps. His soft moans attracted her attention, and she opened the door and called out, "Mister, if you're drunk, you'll have to move along." Leary continued to groan, and Mrs. Hess asked him if he was sick. "No," he replied. "I've been shot twice in the stomach."

"My God!" screamed the lady. "I'll take you inside."

While she was struggling to lift Leary by herself, two men who were passing by came to her aid, and together the trio managed to carry George into the front parlor. They laid him down gently on the couch recently vacated by Mr. Hess. "Hold his head up a moment, please, while I run upstairs and get an old pillow case," requested Mrs. Hess. ("I didn't want to give a stranger one of my good ones," she explained later to the district attorney.)

A half block away the obscure little pedestrian, mission accomplished, stood idly in front of the drug store for a moment. Then he walked to the middle of Spruce Street, retrieved a hat from the center of the car tracks, brushed it off on his sleeve, and placed it on his head. After that he lit the butt end of his cigar, calmly took a puff or two, and strolled over to Delancey Street. He paused in front of the Hess house and surrendered himself to Officer Howard Mulhern of the 38th District just as Leary was being brought out on a stretcher and placed in the patrol wagon.

Every one of Philadelphia's daily newspapers and those outside of the city which carried AP dispatches slanted their stories in McMahon's favor. Chippy saw to that. There was even an editorial in the *Evening Star* praising the bantam saloonkeeper for the courage he displayed in defense of his daughter's honor.

McMahon was held in custody until the morning of May 7, when he was brought before a coroner's jury. Pale and drawn but in excellent control of his emotions, he replied firmly to all questions. The time and place of death were established, and then Chippy proceeded to develop a motive favorable to his client.

"C. Stuart Patterson, Jr. was magnificent," said the *North American*. "His stirring plea of the 'unwritten law' was a tribute to the courage of an outraged father and moved everyone in the room to tears. 'I tell you, gentlemen,' he stated to the jury with great emphasis, 'Frank McMahon did what each one of you would have done under similar circumstances.' "

Coroner Ford, an incumbent up for re-election the following November, after silencing protests of the outraged assistant D.A., spoke his piece.

"You must free McMahon," declared this sworn defender of the Constitution. "I do not ask you gentlemen to take any more responsibility than I myself am willing to shoulder. I am responsible for that act." So reported the Philadelphia *Inquirer*.

The jury, red-blooded Americans, all, duly freed McMahon although not for long.

On May 8, John Leary, George's brother, following a consultation with his attorney, John McClintock, Jr., swore out a warrant for McMahon's arrest on a charge of homicide. McClintock of course knew that private prosecution for capital crimes is not recognized in Pennsylvania. But his action brought headlines, screaming for justice, in the same newspapers which only the preceding day had heaped lavish praise on Ford, the jury, and McMahon.

McMahon was arrested and held without bail. Before being removed to the County Prison he declared, "I am not sorry Leary is dead, for the world is well rid of men like him."

"Mobs in front of Magistrate Doyle's office screamed for vengeance, crying, 'Lynch the Murderer!' " said the *Press* of May 9.

In his cell at Moyamensing the façade of defiance which had protected McMahon broke into pieces. "Oh, my God! Mr. Patterson," he cried out in anguish. "My poor Annie! Her face haunts me night and day. What will become of her now?"

Chippy, like McClintock, recognized the illegality of McMahon's arrest. However, instead of having his client released on a writ of habeas corpus, he decided it would be of more strategic value during the inevitable trial to let the arrest stand. Besides, he was sure Rotan would take over the prosecution from McClintock and McMahon's freedom would be brief.

The *Press* carried the following story on May 10.

"A little man, pale and nervous, stood before Magistrate Morris yesterday afternoon, shielding his face from the battery of cameras aimed at him and heard three witnesses describe how he killed the man his daughter declared was the father of her child. A mob of 3000 persons milled about outside. He was held without bail and remanded to Moyamensing Prison. . . ."

On Monday, May 15, a grand jury indicted McMahon on a charge of murder.

Irate Philadelphians, now convinced Annie was the aggressor and Leary her unfortunate victim, were temporarily calmed. Rotan, supported by the press, said he would push for an early trial, and C. Stuart Patterson, Jr. publicly declared himself in full agreement with the prosecutor. In private, however, Chippy had no intention of permitting his client to be placed in jeopardy while tempers were hot. He told reporters "our defense will be 'Dementia Americana,'" a completely meaningless term coined by counsel for Harry K. Thaw.

Chippy hadn't been to Hollyeva for more than three weeks and had seen Ada and the children only once since Leary's murder. The pressure of his office and the courts never lightened. He maintained the same pace even though he was spending many of his evenings at Moyamensing with the little saloonkeeper, and managed to see Annie every day to comfort her and her mother and to bring messages to them from Frank. From May 1 until May 28, Chippy defended seven men charged with homicide in varying degrees and won acquittals for all.

Ada, tired of being without a husband, swept into the office one evening with two tickets for the theatre. Chippy was delighted to see her, and after dinner at the Bellevue, the pair went to the Forrest, where George M. Cohan and Valeska Surat were performing in a milk-fund benefit.

"It was the first time we'd been alone together for ever so long," Ada said. "Chiff even dressed up for me, although I'd have gone with him no matter how he looked. I was hoping he'd come home after the show, but he didn't. As soon as it was over, he put me on the train for Newtown Square and told me he was going down to Moyamensing to see Frank McMahon. This was after midnight. There wasn't much point arguing. You just didn't argue with him. He wouldn't argue back. He'd smile and that was that."

Chippy's newspaper campaign in behalf of McMahon began with stories in the press of June 1.

"With heart and mind torn between love for the man

who wronged her and love for her father who avenged that wrong," said the *Star,* "Annie McMahon may become the third victim in the tragedy which on May 4 sent George Leary to his grave and sent Frank McMahon to prison to await trial for the murder.

"The girl, whom it is alleged Leary wronged while she was employed in a real-estate office, is sinking rapidly and her condition is so serious, that her grief-stricken mother has begged physicians to hold a consultation in order to save her life."

"The girl's mother," reported the *Telegraph,* "called upon C. Stuart Patterson, her husband's attorney, and pleaded with him to get some eminent consulting doctors to save her young daughter's life. The McMahon home over the saloon represents a startling contrast to the environments of the neighborhood and the longshoremen and stevedores' gathering place in the bar below, where allegiance to Frank McMahon is drunk in foaming mugs by heavy-handed toilers. In the upper floors there is every evidence of refinement and artistic taste with well-filled bookcases containing the highest grade of literature and works of art hanging upon the walls of this home of sorrow."

A hole in Chippy's potential defense came when fifteen-year-old Robert Nerger, who testified at the coroner's hearing that Leary was the aggressor in the fight with McMahon, repudiated his story on June 5. "I made it all up," he told Rotan. "I really wasn't there at all, and I didn't see anything. I just wanted to get out of school for a couple of days."

According to the *Evening Bulletin,* "Attorney Patterson, by the boy Nerger's defection, has been left with practically only the 'unwritten law' as a plea to save his client." This newspaper, as well as the other Philadelphia publications, continued to call for an early trial and on June 6 it looked as though their efforts would be successful.

"With heavy-lined face," said the *Press* on June 6, "already showing the unmistakable prison pallor tinted with a greenish hue, Frank McMahon stood in the prisoner's dock before Judge H. S. Davis, yesterday, and remained mute when asked to plead 'guilty' or 'not guilty' of the murder of George A. Leary. . . . Judge Davis then ordered a plea of 'not guilty' be entered."

The early arraignment meant nothing to Chippy. McMahon went back to his cell for another six months. It was not until November 21, after the case had been re-scheduled perhaps five times, that Chippy told reporters, "We are now ready to begin the trial and hope it will progress without delay. We are prepared to make a strong defense—a full legal defense—without regard to the so-called 'unwritten law' which has so often been discussed. We are going to conduct the case with as little sensationalism as possible and are not likely to call Miss Annie to the stand."

The nation's top-flight reporters were on hand when court convened November 22.

"At nine o'clock, an hour before the time set for the court to open," said the *Ledger,* "the corridors on the fourth floor were choked with men, women and girls, who scented sensations and wanted to hear the story of the girl for the protection of whose honor it is said McMahon killed Leary.

"It was a curious and motley throng that sought to listen to the proceedings. Women were in the vast majority. For the greater part they were poorly clad. They wore nubias over their heads and gabbled on animatedly about the prisoner. Annie McMahon, the daughter of the prisoner, was sought for but not found. Nor the girl's mother who was in her home over the saloon . . . waiting for a time when her testimony will be needed."

All of the first day and part of the second were devoted to the selection of a jury. All but one of the jurors were married. Ten were fathers, with a total of 24 children, 16 of whom were girls. Five of the jurors had daughters between the ages of fifteen and twenty-two. Only one husband on the panel, George Kellmer, was childless.

Once Jean Barrett, who later became a feature writer for the *Evening Bulletin,* reviewing famous old Philadelphia trials, asked Chippy why he'd permitted Kellmer to get on an obviously handpicked jury.

"Kellmer's wife was a hellion," Chippy answered. "I knew that. Skelly's reports on every venireman on the wheel were always thorough. But this was a case I *had* to win, and I was going to play every angle. I reasoned it like this. Here was someone who, given the right motivation, could take a rare opportunity to assert his independence and prove he, too, had red blood in his veins. He was beyond Mrs. Kellmer's reach maybe for the first time since she latched on to him, and now he could be a man again. I played up to him all during the trial. Afterward the foreman told me Kellmer fought hard for an acquittal."

After Crier Hart read the indictment, "with several admonishing shakes of the head and with much dramatic effect," said the *Evening Star*, "Mr. Rotan opened the side of the Commonwealth by first interpreting the law, then defining murder and finally graphically rehearsing the story of the actual tragedy. He then asked the jury to render a verdict of first degree murder. He told them the sentence was death."

Rotan was a formidable opponent, a fact of which Chippy and other criminal lawyers were well aware. He usually made an excellent impression on juries because of his ability to convince them he was motivated solely by a desire to see justice done, a task in which he and the 12 men were made to feel partners.

CHAPTER 28

CHIPPY's opening address impressed even the staid old *Public Ledger*, which heretofore had found only the activities of C. Stuart Patterson, Sr. or his oldest son, George, worthy of its front page.

"C. Stuart Patterson, Jr., counsel for Frank W. McMahon . . . opened the defense of his client in Judge Bregy's Oyer and Terminer Court, and in an address that was short, hard and uncompromising asked the twelve men in the box how far a man might carry his love; how selfishly he might guard the honor of his children, and how much the honor of a girl who trusts, surrenders and is betrayed is worth.

"It was a weary jury to which Mr. Patterson delivered his appeal. It was a body of men who under ordinary circumstances would have been on their way to their homes, their wives, their children. The lonely home-calling hour of the late afternoon had arrived. The minds in the men in front of the lawyer had softened as had the daylight, and in the half-enchanting glow of early evening . . . he shook them and the rest of the court with the tale of a betrayed girl. . . .

" 'Gentlemen of the Jury,' began Mr. Patterson, 'the prisoner, Frank McMahon, is before you charged with murder. He is accused of murdering George Leary. The District Attorney would convince you that McMahon is guilty of first degree murder. . . . You must listen to me and decide for yourselves.

" 'We are going to show you the scene of the shooting. I am going to tear away the veil that enfolds this man, enshrouds Annie McMahon, cloaks the entire affair. It is a duty we owe every woman, every mother, every daughter. You must listen to me and determine what McMahon's mental condition was when George Leary's life was taken.' "

Chippy proceeded to tell the story of the romance between Leary and Annie, beginning with their first meeting in the real-estate office. He led the jury up to the fateful meeting between McMahon and Leary, emphasizing, of course, his client's peaceful intentions. The revolver, he explained, McMahon always carried with him because of a series of holdups which had taken place recently in the vicinity of Second and Spruce Streets. This, Patterson said, he would prove at the proper time. One of the major problems of the defense was to establish, and this at the opening of the trial, the fact that Leary, a big man, was the aggressor in his struggle with McMahon. Chippy carefully laid the ground for this, realizing the Commonwealth would produce many witnesses who would testify to the contrary.

" 'On the evening of May 4,' Patterson continued," said the *Ledger,* " 'McMahon went to the Leary home. He was entering the front yard. He paused irresolutely on the pavement leading to the front porch. As he paused the door opened. Leary came out. The old demands of justice were renewed. Leary sneered again. He laughed at the desperate father. Leary was cold. Together they walked down Spruce Street toward 55th. They talked—the father earnestly, pleadingly, passionately. Leary, coldly, lightly, unmoved. Leary laughed at the suggestion of marriage.

" 'As they reached 55th Street Leary laughed for the last time.

" ' "You're quite an actor, aren't you?" ' he asked McMahon.

" ' "I'm not acting. I don't know how. I'm pleading for my daughter. She's all I have in the world to hope for." '

" ' "You won't be disgraced," ' replied Leary. ' "Nobody will know. You go home and keep your mouth shut, and so will I." '

" 'Then McMahon called Leary a cur and Leary snarled, turned upon the little man and dared him to say that again. McMahon was not afraid of the big man.

" ' "You're a damned cur," ' he replied.

" 'Then Leary pounced upon the little adversary and threw him to the ground. McMahon was beneath. His head struck the asphalt. Doctors will testify he was never responsible for what happened afterward. He fired as he lay beneath this man Leary.' "

Routine testimony of police authorities took up most of the morning of the second day. It was not until after the noon recess that reporters' pencils scratched out the day's first sensation, an initial blow for the defense.

One of the Commonwealth witnesses, Alvin Crawford, had helped Mrs. Hess carry the dying man into her home. Skillfully led by Mr. Gray, the assistant district attorney, he drew a picture sympathetic to the victim and graphically described the agonies Leary suffered as he was placed on the couch.

"How do you know he was suffering, Mr. Crawford?" Chippy asked on cross-examination. "You said he was unconscious."

"Well, he was almost unconscious."

"What do you mean by *almost* unconscious?"

"Why, he was kind of muttering."

"Muttering what?" pressed Chippy.

"I object!" the assistant district attorney called out. "A mutter is an indistinguishable sound."

"A mutter," replied Chippy, "may also be words spoken in a low voice. Webster doesn't say they have to be unintelligible." Chippy turned to Judge Bregy and the jury.

" ' 'Twas whispered in heaven, 'twas muttered in hell. And echo caught faintly the sound as it fell.' Catherine Fanshawe, Your Honor." Chippy glanced at the assistant district attorney. "English Lit Two twenty-one, Mr. Gray. Minor Elizabethan poet," he explained.

Judge Bregy smiled faintly. "Objection overruled! Answer the question, Mr. Crawford."

For another second or two the witness hesitated. Then he gave spectators what they'd been waiting for and handed the working press a new lead for the day.

"I heard Leary say, 'I expected it!' "

"And with good reason, I'd say," added Chippy softly to the jury, which gasped audibly at the witness's words.

Because she claimed to have seen the beginning of the altercation between Leary and McMahon, Edna Shultz was regarded by the Commonwealth as a most important witness.

"This half-frightened girl," said the *Ledger*, "smartly clad in black furs, a big beaver hat with a purple plume, flowing lace cuffs and with a gardenia protruding from her coat was the first witness to tell what happened on that fateful night. She said she was in Appel's Drug Store when the tragedy occurred. She left the drug store and began to walk west on the north side of the street when she saw a tall man coming east. A small man followed him at a distance of three feet. She could not identify McMahon as the smaller man. The tall man continued to the curb. The smaller man followed him. Something impelled her to turn around.

" 'As I turned,' she said, 'I saw the small man draw a revolver. I screamed, "Oh my God!" and that drew the attention of the tall man. He turned. The two seemed to meet. They fell. I heard the report of a gun. The tall man arose first and began to run. The smaller man arose and followed him. I heard another shot. I started to run home but fainted on the pavement. When I came to I was home.' "

Chippy produced two witnesses, S. S. Bliven and Frank McClean, both of whom testified that when the first shot rang out, the girl was still inside the drug store. This was an important point for the defense, which had to show it was after McMahon was attacked that he shot Leary and then only in self-defense. Bliven actually declared Miss Shultz could have seen nothing because she fainted the moment she stepped out of the store and he (Bliven) had to carry her home. Chippy scored one more point against this witness. He asked her if she had discussed the case with anyone.

"Never!" she declared emphatically.

"Never?" pressed Chippy, "and with nobody at all?"

"Well," she admitted, "maybe with a few persons of no consequence," was the phrase the *Ledger* attributed to her.

"I'm not going to waste any more time with you, Miss Shultz," Chippy warned.

Then, according to the *Ledger,* "Miss Shultz calmly stared at several persons, including a clerk in the Prothonotary's office and a reporter from this newspaper whom Mr. Patterson asked to arise and declared she never saw any of them before."

Chippy didn't give an inch without a struggle. He forced every witness to change his story, if only slightly, but he could not deny McMahon carried a gun; that his client had previously threatened to take Leary's life; that he fired a total of four shots, the first of which every witness testified had obviously put Leary *hors de combat;* that when the second, third, and final shots left the barrel of the revolver the real-estate man was running away desperately to save his life.

The testimony of Muir, who was completely self-possessed, could have been damaging to the defense. The pharmacist said that when he rushed out of the drug store, immediately after hearing the first shot, he saw McMahon, revolver drawn, chasing the wounded Leary. He reiterated that he saw no sign of a struggle and that McMahon's clothes were not dusty.

"How far away from McMahon were you when you first saw him?" Chippy asked.

"About fifteen feet."

"What was he doing?"

"He was chasing Leary, running fast after him with his pistol in his hand."

"How long did it take you to get out of the drug store after you heard the first shot?"

"Oh, I guess, not more than five or six seconds at the most. Al Besore and I ran out together."

"Then I say to you, Mr. Muir, you could not have seen whether or not the defendant's clothing was dirty. You heard police say that the first shot was fired approximately fifteen feet away from the front of your store. A man runs at a speed of approximately five miles per hour. If it took you five seconds to get out of the store then Mr. McMahon was about fifty feet away. From that distance you couldn't have told if his clothes were dirty."

Chippy in cross-examination nullified the testimony of Besore, who also declared he saw no sign of any struggle, by involving the pharmaceutical salesman in an argument with Miss Shultz.

"You told the court, Mr. Besore," Patterson went on, "you were right behind Mr. Muir when you rushed out of the store."

"That's correct."

"Were you directly behind him?"

"Yes, Mr. Patterson. I had to brush Miss Shultz away."

"But Miss Schultz said she was outside the store when the shooting took place, Mr. Besore."

"She wasn't, sir. She was standing right next to me at the counter. She didn't go out of the store until after the third or fourth shot was fired, and then she fainted."

At this point Miss Shultz, whose glory was beginning to fade, could stand it no longer.

"He's a liar!" she screamed. "I saw it all."

By the time order was restored, the jury was even less sure of the truth.

The parade of witnesses went on interminably. A good witness for the prosecution was Edward S. McGinley, an alert, sharp-eyed, fifteen-year-old boy, who not only declared he saw McMahon throw Leary to the ground and then shoot him but added that when it was all over, McMahon walked over to him (McGinley), took out 30 cents from his pocket and said, quite calmly, "Go over to the drug store, lad, and get me a quarter's worth of Cincos. You can keep the change."

"Rank bribery," said Chippy, grinning as the boy started to step down from the box. "Wait a minute, please."

"Yes, sir," said Edward, scrambling back again.

"Do you always tell the truth, Edward?"

"Yes, sir," the boy replied, a bit shaky.

"Do you know Edward Nerger?"

"Yes, sir!" he answered, now on sure ground. "We're in the same class."

"Does Edward Nerger always tell the truth?"

"Yes, sir" (pretty firmly).

"Did you know Edward Nerger told a fib to that nice district attorney when he said he saw the shooting and he wasn't there at all?"

"I guess so, sir."

"Did you know Edward Nerger said he made up the story so he could get out of school?"

"Yes, sir" (very weakly).

"Do you have school today, Edward?"

"Yes, sir."

"I think maybe you *are* in the same class as Edward. That's all, son."

Annie McMahon's long-awaited appearance provided spectators with their major thrill on the fourth and final day of the trial. Except to arouse the jury's sympathy, her brief testimony was of little value, a fact of which Mr. Gray was fully aware.

"The entrance of the girl," said the *Telegraph,* "was dramatic; her exit equally so. She appeared to be dazed. She came down the left hand aisle, paused irresolutely before the lawyer's section, turned several times to locate the voice of Mr. Patterson who was calling to her to come toward him, and then hurried on by the prisoner's dock without seeing her father. She took the stand and just two questions were asked her.

" 'Miss McMahon, where do you live?" asked Mr. Patterson.

" 'At Second and Spruce.'

" 'What time did your father leave home on that day?'

" 'About four o'clock.'

" 'That's all,' concluded Mr. Patterson turning to Mr. Gray. 'Cross examine.' "

But the prosecutor was not interested. "No questions," said Gray.

"The girl," continued the *Telegraph,* "left the stand as dazed, apparently, as when she had entered. The father was looking at her jealously, tensely. Tears were streaming down his face and two drops stole over the girl's cheeks, although the blank expression on her face did not change. She hesitated as she neared the prisoner's dock. McMahon waited until she got close and quickly stretched out his hand and touched the furpiece she wore. Then he collapsed utterly and his sobs could be heard in the corridors."

From the moment Annie stepped down from the stand, whatever else happened was anticlimactic. McMahon told his story, his wife told hers, or as much as Mr. Gray would permit. Alienists for the Commonwealth said McMahon was sane. Alienists for the defense said he wasn't. "The defense rests," said Chippy on the morning of the fifth day.

"Mr. Patterson," stated the *Inquirer,* "then launched into a plea which swayed the jury and brought tears to McMahon's eyes. (The little saloonkeeper was apparently the most lachrymose male defendant ever to appear in City Hall.) Once the prisoner burst forth into a violent sobbing fit.

"Mr. Patterson dwelt at length on the testimony of the mental specialists. He depicted the death of Leary with a vividness that was startling, and he spoke of the wrong that the real-estate man had done Annie McMahon.

" 'If he had expected it, as one witness said,' declared Mr. Patterson, 'then he knew he had committed a great wrong. Ask yourselves, can you blame McMahon for what he did?'

"Mr. Rotan spoke in rebuttal and attacked the 'unwritten law' or, as he called it, sympathy.

" 'Sympathy,' he said, 'has nothing to do with our verdict. This case must be decided upon its merits. The law of this State countenances no such defense and to set such a precedent would be to place a blot upon our history of justice.' "

"Judge Bregy's charge," said the *Evening Bulletin*, "lasted an hour. He summarized the evidence and defined murder in all degrees; defined insanity and self-defense as recognized by law. At times it seemed as though he did not place much credence in the self-defense and insanity pleas, and spoke rather disparagingly of the expert testimony. He let it be known he would allow nothing smacking of 'unwritten law' to enter the case."

The jury retired at 4:10 P.M. The moment the 12 men left the box and the courtroom in the custody of the bailiff, Chippy, who'd been listening carefully to every word in Judge Bregy's charge, leaped to his feet.

"Your Honor," he said, "I'd like a sidebar."

Judge Bregy, startled at such a request, unusual at a moment like this, said, "Certainly, Mr. Patterson. Come into my chambers. You, too, Mr. Rotan and Mr. Gray."

About a half hour later they emerged from Chambers and walked back into the courtroom to await the return of the jury. Chippy did not discuss his reasons for requesting the conference. At 5:20 P.M., one hour and ten minutes after leaving the box, the 12, faces grim, filed back to their places.

"Have you reached a verdict?" asked Crier Hart in formal tones.

"We have," answered Howard Richman.

Then Judge Bregy, his jaw set sternly, arose to his full height of six feet four inches, and, towering over the quiet courtroom, turned to the jury. He made what for a presiding judge must have been a difficult confession.

"Mr. Foreman," he said, "listen to me before you announce your decision. Mr. Patterson advised me that I have made a serious omission in my charge to you. The district attorney concurs. I fully agree with both gentlemen and I now wish to correct this error. Jury, I failed to include the testimony of witnesses who spoke of McMahon's good character. This is a very important phase. You must retire again and reconsider your verdict, whatever it was."

The jury went out for the second time and returned with their verdict at 5:51.

"We find the defendant guilty of manslaughter."

It was learned afterward that their first verdict was second-degree murder, but that after Judge Bregy laid so much stress on the importance of a good character, the few who had held out for a manslaughter verdict at first won finally.

Sentencing was deferred pending Chippy's decision whether or not to appeal the verdict.

"It's an outrage!" screamed John Leary, speaking for himself, his father, and his brother's two surviving sisters.

"Justice was served," declared the Reverend Dr. Floyd W. Tomkins, director of Holy Trinity and one of the prominent Philadelphians polled by the press.

"Justice was frustrated," declared the Reverend Joseph Krauskopf, rabbi of Temple Keneseth Israel.

"No comment," said Father D. I. McDermott, pastor of St. Mary's Roman Catholic Church, Fourth and Spruce Streets, where the McMahons were parishioners.

Three days later Chippy decided not to ask for a new

trial. Brought before Judge Bregy, McMahon was given an indeterminate sentence. Five months afterward he was paroled. The saloon at Second and Spruce Streets was sold, and the little saloonkeeper and his family disappeared from sight.

Chippy never saw the McMahons again, although he performed one last legal service for Annie. A month before McMahon was released from Eastern Penitentiary, Leary's will was offered for probate. The meticulous George had added a codicil to his carefully drawn will. The date was August 4, 1911, a few hours after he learned the saloonkeeper's daughter was carrying his child.

"To Annie McMahon, dearer to me than a wife," read Leary's last will and testament, "'I bequeath the sum of $5,000."

CHAPTER 29

THE END of Chippy's marriage was in sight. While Ada did not begin divorce proceedings until June 5, 1913, she knew it had failed long before that.

"There wasn't any point trying to continue," Ada said, "That year, after the McMahon case, I don't think Chiff came home more than a half-dozen times. We were friendly enough, but it was absolutely ridiculous to keep up the pretense of a marriage which no longer existed. My father knew it. Eleanor Patterson knew it. Chiff's parents knew it. The children knew it, and I knew it. The only one who didn't seem to be conscious of the break was Chiff. On the rare occasions he felt like coming home, he came home with complete aplomb. I guess it wouldn't have fazed him a bit to continue the way we were.

"I think the sarge was more upset about it than anybody. He did his damnedest to try to keep us together. Sometimes he'd get his hands on a fee before Chiff could dissipate the money and send me at least half of it and say, 'This is from the lieutenant.' He wasn't fooling me a bit. On my birthday Skelly once had flowers delivered with Chiff's card. But I knew Chiff never sent them. He wouldn't have remembered my birthday or any other occasion. The man just wasn't cut out for marriage. I was, and I wanted a fresh start. I was determined to have it.

"The last straw was Christmas of nineteen twelve. For months I'd planned a real family dinner, the very first one we would have had since we were married. My father, C. Stuart, Ellen, and Eleanor were coming, and I even went so far as to ask the George Stuart Pattersons. I don't believe Dike and Edith came. I think they were abroad at the time. I kept hammering at my husband to be sure he came. Only the day before, I talked with him, and he faithfully promised he'd be at Hollyeva on time for Christmas dinner. The sarge said he'd keep after Chiff, too, and that he'd have Buck Callahan deliver Chiffy to the door. Buck was a cab driver who used to chauffeur Chiff all over."

Ada was lost in thought for a moment, then she smiled gently and continued.

"I guess it sounds funny now, but believe me it wasn't then. Oh, we had our Christmas dinner all right. Everybody was there except Chiff. We had cocktails and talked and waited and waited and waited. Finally we sat down to eat. We were having coffee and dessert when I heard the sound of not one but several cars out in the driveway. A couple of moments later Willis, our houseman, opened the door, and in walked Chiffy and about twenty of the oddest assortment of men I ever hope to see."

She chuckled at the recollection and went on.

"They were all from Kirkbride's. Chiff had stopped in there on his way to Hollyeva and brought them home for Christmas. Each of them had a gift for me, all wrapped up, and I suppose that's why it took so long for them to get to Newtown Square. There were wooden carvings, potholders, towel racks, and one man, I remember, brought a complete shoeshine kit. They'd made them in their therapy shop. Although they sure knocked the hell out of that dinner, there was something awfully sweet about what Chiff did for those homeless gentlemen from the highball annex. If he'd only have told me about it first!

"As you can imagine, our regular dinner guests didn't linger. As soon as they left, which was practically right away, I had the table cleared, the liquor removed, and we served the men. Eleanor stayed, and I guess it was fun at that. But this just wasn't the way I wanted to live."

Unless you except the great train shed at Broad Street Station where C. Stuart had his suite of offices and Chippy set up temporary quarters in a telephone booth on the second floor after he was evicted from #1523 for non-payment of rent, that Christmas dinner at Hollyeva was probably the last time father and son were together under the same roof.

The first of the many times Chippy was forced to depend upon quasi-public facilities for the operation of his office following evictions might have come as a shock even to the clients he represented. But after a few occasions no doubt they became inured to waiting their turns while seated on rows of the hard benches the P.R.R. thoughtfully provided for its passengers. With the help of Skelly and the connivance of Bert Edwards, a friendly railroad detective Chippy once represented, two telephone booths were pre-empted and turned around so that they faced each other. In the semi-darkness beneath the high, cathedral-like ceiling which covered the huge train shed, the atmosphere was not unlike that of the confessional, with lawyer in one booth and client in the other, the latter pouring out truth and hoping for future courtroom absolution.

One of Chippy's favorite and frequently well-paying clients of that era was Frank Watkins, alias Frank Moore, alias Doctor Jackson. Chippy preferred the last one, and as Doctor Jackson of Boston, Mass., Montreal, Canada, or London, England, Frank was introduced to all of Chippy's friends, from Ikey Pinwheel, a City Hall character so named because of his enormous flapping ears, to Mr. George Wharton Pepper. No one knew the "doctor's" real name until years later when, according to the *Evening*

Bulletin of February 27, 1923, "the bullet-riddled body of this super-confidence man, wanted by police of both continents, was identified by his father, a trembling old man with a shock of white hair, as Peter Pelquin, of Worcester, Mass. Pelquin, known to the underworld as 'Doctor Jackson' was a soldier of fortune, a professional gambler and a college graduate with an almost perfect command of English. With his well modulated voice he could have passed muster in any of this city's most aristocratic clubs."

But Pelquin, or Watkins, or Moore, or Jackson, had decided to augment his funds by "working" the first-class passenger list of a swank trans-Atlantic liner. Traveling under still another alias, he sailed from England April 11, 1912. He picked the wrong ship for his base of operations, and four days later he was lucky to be one of the 711 survivors of the *Titanic*. Since he was traveling under a forged passport and was wanted by the police of many cities on both sides of the ocean, he was in no position to make any claim against the White Star Line and was glad to be able to slip away from photographers into penniless oblivion.

Within a year the resourceful Dr. Jackson had recouped his losses and decided to return to Philadelphia to revisit the scenes of his more successful ventures. He was eager to call upon his friend and counselor, C. Stuart Patterson, Jr. Dressed in the height of fashion, swinging an ivory-topped cane and looking like the sporting gentleman he undoubtedly was, he stepped from his bedroom on the Broadway Limited one morning in the spring of 1913. With redcaps behind him carrying his matched luggage, he strolled into Broad Street Station.

It must have come as an unpleasant surprise as well as a sad commentary on man's ingratitude to man to find the counselor whom he proclaimed, wherever he went, "the finest member of the bar and most distinguished gentleman in America" forced to practice his profession under such unpleasant circumstances. The elegant Dr. Jackson refused to consult with his lawyer until Patterson was reinstalled in his own offices. This was accomplished almost at once. The Doctor simply handed his counselor a generous annual retainer, saying, quite correctly, "Chip, you know you'll earn all of it before the next twelve months are up." It's likely that while Chippy didn't particularly care where his shingle hung, provided he could practice law, he still preferred the semi-privacy of his own offices to the train shed and was probably glad to return to #1523.

There was even enough money left over for the long-suffering Bellevue-Stratford, where Chippy had run up an enormous bill, and to pay a few months' rent in advance on a small but elegantly furnished house on Sansom Street. Chippy was comfortably installed there in the master bedroom on the second-floor front, and Dr. Jackson set up quarters above. Among his other accomplishments this confidence man was a superb chef. The house had a large, well-equipped basement kitchen, and the meals he enjoyed preparing there for his attorney and their many guests of both sexes were as fine and varied as those served in Philadelphia's best clubs.

For the very few Chestnut Hill gentlemen who still remained Chippy's friends, the house on Sansom Street became a haven of infinite delight, with a variety of titillating pleasures awaiting those made welcome there. The food was superb; the liquor excellent (Dr. Jackson would serve nothing but vintage wine); and there was usually an attractive woman available. Unfortunately for Chippy, his long hours in the office and the Hall gave him little time to relax at his Sansom Street home, but the debonair Dr. Jackson, whose chores were less arduous and more profitable, was around to act as substitute host, a function he performed most graciously.

Early one afternoon, not long after Dr. Jackson's return to Philadelphia, he and Chippy were again in Broad Street Station making sure a former associate of Dr. Jackson and present client of C. Stuart Patterson, Jr. carried out his obligation in a choice given him the day before by Judge Barratt to "get out of town within twenty-four hours or go to jail for six months." The westbound train, with client safely aboard, had just steamed out of the shed, and

Chippy and Dr. Jackson were about to leave when they heard a page boy scurrying through the station call out, "Mr. Patterson! Mr. C. Stuart Patterson!"

Dr. Jackson turned to his lawyer.

"That's for you, Chippy, isn't it?"

"I doubt it. It's probably for my father."

"Well, let's find out. Do you mind?"

"Not a bit. Go right ahead," Chippy answered.

Dr. Jackson beckoned to the boy. "What's the message for Mr. Patterson?" he asked.

"Are you Mr. Patterson?" questioned the lad.

"No, son, I'm not. That's Mr. Patterson over there," he said pointing to Chippy, who had withdrawn a few yards. Puzzled by Chippy's appearance, the boy hesitated a moment.

"Go on. That's Mr. Patterson, all right."

The young man looked at Dr. Jackson, who much more easily could have been C. Stuart, shrugged his shoulders, then delivered the message.

"Mr. Patterson is to telephone Admiral Wilson at the Navy Yard right away."

"Thank you, son," said Dr. Jackson, handing the boy a dollar bill. "I'll see that Mr. Patterson gets the word right away."

Dr. Jackson walked over to Chippy and repeated the message.

"May I see what the admiral wants?" he asked Chippy.

"Certainly," Patterson answered, and his companion entered a telephone booth, engaged in animated conversation, and emerged about five minutes later with a broad grin across his distinguished face.

"You'll be happy to know," he told Chippy as soon as he could control his laughter, "you and I are playing hosts to sixty-nine cadets on the Argentinian warship, *Rivadavia*. Fortunately for us both, I speak Spanish fluently."

"Of course the message wasn't for me, was it?"

Dr. Jackson shook his head. "I didn't ask."

"Okay," Chippy went on. "What's it all about?"

The Argentinian warship, on its shakedown cruise, Dr.

Jackson explained, had made Philadelphia its first foreign port of call. The cadets, all of whom were scions of Argentina's best families, and whose ages ranged from seventeen to twenty-one years, were to be guests of honor at a "thé dansant." It was to be given by the Junior League. That year's "buds" were to be hostesses, and the affair was to be properly chaperoned by the hallowed patronesses of the Assembly itself. At the conclusion of the dance, the Argentinians were to be given a formal dinner at the Union League. C. Stuart Patterson, Sr., then president of the League, was in charge of arrangements.

With war clouds gathering over Europe, the visit of a warship from America's friendly neighbor to the south, and the entertainment of cadets who soon would be naval career officers, had high United States government approval. As a matter of fact, the President of the United States, William Howard Taft, himself, had written a personal note to his friend, C. Stuart Patterson, Sr., urging everything be done to make the cadets happy.

For the first 48 hours the *Rivadavia* was docked at the Philadelphia Navy Yard, everything went according to plan. Then, for some long-forgotten reason, routine was fouled up and the cadets, as Admiral Wilson pointed out to Dr. Jackson, were set to leave Fourth Naval District Headquarters several hours ahead of schedule. What the commandant wanted to know was whether Mr. Patterson could arrange to have the P.R.R.'s special car, which was to carry the young gentlemen from the Navy Yard to Broad Street Station, arrive sooner.

"That," said Dr. Jackson, who knew the limit of even his capabilities, "will be impossible." But he assured the worried naval officer other transportation arrangements would be made forthwith and the cadets should be at the gate, ready to leave, within an hour.

"I have asked the Honorable Frank Jackson, former Minister to the Republic of Bolivia and a close friend of the President of the United States, to act as my representative," "Mr. Patterson" told Admiral Wilson. "Dr. Jackson speaks Spanish fluently. He will be delighted to escort the young men to the dance and the Union League dinner. No other escort, military or civilian, with be necessary."

Not more than 45 minutes later, led by Buck Callahan driving a rented Packard landau with Dr. Jackson seated haughtily inside, a fleet of cabs pulled up in front of the Navy Yard gate at the south end of Broad Street. The former "Bolivian Minister," attired in high silk hat, morning trousers, frock coat, and sporting his ivory-topped cane, graciously stepped down from the car. In pure Castilian he introduced himself to the Argentinian officer in charge, a lieutenant commander. With that gentleman sitting by his side and five cadets quickly distributed in each cab, the military entourage drove north, hurriedly turning off Broad Street as soon as it reached Oregon Avenue. By a devious route it arrived, a half hour later, not at the ballroom of the Bellevue-Stratford Hotel, where the year's debutantes were about to assemble, but at the side entrance to Rose Hicks' Girard Avenue Palm Garden.

Chippy, meanwhile, carried out the assignments Dr. Jackson had given hin. It was a legal holiday of some sort (Tom McBride, the former state's attorney general and Justice of the Supreme Court who represented Dr. Jackson in later years, said he would like to think it was Mother's Day), and court was closed. The moment Dr. Jackson left Broad Street Station, Chippy telephoned a client, Rose Hicks, a madam who not only operated one of the largest and choicest "stables" in Philadelphia, but also was gifted with a sense of humor and a flair for the dramatic.

Although she had less than two hours' time between Chippy's call and the arrival of the former "Bolivian Minister" with a handsome lieutenant commander and 69 eager young cadets in tow, Madam Hicks had done her job most efficiently and everything inside the Garden was in readiness. On the stage of this gigantic bawdy house, which occupied nearly a quarter of a city block on Girard Avenue between Seventh and Eighth Streets, a ten-piece all-female string orchestra, culled from the city's best parlor houses, struggled bravely with the Argentine national anthem as the doors were thrown open and the young gentlemen entered.

The sounds, sights, and smells which greeted the embryo officers as they entered the gaily decorated Garden must have given them thrills they would never forget. The place was teeming with scores of beautiful girls, all fragrantly scented and lined up demurely behind the trio of fashionably gowned hostesses, Rose and two of her colleagues. The three women stood beside the entrance graciously acknowledging the formal introduction of each young gentleman, whose name was relayed from the lieutenant commander to the unsmiling, dignified former Bolivian Minister, to Misses "Rush," "Cadwallader," "Biddle," "Borie," "Norris," "Wister," etc. Since he was no snob, there was even an "Elkins" and a "Widener."

Then Dr. Jackson mounted the stage and introduced "Your host, ladies and gentlemen, the distinguished Philadelphian, Mr. C. Stuart Patterson, Jr." Most of the females present knew Chippy. In fact he'd represented many of them in magistrate's court, and they were aware of his peculiarities of dress. But it's difficult to imagine what the cadets thought when the oddly attired Patterson stood next to the sartorially perfect Dr. Jackson. Perhaps they were too busy considering other more intimate ideas to notice the fishing boots, baggy trousers, and nondescript jacket. In any event Chippy's speech of welcome was brief.

"I am sure," he said, "you handsome officers from the Republic of Argentina will have fun and take back with you something to remember about the City of Brotherly Love." It's more than likely he was right on both counts. After the polite accolade, Dr. Jackson proposed a toast, first in Spanish and next in English, to "Our brave Argentinian heroes!" It was drunk in punch, heavily spiked with 100-proof Overholt. As the sound of the "Vivas!" reverberated through the hall and up into the bunting-covered rafters, the former "Bolivian Minister" turned to the young lady in charge of the ensemble. "Music, maestra," he said. "Let the dancing begin!"

It couldn't have taken even a virginal cadet long to discover that beneath the gown his lovely partner wore there was nothing but bare flesh. Nor could the sinuous gyrations of the girls be misinterpreted. One by one the pairs of partners drifted off the dance floor and arm in arm climbed the stairs to the second and third floors.

By about six o'clock Dr. Jackson believed it was time to call a halt to the pleasant afternoon before international complications could develop. He felt, and here as later events proved, he was absolutely correct, that within a few hours of the cadets' failure to appear at the Bellevue's "thé dansant" Philadelphia police would begin a discreet investigation into the strange disappearance of 69 cadets and an officer of the Argentine Navy.

Only the piercing cries ("Front and center, girls!") of Rose and her associates broke up the party and brought reluctant stragglers downstairs to bid grateful "Adios" to their duennas, so *simpatica*. At 6:15 the motor cavalcade, bearing the sated, but contented cadets, unbelievably impressed with the sample of Philadelphia's hospitality, arrived at the Union League. There they were welcomed with undisguised relief by Governor John K. Tener, Mayor Rudolph Blankenburg, and Mr. C. Stuart Patterson, Sr.

It's reasonable to believe that even the Union League's impressive table settings, superior food, and flowery speeches did not do as much to cement Argentine-American relations as the impromptu entertainment arranged by Dr. Jackson and Christopher Stuart Patterson, Jr. But from that day forward, C. Stuart no longer spoke to his son when they passed on the street.

Although life at Hollyeva was over, the cottage sold, and Ada back at her father's Chestnut Street home with the children, things were much the same at the office. Before the years 1913 and 1914 ended, Chippy defended the usual number of clients, including 38 men and women charged with murder in varying degrees.

Long after these homicides were forgotten, Chippy was remembered for a comment he made that same year during a trial so unimportant no newspaper thought it worthy of a single paragraph. He was defending, at a juryless trial, a young man charged with rape. This was probably the third or fourth defendant Chippy had represented on the same charge that day. The prisoner was no more than eighteen years old, and his "victim" over twice that age. Those members of the press assigned to follow Chippy wherever he went recalled that the plaintiff was singularly unattractive.

"Entry" was admitted, and the only question to be resolved was which of the pair, caught in *flagrante delicto* by the lady's husband, was the true aggressor. Chippy's plea was brief. At its conclusion he raised his eyebrows quizzically and glanced up at the Judge.

"Your Honor," he said, "I ask only that you look appraisingly at my client's accuser before passing sentence and then tell me how the charge could possibly be rape."

The Court followed counsel's suggestion, and his eyes lingered for a moment or two on the short, fat, middle-aged plaintiff. Then he turned to Chippy.

"All right, Mr. Patterson," he said. "What would you call it?"

Without a moment's hesitation Chippy replied, "Your Honor, I'd call it felonious gallantry."

CHAPTER 30

THE YEAR 1915 was an eventful one for Chippy. Ada's final divorce papers were issued January 20. Less than a week later, on January 26, the *North American* reported Patterson's engagement to Miss Cesira Marie De Guglielmo Vizale, of Jefferson Street. This news came as a shock both to Chippy and to his sister Eleanor. Nora, upon reading about the alleged betrothal, was prompted to remark, "At least Chiffy's following the family traditions and living off breast of guinea."

With Dr. Jackson's hurried departure for the Far West some time previously, there was no money to keep up the pleasant *pied-à-terre* he had established and ran so well. Miss Vizale, who must have been the possessor of a small dowry, stepped into the breach, took Chippy out of hock to the Hotel Stenton, and set up housekeeping in a charming two-and-one-half-story house on Van Pelt Street. Although Miss Vizale was an attractive, well-rounded brunette and certainly looked as though she could have made someone a good wife, the other Philadelphia newspapers were far more skeptical than the *North American*, refused to believe in the validity of this betrothal, and consequently made no mention of it in their columns.

There's a yellowed snapshot in the morgue of the Philadelphia *Record*, one of the skeptics. The photograph, apparently taken in front of what might be a resort hotel, reveals the attractive Miss V. holding a huge picture hat in her hands and dressed in what looks like a lacy, light-colored gown. An immense St. Bernard sits obediently at the lady's feet. By her side stands Chippy, dressed as usual, cap in hand, shoestring tie pulled to one side, nondescript ill-fitting jacket with a hole showing on one sleeve, and fishing boots. Just the merest shadow of a smile appears on his lips.

Since nobody except the normally distrustful *North American* took the announcement seriously, nothing came of it, and the relationship between Miss Vizale and Chippy never reached the status of permanency. The lady was followed by innumerable successors, all of whom seemed willing to share not only Patterson's bed but his financial problems as well.

Some time in February of that meaningful year of 1915, the faithful sarge and his lieutenant parted company. Skelly, at an age when most men are either dandling grandchildren on their knees or have become so accustomed to a life of bachelorhood that any change would be abhorrent, fell in love. The object of his affections was a twenty-year-old client. Within three weeks of the girl's discharge (a first offense), she and Skelly were married. The ceremony was performed in chambers by Judge Audenreid in the presence of as prominent a company of gentlemen as ever attended the most exclusive wedding held at Holy Trinity.

Mr. C. Stuart Patterson, Jr. was best man and no less a Proper Philadelphian than Mr. George Wharton Pepper, who happened to be passing through the sixth-floor corridor of City Hall when Chippy corralled him, gave the bride away. Witnesses, all distinguished members of the bar, community leaders, and members of the bench, included two Justices of the State Supreme Court, the mayor of the city of Philadelphia, assistant district attorney John H. Maurer, the Messrs. Norris Barratt and William Cadwallader. The only other lady present was the bride's former employer, the aforementioned Miss Hicks. Unaccustomed to be on eye level or in such completely unfamiliar juxtaposition with any judge, Miss Hicks forgot herself long enough to shed a sentimental tear when His Honor pronounced the pair man and wife. Following the ceremony, Chippy gave a dinner at the Bellevue-Stratford in honor of the bride and groom.

The marriage, it is a pleasure to report, was a long and happy one. Skelly and his bride moved to Southern California, and the sarge, before his death in 1943, was able to dandle his own grandchildren on his knees. Snapshots of his children, then his children's children, sent to Ada over the years are offered in evidence.

Whatever slight control the sergeant had been able to exercise over his lieutenant departed with him. From then on Chippy's life ran its course without restraint from anyone. Skelly's successor was Charlie Phillips, called "Happy" or "Hap" by everyone. Phillips, nearing sixty now and still able to smile despite many years spent in the service of the Republican Party, was only fifteen when he became an employee of C. Stuart Patterson, Jr., doing a job, frequently payless, he was to hold for six years.

Happy was a Western Union messsenger boy when Chippy sounded the "call."

"My salary with the company was two dollars a week," reminisced Happy, adding with a sigh, "but it had one big advantage—it was regular. One day in nineteen fifteen I delivered a telegram to Mr. C. Stuart Patterson, Jr. He opened the envelope, and while he was reading the message I stood around hoping maybe I'd get a dime, although after one look at the way he was dressed I wouldn't have been surprised if *he* asked *me* for a dime.

"I had never seen Mr. Patterson before, so I didn't know what to expect. Well, after he finished, he looked down at me, thanked me very politely, took out a wad of money from his pocket, and handed me a five-dollar bill. I must have turned white with shock. The biggest tip I'd ever gotten before was fifty cents. I know for a moment I couldn't talk even to thank him. Then in a couple seconds I blurted out something about didn't he make a mistake. This made him smile again. He asked me my name and I told him. Then he pulled my cap down over my eyes and up again kiddingly, gave me a little push, and said, 'You're all right, son. Your mother ought to be proud of you.'

"The way he said it I knew he was a real gentleman, and believe me, it wasn't the five-dollar tip that did it. I think right then and there I'd have done anything he could have asked me to do, and I guess later on I probably did. After that I kept hoping to see Mr. Patterson again, and a couple weeks later I saw him on Broad Street. I'd just delivered a telegram to somebody in the Girard Trust, and I was coming down the steps when I spotted Mr. Patterson. He was walking with some guy, so I didn't say anything. He saw me and called out, 'Hello, Happy, how are you?'

"I answered, 'Fine, Mr. Patterson, how are you?' Then he said, 'Where's your bike?' and I told him I didn't have one. He turned to the guy he was with and said, 'Shooey, can't we do something about this?' The guy grinned and answered, 'I guess we could take care of this little matter, Chippy.' So then Mr. Patterson asked me where I lived and I told him. The other man wrote it down. Well, the next afternoon I got home, ready to sit down to supper, when a cop comes to the door and asks for me. I hadn't done anything wrong that I knew of, but I got so scared I nearly wet my pants. 'It's all right, kid,' he said, 'we just want you to identify something.' He turned to my mother who was standing there pale as a sheet and told her, 'I'll have him back in an hour.'

"The cop had a motorcycle with a side car, and he told me to climb in. We rode out Jefferson Street to Tenth and stopped at a big warehouse there. There was another cop outside, and he let us in and turned on the lights. I could hardly believe my eyes. There must have been a couple hundred bikes there, all lined up with a tag on each one of them. Many were brand new.

" 'Go ahead, boy,' the cop told me. 'Shooey Malone (then a lieutenant, later Director of Public Safety) says you're to take your pick.' I chose a Schwinn racer, practically new. The cop tore the tag off, and I rode home to tell my mother. That Saturday I quit Western Union, and I went to work for Mr. Patterson two days later. My pay was eight dollars a week—when I got it, which wasn't often. But the experiences I had! I wouldn't trade them for the world."

When Ada, Skelly, and Miss DuBarry were around, there was some semblance of order at #1523. Attempts, successful a fair percentage of the time despite Chippy, were made to operate his office in a more or less routine fashion, although to handle the tremendous volume of business properly, Chippy's legal contemporaries estimated he should have had a staff of at least ten, not including a half dozen "juniors." With Ada divorced, Skelly in California, and Miss DuBarry long since departed, Happy Phillips became the sole official employee of C. Stuart Patterson, Jr. The rest—stenographers, investigators, clerks, messengers, etc.—were volunteers from the district attorney's office, the Courts of Oyer and Terminer, police and sheriff's offices, Probation Bureau, newspaper reporters, and the underworld. In fact everyone who could be pressed into service was used to help Chippy prepare his cases and handle the never-ending flow of clients.

Harry Ogden, the fastest stenographer in Criminal Courts, took Chippy's dictation and helped prepare his briefs (supplying paper, pencils, notebooks, and blue backers) after his own work day ended at City Hall. "Hell, I knew Chippy'd never pay me, but I just couldn't refuse that guy nothing. In fact *he* never asked *me* to help. I was the one who volunteered," Ogden said. "What did I get out of it? Well, Chippy's friendship, some wonderful fishing trips with him at Corson's Inlet, lots of good laughs, and I guess that was enough for all of us. Zeke Hackney, chief probation officer, Bob Comber from the *Bulletin,* Jimmy Day from the *Inquirer,* Charlie Gordon, first assistant district attorney, cops, deputy sheriffs, and half the goddamned underworld, or that part which wasn't in jail, would go over to fifteen twenty-three and pitch in. We'd take any assignment Chip would hand out. Sometimes there'd even be a cop teamed up with a thug he'd arrested one time or other, digging up evidence for a Patterson client."

Not a client had paid Chippy a fee of any size for weeks and his finances were at a particularly low ebb when the fifteen-year-old Phillips took over office management. The Bell Telephone Company, its patience exhausted, had finally suspended service, and Clement C. Love, the landlord, threatened eviction again, swearing that if he ever got C. Stuart Patterson, Jr. out of his building, he'd never be persuaded to let him come back. Merchants, foolish enough to have extended credit or perhaps misled by the magic name of Patterson, kept dunning for long overdue payment of bills.

This almost perpetual state of fiscal vacuum never seemed to bother Chippy, but his financial irresponsibility distressed those who were close to him. From time to time his friends and associates made sporadic attempts to straighten Patterson's finances by holding out a fee and using the money to pay the most pressing bills. But after a while they gave up and resigned themselves and Chippy to whatever the fates, frequently in the form of a constable, had to offer.

Young Phillips' first duty, as he recalls, was to act as a lookout.

"I used to get to the office about seven o'clock in the morning, to sweep up," he said, "and had to buy my own broom. Sometimes when I arrived there'd be bill collectors waiting outside the office door. They must have been there all night, I guess. Mr. Patterson would be due to get in about seven thirty. We had a signal worked out. Buck Callahan drove him from the Bellevue along Chestnut Street in his cab and always slowed down to give Mr. Patterson a chance to look up at the head of the stairs. You could see it from the street. If there was nobody around but clients—pretty soon I could tell the difference between them and collectors—I'd stand at the top of the stairs and hold my broom the regular way. That was the all clear. But if a constable or someone like that was around, I'd hold it upside down. That was the distress signal, and Mr. Patterson would drive around the block a couple of times, or maybe he'd sneak up the back entrance through the alley.

"I don't know what the constable would have levied on if he could have made service. We had three rooms, and there wasn't two dollars' worth of usable furniture in all of them. There were plenty of chairs, but they were all broken and scratched, and clients felt safer standing up. There were no files or law books. He did have a desk he managed to take with him wherever he went. It was a great big rolltop. I think his father gave it to him. D. J. Callahan, the assistant city solicitor, had his offices on the back part of our floor, and I often wonder what he thought of what went on. There was Goodman's Barber Supply Company on the first floor and an art gallery, I forget whose, on the third.

"Once when I was out sick or something and Mr. Patterson had no way of telling who was upstairs when he came to work, he borrowed Mr. Goodman's overcoat and a thick black wig, climbed up the stairs, and looked around. He didn't like what he saw, so he went up to the third floor and spent a while there looking at the paintings until it was safe to come down."

Happy recalls a particularly persistent constable named Schlemmerer, hired by Mr. Love to get Chippy out, regardless of the expense.

"I think," recollected Phillips, "the job must have been

given to him on a cost-plus basis, because even if he could have collected all the past-due rent it still wouldn't have nearly paid him for the time he gave. Clients got to know him as well as they knew Shooey Malone. Why, every time I looked around, there was Schlemmerer. During his 'campaign,' Mr. Patterson used the back entrance as much as he used the front.

"Something happened to Schlemmerer, and he got sick and died. Very late one night we were sitting around the inside office, Mr. Patterson, me, and a few underworld characters, automobile thieves and gunmen. Nobody was talking, and it was very quiet. All of a sudden the window slammed shut with a hell of a bang. We nearly hit the ceiling.

" 'Relax, gentlemen,' said Mr. Patterson. 'It's only the ghost of Schlemmerer!' "

Chippy saw his mother for the last time in July, 1915. Because of Ellen Patterson's rapidly failing health, she and C. Stuart decided not to spend the summer at Newport. One afternoon when Chippy returned to #1523 from court, Happy Phillips knocked on his door to announce the presence of "two respectable old ladies." One was Nurse Johnson and the other Ellen Patterson. Against C. Stuart's wishes, or perhaps without his knowledge, Ellen had come to say goodbye to the son who had caused both of them so many heartaches. It was the first time Chippy had seen his mother in nearly three years.

It's hard to imagine what Philadelphians who knew the Pattersons' recent history thought as mother, son, and Nurse Johnson slowly strolled up tree-lined Walnut Street, the Patterson limousine, liveried chauffeur behind the wheel, following discreetly a few hundred feet to the rear. When the three arrived at Rittenhouse Square, they sat on a bench near the fountain. What they talked about no one will ever know. In a half hour the two women, their pilgrimage ended, returned to Gracehill. Ellen Patterson died less than a month later, and her ashes were buried in the family plot at the base of a monument in the churchyard of St. Thomas in Whitemarsh Township. Chippy did not attend the funeral.

CHAPTER 31

THE FOLLOWING YEAR Chippy began and ended his brief and limited association with as unlikely a colleague as could be found in the roster of the Philadelphia Bar Association: Henry Stevenson, Penn Charter '94, Princeton '98, and Penn Law '02, son of the distinguished Judge Maxwell Stevenson.

Henry Stevenson was a lawyer's lawyer, a master of technicalities and an expert on appeals. He was aloof, methodical, never permitted the slightest familiarities from clients, demanded high fees in advance, and paid his bills promptly. He was a firm believer in and practitioner of monogamy, frowned upon immorality in others, and detested alcohol and tobacco. His saving grace was a superb sense of humor. He and Chippy shared enormous respect for each other's abilities, and this team, during the short period of its existence, became a nightmare to the district attorney's office, which did not win a single conviction against it in 14 capital cases. Stevenson supplied what Patterson lacked, and if this loose partnership had lasted it would have been as simple to beat a homicide rap in Philadelphia (for a Stevenson-Patterson client, at any rate) as to fix a parking ticket.

The only serious difficulties Chippy experienced in his handling of cases arose when adverse decisions of the lower courts had to be appealed to higher jurisdictions, or, to use a phrase current then, Patterson was "cooked upstairs." There were good reasons for this. In the first place, trial notes had to be current and detailed, and Chippy made only the most cursory jottings, which he either destroyed or lost once the verdict was in. Then, too, complete stenographic records were requisites of an appeal, and, like formal briefs, also had to be paid for in advance. Most of Chippy's clients rarely had funds to pay court stenographers and printers. Besides, though Chippy was a trial lawyer with enormous attractions for judge and jury, he certainly was no student of the law. As a result of his normal failure to pursue verdicts beyond the lower courts, he was forced to abide by many a decision which might well have been reversed at a higher level. While the percentage of cases he lost remained small, the actual number was sizable because of the huge volume of business he handled.

It was when Chippy was associated with brilliant, methodical men like Waln, Stevenson, or, later, Lou McCabe, Tom McBride, and Benny Lemisch that the physical requisites for appeals were present. The tenuous combination of Patterson and Stevenson handled no earth-shaking cases. The significance of their short tie-up lay in the fact that because of Stevenson's peculiar abilities, verdicts which Chippy would have been forced to accept were carried to higher courts. Convictions in five homicides were set aside, and when new trials were granted, clients who'd been found guilty of murder in varying degrees found themselves exonerated completely. Fortunately for the sake of justice, incompatibility forced the team to disband in three months.

Those members of the bench who enjoyed brilliant jousting were sorry to see the association broken; while it lasted, they never dared relax for a moment when this pair was engaged in a trial. Every one of them knew that any lapse on his part would be noted and used for an appeal, thus spoiling his record.

One rather stuffy judge, Thomas O. Finletter, who was a close friend of C. Stuart and George, actually upbraided Chippy in open court for not making sufficient effort to continue his association with Mr. Stevenson. An old friend of the family, he seemed to usurp the forgotten duties of Chippy's father and delivered a lecture in which he praised Stevenson for qualities of reliability, dependability, and responsibility, virtues which by inference his recent associate did not possess. His Honor concluded his brief, though long-remembered harangue, with a statement to the effect that every member of the bench trusted Mr. Stevenson implicitly, while the actions of Christopher

Stuart Patterson, Jr. were always scrutinized. This, of course, was not true, and no member of the bench, including Finletter, doubted Chippy's integrity, even though the Court frequently deplored his *modus operandi.*

In any event, the subject of the diatribe listened with bowed head, and when Judge Finletter concluded, left the room. But the following morning before court convened Chippy, with the connivance of Finletter's secretary, slipped his own petition into a stack of others which Harry Stevenson had left on His Honor's desk for his signature. Shortly before the noon recess, during that brief period in which the district attorney decides whether to put on another case before lunch or ask for an adjournment, Judge Finletter normally signed the petitions before him. Like most of his colleagues he considered lawyers officers of the court and gave the papers no more than a cursory glance before affixing his name at the bottom. Occasionally, when the attorney on the backer was unfamiliar, he might regard the document he was about to sign with a bit more care.

That morning was no different from others, and without a thought Judge Finletter signed several dozen petitions. When he concluded he looked up over the top of his pince-nez to see Chippy standing in front of the bench.

"Well, Mr. Patterson," Finletter asked kindly, perhaps a bit upset by his own words of the previous day, "what can I do for you?"

"I would appreciate it, Your Honor," Chippy answered, "if you would read one of Mr. Stevenson's petitions you have just signed."

Judge Finletter squinted and drew his heavy eyebrows together in a puzzled fashion, leafed through the papers on his desk, and pulled out those with Mr. Stevenson's name on the backers.

"Which one, Mr. Patterson?" the Court asked.

"It's only a single page."

Judge Finletter flicked the papers rapidly and came to the one he wanted almost at once, and read, for the first time, the paper to which he had affixed his signature. He frowned deeply, grew beet red, and seemed to gasp for breath. No one knew quite what to expect from this frequently irascible member of the bench, and court attachés who had been present the preceding day and heard His Honor's blast at Mr. Patterson were afraid something far worse was about to happen. There was deep silence for a few moments, then Judge Finletter's rigid shoulders sagged, and unexpectedly he smiled.

"Gentlemen," he said looking down from the bench, "some of you may be pleased to know I have just signed an irrevocable petition for my own commitment to Pennsylvania Hospital for the Mentally Ill."

About this time Chippy formed his famous one-man "Patterson Athletic Club," under the aegis of which he and others were able to give anonymous help to families of prisoners and the prisoners themselves when they won their freedom. Frequently, assistance was given by the very judges who had passed sentence but who wanted to aid convicts' families if it could be done without public knowledge. The first act of the Patterson A.C., which held no meetings, owned no clubhouse, and solicited no members, was to purchase a cemetery lot for the burial of penniless ex-convicts.

The burial ground of the Patterson A.C. was in undedicated land adjacent to the New Cathedral Cemetery on Nicetown Lane near Second and Butler Streets. It was bought very cheaply because of Chippy's friendship with Monsignor Cavanaugh, pastor of nearby St. Michael's Roman Catholic Church, and had room for 150 graves. The prelate, who had considerable experience with the purchase of real estate, helped Patterson, who had none, prepare the deed, which was duly registered at City Hall. Monsignor Cavanaugh was a kindly man with deep feelings, even for those not of the faith who wound up their dreary lives buried in unconsecrated ground.

The Patterson A.C. had many uses other than to provide a last resting place for Patterson clients. Over the years it became a cloak to cover anonymous gifts of coal, food, and clothing to destitute families of prisoners. Frequently, a judge who wanted to reward a convict for good behavior by granting a parole but was unable to do so until a sponsor was found, at Chippy's suggestion would place the convict in the custody of the P.A.C., knowing, of course, this institution was close to being fictional.

Later, during the bitter political campaign which developed between Mr. Pepper and Gifford Pinchot, the Patterson Athletic Club was forced to occupy a position for which it was hardly prepared. In the vitriolic exchange of letters between Senator Pepper and the man who was twice elected governor of the Commonwealth of Pennsylvania, the fertile imagination of Pinchot's fiery-tempered, red-headed wife, Cordelia, called the P.A.C. a "gathering place to rally prostitutes' forces for Pepper." Years afterward, Ira Jewell Williams, Pinchot's campaign manager, and his opponent, George Wharton Pepper, old men with bitterness long since forgotten, were both delighted to recall the innocent remarks which pushed Chiffy Patterson, who never voted in his life, into becoming an important political issue.

The incident occurred, Mr. Williams said, during a reunion of the class of '97 held at the University Club.

"We'd all urged Chiffy to attend—we loved him very much—and didn't care how he looked. At first he said 'no.' But Isabelle Darlington asked him, and you know Chiff could never refuse a woman anything, so he came, drifting in late and dressed as usual. The rest of us, about eighty, were in formal clothes. Somehow or other someone adroitly maneuvered the innocent reunion into a gentle political rally in behalf of Mr. Pepper, then a Professor of Law at the University."

What happened from this point on, Mr. Williams explained in a letter he wrote to the *Shingle,* April, 1948.

"Chiffy must have had a high regard for George Wharton Pepper . . . and he volunteered to speak and work for him. His words illustrated his wit: 'I have a very unusual practice,' he said. 'It is principally in the red-light district. Many, if not most, of my clients there are members of Mrs. Warren's profession. But while most of them live in the Eighth Ward, they have votes. And these votes I shall try to secure in the name of the Patterson A.C. so that these ladies will form a street parade for Mr. Pepper and carry banners with large letters: PEPPER AND PURITY!' "

CHAPTER 32

ALTHOUGH Chippy handled an unbelievable number of cases during his 30-odd years of practice (Benny Lemisch's estimate is 125,000), records of only comparatively few exist today. These are to be found in the homicide dockets of the district attorney's office. You may open these books at nearly any place and turn but a few pages before you run across the name of C. Stuart Patterson, Jr. listed as counsel for the defense. To find a typical period in the professional life of Chippy Patterson, these dusty volumes, stacked high in a City Hall storeroom, apparently provided the only clue, since the working press of the day considered most of his homicides so routine they didn't rate even a paragraph.

There's no compelling historical reason to choose the months between April 20, 1915 and December 21, 1917, except that everything about the murderers he represented then, the manner in which they committed their crimes, and the resulting verdicts were average. No notorious criminals were involved; no man or woman of importance, except to himself and his family, was murdered; and no unique method of killing was developed. Chippy's box score for those months also was average. Of the 24 men and women he defended on charges of homicide in varying degrees, 16 were found "not guilty"; six received sentences ranging from one to three years; one defendant was sentenced from 10 to 12 years (he was out in five); and one went to Eastern Penitentiary, where he remained for 14 years. Nobody got the chair.

During at least part of this busy period and for some time afterward, Chippy's problem of trying to hang on to enough money every day for food and lodging, to say nothing of office expenses, was solved through the combined efforts of a trio of successful South Philadelphia thieves, the Nelson brothers. Rather than have their attractive young wives on the loose while they served two- to five-year sentences at Eastern Penitentiary, the three brothers, clients of Chippy's, rented a house, where they installed their counselor and their spouses. Before entering prison they arranged with a bank to mail a check on the first of the month of sufficient size to pay all reasonable expenses for a 30-day period. Hard-working and thrifty themselves, they were aware of Chippy's propensity for getting rid of all cash he had on hand, and accordingly had the money sent to the oldest brother's wife, Clara, a frugal housekeeper. Clara was under strict instructions never to exceed Chippy's allowance of $2 a day, cabfare downtown and return.

It was a happy arrangement for everyone concerned. For Chippy it was ideal. Even though Mr. Love finally succeeded in evicting him permanently from #1523 and the Bell Telephone Company was adamant in its refusal to re-install equipment until all past bills were paid, Chippy was content. He had no immediate problems of food or shelter and could give away every dollar he earned. With three attractive women present at all times, day and night, the household situation was strongly reminiscent of the delightful week Chippy had spent under Mrs. Stone's roof some years before.

For the girls it was a pleasant interlude. Chippy was a gentleman, and obviously appreciative of all favors. On the table at every meal were flowers provided by Chippy. He understood the attitude of the brothers Nelson, and while he never brought male guests home to share the hospitality, he was a superb raconteur and life was far from dull. With little to do until their husbands returned, except to provide for the wants of C. Stuart Patterson, Jr., each meal became almost festive, and the sisters-in-law tried nightly to outdo each other in tempting Chippy with examples of culinary skill.

The setup served the Nelson brothers best of all. With plenty of money stashed away outside and more where that came from for craftsmen as skillful as they, the future held no terrors. "Inside" they had a supply of cash sufficient to meet all their needs and to buy favors. While they had no illusions about their wives' chastity with Chippy around, at least they knew the girls were not on the town, sharing favors promiscuously.

Neither Gopsill's City Directory of Philadelphia, nor its successor, Boyd's, ever caught up with Chippy, and throughout most of the years he continued to list his residence as Gracehill. Occasionally, however, they did manage to place his shingle over the right door, even though some of the time he was supposed to have a suite in a downtown building, his office, quite literally, was in his hat, or rather his cap. One day, in the midst of a case he was trying, an important witness subpoenaed by the defense did not appear. Judge Charles Brown, annoyed, questioned the court representative to find out if proper service had been made. Told that the notice was left in the mailbox at the witness's last known address, Judge Brown turned to Chippy and asked him if he had a more recent one.

"I believe I have, Your Honor," Chippy replied. "It's in my office."

"Shall I declare a half-hour recess while you get it, Mr. Patterson?"

"That won't be necessary, Judge. It shouldn't take that long."

So saying, Chippy reached for his tattered overcoat, which had been draped over a chair, and while everyone grinned, he began to pull papers from its pockets, glance at each rapidly, then dump them on counsel's table in front of the bench. When he'd emptied his overcoat, he reached into the jacket he was wearing and continued the process until the table was heaped high. Finally he found what he wanted, an address scrawled on the back of an old envelope.

"I have it, Your Honor," he said, looking up at Judge Brown triumphantly.

"Thank you, Mr. Patterson," the Court replied without a smile. "Your efficient filing system and the proximity of your office have saved us twenty-five minutes. We're all grateful to you. The case will continue."

CHAPTER 33

THE NELSONS behaved like gentlemen at Eastern Penitentiary, and Chippy, with an assist from Warden McKenty, was able to persuade the Pardon Board at Harrisburg to parole all three in January, 1919. One by one they came home to their wives. Leon, the baby, was last out and just made it in time to join the family group to celebrate the passage of the 18th Amendment, January 29. Although they did not realize it at the time, a new career had been opened for them.

Chippy was on his own again, the base of his legal activities in Broad Street Station and his living quarters once more on the eleventh floor of the patient Bellevue-Stratford Hotel.

Quantitatively speaking, April was the most successful in that section of Chippy's career devoted to the defense of murderers. Nobody quite knows how he did it, but if the docket book in the district attorney's office is accurate, then he represented nine men and women charged with varying degrees of homicide between April 6 and April 30. The results were impressive: five were acquitted, two received sentences of less than one year on charges of involuntary manslaughter, and two went to Eastern Penitentiary, where their stay averaged less than six years.

Chippy also continued his usual rounds of the lower courts and was seen daily at all hours pleading his cases before those of the city's 14 magistrates who handled criminal matters. Early on the morning of April 29, Chippy gained a client's freedom in a surprisingly unorthodox fashion. According to Ralph B. Umsted, a former deputy attorney general, the incident occurred in the 9th District Police Station where the late Magistrate Edward ("Carnation Eddie") Carney was conducting hearings.

"The only reason I remember the date so well," Umsted recalled, "was that I was about to represent my first client, who'd been picked up the night before for drunken and disorderly conduct. I was a little nervous when I reached Twentieth and Buttonwood where the Ninth used to be. The courtroom, which was really the officers' roll room, was jammed, and it stank. There must have been fifty drunks there out on copies, waiting for Carnation Eddie to make his appearance.

"I didn't see my client, and I wasn't sure what I was supposed to do next. I turned around, and there was Chiff Patterson standing next to me. I said, 'Good morning, Mr. Patterson,' and he answered, 'Good morning, Sir.' We could hardly hear each other it was so noisy, what with the chatter of wardheelers, committeemen, bondsmen, and all those drunks up for hearings. You had to scream to make yourself heard.

"Mr. Patterson was standing next to a well-dressed man, although maybe he only appeared to be because nearly everyone who stood next to Chiffy looked like Beau Brummell. Over the din Mr. Patterson told me the fellow's name was George Burrows. He was a client of Chiffy's arrested on suspicion of stealing five thousand dollars' worth of diamonds. I was going to ask Chiff what I ought to do about my own client when the 'judge' walked in. He was in a bad mood, and he looked like he was nursing a beautiful hangover. Even the flower he always wore in his lapel drooped."

Umsted chuckled at the recollection and went on.

"Carnation Eddie took one look around the room and addressed the crowd in his usual dignified fashion.

" 'Quiet, all you bastards!' he screamed. 'Let's have order in the court!' There was no lessening of the din, and Carney held his head with both hands and rocked it back and forth as if he was in actual pain. I suppose he was. He'd probably been out drinking all night and hadn't gone to bed. He tried again.

" 'Will you sons of bitches keep quiet!' he yelled. 'I can't stand it.' Nobody paid any attention to Carney. Finally, in desperation he stood up and shouted at the top of his voice, 'Get the hell out of this room, every —— one of you.'

"Chiffy grinned and turned to his client. 'George, you heard what the man said.' And they both strolled out of the Ninth District. As far as I know that was the last Philadelphia heard of George Burrows."

On May 22, Albert "Reds" Murphy, Chippy's friend and fishing companion, was an active participant in a murder stick-up. Murphy was a gangster, gunman, and all-around thug, but he was polite, possessed a well-developed sense of humor, and had enormous respect for his counselor. The late Walter Capelli, who used to work on the *Bulletin,* recalled the many stories told about Reds.

"Murphy," said Capelli, "was a real tough monkey, but you'd never think it to look at him. He wasn't very big, and he didn't look strong, but that was deceptive. One day another rough guy, Joe Breslin, and his wife, Bessie, were drinking in a saloon at Eighth and Vine. Suddenly Bessie's husband clouted her just as Reds walked in. Reds socked the husband, took one look at Bessie, and led her out of the saloon, beginning a romance of many years. Bessie was a beautiful, baby-faced blonde whom Chippy described as a 'China Doll.' In their own peculiar fashion she and Reds were faithful to each other while it lasted. Chippy represented them both in their various dealings with the law.

"Early one morning, it must have been about one A.M., when Chippy was living at the Hotel Stenton, there was a knock on his door. A dapper cocky little man came in and introduced himself as Wilfred Carpentier. He said he was a messenger for Ownie Madden, who wished to offer the services of the Madden mob to Mickey Duffy, the Philadelphia gangster then serving a sentence at Cherry Hill. Bill Fallon, Carpentier told Chip, was the source of the Patterson recommendation. I'm inclined to think the kind of service Madden volunteered was in the nature of temporary leadership, Ownie hoping this would become permanent. With an assassination or two, he and his New York gang might take over Duffy's Philadelphia and South Jersey mob.

"I'm sure Chip never gave him the chance to be

specific. He probably thanked Carpentier politely and sent him on his way. That was the difference between C. Stuart Patterson, Jr. and gang mouthpieces. Those boys forgot the ethics they learned at law school. They'd sit in on mob sessions just like they do in the movies, and help the gang plan crimes."

Capelli shook his head vigorously.

"Chippy'd have none of that. It's true he'd represent anyone in need of a lawyer, and he defended many a mobster. But that was *after* the crime, something even George Wharton Pepper would have done if he'd practiced criminal law. You can be sure Chippy'd never allow anyone to discuss future criminal plans in his presence. Before they could say very much, Chip would remind them he was not only a member of the bar but an officer of the court and that he would report any intended violations of the law to the proper authorities. I'm sure he would have without the slightest compunction.

"As far as Mickey Duffy is concerned, Chippy never represented him at all, although Duffy would have liked it. I know for certain that once, after Mickey and Boo Boo Hoff took over all the rackets in Philadelphia and South Jersey and pocketed millions every year, they offered Chip an annual retainer of two hundred fifty thousand dollars. All he'd have to do was drop his other practice and handle just them. Chip said 'no' even though at the time his office was filled with non-paying clients."

As Capelli recalled, after Carpentier left the Stenton that night, he wandered down to Eighth and Vine Streets and into a saloon which then was a hangout for many Philadelphia gangsters, including Reds Murphy. Carpentier apparently knew Murphy by sight and reputation and walked over to his table where Reds and several companions were drinking.

"The moment he sat down," Capelli said, "Carpentier began bragging about how tough and wide-awake Ownie Madden's gang was and how weak and sleepy the Philadelphia mob was by contrast. He kept it up and kept it up while Murphy and the rest of the killers listened in cold silence.

"Finally one of them said they'd let Carpentier come along the following day and help them on a stick-up in West Philadelphia to show the Philly boys how it should be done. The boys certainly didn't need any outside help. They were out to get Carpentier so that the word would be passed on to Madden he'd better stay the hell away from the City of Brotherly Love."

The robbery took place as scheduled. According to the Philadelphia *Record* of May 22, "An alleged gangster was killed yesterday when Harry Peterman, a collector for the American Stores Company was held up at 51st and Arch Streets. He had a large sum which he had collected from stores of the company. . . . Just as he left the place an automobile, in which three men were riding, drove up alongside.

"One of the men jumped from the car and demanded the bag of money. Peterman resisted and in a scuffle that followed a shot was fired and the bandit who left the automobile was wounded. The two men who remained in the automobile pulled their comrade in with them and the machine was driven away.

". . . the automobile was found abandoned at 13th and Callowhill Streets. The bandit who had been shot was in it, dead. He was identified as Wilfred E. Carpentier, a former convict, of Boston."

Murphy was arrested a few days afterward and pointed out by an eyewitness as the man who fired the fatal shot. The grand jury held him without bail on a charge of murder. There would be no Saturday fishing at Corson's Inlet for some time to come. Chippy, of course, entered his name as counsel for the defense. Afraid this one might go against him in Oyer and Terminer, he took as co-counsel Thomas J. Minnick, an old-time criminal lawyer who had piled up a record of success in appeals to the higher courts. But before Murphy could be tried for murder, he had several other charges to face.

"This was a day of trials for Albert 'Reds' Murphy, suspected bandit slayer," said the Philadelphia *Record* of

June 13. "Murphy was brought from Moyamensing Prison, where he is held on charges of murder, and placed on trial first for punching a garage man and then for 'sticking up' a motorist.

"Murphy was convicted of assault and battery and sentenced to six months' imprisonment. He was acquitted of assault and battery with intent to kill and carrying concealed deadly weapons. He was immediately placed on trial on the charge of holding up a motorist at 46th and Chestnut Streets and was acquitted.

"L. R. Baker, proprietor of a garage at 57th Street above Chestnut, identified Murphy as one of the two men who held him up on the morning of April 30. Baker gave a hair-raising account of motor piracy on West Philadelphia streets. Murphy laughed heartily while Baker was testifying. He continued to smile when Baker said he could not be mistaken in his identification."

While other witnesses for the defense, unsavory characters at best, alibied Murphy, it was of vital importance for Chippy to break down this strong witness for the prosecution. He had to consider the probable effect a conviction here would have later when Murphy faced a jury on a charge of murder. If a Commonwealth witness could be discredited and Murphy acquitted, it would prove Chippy's contention that, as the *Record* quoted him, ". . . trying my client on a minor charge shows the police case against Murphy in the murder accusation must be weak."

On cross-examination Chippy made Baker repeat his story. He told it with great confidence. There was no doubt in his mind, he reiterated, that one of the hold-up men was Murphy, whom he identified by his bright red hair. The other thug, Baker said over and over again, was tall and thin.

"You're sure you couldn't be mistaken about either, Mr. Baker?" Chippy asked.

"No, *sir,*" the garageman answered emphatically. "I'll always remember to my dying day the faces of the guys who pulled guns on me and said they'd blow my brains out if I didn't hand over my dough. I'd *never* make any mistake about that."

"Never, Mr. Baker?"

"Never," answered the witness.

Chippy then recalled Chief of Detectives James "Shooey" Malone to the stand. Malone felt he had a good idea of what was coming. "That witness was so damned sure of himself," he said. "I only wish Morrie Speiser could have figured out Chip's next move, because Murphy was a bad actor and he should have been burned. The son-of-a-bitch killed Carpentier deliberately. No question about that. Murphy and the 'boys' hadn't the slightest intention of shooting the watchman, otherwise they'd have blasted him right away.

"The plan was to bump Carpentier off and send the body back to New York. Somebody was going to deliver it right to Madden's doorstep with a note so he'd know, even if Mickey Duffy was in jail, nobody else was going to take over.

"Well, Chip got me on the stand and asked the usual questions like was I chief of detectives, my reputation, etc., and all the time I'm waiting for the lead-in. Finally it came.

" 'Have you ever committed armed robbery, Mr. Malone?' he asks.

"Up jumped Morrie Speiser. 'I object!' he screamed.

" 'Objection sustained!' Judge Audenreid said, very angry, and he bawled the hell out of Chip for trying to impugn my character. I knew damned well Chip wasn't trying to do that. We were good friends every place except in the witness's box. He ordered Chippy to apologize to me. Chip did that very gravely, but he gave me a slight wink. Then came the next one.

" 'Have you ever been *accused* of armed robbery?'

"The D.A. was up on his feet in a second. 'I object!' he shouted at the top of his voice.

"This time Audenreid went white with anger, and his lips trembled. I thought he'd never be able to control himself. He tongue-lashed Chip and said he ought to hold him in contempt and couldn't understand why a lawyer of

Patterson's reputation would deliberately incense the Court for no apparent reason. Maybe the reason wasn't apparent to them, but it was to me. Chippy stood in front of the bench with his head bowed and never said a word. His Honor finally cooled off and looked over at me and did what Chip planned all along.

" 'Mr. Malone,' he said, 'I'd hate to have anyone in this courtroom think for a single moment you would have had the slightest hesitation in answering either question asked by counsel for the defense. I know as well as Mr. Speiser and Mr. Patterson what your answers would be.'

"I thanked the judge and hoped he'd let it go at that, but he didn't.

" 'Well then, Mr. Malone,' he said, 'over the objections of the district attorney I'm going to permit you to reply. Mr. Speiser may take an exception, and it will be so noted on the record. Go on, Mr. Malone.'

" 'I've never committed armed robbery, Your Honor,' I answered and thought that would stop His Honor. Whatever tension was built up in the room broke then. But the judge couldn't let well enough alone.

" 'Have you ever been *accused* of armed robbery?' he asked, and I had to answer, 'Yes.'

" 'By whom?' asks His Honor.

" 'By Mr. Baker,' I said.

" 'The witness Baker?' says the Judge.

"Up jumped Speiser again. 'I object!' he yelled.

" 'Sit down, Morrie,' ordered Audenreid. 'Go on, Mr. Malone.'

" 'Yes sir,' I said, and the Court said, 'Tell us the occasion.'

" 'During the line-up, Judge,' I answered. 'I stood up with about seven or eight men who answered the general description of the second man.'

"Chip was on his feet now, and the judge didn't interrupt him. 'Exactly what did Mr. Baker say, Mr. Malone?'

"I looked up at Judge Audenreid, and he nodded his head.

" 'Mr. Baker picked me out right away and said,

"That's the man. I'll always remember to my dying day the faces of the guys who pulled guns on me. . . ." ' "

The jury stayed out of the box less than half an hour before bringing in a verdict of "not guilty." Murphy was sent back to Moyamensing to await trial for the murder of Wilfred Carpentier. This was held February 25, 1920, and Mr. Minnick's services as an expert on appeals were not used. A confused jury gave "Reds" his freedom, and the gangster once more was returned to society and Chippy's Saturday fishing parties at Corson's Inlet.

There was no chance of an appeal, however, from a bullet fired into Reds' heart by John Ruth, a watchman, October 4, of that same year. Murphy was buried with full honors, and C. Stuart Patterson, Jr. was one of a dozen distinguished honorary pall-bearers.

A touching note of gratitude for a job well done is to be found in the *North American*'s obituary.

"Among the floral tributes which filled five motor cars," said this newspaper, "was a harp of flowers sent by Mickey Duffy, who is serving five years in the Eastern Penitentiary."

On January 2, 1921, Orphan's Court probated the will of Nurse Johnson, who died December 20, 1919, after more than 50 years of service in the Patterson household. She left Chippy, her favorite, $1,000, with the proviso that it be spent under Eleanor's direction. Nora promptly took her brother out of Broad Street Station, leased an office for him a few doors away from the Philadelphia Club, and paid a year's rent in advance. Chippy moved his residence from the Hotel Stenton to a two-story row house on Walnut Street, some five or six miles to the west.

CHAPTER 34

MANY STRANGE PEOPLE hung about the streets of the city in those days, "characters" to most Philadelphians, but friends and often non-paying clients of Chippy's. Because they were constantly exposed to the public and missed little of what went on in the city's streets, some of them became Chippy's unofficial "runners" and the number of cases they referred to him was considerable.

One such "character" was the "potholder lady," seen over the years, 45 of them, by millions of Philadelphians. To most passers-by, many of whom remembered her from their own childhood, she was merely a dowdy old woman, always dressed in black satin, who sold her products on a spot near the southeast corner of 13th and Chestnut Streets. Like the "giant" sandwich man who walked up and down Market Street advertising typewriters, people took the potholder lady for granted and "saw" her only when she was there no longer. But to Chippy she was Mrs. Henrietta Broadbent, a person and a friend. When she needed money for a stay of eviction from her home she got it from Chippy, who at the time was practicing his profession without benefit of office.

Arthur Brooks, the original "lavender man," a childhood polio victim, was another. For 30 years he sat, rain or shine, perched on his stool in front of 1600 Chestnut Street, box filled with lavender—"It keeps your clothes sweet and pure"—hung from his shoulder. Brooks, as Chippy but few others knew, was an omnivorous reader of the classics, many of which were given him by Chippy. Busy as Chippy was, he never passed Brooks without pausing for a moment to play a game which, 30 years or so later, became "Information Please." Chippy would call out, "What was the name of Silas Marner's golden-haired foundling?" or "Give me the last line in *The Mill on the Floss.*" With no hesitation Arthur would grin and answer, "Eppie," or "In their death they were not divided."

Ikey Pinwheel was another friend of Chippy's, his protector against crude wardheelers and committeemen who regarded the "hot foot" as the quintessence of humor. Ikey was gentle, harmless, and probably not very bright. His ears were large, thin, and protruded so far that his contemporaries swear they actually flapped in a high wind. During the day, he operated a quicklunch stand (one of eight which flourished in City Hall until 1927) on the southeast corner of the sixth-floor corridor near Central Police Court. At night he hung around the fringes of the underworld and became its messenger.

Despite his limited mentality he was a better businessman than his hero, C. Stuart Patterson, Jr. Frequently a man or woman, unaccustomed to the courts and in need of an attorney, would wander aimlessly along the sixth-floor corridor and finally approach Ikey behind his counter, asking him if he knew a good lawyer. "Have you got fifty bucks on you?" was Ikey's first and only question. If they answered affirmatively, he referred them to Chippy. If they said "no," Ikey shook his head sadly and sent them on their way.

City Hall has four giant archways through which pedestrians must pass in order to continue in a direct line north and south on Broad Street or east and west on Market. Quite recently, in keeping with Philadelphia's program of municipal face lifting, an effort was made to brighten City Hall both inside and out, although business goes on inside almost, but not quite, as it did under the Republicans. But for years, naked, low-wattage bulbs hanging from the vaulted ceilings did little to dispel the perpetual twilight inside these dark and musty corridors. Three of the high, gloomy tunnels, untouched by the sun except at their outer edges, lead into the Hall itself.

The fourth, the one facing South Broad Street, goes nowhere except into the courtyard. The doors here, through which access was gained to a front-floor corridor, have been bolted shut for no one knows how many generations. Even the pigeons which flit through all the other archways seem to shun this one, and its stone gargoyles, hidden beneath the tall columns which help block out the light, remain unfouled. Sometimes pedestrians, squinting after a plunge from sunlight into the semi-darkness of the fourth corridor, are dimly aware of a man standing motionless there in the shadows, partially concealed by one of the stone columns. Chances are they are looking at Nick Hayes, who has made this depressing spot his headquarters for almost a half-century.

Nick looks more than a little like the late W. C. Fields, same eyes, same nose, less bulbous perhaps, and same coloring. A neatly folded newspaper protrudes from each of Nick's overcoat pockets. Summer and winter he wears a shiny black derby, green at the rim; high starched piccadilly collar, about which is tied a bright green bow; nondescript trousers; gray spats; and patent-leather shoes. A wet, half-chewed cigar stump usually sticks out of one corner of Nick's mouth. Nobody knows exactly what Nick does. Some of the working press think he used to be a newspaper man himself, and there are stories he was a tipster for the *Sunday Transcript,* Clem Congdon's scandal sheet. While his name was never on the masthead, a few reporters believe he actually was this paper's copublisher. At one time he edited a boxing news tabloid. He's not a "runner" or a numbers writer, nor does he engage in any illegal activities.

Nick is hardly one to talk about himself or anyone else, and a conversation with him can be a highly frustrating experience. In the first place he volunteers nothing, and the introduction of chit-chat and small talk—sports, politics, the weather, sex—is greeted with a distant stare from Nick's cold, blue eyes. In the second place, and this becomes most disconcerting, he pauses for long periods of time in the middle of his sentences.

You join Nick in his shadows of the fourth corridor and ask, "Did you know Chippy Patterson well?" and he answers, "Yeh! I knew him for twenty-five years. He used to . . ."

You stand and wait while Nick looks around, not furtively or any other way. He just looks around. The seconds go by and they seem like minutes. You think he's forgotten all about you when suddenly he continues, ". . .

play billiards at Joe Payne's Pool Room on North Eighth Street. He was a real expert, and one time I remember . . ."

Now you're sure you've got Nick going, but he doesn't even bother to conclude the one sentence. You wait again. After the recess he goes on, ". . . he amazed a crowd there by taking five racks without a miss."

You think that if Nick leaves his normal habitat he might be more communicative, and you both walk to the nearby Automat for a cup of coffee. You cross Market Street, and on the way you're surprised at the number and variety of people—cops, lawyers, racketeers, reporters, ministers, prostitutes, judges, and pimps—who know your companion well enough to say "Hello, Nick." This only adds to the confusion. H & H is no better and may even be worse because now Nick pauses not only in the middle of his sentences but also in between sips of coffee. It takes a long while and a considerable amount of patience to extract from Mr. Hayes the fact that "Mr. Patterson was a . . ." (several glances about the basement restaurant, two or three sips of coffee, a rest of about eight bars) ". . . great friend of Bill Fallon."

In much the same manner you find out from Nick that Mr. Patterson was a chain smoker on Rameses #2 cigarettes; that he went fishing with a crowd of reporters, assorted gunmen, lawyers, and court attachés every Saturday at Corson's Inlet; that the girls were crazy about him; that he (Nick) once persuaded a landlord to give Mr. Patterson a couple of rooms and got him off the streets; that the Olney Bank case broke Mr. Patterson's heart; and that the greatest victory Mr. Patterson ever won was . . . (and now I could almost feel the perspiration rolling down my forehead as I waited and waited and waited) . . . the Peter Treadway case.

"Head battered in," said the *North American* of Tuesday, November 23, 1920. "The body of Henry Peirce, a well-known businessman, was found yesterday morning in a small apartment he had just rented on Market Street. . . . A heavy wrench, believed to have been the murder weapon, was found nearby. The only clues are that a plump girl was the last person seen with Peirce and that his automobile disappeared. Because of the peculiar shape and color of the car (this was an understatement), it would be recognized anywhere.

"The room bore no evidence of a struggle. Peirce's body was found lying on the floor by Patrolman Sloan. The position indicated the murder might have been committed by someone who sprang from behind the door as Peirce entered the room. Sloan claimed the gas was turned on full in a small gas radiator as if the slayer, not content with battering his victim's head, relied upon gas to make death certain."

It was discovered that $100 in cash, a diamond stickpin, two watches, and a Masonic ring were missing. Peirce had been a successful industrial engineer, the father of five sons, and police had no trouble tracing his movements up to 11:30 on Saturday night, when he was seen to enter the apartment back of his office through the office door in company with a woman and one or two men. Neither Detective Belshaw, head of the murder squad, nor his aides, were able to find anyone who saw Peirce after that time.

Peirce had recently rented the apartment; if his intentions were such as might displease his wife, at least he was no sneak. "His car, an underslung Stutz Bearcat," said the *Evening Ledger,* "was equipped with a boat-shaped body and painted bright red."

Dr. William Wadsworth, coroner's physician, revealed Peirce had 25 head wounds and six fractures of the skull, enough, he added, "to kill six men."

Interrogation of scores of men and women resulted in suspicion pointing to Peter Treadway, a casual acquaintance of Peirce, and two or more companions. On Wednesday following the murder, Treadway and Susan "Boots" Rogers were taken into custody in a Wheeling, West Virginia, rooming house. The third man, Joseph Moss, was caught in Pittsburgh three days later. The fourth member of the quartet, Marion Elliotte, was not apprehended until six years later.

Since the killers had refused to give up Peirce's hardly

inconspicuous automobile although they must have known it could lead only to disaster, their movements were easy to trace. After leaving Peirce's body where it fell, the quartet rushed downstairs and piled into their victim's car. They stopped at each member's furnished room to pack suitcases, then all four drove to a West Philadelphia garage to fill the tank with gasoline.

This was no car full of morose guilt-ridden murderers. On the contrary, the quartet, fortified by bootleg whiskey, acted like a party of jolly picnickers. Gleefully Susan offered a drink "right off the boat" to Michael Hawkins, who serviced the car at pumps outside of his garage. He refused, but a passing policeman accepted Boots' generous gesture. Moss, described as a "swarthy Levantine," was also in a gay mood. He kept singing verse and chorus of "Ireland Must Be Heaven Because My Mother Came From There."

Even the ride to Baltimore, where they pawned Peirce's jewelry, and the trip west over the Cumberland mountains through a raging snowstorm, were accepted with good humor. "Most of the way," said Boots, "the men kidded me about Peirce. They said I had killed him after he'd made love to me and teased me about which was more fun."

A slightly petulant note reached Miss Rogers' ears as they entered Morgantown. "It was either Moss or Elliotte," she testified at the trial, "I don't know which, but somebody in the back seat said Peirce was the hardest bastard to kill they had ever seen."

The trial was begun the morning of March 15.

"Treadway, the first of the three defendants to be brought into the courtroom," said the *North American*, "strode to his seat behind his counsel, C. Stuart Patterson, Jr. and Thomas J. Minnick, Jr., and sat down with an air of self-assurance. Behind Treadway came Susan Rogers with the same I-don't-care-what-happens attitude that characterized her appearance when she was first arraigned. Moss was a somber figure in a dark suit. There was a scowl on his face."

In his opening address Speiser quietly but methodically

described Peirce's death and the actions of each participant. He declared he would prove (as he did to the satisfaction of everyone but the jury) that the murder was premeditated. Since it was clear that defense strategy would attempt to throw the blame for the actual killing on the missing Elliotte, Speiser had to forestall this by making Elliotte and Treadway equal partners in the murder itself. At the same time, because the girl and Moss had turned witnesses for the Commonwealth, he must prevent resentment against them for "ratting."

"We will prove to you," said Speiser, "that Peirce first opened the door leading to his private room, and the girl, then Treadway, followed him in. Treadway then motioned to Moss and Elliotte, loitering outside by prearrangement, and as they were going up the stairs, Treadway gave a revolver to Elliotte.

"Elliotte struck Peirce with a blackjack and then beat him so hard repeatedly with the butt end of the revolver that the rubber pieces on the handle flew off. Moss and the girl left the room, leaving Treadway and Elliotte with the stricken man, Treadway placing a towel over the victim's head and turning on the gas to make his death more certain."

At this point, according to the *Public Ledger,* "a shudder of horror swept the courtroom as jury and spectators looked at Treadway with utter revulsion."

Commonwealth witnesses traced the movements of each participant in the crime, from the beginning of Peirce's last night on earth until the criminals' capture several days later. With the exception of that half hour during which the murder was committed, Speiser accounted for every minute of the prisoners' time.

A sensation the fourth day of the trial was the appearance of Boots Rogers on the stand as a witness for the prosecution. This was the important witness Chippy and his associate Minnick, seated by Treadway's side, had to break. The *North American* said:

"The hush that pervaded the courtroom was absolute as she began the dramatic recital—dramatic because she made it so—of her meeting with Treadway, the murder of Peirce, and the wild automobile flight. . . .

"She told how, on the night of the murder, she and Treadway went to a movie, bought some newspapers, and returned to their apartment at 11:30 . . . how Moss and Elliotte came to the house and insisted they go to a café . . . how they met Peirce . . . who waited in his automobile on Walnut Street. . . .

" 'Peirce drove us around to his room . . . and we went upstairs—to the third floor,' the girl said. 'Peirce went in first, I followed, and then Treadway. There were three empty glasses on the table in the room and Peirce poured Treadway a drink and one for me. Treadway said I must drink it to be sociable, so I did.

" 'Peirce then filled the glasses a second time, but he got sick and had to go to another room. . . . Peirce came back immediately and insisted on having a third drink, despite Treadway's plea that he better lie down.

" 'Just as Peirce said, "Let's have another," in walked Elliotte and Moss, Elliotte with a revolver in his left hand and a blackjack in the right.

" ' "Hands up!" Elliotte said to Peirce, but Peirce either didn't hear him or thought he was joking because he didn't put up his hands. Then Elliotte hit him over the head with the blackjack, sending Peirce's glass of whiskey flying across the room. I screamed and covered my face with my hands. I ran out of the room.

" 'Moss followed me and took me back to the apartment. I was lying on the bed and Moss was sitting on the side when a half hour later Treadway and Elliotte came in.

" 'Treadway said, "Up kid, we're going west. Don't argue. Get your things on. Quick!" ' "

It was obvious that Boots' testimony had a telling effect on the jury, and Chippy tried to break it down. After hours of grueling cross-examination, she admitted she might have been mistaken about the ownership of the murder weapon; which at first she said was Treadway's. This was the only point the defense scored with Boots. As it turned out, the gain was important, and the jury in its deliberations weighed this carefully.

On the fifth day of the trial, Treadway went to the stand. He remained there with an air of confidence for three and one half hours. He described in detail the events preceding the actual slaying, claiming that after Elliotte had begun to beat Peirce, he (Treadway) pleaded with him to stop. But Elliotte, who he claimed was under the influence of drugs, said to him, "Shut up or you'll get the same."

Chippy closed for the defense immediately after Treadway stepped down.

"Where is the proof," asked Chippy, addressing the jury, "that Treadway entered into the conspiracy with Eliotte? All the inconsequential details in the case, all the evidence of the flight after the crime—there was no necessity for that. Treadway said that he went away after the crime. The district attorney said Treadway fled because he was guilty of murder, that Susan fled because she was forced to, and Moss—well, they don't explain why *he* fled.

"I'll tell you. They all fled because they all were guilty of something—they stole that automobile belonging to Peirce; they all stole it, and fled in it. They could have been brought here and indicted for stealing that car, but that is no question in this case. They might all have fled with Elliotte and helped to carry the booty—but that does not fasten the guilt of this crime."

Chippy traced the movements of the quartet up to the time they fled. Then he belabored the district attorney for telling the jury neither Moss nor Susan had anything to gain by their testimony.

"My friend, Mr. Speiser, tells you that Moss is an innocent man and that he has nothing to fear and nothing to gain. He forgets how you, the jury, were selected. He says you are proud and intelligent—yet he insults your intelligence by telling you Susan and Moss have nothing to gain when they have been indicted for murder and may be tried by this same gentleman for their lives."

Chippy pilloried Boots' statement that she identified the

murder pistol (testimony which she later admitted was false) and brought out the fact police could find no trace of the gun.

It took Chippy nearly two hours to bring his summation to an end, but during the entire time, said the *Evening Ledger*, "the jury and all the rest listened with rapt attention, their eyes never straying for a single moment from this tall, eloquent and earnest gentleman pleading so desperately for his client's life.

" 'Will you brand this defendant with the taint of a felon,' asked Patterson, 'and send him to the electric chair on the testimony of Moss, whom Mr. Speiser calls a drunken, maudlin fool, and Susan Rogers, both of whom are seeking their liberty?

" 'In the name of justice I ask you men to ask yourselves if the Commonwealth has proved a conspiracy to rob Peirce. Try this on your conscience, and don't let that conscience turn back on you in the still watches of the night.' "

Speiser's rebuttal was brief. He tried to shatter the pleas of defense for sympathy with the declaration that "the state is not seeking a victim, nor should the jury seek a victim."

"Judge Audenreid," said the *North American*, "in his charge pointed out that while nobody saw Treadway hit Peirce, it has been argued that no *one* man could have inflicted as many blows as were indicated on the victim's head and face. The case of the Commonwealth does not rest entirely on the claim that Treadway personally inflicted the violence.

" 'If Treadway was concerned in the commission of the robbery, he is just as guilty of Peirce's death, even if he didn't strike him, as the man whose blows brought Peirce's death about. As to Treadway's share in the murder it has been testified he was present at the killing; that he remained in the room while Peirce was killed, and that he said after the killing, "We killed him and I turned on the gas." Treadway also participated in the theft, shared in the proceeds of this theft, and was wearing a stolen suit of clothes belonging to the dead man when he was arrested.' "

Judge Audenreid declared a recess until 2:30. It was obvious to experienced courtroom observers that His Honor, sensing an atmosphere of guilt, expected a verdict to be returned by then. But the time came and went and the jury was still out. At 4:31 P.M. the panel filed back to the courtroom and the foreman announced a verdict had been reached.

"Guilty of murder in the second degree," he stated in a firm voice.

"With brows lowered," said the *North American,* "Treadway received the verdict without the move of a muscle. . . . On the way to the elevator, the defendant was visibly elated and threw his arms about counsel's neck crying, 'J . . . .! I feel like a new man.' "

His Honor's reaction was quite different. Face flushed with anger he turned to the jury and exclaimed, "Gentlemen, don't ask me what I think of this prisoner's guilt. Someday you will be sorry for what you have done!"

Judge Audenreid sentenced Treadway to not less than 19 years and six months nor more than 20 years in Eastern Penitentiary.

On March 30, Moss went on trial before the same judge. By direction of the Court he was acquitted of murder, but after pleading guilty to being an accessory after the fact, was sentenced to a term of two years at Eastern Penitentiary. Boots went on trial March 31, 1921, and was found "innocent" of all charges. "I vamped the jury!" she exclaimed as she was turned loose into the arms of her waiting husband.

Elliotte was captured in Detroit, July, 1927, and brought back to Philadelphia. He was found guilty of murder in the first degree with a recommendation of mercy and sent to Cherry Hill for a term of what is known optimistically by the People as "life."

This by no means wound up Treadway's career. He lived to make those members of the Peirce jury still alive in 1934 regret their decision. He was released after serving only ten years. As soon as he gained his freedom he left Philadelphia and got a job in a Cleveland gasoline station. After a series of minor crimes, less than two years out of prison, he kidnapped, raped, and murdered Mrs. Ruth Gillmore Steese, a Cleveland social worker. He was caught, tried, and convicted. On June 1, 1935 he was executed in the electric chair at Columbus.

In Chippy's old rolltop desk, which Ben Zion has in his apartment, are two of the very few physical remembrances of C. Stuart Patterson, Jr. One is a limp-leather edition of *The Short Stories of Robert Louis Stevenson* with Chippy's inscription scrawled on the flyleaf, "To Ben—*Semper Fidelis*"; the second is an envelope containing $1,000 in Confederate money. The latter, Ben explained, was all defense counsel ever received for representing Peirce's killer.

"I began to work for Mr. Patterson the day the Peirce case ended, and when it was over he came back from City Hall, tossed the bills to me, and said, 'Here's my fee, Ben. You keep it as a souvenir.' Then he grinned and looked down. 'I wonder what ever happened to the good five-dollar bill it was wrapped in. We could have used that, couldn't we?' "

CHAPTER 35

BEN ZION was the third, last, and most devoted of Chippy's major-domos. He stayed with him through the final, chaotic period of Patterson's life; ran his errands; looked up the law; entered his appearances in court; protected his health, or tried to; fought his landlords; operated his office; collected his debts; stalled his creditors; kept his jealous mistresses apart; and when the end came, watched him die.

Ben is short and slight, the son of poor Orthodox Jewish parents. He was born and raised in South Philadelphia, and he has earned his education the hard way—night high school, evening classes through college, and finally, Temple Law. Like his predecessor, Happy Phillips, Ben was a Western Union messenger boy when Chippy met him.

"Better say I was an ex-messenger boy when Mr. Patterson handed me a job. W.U. was on strike, back in the spring of nineteen twenty-one, and I was out of work. We got seventy-five cents for a twelve-hour day, and we wanted a buck. But they said 'no.' At any rate I was trying to get upstairs to the second floor of Broad Street Station where the office I worked out of was located. My bike was there, and I wanted it, but there'd been some violence, paint throwing or something, and the police wouldn't let us through. One of the cops standing at the Fifteenth Street entrance was giving me a hard time when Mr. Patterson walked up. I knew him from delivering messages, he was a big tipper, and he remembered me.

" 'What's the matter, son?' he asked. I told him. He turned to the policeman. 'Let him through, Joe, will you?' The cop said, 'It's all right with me, Mr. Patterson, but he'll only get inside as far as the stairs. The railroad dicks won't let him up.'

"Mr. Patterson put his arm around my shoulder and the cop opened the door for both of us. We bypassed the steps and walked over to the elevator, which we weren't ever allowed to use. There was a plainclothes policeman named Edwards in front of it.

" 'Hello, Mr. Patterson,' he said.

" 'Hello, Bert,' Mr. Patterson answered. 'We'd like to go upstairs.'

" 'Please don't ask me to let the kid up. I could get fired. Your father's orders, Mr. Patterson. No strikers, he said. It ain't as though he's against the boys. None of us are. Just don't want any claims against their railroad if there's trouble.'

" 'Ben's no striker, Bert. He needs his bike. He works for me. My office, you know, is temporarily upstairs,' he said with a smile.

"Bert grinned, the elevator doors opened up, and well, that's the way it started. Lots of times I took home less pay to my mother than what I was striking for, but I wouldn't swap those next twelve years for anything in the world. Then again, there were days I'd walk out of the office with a hundred dollars in my pocket, which was something for a kid of eighteen. 'Your back pay, Bennie,' he'd say when a 'fat' client came through, which happened once in a while."

Shortly after Ben Zion began his association with the lawyer, Chippy, through a kind of barter arrangement, was able to reestablish his office, as well as set up new living quarters. A client, Harry Espinshade, referred to Chippy by Bill Fallon, had opened a Philadelphia branch of his New York bucket shop in the Ludlow Building. When he had more than two years to go on a three-year lease, paid in advance because of the nature of the business, the law caught up with him. Chippy was able to save him from doing time only by closing the shop and getting Espinshade to leave Pennsylvania's jurisdiction. Chippy's fee was a transfer of the lease, and as Espinshade moved out, Chippy moved in, safe from landlords for 31 months.

Philadelphia's best colored hotel at the time was at Thirteenth and Lombard Streets. Its manager, Asa Winters, grateful to Chippy for successfully defending a close relative, offered Patterson, in lieu of a fee, a third-floor corner room and bath for as long as he cared to stay. Chippy accepted gratefully and moved his few personal possessions from the Bellevue to the Evans.

The year 1921 was a good one for Philadelphians other than Chippy, to whom it brought temporary stability. Archbishop Dougherty was made a cardinal that March 7. C. Stuart Patterson, Sr., on May 23, was named to head a committee which feted Madame Curie, and on June 5, Patterson, Sr., with Senator Knox and the Union League, entertained President Harding. William T. Tilden, 2nd, lanky Germantown aristocrat, won the national tennis championship at Manheim Cricket Club, September 19. E. T. Stotesbury opened Whitemarsh Hall, his $5,000,000 palace modeled after Versailles.

But it was a bad year, a "panic" year, for the nation, and it brought unemployment and lowered wages to millions. It was a bad year for Mrs. Emma C. Bergdoll, mother of the infamous draft dodger. She was sentenced on May 17 to a year in jail and fined $7,000 for helping her son escape. It was a bad year for the schoolchildren of Philadelphia, whose right to be spanked by their teachers was upheld in a suit brought before no less a dispenser of justice than Magistrate Carney, September 30. And it was a very bad year for four Patterson clients who stood within the umbra of the electric chair at Bellefonte. Undoubtedly, since Chippy managed to save their worthless lives at the very last minute, things for this quartet were not so bad that they could not have been worse.

Two of the homicides were tried in January before Ben arrived, while the other pair of near misses came after his stewardship had begun, one in May and one in December. One client came so close to his execution that the chaplain had already followed on the heels of the prison barber. Another, who thought he was spending his last hour on earth some 38 years ago, is still alive.

The year got off to a poor start for Chippy. He lost the only two homicide trials he handled in January. The first was when he defended James Priest, charged with shooting his wife to death. Priest was found guilty of murder in the first degree with no recommendation of mercy. On April 28 Judge McCullen, sitting in Oyer and Terminer, sentenced him to die in the electric chair. This was the first major defeat Chippy had suffered in a homicide case, and he had no intention of letting the Commonwealth spoil his record.

In order to appeal for a new trial or stay of execution, notes of testimony were necessary, and since neither Chippy nor his client had money to pay for professional services, one of Ben Zion's first jobs was to copy in longhand—he couldn't type—hundreds of pages of the court stenographer's trial records. To accomplish this, Ben said he worked 72 hours without sleeping. The original date of Priest's execution was set for June 30, but Chippy's plea for a new trial delayed it until the following April 25. On April 19, Chippy succeeded in having Priest's death sentence commuted to life imprisonment.

The second of Chippy's 1921 defeats occurred when he defended six gangsters charged with murdering Michael Orsak, of Newark, New Jersey, the preceding June 1. Only one was found guilty of murder in the first degree with no recommendation of mercy, but on a retrial was found guilty of murder in the second degree. Chippy succeeded in getting second-degree sentences for all the other thugs.

Christopher Murrano, a "cop killer," was the third murderer who escaped the chair not once but twice, the second time after he had received last rites of his church and had his head shaved. Two juries found him guilty of murder in the first degree with no recommendation of mercy, and the State Supreme Court upheld the sentences. The first time, Murrano had less than 24 hours to go when Chippy persuaded Justice Shaeffer to grant him a stay of execution and a new trial. He was again sentenced to die in the chair. Then, 50 minutes before the death sentence was to be carried out, Patterson induced Governor Sproul to commute the sentence to life imprisonment. Murrano served 12 years in Eastern Penitentiary. When last heard from in 1957, he was spending his declining years in his native Sicily.

The last of Chippy's 1921 near misses was a double in which he shared honors with the famous team of Witkin and Egan, two of the shrewdest criminal lawyers in the city. Even the combination of Witkin, Egan, and Patterson wasn't enough to convince two juries that George Jaekel and Harry Lessner should not die in the electric chair for killing Isadore Rabinowitz, an innocent bystander in the holdup of a South Philadelphia jewelry store.

Both were found guilty of murder in the first degree with no recommendation of mercy. On February 1, 1922, they were removed to death cells at Bellefonte and scheduled to die two days later. On February 2, Jaekel was granted a new trial based on technicalities Egan had evolved. The execution of both prisoners was stayed. On May 2, the trio of lawyers had better luck with a jury that found Jaekel guilty of second-degree murder, and on May 19, 1922, Lessner's sentence was commuted to life.

In passing it might be noted that the fee, exclusive of costs, for the services of Witkin, Egan, and Patterson, was $30,000, a fair sum to pay for the lives of a couple of worthless characters. Witkin and Egan no doubt spent their share judiciously and, since each was generous, gave a fair measure to charity. Chippy, as usual, got rid of much of the $15,000 he received almost at once but managed to put enough aside to move out of the Evans; furnish a large apartment on Pine Street for himself and Virginia Wendell, the woman he was then living with; and carry on his brief but expensive romance with Jeanne Eagels.

CHAPTER 36

BEN ZION was talking about the women in Chippy's life.

"I don't know how many there were, and all I saw were beautiful, but there wasn't one, in my opinion, who could touch Virginia Wendell, the first I met," he said. She was a model and absolutely magnificent. Like most of the girls he liked—Jeanne Eagels was the exception—she was tall and very full-bosomed. She had jet-black hair, dark eyes, and an olive skin. She used only lipstick, but there was always a little color, a sort of flush, on her high cheekbones.

"He spent a hell of a lot of money on her—it must have cost ten thousand dollars to furnish the apartment—and yet I think she'd have been satisfied to stay with him any place at all. I guess he was fond of her in his own way, but that did not include marriage. Many a time she used to take me aside and say, half kidding, half serious, 'Ben, what can I do to make this permanent?' and I'd answer truthfully, 'I don't know.' And I didn't. Nothing, I suppose.

"All the time from nineteen twenty-two to about nineteen twenty-five or twenty-six, while he was living with Virginia, he had lots of others. He couldn't stay away from them, and they couldn't keep away from him. There was a young schoolteacher to whom I used to deliver messages. Then when he had his place on Pine Street, he'd take a room at the Bellevue and spend the night with a very attractive Chestnut Hill matron whose husband used to go to Europe a lot. I met her only once, and that was to let her know Chippy couldn't make it.

"There was a set of gorgeous twins who used to share Mr. Patterson between them in their aunt's apartment when she went away weekends. I can't tell you how many more—he had a woman with him even on his dying day—but as I said, they were all beautiful, only some more so.

"To get back to Virginia. She was jealous as hell and would have liked to scratch the eyes out of any women who ever looked at Chippy. They'd been living together for maybe a couple of months when Mr. Patterson met Jeanne Eagels, and for two weeks after that he didn't pay much attention to Virginia."

No great romance developed between Miss Eagels and Chippy. For the actress it was probably a brief and pleasant interlude with a man considerably older than herself. She was about twenty-eight when they met and he was her senior by nearly 20 years. He was obviously different from the usual run of "stage-door Johnnies" who besieged the slight, gray-eyed blonde. She was fascinated by his "performances" at City Hall, where Ben Zion took her to watch Chippy defend a murderer and where she created considerable stir herself.

They met the day after she opened as Sadie Thompson at the Garrick in Philadelphia, October 12, 1922. In the eyes of the Reverend Gordon Forney, Secretary of the Lord's Day Alliance (he never saw the show), *Rain* mocked religion and its practitioners, and apparently someone had clarified the meaning of "the hills of Nebraska" for him. Dr. Forney, backed by the Philadelphia Ministerium, demanded that the district attorney close the Garrick. The Garrick management, which would have benefited by a loud public protest against *Rain* providing it didn't force the show's closing, got in touch with Chippy.

The district attorney, Reverend Forney and his group conferred with Chippy, who represented the Garrick for this one occasion, an attorney whose name is lost to posterity representing Mr. Maugham, and Miss Eagels, who represented herself. She came along just for the hell of it. Whatever might be said about the Reverend Forney's methods of eliminating sin, no one could honestly question either his sincerity or his willingness to admit he could be wrong. The upshot of the meeting was that the Lord's Day Alliance withdrew its objections, a slight face-saving script change was made, and the show went on.

For the next two weeks, while *Rain* played to capacity houses, Chippy attended every evening performance and each night was Miss Eagels' supper escort. When there were no matinees, she watched him in Court.

Ben Zion's most pleasant recollection of the Eagels interlude was the last day she and Chippy were together. It was a Sunday, and almost the only public entertainment the Reverend Mr. Forney, who believed in strict adherence to Pennsylvania's Blue Laws, permitted, was a ride on the open Fairmount Park trolley. They took Ben with them.

"It was a very mild day for that time of the year," Ben recalled. "Eleven o'clock in the morning Buck Callahan picked me up at home in Mr. Patterson's cab and drove me to the Bellevue just as he promised me he'd do the night before.

"He was all dressed up. Chippy, I mean. Those two weeks *Rain* played he really went to town on clothes, but only in the evening. During the day in the office he looked like a bum, as usual, and I wonder what Miss Eagels thought when she saw him dressed that way the first time she went to court. But at night! It was tails and top hat and all that goes with them. He was really something! Philadelphians hardly recognized him when he walked down to his seat in the theater or afterward when they saw them together at the L'Aiglon or the Bellevue Roof. Or once when I know they drove down to the Brighton in Atlantic City.

"Well, the Sunday we went riding in the park he was

all rigged out in sports clothes from Jacob Reed's. Gray tweed jacket, a kind of a soft English hat, and wide brogues and knickers. He gave them to me the next day, the whole outfit. They were all too big to wear or have cut down to size, so I kept them around for a while, then sold them to an old-clothes man.

"Miss Eagels was staying at the Ritz across the street from the Bellevue, and we went over to pick her up. She was gorgeous. I can't remember how she was dressed, but she took your breath away. She was very sweet to me and didn't seem to mind a bit my coming along on the last day she and Mr. Patterson were to be together.

"Buck drove us up Broad and out to the park trolley stop at Thirty-Third and Dauphin Streets and parked his cab. Chippy said for him to wait and we went on the trolley. The trollies weren't very big and they rattled like Toonervilles. The conductor walked around the car on a little ledge, collecting fares with one hand and pulling the gong with the other. We used to wonder how he could balance himself without holding on while the trolley rocked up and down over the bumps. The car was filled. Looked like everybody in Philly wanted to get one last ride through Fairmount Park before the long winter set in, and those that got on our car were sure lucky.

"We sat in the back seat, and pretty soon Miss Eagels was singing and everyone joining in, even the conductor and motorman. They were having a wonderful time. They all knew who she was and Chippy, too. When we reached West Philly, nobody got off, and we came back to Strawberry Mansion with the same crowd we started with. We'd slow down on the curves and speed up along the straightaways, and Miss Eagels' long, blonde hair was flying in the breeze. People all along the right of way, children near the zoo, and men and women on horses, would wait beside the bridle paths to watch us whiz along.

"This must have kept up for a couple of hours, back and forth, back and forth, with the kids hopping off to comfort stations at each end of the line, and to buy hot dogs and sour pickles, while their parents held places for them 'til they climbed aboard again.

"After a while Mr. Patterson started to join in on the chorus. I didn't even know he could carry a tune. He used to say he wouldn't be caught dead at the Opera or at the Philadelphia Orchestra. He had a wonderful voice, a bass baritone. We wound up the afternoon with Chippy singing a solo, or at first it was a solo, before everybody started to sing it with him. It was pretty popular then. Called the 'Song of the Trolley.' It was written for those big, fast inter-urban street cars they used to have, not our dinky Toonerville."

Ben smiled at the recollection and continued.

"We sang it over and over again, verse and chorus, everybody did, and by the time we got off the car and people went to their homes, the words must have been imbedded in their minds. I'll bet a lot of the people on that particular car, especially the young ones, remember it and that ride to this day. I know I do."

He cleared his throat.

"Don't worry. I'm not going to try to sing it for you but these are the words.

> " 'I am coming, I am coming, hark you hear my
> motor humming,
> For the trolley's come to conquer, so you
> cannot keep it back;
> And Zip! the sparks are flashing, as the car
> goes onward dashing.
> While the wheels are whirring smoothly along
> a perfect track!' "

Rain moved from Philadelphia to Broadway to become the hit show of the decade, and Miss Eagels was its star. As far as Ben or anyone else knew, Chippy never saw her again, and when she died of a nervous disorder in 1929, he was a sick man himself. As an afterthought, Ben added that Miss Wendell was most unhappy about her estrangement from Chippy, even though it lasted only a couple of weeks.

"Actually she was furious, and she had a devil of a temper," he said. "I wasn't there when it happened, but one day, shortly after Miss Eagels went away and Mr. Patterson was back at the Pine Street apartment every night, he came into the office with his right hand bandaged. He laughed when I asked him what was the matter, and Virginia got red as a beet when I asked her. John Wickas, Mr. Patterson's favorite waiter at the Bellevue, told me."

The night before, Chippy and Miss Wendell walked into the main dining room together, Chippy clad in his usual raiment once more. There was always a question of where the captain should seat Chippy so if any other members of the family came in, they would not have to be embarrassingly close to him. Most of them ignored Chippy, and their young offspring weren't allowed to talk to him. A further problem was that Chippy had to have the best available table, and that, for him, was *never* near the orchestra which played dinner music.

As soon as the pair was comfortably seated, Chippy pulled out a cigarette, and the waiter, who was standing by his side waiting to take the order, lit it for him. Mr. Patterson, he added, seemed to be perfectly all right, but the girl appeared to be disturbed.

" 'There was something wrong there,' " Ben said Wickas told him. " 'She seemed okay on the surface, sat there tall and straight, but when you've been waiting on tables as long as I have, you get to sense things. The moment I lit that cigarette for Mr. Patterson, she reached over and pulled it out of his mouth. She took one puff herself—we didn't used to allow ladies to smoke in any of the hotel's public rooms—and then she held Mr. Patterson's hand in hers.

" 'She took that cigarette in her other hand and stuck it in his palm and kept it there. I shuddered and thought I'd get sick. I couldn't tear my eyes away. Mr. Patterson didn't say a word. You could smell the flesh burn, but he never moved his arm, and you could see the sweat pouring off his forehead. Finally, it seemed like an hour, although I guess it wasn't more than a minute, the woman lifted the cigarette from Mr. Patterson's palm, put it to her lips, took another puff, then squashed it on an ash tray.

" 'I didn't know what to do, and the girl was shaking like a leaf. I wouldn't have been surprised if she let out a scream, but she didn't. Mr. Patterson ate his dinner just like nothing happened, but I was so nervous I almost dumped the oysters on their laps. The next morning when he came in to breakfast his hand was all bandaged. I guess you knew all about that, Ben. I served Dr. Vaux, Mr. Patterson's cousin, that day for lunch and told him what happened. I hadn't gotten over it yet. I figured he'd treated the burn but that he hadn't been told the truth of what caused it. I was right. The doctor said Mr. Patterson's flesh was burned damned near to the bone. He carried that scar with him to the grave.' "

Sometime in 1922 Patterson's staff was augmented by Harold Gordon, a young university senior who was fired with ambition to practice criminal law. Chippy became his preceptor, and for three years Gordon gave Ben Zion a hand whenever he could. It was a strange office for an idealistic "junior" to begin a career, and what he learned helped him decide that the defense of criminals was not for him.

"The calm routine of a firm which handled only corporate law or even negligence might have sounded dull to me once," Gordon recollected, "but after a few mad years under the wing of Mr. Patterson it held a quiet charm I never realized existed. When I was a kid I used to dream of becoming a great criminal lawyer, saving innocent men and beautiful women from the chair.

"I pictured I'd have an impressive corner suite high up in the *North American* Building and a large staff. All the men in my Utopia would be rich, and the women grateful. From what I saw in the newspapers this was exactly the kind of life Mr. C. Stuart Patterson, Jr. was leading. When I'd get an hour or two to spare from work or class, I'd hurry down to the Hall and watch him. He was a real master of persuasion, and he played with the jury the same way I hoped I'd do some day. It's true his attire was odd, to say the least, but I figured this was some harmless eccentricity I wouldn't have to follow."

Gordon glanced unconsciously at his freshly pressed suit and newly shined shoes.

"One day I got up enough nerve to approach Mr. Patterson and ask him if he'd be willing to become my preceptor. The request, undoubtedly the first of its kind, must have startled him. He paused, looked down at me for a moment and said, 'Son, are you sure you know what you're doing?'

"When I look back now, I should not have been so certain of my answer. I told him I knew exactly what I was doing and that I'd rather work under him than any other lawyer in the city.

" 'Okay, son,' he said, 'tell the Dean to send me your papers and I'll sign them!' "

A few weeks later Gordon reported for work.

"I don't know what I expected, but when I knocked on the door and walked in timidly, it certainly wasn't what I got. The place was a shambles, filled with an assortment of characters, standing around or sitting on beaten-up old chairs. They'd have done Dickens proud. Each of them looked as if he could be guilty of practically every crime on the books. From what I learned soon afterward, they were.

"I was completely befuddled, looked around the room, and got ready to walk the hell out as fast as I could. A young little guy came over to me and introduced himself as Ben Zion. 'You're Harold Gordon, aren't you?' he said. 'Mr. Patterson's expecting you. He's in court now, but he'll be back in time to take you to lunch if you're free.'

"I stayed to lunch, and I stayed for three years after that. Maybe I'd have been better off if I had walked out that first day. Not that the experience wasn't fascinating. It was. But as for doing what I was supposed to do, learning the practicalities and ethics of the law, I wasn't. Nobody in the world practiced law like Mr. Patterson. I guess no one could. As for my ideals about the defense of the innocent! In criminal law you can't restrict your practice to those who are unjustly accused. If you did, you wouldn't have much of a practice. Damned few of those who came into Mr. Patterson's office were innocent. More murderers, dope addicts, abortionists, thieves, gamblers, rapists, whores, bootleggers, and so on were roaming about the streets of Philadelphia than there would have been if they hadn't retained C. Stuart Patterson, Jr. They'd have been where they belonged—in jail.

"I'm not trying to belittle Mr. Patterson. He was a great man and a tremendous lawyer, and when he died he left a gap which has never been filled. He had a very high standard of professional ethics. I'll tell you about an incident involving a guy whose name I recall was Joe Baily. It occurred shortly after I started to work for Mr. Patterson."

Until he was arrested for murder, Joe Baily was an unimportant professional thief. In the midst of an argument with his wife one day he rushed to the bedroom, pulled a loaded revolver from a closet shelf, and fired. His aim was poor. He missed Mrs. Baily and instead fatally wounded his five-year-old daughter. Following his arrest on charges of homicide, he asked Chippy to defend him.

"I was assigned to the investigation," Gordon said, "and I think Mr. Patterson could easily have gotten Baily an acquittal on the strength of the evidence I dug up. He'd beaten much tougher ones than this. We'd just about started the trial before Judge McDevitt. The jury'd been picked and locked up for the night and we were leaving the courtroom. A shady-looking guy walked over to Mr. Patterson, took him aside, and whispered something in his ear.

"I couldn't hear what was said, but I could see Mr. Patterson was getting angry and that was unusual. He brushed the man aside, pointed his hand at the exit. The guy left in a hurry, and Mr. Patterson walked to the bench. He told McDevitt the jury was 'spotted,' which meant one juror had been fixed. Mr. Patterson asked for a dismissal of the panel and withdrew from the case. It was a fine thing to do, and Harry McDevitt praised him for it."

Not too long after the Baily incident, and when Chippy

had become friendly with McDevitt, the judge was the innocent means through which Patterson was able to borrow money and at the same time outsmart a gambler he disliked. Chippy's victim was Richard "Dicky Boy" Kaelker, a blowhard, oleaginous racketeer who was always happy to bet on a sure thing, take a "sucker," or seduce a woman, and certain to brag about all his achievements afterward.

One day, as Thomas P. "Tip" O'Neil, who used to work for the *Record,* recalls, "Chippy was broke as usual and needed money to get someone out of a hole.

"Not for himself," Tip said thoughtfully. "He wouldn't have gone through such pains for that. He needed a thousand bucks in a hurry, and nobody in Philly with any sense would lend it to him, and the rest didn't have the thousand. That would have been like tossing money in the Schuylkill. You might recover it with a dredge, but the effort wouldn't have been worth it.

"This was about the time the Kaelker brothers first got into trouble, and they were worried. Afterward they got used to getting slapped down by both sides—the law and the associates they double-crossed. They were slick gamblers who'd bet on anything and wanted a hundred back for every buck they 'risked.' Chippy was riding high in those days, and the Kaelkers had been after him to represent them. But for some strange reason, Chip, who'd represented scummier clients than the Kaelkers, didn't want to and for a while kept sending them to John R. K. Scott.

"For all I know, maybe he'd already begun to represent them when he tried to touch Dick for the grand. Whatever retainer he might have gotten, you can be sure was spent, and I can imagine Dicky Boy saying, 'We'll see, Mr. Patterson. We'll see,' in the meantime having no intention of lending Chippy anything at all. Well, Chippy was bound to get that thousand, and so one afternoon he walked up to Harry McDevitt, handed His Honor $100 he'd gotten somewhere, and said, 'Judge, would you mind holding this for me? I'll need it later on, and I'm afraid I'll spend it.'

" 'Give it away, you mean, Chip,' McDevitt answered. 'All right. I'll keep it. Let me know when you want it.'

"The next day Chippy and Dick Kaelker were walking along the sixth-floor corridor when McDevitt got off the elevator.

" 'Good morning, Judge,' Chippy said, going over to him. 'Would you let me have fifty dollars?'

"I guess Kaelker must have gasped for breath at this kind of nerve, which even he didn't have. McDevitt, who used to work for the *Press* before he got into politics, had been around plenty, and even before he started his career on the bench, he had a reputation for being a tough skeptic.

" 'Of course, Mr. Patterson,' Harry answered, unbuttoned his hip pocket, removed his wallet, and counted out fifty dollars, which he handed to Chippy.

" 'Will that be enough?' His Honor asked.

" 'That will be plenty for the time, Judge,' Chip answered, and thanked him."

O'Neil stopped to chuckle before going on.

"Kaelker," he continued, "who was within earshot of the transaction, by this time was probably stupefied with shock. When he got his wind he must have said to himself, 'Now, I've seen everything. If a tough nut like McDevitt will lend him the dough, who the hell are the Kaelkers to say no?' And whereupon he turned to Chippy right before going into court and said, 'Was it a thousand bucks you wanted, counselor? Are you sure that will be enough?' "

Chippy had other ways of raising money when he needed it desperately, although not in such a large amount as he got from Kaelker. One method he developed, Tom Finney labeled the "Patterson beefsteak habeas corpus." Finney used to run the City Hall court "combine," an economical device operated by two men whose job it was to brief all Philadelphia city editors on the day's Hall activities so they could decide how best to distribute their limited staffs of reporters throughout the many courtrooms.

"The beefsteak habeas corpus was worked this way,"

Finney explained. "Suppose Chippy needed twenty-five or fifty bucks in a hurry. Well, Ben Zion would cull the list of clients down in Moko waiting trial, which might be several months ahead. They'd have some dough, not enough to pay for big bail, or it might even be they felt safer in prison than on the streets. But after a few weeks they'd be sick of the food and would give almost anything for a good meal. So Ben would talk to one of these guys and ask him how he'd like to get out for a day and eat whatever he wanted and probably get laid, too.

"All it would cost him, Ben would say, was fifty dollars for Mr. Patterson, exclusive, naturally, of what the prisoner spent on himself. He'd have to promise to be a good boy and surrender voluntarily within twenty-four hours. If he agreed, then Ben would report to Chip, who'd apply for a writ of habeas corpus before a judge. If the crime wasn't too serious, particularly if it was a bailable offense, no judge would take the trouble to refuse this opportunity for a prisoner to 'develop fresh evidence on his behalf.' So the writ would be granted, the district attorney's office notified, and a hearing set for the following day.

"In the meantime, Chippy got his fifty dollars, the prisoner was 'on the bricks,' had his steak, and everybody was happy. Naturally the petition would be knocked out the next day and Chippy's client back in Moko. But he'd had his fun, and waiting wasn't as tough as it might have been without that twenty-four-hour break."

Chippy handled 14 homicides in 1922 and won acquittals for five defendants and for the balance secured verdicts of less severity than the Commonwealth demanded. The only trial which might have been newsworthy ran into tough competition and was barely mentioned. On the day it opened, crime reporters, sob sisters, and photographers were all some 60 miles away to the north, outside of New Brunswick, New Jersey, where the Reverend Edward Hall and his lady love, Mrs. Eleanor R. Mills, the sexton's wife, were found murdered beneath an apple tree in De Russey's Lane.

Before that year ended two Philadelphians of note died. Chippy attended both funerals, highly unusual gestures for him. The first, November 22, was for his famous uncle, T. DeWitt Cuyler, retired chief counsel for the P.R.R., a man who, Chippy claimed, possessed "the most orderly legal mind of the generation." The second funeral, December 12, was for John Wanamaker, whom Chippy respected greatly and with whom he used to talk when they met infrequently in the store's first-floor bookstore where Chippy often read the books he did not have the money to buy.

CHAPTER 37

ON FEBRUARY 26, 1923, Philadelphians, whose tolerance for infractions of the law had been raised considerably by four years' exposure to prohibition, were startled out of their complacency.

"One of the most daring kidnapping cases in a long time," said the *North American,* "was that of Lillian Gilmore, six, and her sister, Dorothy, five, from in front of their home. . . about 3:30 o'clock yesterday afternoon.

"The children were playing when a man drove up in an old Ford sedan, grabbed the children, and threw them into the machine. Neighbors were attracted by the children's screams.

". . . About six o'clock last night, Dorothy was found wandering about the streets . . . in a half frozen condition. The little girl told her parents and police the man who put her and her sister into the machine had taken them for a long ride. Later, according to the little girl's story, the kidnapper returned to the vicinity of the home and put her out of the automobile. At the same time, Dorothy said, he assaulted her older sister."

The family's financial condition (Gilmore was a hatter and was supporting his wife and seven children besides Lillian) did not warrant, even momentarily, consideration of kidnapping for ransom. Lillian was still missing the following morning, and only then did police mobilize fully to search for her and her abductor.

"After an all-night search," the *North American* continued, "police arrested Wylie Morgan, of Maud, Texas, as the kidnapper, after little Dorothy had dramatically accused him of the crime. . . .

"Morgan, after his detention, was placed among twenty-five civilians, prisoners, policemen in plain clothes and detectives. Dorothy was asked to see whether she could find the man who took her away.

"Robert Gilmore, the father, held Dorothy in his arms as she moved along the line. She passed ten men without recognition. As she reached Morgan she shuddered.

" 'Pop, that's him,' Dorothy cried, pointing an accusing finger at Morgan.

". . . Later police let it be known that after they had taken Morgan into custody his clothing had been examined and blood spots were found on his trousers, undergarments and shirt.

"Morgan denied kidnapping the children. He gave alibis in which the police do not place much belief, but which they are checking."

None of Morgan's alibis held up, and detectives found blood stains on the seat of a friend's automobile he had borrowed. It was identified as the Ford sedan the two children entered.

Morgan admitted nothing. Despite constant grilling, day and night, he did not break. Lieutenant Belshaw placed him in a cell with an alleged dope peddler booked as "Barney Ford," who, in reality, was county detective Edward Hill. Within 24 hours the Texan not only admitted to Hill that he had killed Lillian but also expressed regrets he had not done away with her sister as well.

When Belshaw confronted Morgan with his revelations to "Ford," the Texan made a formal confession and agreed to lead police to the spot where he said they would find Lillian. A procession of six automobiles, filled with detectives, technical experts, reporters, and photographers skidded along streets glazed with ice from a freezing rain which began to fall at dusk. At Morgan's instructions, they stopped at a point some six miles north of Philadelphia. There Morgan led police to the place where he had thrown the child into Neshaminy Creek. In the cold dark they searched for and found the child's body. Her underclothing was drenched with blood.

When Morgan was returned to the police station, police had to rush him through a huge crowd gathered there, shouting for his death.

What position the defense would hold was prophesied in the *North American.*

"Lawyers who discussed the case," said this paper, "expressed belief insanity was the only defense that Morgan may invoke. Yesterday afternoon two alienists, at the request of Mr. Rotan, examined the prisoner in his cell at central station."

On March 12, less than three weeks after the crime, Morgan was arraigned before Judge Henry C. Quigley and pled "not guilty" to the charge of murdering Lillian De Haven Gilmore.

Chippy was in another courtroom trying a case on March 16 when he was called into Judge Monaghan's chambers in Quarter Sessions. He had been half-expecting the summons and was not surprised when Monaghan asked him if he'd represent Morgan.

"Nobody else will, Chip," the Judge admitted. "It's a tough one, I don't have to tell you, and Morgan's taken the pauper's oath, so there won't be much money."

Chippy smiled. "It doesn't matter, Your Honor. I'll take the case."

Monaghan told Chippy to choose any member of the Philadelphia Bar he wished for co-counsel.

Chippy chose Minnick.

Chippy spent several hours with Morgan in his cell at Moyamensing the next day.

"This man's not responsible for his actions, Tom," he told Minnick that evening. "He doesn't know what he's doing or why and is not oriented at all. I know he's not trying to put on any act with me. I'm going to talk to Kelley (the assistant district attorney) and Monaghan and see if we can't arrange to have Morgan committed to a mental institution."

Kelley's answer, as Minnick and Patterson fully anticipated, was an unequivocal "no!" Counsel pleaded with the district attorney, Rotan, to agree to a postponement of at least one month to give the defense enough time to prepare its case properly. But the public was deeply angered and demanded speedy "justice." The district attorney, subjected to enormous outside pressure, refused to go along with the request, and Judge Monaghan denied Patterson's and Minnick's formal plea for an extension.

The only possible defense, and on this Patterson and Minnick were in complete agreement, was insanity. A minimum of two alienists would have to be engaged to attempt to refute testimony of alienists hired by the prosecution. Then Morgan's background, antecedents, and family would have to be checked thoroughly. This was the kind of investigation which would require months of skilled research, backed by a considerable amount of money.

Morgan was unco-operative. Apparently incapable of remorse, he sat in his cell, day after day, staring at the walls in what seemed to Chippy like a state of catatonia. The day the indictment was handed down, counsel sent a telegram to Morgan's father, urging him to come to Philadelphia at once and bring with him any documentary medical evidence of mental disturbance in his son's past.

For five days Chippy and Minnick waited for an answer. They checked with Western Union and found the telegram had been delivered, but when they attempted to telephone Morgan's family, they were told the nearest telephone was miles away. On the eighth day there was a badly scrawled note from Wylie Morgan's father. He was sorry for what had happened to his son, he said, but since he was only a tenant farmer he had no money to come north or send anyone else. He hoped "kind friends would send his boy's body back to Maud to be buried."

"Well, Chippy, what do we do now?" Minnick asked.

"One of us goes to Texas," he answered, "as quick as he can."

" 'We tossed a coin,' " Ben Zion said Chippy told him, " 'and Minnick lost.' " The total fee and expenses allotted by the Court for Morgan's defense was $750; Minnick's trip cost $600. He spent three days interviewing Morgan's family, friends, and doctors and came back to Philadelphia five days before the beginning of the trial.

He brought back depositions showing Morgan had received a serious head injury when he was ten years old, but the family, according to a local doctor who treated the boy, couldn't raise $130 to pay a surgeon for a brain operation advised at the time. They added that Morgan "hadn't acted right ever since," that his mother had died in an insane asylum, and that a maternal aunt had been an inmate of a state mental institution for 25 years.

"If I could have brought the family doctor with me and a couple more witnesses and explored the family history of insanity further we'd have a case," Minnick advised Chippy. "Since I couldn't, we're going to have to be satisfied with what we have."

CHAPTER 38

WHEN THE TRIAL of the Commonwealth vs. Wylie Morgan opened, the prosecution called Dr. Wadsworth, coroner's physician, to refute Morgan's refusal to admit rape.

"Lillie Gilmore died as a result of a criminal assault," he testified.

Lillian's parents were next called to the stand. Her father burst into tears when asked to identify Lillian's clothing, and her mother, near fainting, had to be taken from the courtroom.

It was obvious to observers that the jury was deeply affected.

As the fifth day of his trial began, the only participant who seemed to be holding up well was the prisoner.

"Morgan has not been visibly affected," said the *Rec-*

ord. "No emotion can be seen on his face, and when any of the witnesses in the case makes a remark which seems funny he joins in the laughter of the spectators and jury."

Chippy and Minnick, said the *North American,* ". . . sought to bar testimony relating to the obtaining of the information which led to the finding of the body on the ground that the police had resorted to deception. The deception consisted in part of the signing of a copy of the charge by Lieutenant of Detectives William Belshaw, head of the murder squad, which Morgan, it was contended, was led to believe would get him his liberty if he disclosed what had been done to the child.

"After argument by Assistant District Attorney Kelley and defense lawyers, Judge Monaghan ruled the authorities had not resorted to 'fear or hope' within the meaning of the law relating to the inadmissibility of certain evidence.

"Lieutenant Belshaw, under cross examination, readily admitted he had resorted to trickery to find Lillian's body.

" 'I'd have told him anything to find that kid,' Belshaw testified. 'It's the first time in my life I ever tricked a defendant, but we wanted to find out where the child was.' "

The defense suffered another blow when Judge Monaghan, over Chippy's objections, permitted to be read into the proceedings the confession Morgan made to "Barney Ford," identified then as a policeman, county detective Edward Hill.

Morgan was aroused from his lethargy when he learned Hill's identity for the first time and heard the detective repeat, on the witness stand, the Texan's "confession" to him. Chippy objected strenuously and accused the Commonwealth of "making fraudulent representations to a defendant and then trying to take advantage of them." He was overruled. The Court also admitted into evidence a 45-page confession obtained by Major Wynne, chief of county detectives. It was brought out in direct testimony that when the major interrupted Morgan during his interrogation to ask him why he killed the child, the prisoner replied, "God knows. I don't."

Chippy never placed Morgan on the stand. Instead, Minnick read into the record the depositions taken at Maud. The jury was unimpressed, and although they may have been stirred by Chippy's eloquent plea to "spare the life of this mentally deficient boy," the panel had long before made up its mind.

Kelley's address to the jury was short and strong. He graphically described the manner of Lillian's death, repeated the most damaging parts of Morgan's confession, and hammered at the insanity angle. He demanded the death penalty. His Honor's charge was fair, and most of the 12 exceptions Patterson and Minnick noted later were tenuous.

At five o'clock in the evening of the eighth day of the trial, the jury retired. Four hours later they re-entered the courtroom, and David Tobin, the foreman, announced a verdict of guilty of murder in the first degree.

Chippy and Minnick, who had never left the courtroom from the moment the jury retired, waited hopefully for the phrase "with a recommendation of mercy," but it did not come.

Defense counsel filed the usual request for a new trial. This was denied, and on May 5, Judge Monaghan sentenced Morgan to die in the electric chair, August 25.

An appeal to the Supreme Court of the Commonwealth of Pennsylvania, paid for by Patterson and Minnick out of their own pockets, delayed the execution. It was rejected February 18, 1924, only a few days less than a year after the murder.

Morgan was re-sentenced to die the week of April 24. Chippy made a futile appeal to Governor Pinchot, who refused to commute Morgan's sentence to life imprisonment. On April 23, the Texan was removed to the Western State Penitentiary at Bellefonte, where he was placed in the death house. Chippy, his only visitor, spent several hours with him on the afternoon of April 27, but communication between the two was almost impossible.

Morgan seemed to be in a daze from which he could not be aroused. Chippy told Minnick when he came back to Philadelphia that evening, "He's a sick man, not a murderer."

Silently, as though in a trance, Morgan walked the 13 or 14 steps (that much publicized "last mile") from his cell through a narrow opening to a chamber containing the chair. In the presence of six witnesses and an equal number of newspapermen, Morgan was executed. An autopsy performed the next day revealed a massive brain tumor of long duration.

CHAPTER 39

EARLY on the morning of June 11, 1923, Arthur Stewart, a professional car thief and long-time client of C. Stuart Patterson, Jr., asleep in his lower berth "set out" at Broad Street Station, was awakened by the smell of smoke. He raised the heavy green shade and looked out the window. Before he could see what was happening, his car gave a sudden jerk, only a bit more powerful than the violent convulsions with which P.R.R. engineers traditionally begin their runs. Arthur, assuming this was the start of his trip to Pittsburgh, lay back and relaxed.

A few minutes later speed diminished. Then, with the usual slamming of brakes, the car came to an abrupt stop and Arthur's skull was thrown against the two pillows which he, a seasoned P.R.R. traveler, always placed for his protection at the head of the berth. Arms and legs braced in preparedness for anything, he waited tensely for the customary lunge. But the train did not move, and the sound of voices outside aroused his curiosity. Arthur slipped on his robe and stepped down from the car to join fellow passengers standing beside the motionless car and looking to the east. Huge flames lit a sky filled with billowing black smoke.

"George," he asked his porter, "where's the fire?"

"The whole Broad Street Station's going up in flames, Mr. Stewart," was the answer.

"My God!" exclaimed Stewart, stunned. "Now what will Mr. Patterson use for his office?"

There's one more story about C. Stuart Patterson, Jr. and the Broad Street Station fire, which burned for three days, cost $6,000,000, and overcame scores of fire fighters.

This one, which concerns a district "leg man" from the *Inquirer,* might be regarded as apocryphal if its source were not John "Cap" Cummings, a newspaperman of unquestioned veracity.

"Reynolds Moorhead was on the night desk," Cap recalls. "Moory was a rigid disciplinarian who rarely unbent, never lost his temper, and ran a city room full of hard-drinking newspapermen as though he was their stern unyielding guardian. One of his particular tribulations was George Dixon, now a distinguished columnist for the Hearst chain but then covering 'central' for us. His headquarters were the 19th District at 12th and Pine, and his beat was everything in mid-Philadelphia from the south side of Race Street to the north side of South Street and from river to river. In dead center of George's domain was Broad Street Station."

For the efficient gathering of news, Philadelphia used to be divided into six districts, north, south, west, northeast, northwest, and central, the last by far the most important. For example, a fire in the vast, unpopulated stretches of the great northeast might be brush burning on a vacant lot, but in downtown Philadelphia, where there are no vacant lots, chances were that even a one-alarmer in a hospital or a bank could turn out to be a front-page story.

District or leg men for morning newspapers went to work at 5 P.M. and went off at 3 A.M. after the last edition was put to bed. In order that the man on the desk could keep his finger on the pulse of the city at all times, leg men called in by telephone every hour, unless, of course, a story broke in their territory, and then they reported instantly. The job of the leg man was to gather the news and to turn it over as quickly as he could to a rewrite man. If, in the opinion of the city editor, the telephoned story warranted better coverage, a more experienced reporter and perhaps a photographer were dispatched to the scene.

A conscientious leg man covered his district—hospitals, firehouses, police stations, etc.—personally or by telephone seven or eight times each tour of duty. After he'd made his check he'd pick up any free phone he could put his hands on and call the desk. His manner of letting the "Man" know he was alive and sober, providing he had no news to give, would be, for example, "Lewis. South. Nothing." The deskman would answer, "Right," or "Okay," and each would hang up. Occasionally, either because the city editor wanted to spot-check his wandering leg men or perhaps because a tipster might have telephoned the paper with information of potential value and the story merited investigation, before hanging up after the leg man's terse call, the deskman might say, "Where are you? Give me your number and I'll call you back."

Fortunately for a fair proportion of the so-called working press who frequently wandered far from their assigned territories in search of greener fields, most of the communications between desk and leg men were purely routine.

A few minutes after 11 P.M. on the night of June 10, 1923, railroad firemen who'd been attempting to quell what they thought was a slight smouldering between tracks 11 and 12 decided the job was too much for them. They telephoned the city fire department for help. By 1 A.M., after fire alarms had been pulled, a fire in one of the largest railroad passenger terminals in the world was out of control. As Frank H. Weir of the *Inquirer* put it, "Flames raged through the cavernous shed, 300 feet wide and nearly 600 feet long, spreading along the floor, up the side walls along Market and Filbert Streets, and over the graceful arch of steel and glass, feeding on paint, the wooden deck planking, its covering of asphalt, the partial roofing of tar-coated wood, and oil that had dripped from cars and locomotives for decades.

"Twenty miles away, watchers thought they were seeing the flare of a Great Fire of Philadelphia that would rival London's of 1666. On the ground it was the firestorm in the shed, with its intense heat and the mad howl of its forced draft, that fascinated spectators. At one time 30 firemen lay stretched out, exhausted and all but smothered by the smoke. . . ."

Broad Street Station was well within Mr. Dixon's assigned beat, but he was nowhere in sight.

"Moory," continued Cummings, "hadn't heard a word from George for about six hours. He hadn't even bothered to call in. Naturally we knew about the fire without him, and one after another the Man sent every available reporter and photographer to Broad Street Station. Even the p.m. papers, which wouldn't be going to press for another eight hours, had reporters there. The city room was a madhouse. Typewriters were clacking away, and copy boys were running like crazy between the machines and the desk.

"We were on the streets with our first extra a little after midnight. They kept running new lifts every half hour. Papers were grabbed up right away by thousands of men and women lining Broad Street as far north as Erie Avenue, watching the flames and smoke and listening to the screams of fire sirens and ambulances. It was too hot for them to get closer than Arch.

"At exactly three A.M., in the midst of all the mad commotion in the city room, the Keystone on Moorhead's desk rings. It's George reporting. 'Dixon. Central,' he says. 'Nothing.'

" 'Hold it a minute, George,' Moorhead answered calmly. 'Where are you?'

" 'I'm in Broad Street Station, Mr. Moorhead.'

" 'What are you doing there, George?'

" 'I'm with Chippy Patterson. We're working on a Sunday feature.'

" 'Really,' said Moory quietly, watching a Philadelphia sky lit up as though it were morning. 'You better get the hell out fast, George, and take Mr. Patterson with you. The god-damned place is burning to the ground.' "

Although badly shaken by losing a client to the chair for the first time, Chippy recovered his poise sufficiently to defend 15 more murderers before the year ended, bringing his 1923 total to 28. Most of these were found not guilty; the balance went to jail for sentences ranging from six months to 12 years. Minnick's bad luck continued for at least another six months, and in December he had the misfortune to be beaten once more by Kelley. What was even worse than the Morgan case was that Minnick's client, while guilty of other gang killings, was innocent of the one for which he was executed. As it happened, the murder was committed by a client of C. Stuart Patterson, Jr.

"One of the unwritten laws of gangsterdom," recalled Walter Capelli of the *Bulletin*, "was that when one guy was arrested falsely, say for bumping off somebody, the real killer had to do everything in his power to help, save confessing. If the other guy went on trial, then the killer had to raise funds to hire the best lawyer he could get. And if the innocent man went to the chair, then the killer had to contribute to the support of the widow and take care of any kids she might have.

"Well, this client of Tom Minnick's, who must have machine-gunned half a dozen rival racketeers and dumped their bodies all over South Philly, was picked up for one he didn't do. He was tried, convicted, and sentenced to die in the chair. Chippy represented the real killer, who was never even questioned by police although Chippy had strong suspicions he knew a lot more than he'd say.

"This guy, whom I'll call Frank, was the tightest, cheapest creep in the world. He wouldn't part with a dime for anybody except himself. Nothing for Minnick and nothing for the wife and kids. Even when the appeal was turned down and the day for the execution set, Frank still didn't budge. Finally, the night before Minnick's client was scheduled to go to the chair, Chippy sent word for his client to come to the office. By now Chip was certain he was the murderer, but he had no proof and even if he had, I don't think he would have done anything. But he did expect Frank to live up to some of the self-imposed gangster obligations and was astonished when he didn't.

"He rebuked Frank in no uncertain terms and wound up saying, 'Aren't you going to do *anything?*'

"Frank looked downcast and embarrassed for a couple of moments, then his face broke into a smile.

" 'I'll go right down to St. John's, Mr. Patterson,' he replied, 'and light a candle.' "

Gangsters and subsequent gang killings, by-products of prohibition, became more and more integral parts in the lives of most American communities, and Philadelphia was no exception. Almost daily the "bloody angle," where Passyunk cuts across Washington Avenue, the railroad tracks, and Sixth Street in South Philadelphia, became a depository for machine-gunned bodies dumped there from speeding automobiles in the middle of the night.

Police on every level, for years forced to supplement starvation wages from the apple cart, were close enough to real money to smell it. All they had to do was to look the other way and ignore the activities of Max "Boo Boo" Hoff, the Lanzetti Brothers, and Mickey Duffy, who controlled the mobs which provided a thirsty metropolis with more liquor per capita than it ever consumed before the 18th Amendment was passed. Immunity on a high level was provided by the Vare-controlled Republican machine, which took over the city upon the death of Boies Penrose.

Stocked with enough good liquor to outlast their oldest and hardest-drinking members, the Philadelphia Club, State in Schuylkill (creators of Fishhouse Punch), Manheim, Germantown Cricket, and Racquet Clubs decided to withdraw deeper into their impenetrable shells and let the *hoi polloi* go to hell in its own fashion. Even the Union League, ancient *sanctum sanctorum* of the Party itself, and within breathing distance of the stench which emanated from City Hall, sat on its hands while the most corrupt machine in Philadelphia's history ran the show.

Despite the rapidly spreading corruption which contaminated so many of the city's men in power, by the end of 1923 there remained enough public-spirited citizens, including a few Proper Philadelphians, to badger Mayor W. Freeland Kendrick into making an honest attempt at law enforcement. Kendrick was truly a man in a quandary. On the one hand he was being driven to desperation by the loud and persistent cries of the Anti-Saloon League; the Philadelphia Ministerium; the Masons, of which he was an active member; and the hundreds of thousands of decent Philadelphians who wanted their city rid of the scum taking over. And on the other he had an obligation to the Organization, which that year had elected him to high office with a plurality of 249,331 over his Democratic opponent, in a total vote of only 286,350.

Driven to desperation, Mayor Kendrick called in the Marines, or rather their representative in the person of Major General Smedley Darlington Butler. On December 7, the Corps granted a year's leave of absence to Butler, one of its commanding officers, and ten days later Mayor Kendrick announced the general's appointment as Philadelphia's Director of Public Safety. Butler, a Hicksite Friend, belonged to a Chester County family as ancient and as honorable as any on Chestnut Hill. One of the very few living recipients of two Congressional Medals of Honor, the general was hardly the man to be afraid of sawed-off shot guns in the hands of Hoff, Duffy, or Lanzetti and for more than a year did his best to make Philadelphia a "closed city."

Before the machine was aware of what was going on and could take the steps which finally led to Butler's ouster, the general fired five police lieutenants and three sergeants (January 5); closed the city's estimated 13,000 speakeasies for 48 hours (January 7-9); revolver in hand, personally ejected seven gangsters from their Tenderloin hideout (January 15); and with a picked body of honest policemen, swooped down on houses of prostitution, arresting 1,077 Philadelphians, not including the girls, in one city-wide raid (January 20).

Philadelphia was too small for both the general and the

Organization, and one or the other had to go. The job of Director of Public Safety was appointive, not elective, and while enough well-meaning citizens came to the general's support when the Mayor tried to fire him the first time, the Party sat back and waited, knowing what would happen. By the time a second ouster attempt was made, public apathy had set in and Butler was not reappointed. He was succeeded by a series of puppets whose every movement was controlled by strings in the pudgy fingers of the Vares.

Part of the peculiar flotsam of that era drifted into Chippy's office. Paid assassins occasionally got caught so red-handed there was nothing else the district attorney could do but prosecute. Most of these luckless killers were represented by the mob's regular lawyers, but on many occasions the man whose life was in jeopardy preferred to be defended by C. Stuart Patterson, Jr., whose reputation for success was an acknowledged fact within gang circles. And infrequently the mob itself would decide to eliminate legally, if possible, a disgruntled employee and deliver sufficient evidence to establish a prima facie case of murder. In this way a double purpose was accomplished. First, the police had a victim to prove to the public they were on its side, and second, the gang could teach a lesson in versatility and co-operation to potentially recalcitrant members.

As entries in the district attorney's docket book show, the prohibition era brought more and more hired killers into Patterson's Ludlow Building suite, where they awaited their turns seated next to or standing between representatives of the lowest orders of crime. Many of his homicides began to bear the unmistakable earmark of the professional—death by machine gun, sawed-off shot gun, flaming gasoline, concrete mixer. Chippy continued to draw the line between counsel and client and only rarely had any social contact with the gangsters whose worthless lives he saved. The exceptions were the men of whom he was genuinely fond and who themselves knew just how much they could reveal to their peculiarly ethical lawyer, or how far they could unbend with this distinguished, now graying representative of the upper classes.

Much of what little spare time Patterson had then he was spending at Eastern Penitentiary, visiting clients happy to be alive even though their freedom of movement was highly restricted. Chippy had the run of the prison. Colonel Groome, his old friend, had been appointed warden by Governor Pinchot, and whatever information Patterson, Jr. needed was his even without the asking. Chippy was also beginning to develop a friendship with one of the very few men in his life with whom he became intimate. He was Father Francis Hoey, prison chaplain.

"Chippy was a great man and a great humanitarian," Father Hoey said. "His death was a blow to me personally, and I know it must have been a severe loss to hundreds of poor devils he used to represent."

An excellent dinner digesting beneath his black robes, Father Hoey leaned back in a chair in the dining room of the parish house adjacent to St. Joseph's Roman Catholic Church, Ashland, Pa., ten miles west of the work camp where Chippy had spent a summer so many years before.

"I wish someone had taken the trouble to understand Chippy when he was a lad," Father Hoey said. "I think perhaps his course in life would have been different. You know, I'm not at all sure what he believed in. An Almighty God, I guess, but that's as far as he went. We never did discuss philosophy very much. It was always people. The poorer off they were, the better he liked them. That's why, I suppose, prisoners and criminals had so much appeal for him. They were in worse trouble than he ever was.

"I don't know if you've ever walked through a prison yard when the convicts are having a recreation period. It could be frightening to a stranger. They don't like strangers. They stand around in little groups, and some are off by themselves. When a visitor comes by with the warden or a couple of guards, they clam up and glance at the stranger out of the corners of their eyes. These are the men who have sinned against society—murderers, thugs, wife killers, rapists. A pretty tough and desperate lot altogether. Many of them are on edge all the time, and it wouldn't take much to have one pull a 'shiv' and work on someone he didn't like or thought was laughing at him.

"Chippy used to walk through that yard as unconcerned as though he were strolling on Chestnut Street, pausing here and there to say 'hello' to a particular friend. He asked me once if I wasn't afraid to go around unarmed and didn't I think some atheist might try to kill me. I told him a lad brought up in the streets of Conshohocken as I was had little to fear. 'But what about you?' I said. 'Well,' he answered, 'I defended most of them, and they know me.' It wasn't so much of an exaggeration. I'd say that at all times there'd be at least four or five hundred men there he'd represented at some time or other."

Father Hoey poured a brandy for his guest, refused one himself, and went on.

"It was incredible, the number of people he knew intimately who had been raised in as different a world as possible from his own. He used to say there was far more charity among the men on the 'inside' than on the 'outside.' It never ceased to give him satisfaction when he learned what many of the cons, lucky enough to work in the laundry or jute mill, did with their money.

"They got paid six dollars a month. By giving up smoking and candy they'd accumulate as much as two hundred dollars in maybe five years. This they'd willingly turn over to some other con who might need it for an appeal or for his family, and they'd pass on the money to Chip to handle for them. He never kept a cent for the appeal, which he'd try for but which he knew beforehand was impossible. The cash he'd turn over to the prisoner's wife and kids and likely as not add some of his own.

"I came to Cherry Hill in nineteen twenty, but it was a couple of years before Patterson and I got to be friends. I remember the first time I was introduced to him. Chippy wished me success and smiled down at me in that friendly way he had. Then he said, 'If you wouldn't resent a word of advice, Father, take it from one who's been coming around here for a long time. Don't read any books about prison life until you've been here at least five years.'

"Actually, even for a chaplain, it takes a couple years before you're accepted by the cons. I wasn't, I know, until once when I was refereeing a football game, my clerical robes were torn so badly in a scrimmage I had to borrow prison attire. After that everything went fine and they stopped trying to fool me by getting 'prison religion,' meaning the religion they get in jail to win the chaplain over to their side for a pardon.

"There was one thing that used to disturb me very much in my early days at Cherry Hill. Walter Tees, Major Tees—he became warden later on—was stationed at the gate back in nineteen twenty and nineteen twenty-one. Consequently he was the first official to interview visitors when they were passed through. It was what happened to the women particularly, and it was always on their first visit to the prison, when I thought they should be treated most kindly and with the greatest understanding. I'd watch them come out of the major's office, mothers, wives, daughters, the ones most affected by the crime, and they'd be boiling mad and stalk off to the visitors' room so angry they could hardly see straight.

"Often I was going to complain to the warden about this, but then I figured he must know what was going on. He didn't miss much. I figured it was none of my business. The warden had his job to do and I had mine. One day, I couldn't keep it in any longer, and I mentioned Walter's 'abuse' of female visitors to Chippy.

"He listened to me quietly, then he said, 'You know by now, Father, I'm sure, that the toughest visit, especially for a woman, is her first one. She doesn't know what to expect. Her son, or husband, or father's been bad and he's being punished. She thinks all this will be reflected upon her. She's ready to break into tears any second. If she gets sympathy she'll go to pieces, and that would be dreadful for the morale of the man she's going to see.

" 'What Major Tees does is to ask that female visitor a lot of embarrassing questions, all of which are needless. By the time he's finished with her she's absolutely furious.

She's too angry to cry. It's a far better way for her to be when she sees her man than if she greeted him with tear-filled eyes.'

"What Chippy said made a great deal of sense. I discovered that the idea was his and he'd suggested it many years before. Chippy really understood prison psychology. He used to tell me there were only two questions a con wanted answered. 'When do I eat?' and 'How soon can I get out?' I guess he was right at that.

"We spent many an hour together throughout the years, mostly at Cherry Hill, but sometimes we'd meet on the outside. I was with Chippy about a week after his father died. He stayed with me all night at the Hill, and he really talked. He told me much about his childhood—things I can't tell anyone. I felt they were almost in the nature of a confession. But I know this. He loved and respected his father as much as any son could. He felt he'd been rejected, although he wasn't bitter at all. Despite the thousands of men and women who called him friend, he was essentially lonely."

Father Hoey paused, and looked into the distance beyond the windows.

"He was the loneliest man I ever knew."

CHAPTER 40

"MAY twenty-seventh, nineteen twenty-five," recalled Ben Zion, "is one day I'm not likely to forget, and I don't believe Mr. Patterson forgot it in a hurry either. Most of the days I spent in his office were so crowded with action it was hard to distinguish one from the other. But this particular twenty-four-hour stretch had just about everything."

May 27, 1924, was a day of special interest to others besides Ben Zion and C. Stuart Patterson, Jr. It was the beginning of a nightmare which was to last a lifetime for a number of Chicagoans, including two brilliant University students aiding the police search for thirteen-year-old

Bobby Franks, missing from the Northside home of his wealthy parents. It was the day news of Victor Herbert's death reached a saddened world. It was the day the law finally caught up with the "Great Mouthpiece" and the district attorney of New York issued a peremptory summons for the arrest of William J. Fallon.

"Shortly after midnight," Ben Zion continued, "I was in the office when things began to happen. Usually it was peaceful at that time of the night. There'd be no clients around. The majority of our late evening 'customers' by then would have polished off their wine and be sleeping in a skid-row gutter or doorway. Mr. Patterson was out. I didn't know where, but he'd be back. He always dropped in before going home.

"The phone rang. It was Mr. Joseph Sims, the architect. Could I reach Mr. Patterson right away? It was very important. I said I expected him soon and might I take a message. 'Yes,' was the answer. 'Would Mr. Patterson meet Mr. Sims and Dr. Vaux at the Sixth District Police Station as soon as possible?' Ten minutes later the phone rang again. Mr. Ah Hung, a client, and a good paying one, needed Mr. Patterson right away at the Sixth District. Mr. Ah Hung was in trouble.

"About one A.M. Mr. Patterson walked in alone. I gave him the messages. We went downstairs, and Buck Callahan drove us to the Sixth. It was mobbed with Chinese, cops, three Federal narcotic agents I recognized, a couple of hysterical white women in evening gowns, and Dr. Vaux and Mr. Sims. They were waiting for Chippy. So was Hung, who looked much the worse for wear. He was a big man, over six feet, and his collar was torn, his head bleeding, and he was shackled to a city detective. Mr. Sims, Dr. Vaux, and Mr. Patterson went into a huddle."

Ben said it was easy for him to figure out most of what had happened and the rest he was told later.

"The Federal agents, working with city police," Ben said, "had staged a raid on Hung's laundry on Fifth below Race. This was only a front for his opium den. Hung must have resisted, got beaten up and all his customers shoved in the wagon and taken to the Sixth. The women were from Chestnut Hill, big names I found out afterward. Both were Hung's regular patrons and often used to take what they called 'trips to poppyland.' One was a patient of Dr. Vaux, who was trying to cure her. He and Mr. Sims were together when she called him. That's when they telephoned Mr. Patterson.

"The three cousins came out of their huddle and Mr. Patterson talked with the ladies in evening clothes. He quieted them down. Then he spoke with the agent in charge and the lieutenant, who nodded their heads. The women were released and walked out with Dr. Vaux and Mr. Sims. Chippy next had a conversation with Hung, who was all excited. He calmed down when Chip said he'd represent him at the hearing. After that they took Hung away to Ninth and Chestnut, where he was booked. City police handled the patrons, and we got about five or six of them out on copies. By this time it was past four A.M.

"We had a murder case coming up at ten A.M. and a couple of hearings in Central Police before that. I wanted to go back to the office to see if at least the homicide case was ready for Mr. Patterson. But he said we'd worry about that in the morning and told me to come back home and spend what was left of the night with him.

"When Buck pulled up in front of the place and we got out of the cab, a little guy hopped out of the shadows to Mr. Patterson. He was Walter something or other—I just forget his last name, everybody called him 'Wee Willie.' He was a cut-rate professional killer. He wasn't very neat in his work, but then he didn't charge going rates. He had no gang connections, and he'd hire out for anybody who'd pay him. He messed up quite a few jobs."

Ben shuddered at what must have been extremely unpleasant recollections and went on.

"Wee Willie was shivering like a leaf, scared half to death. He'd been hired by one of the Duffy mob to bump off somebody. It was not a gang killing, otherwise the mob would have taken care of the matter themselves. This was a private affair; the victim who'd been fingered for Willie had been playing around with the other guy's wife. Wee Willie always used a .38 with a silencer. It's awkward but effective. He made a mistake, got nervous, and killed the wife, too. The husband was after him, the police were after him, and Duffy was after him. Chippy told him to come upstairs with us and he'd try to see what could be done in the morning.

"When we got upstairs, the place was dark and empty. There was a note from Virginia saying in effect that she'd had it, had packed up her belongings, and was off to Tulsa to marry an old sweetheart. 'That's that,' said Chippy. 'Let's get some sleep. We have a big day ahead of us.'

"I woke up at eight A.M., but Mr. Patterson had already left and taken Wee Willie with him. Later in the day he told me he'd persuaded the little killer the best thing was to turn himself over to Belshaw, who'd give him a square deal."

(The case of the Commonwealth vs. Walter "Wee Willie" Phillips was tried before Judge Barnet on September 15, 1924. C. Stuart Patterson, Jr. was counsel for the defense. Phillips was found guilty of voluntary manslaughter, sentenced to from three to five years, and was out in 30 months.)

Ben continued.

"I went right down to the Bellevue and thought I'd catch Mr. Patterson before he finished breakfast, but John Wickas said he'd been there and gone. I grabbed juice and coffee at H and H and walked over to Sixteenth Street. Chippy was there. He'd worked through half the customers by the time I arrived. This was around eight thirty, and I helped him take care of the rest while he looked over the day's schedule I'd made up for him. I only had the roughest kind of notes ready for the homicide and apologized for their brevity. He said, 'It's okay, Ben, we'll get by,' glanced at them for a couple of minutes, stuffed them and the schedule in his pockets with some other memos, and then Buck drove him to the Hall.

"He had about six or seven in Central Police—drunks,

disorderly conduct, solicitation, streetwalking, the usual run. Then he rushed over to Magistrate Carson's at Twelfth and Arch for two or three more. Then back to the Hall for the homicide in front of Judge Bartlett.

"The case was over a little after noon. Mr. Patterson could have tried another homicide listed that day if we'd have known it would be over that early. But I'd already asked for a twenty-four-hour continuance and we didn't go on trial for that one until the following morning.

"We went back to the office together. It was filled up again, and we were working through clients when Arthur Stewart, a professional automobile thief, busted in. He was all excited, and for him that was highly unusual. The man was normally cold as ice. We went right into the private office. 'My God! Mr. Patterson,' he shouted. 'I've kidnapped a little girl accidentally. What the hell am I going to do?'

" 'Where is she, Arthur?' Mr. Patterson asked.

" 'I got her in the back of a car parked right outside your office. She's sound asleep.'

" 'Ben,' Chippy told me, with a straight face although I knew he was barely controlling his laughter, 'go downstairs and sit in the car with the child and keep her quiet if she wakes up while I figure out what we ought to do.'

" 'It's a nineteen twenty-four red Reo Sports Phaeton, Ben,' Stewart called to me as I went out the door. 'You can't miss it.' "

What had happened, Stewart told his lawyer, was that he had been up in the northeast section of Philadelphia, where he'd spent the night with a friend whose husband was away. He left shortly after noon and while on his way to a cab stand he saw the Reo. "I had no intention of working that day, Mr. Patterson, but I couldn't resist. The motor was actually running." Stewart stepped into the automobile and drove off. He was halfway downtown to a garage which would have taken the car off his hands for a consideration when he heard a child cry.

"I turned around," he said, "and my hair stood up straight when I spotted a little girl, all wrapped up in a blanket on the back seat, screaming her head off. You know I wouldn't harm a kid for anything in the world, let alone take one for ransom. I'd die first. I didn't know what to do. I was afraid she'd start yelling out the window and the cops would come along and I'd get mobbed.

"We were travelling south on Twelfth Street when I saw a baby carriage in front of a house. I jammed the brakes, stopped the car, got out and looked into the coach. I was desperate. Sure enough there was a doll inside but no baby. I grabbed the doll and handed it to the kid in my car, and she stopped crying right away. By the time we got here she was asleep. What do I do now? The girl's parents'll be going crazy with worry."

"How long is it since you took the car, Arthur?" Chippy asked.

"At most, forty-five minutes."

"All right. Chances are the district's just been notified and there'd be no general alarm out yet. Let's see what I can do if we work fast."

Patterson picked up the Keystone and called Hurley Motor Company, the Reo agency, and asked one of the co-owners, Frank Evans, if he had a '24 red Sports Phaeton on hand. Evans answered "yes" and agreed to lend the automobile to Chippy for an hour and balked only when he heard who was to pick it up.

"Not Arthur Stewart, Mr. Patterson, please!" he remonstrated but relented when Chippy promised not only that the car would be returned within a few hours in good condition but guaranteed the agency immunity from Stewart's further depredations. Chippy then sent Stewart to Hurley Motor Company. He returned with the other Reo in about five minutes and parked it behind the one in which Ben sat. The little girl was still sleeping peacefully, hugging the doll close to her.

From the officeful of clients Chippy picked Gerald Taylor, an out-of-town confidence man dressed well enough to look as though he might own a $4,000 car. He told Taylor what to do, and in a couple of minutes, with Taylor at the wheel and Stewart by his side to direct him, the pair drove out to the northeast. Ben followed in the stolen Reo. When they were about a block from the spot where Stewart had taken the car, the automobile thief got out and left the neighborhood. Taylor then parked the car he was driving; Ben walked away; and the confidence man drove that Reo in front of the home from which Stewart had driven it slightly more than an hour before.

There was a little knot of people, including the missing girl's father, gathered around a patrolman on the sidewalk when Taylor stepped out of the car.

"Officer," he said rushing up to the policeman, "I've made a terrible mistake!"

Almost before he finished talking, the child's father flung open the door of his car and gave a cry of relief as he picked up his daughter, who awoke, blissfully unaware of much of the last hour's events. An explanation was simple, Taylor insisted, taking both the patrolman and father to "his" car, a few hundred yards away. He pointed out the strong resemblance between the two vehicles.

"A natural mistake. No harm done," said the father, eager to forget the whole episode before his wife found out he had left the motor of his car running while he went inside. The officer agreed, and since not even the district had been notified, the matter would have ended there but for the unexplained presence of the doll. This puzzled the little girl's parents. Some months later Harry Hoffman, whose car it was that Stewart had stolen, related the incident to an acquaintance, Arthur Mostyn. Mostyn was a detective attached to the automobile theft squad. Hoffman's three-year-old daughter, Virginia, hung onto the doll and kept talking about the man who took her for a ride. She vaguely remembered other bits of her trip.

Mostyn, more out of curiosity than anything else, did some checking; took latent fingerprints on Hoffman's car; and talked with all Reo dealers, including Hurley Motor Company. He deduced what had happened, arrived at a reasonably close version of the truth, and submitted his report. It was turned over to the district attorney's office. Maurice Speiser shook his head. "We'd never be able to establish a prima facie case," he said. Thereupon thoughts of prosecution were discarded, although once

Speiser, who was having lunch at Kugler's with Chippy and Speiser's son, Raymond, told the story in an anecdotal fashion. He watched closely for Chippy's reaction.

"No comment, Maurice," said Chippy, grinning.

It was only a little past three that May 27 when Ben, Taylor, and Stewart were all back in the Ludlow Building. Chippy, meanwhile, had concluded interviews, sent all clients on their diverse ways, and left for late-afternoon hearings in Magistrate Carney's Court, where he represented his usual allotment of a dozen unattached prostitutes. He was in the grand-jury room dictating an appeal to Rupert Razer, the official court stenographer, at seven o'clock when Judge McDevitt sent word that he wanted C. Stuart Patterson, Jr. to represent Violet Dickerson, the "flapper bandit," accused of murdering an elderly shopkeeper the preceding November 8. This became one of Patterson's most famous cases. He and Ben discussed it until about 11 P.M., when the pair finally sat down to dinner at the Bellevue.

"We'd just finished our soup when the captain came over to Mr. Patterson and told him he was wanted on the phone. He got up and returned a couple of minutes later.

" 'I'm sorry to leave you, Ben,' he said. 'My sister called me to say father's had a slight stroke. I'm meeting her at Jefferson Hospital now.'

"He signed our check, left a bill for the waiter, and was about to walk away when he reached in his pocket and took out an envelope.

" 'Happy Birthday, Ben,' he said, handing it to me. 'Here's a little something for your twenty-first.' There was a thousand-dollar bill inside. What a man!"

CHAPTER 41

To C. Stuart Patterson, Jr. the prime objective of a trial was to convince a jury it should allow his client to walk out of the courtroom a free man. Next best was a sentence which would let him do as little time as possible. Frequently his opponents, ambitious district attorneys and their assistants, had reasons other than the pursuit of justice for wanting to win. In the history of American politics many a prosecutor has stepped right into the governor's mansion, and on one occasion, as Tom Dewey has good reason to recall, almost made the White House, after a series of well-publicized courtroom victories.

Two victims of Chippy's successes were Maurice Speiser and Charles F. Kelley, brilliant, ambitious, and politically unfortunate members of the district attorney's staff. Both wanted to rise far above their jobs. Kelley had been winning case after case, was receiving excellent press notices, and looked as if he were on his way up, when he had the misfortune to tangle with Chippy in the case of the Commonwealth vs. Violet Dickerson.

Although nobody can prove this since all the principals are dead, the day after the jury returned its verdict, Kelley is supposed to have said to Judge McDevitt, "My God, Harry! With eighteen hundred lawyers to choose from, why the hell did you pick Chippy Patterson?"

A few minutes past eight o'clock on the cool, clear evening of November 8, 1923, sixty-four-year-old Louis Hirsch sat behind the counter of his Army and Navy store on Market Street reading the *Jewish Times*. He was weary, although not many customers had come into his place of business that day. Now he was waiting for his wife, Rose, to help him count the cash and close up shop. Rose was a bit later than usual.

About a quarter after eight a man in his mid-twenties and a girl in her late teens, later described as a "nice-looking flapper, with bobbed, brunette hair," strolled in.

Hirsch glanced up as the pair walked toward him. He thought the girl looked familiar, but there was so much action during the next half minute this important fact was forgotten until many hours later. There were three people in the store: Hirsch, the "flapper," and her escort, and three different versions of what happened in the ensuing thirty seconds emerged.

" 'The man asked to be shown a pair of pants,' " Hirsch told detectives, according to the *Evening Ledger* the following day. " 'I turned around to get them when I heard him say, "Hands up!" I looked and seeing no revolver in his hand, I decided to take a chance.

" 'I started for the door and began to yell "Police!" Before I had the word out of my mouth the man yelled to the girl, "Shoot him!" About the same time I fell. She certainly was cool.' "

Hirsch stuck to this story with only minor variations. After being informed by Magistrate Dennis Fitzgerald, sent by police to take a death-bed statement, that he had only a few hours to live, "the victim," said the Philadelphia *Record*, "whispered to the girl, brought to the dying man's side, 'You are the woman who shot me. Why did you do it? You are Violet Dickerson. I knew you when you were a little girl. You lived next door to us when we lived on Salford Street. I never thought you'd do such a thing.' "

Violet's companion, identified as Charles Oeffinger, alias Charles Bates, was captured a few minutes after the shooting by two passing detectives, Ferris and Silber. A shot fired by Silber at the fugitive's feet brought him to a halt. Oeffinger told several variations of the holdup, including one which unsuccessfully attempted to involve a young Negro as the "finger man." But in one essential point he stood firm. He continued to swear that Violet fired the fatal shot, even on the night he was told Governor Pinchot had refused to grant clemency and he knew he would die in the electric chair by morning.

Violet told any number of stories, some of which might have come from the pen of Mrs. E. D. E. N. Southworth.

The most romantic one was related in the *Evening Ledger* of November 10.

"Violet Dickerson, the flapper bandit held without bail today when charged with shooting Louis Hirsch in his store . . . unfolded a strange tale of the hypnotic power exercised over her by her sweetheart who she says compelled her to shoot an old man she had known since childhood," said this newspaper.

"Choking with emotion and with tears streaming down her cheeks, Violet related her version of the shooting and what led up to it.

" 'I met Bates two weeks ago and I have been in his company ever since. Immediately he seemed to have me under hypnotic control. He at once could make me do anything. Up to the night of the shooting he could exercise that power.

" 'We have been living on North 18th Street. Thursday evening Bates and I met George Howard. (Howard was completely exonerated and was shown to have only a nodding acquaintance with Oeffinger and Violet.) During our conversation with Howard, Bates and I mentioned we had no money.

" 'Howard said I know where you can get some. An old man who has a store always keeps plenty of money about him. The robbery was planned. Howard gave Bates some money. We went to an Army and Navy store on Market Street and Bates selected a revolver.

" 'We got in a taxi and went to a restaurant and had something to eat and began talking about the proposed robbery. We left Howard, and Bates and I went to our room. There Bates showed me how to use the revolver. I don't want to do anything like that I told Bates and he said, "You must do it."

" 'We entered the store and talked with Mr. Hirsch. At first I did not recognize him as a former neighbor—a man I had known as a little girl.

" ' "Shove the gun against his back," Bates shouted.

" ' "I can't do it." I said.

" 'But again his hypnotic power seemed to influence

me. I took the revolver from my pocket and told Mr. Hirsch to hold up his hands.

" 'Mr. Hirsch, to my surprise, turned around and smiled at me. "That's no way to talk to an old man," he said. "You're only a little girl. You wouldn't hurt me. Put that pistol down."

" 'Hirsch ran to the door. "Pull the trigger," Bates yelled at me. "I won't," I insisted. Bates grabbed the weapon out of my hands and said "I'll pull the trigger then." He leveled the revolver at Hirsch. I screamed. I became so terribly frightened. I was nearly out of my mind.' "

Violet, however, was self-possessed enough to separate from her accomplice the moment she reached the side-walk, fade into a crowd that had gathered, and hop into a cruising taxi. She directed the driver to her room, where she collected her clothing. Then, changing cabs, she was driven to the ferry at the foot of Market Street. Arriving in Camden 15 minutes later, she went by bus straight to the home of her fiancé in Brooklawn. There, according to a story in the *Evening Ledger,* she confessed to her fian-cé's mother that she had shot Hirsch.

Oeffinger, alias Bates, was present during Violet's "con-fession" to the police. By the time she concluded he could no longer restrain himself, although detectives had warned him to be quiet. "You're lying!" he shouted.

On Saturday, Violet and Oeffinger were arraigned be-fore Magistrate Holland in Central Police Court and held without bail for action of the grand jury on charges which included highway robbery and atrocious assault and bat-tery. Hirsch's youngest daughter, Etta, testified that she and Violet used to play together as children. Oeffinger and his companion were re-arraigned, this time charged with murder. Hirsch died in Medico-Chi Hospital, Mon-day, November 12.

Oeffinger was tried before Judge McDevitt on Decem-ber 19. Violet was granted a severance. Oeffinger's coun-sel, Thomas E. Cogan, attempted to prove the girl had fired the fatal shot, using as his strongest argument the victim's death-bed statement. But Kelley, aware that only one of the pair could have pulled the trigger and that the case against the man looked stronger than that against the girl, produced several witnesses who claimed they saw the former kill Hirsch. Oeffinger refused to submit any defense. The jury was out less than three hours before returning a verdict of "guilty as charged." There was no recommendation of mercy.

Chippy's first attempt to see his client a few days after his appointment as her counsel failed. She was otherwise engaged—in giving birth to a boy in the Moyamensing Prison Hospital. To the surprise of any number of South Jerseyites and Philadelphians, including the wife of a well-known businessman, Violet named neither her fiancé nor Oeffinger as the putative father of her child.

"Immediately after the baby was born," concluded the *Bulletin,* "prison authorities notified the Municipal Court and the district attorney. They will co-operate to investigate charges made against a West Philadelphia contractor by the mother."

Chippy was able to delay Violet's trial for nearly a year after her companion was convicted. It was not until Monday, October 13, that the girl faced the same judge who had presided over the case of the Commonwealth vs. Charles Oeffinger. No one looking at a sedate Violet, who entered the courtroom modestly attired in a simple dark dress, would have thought of her as a "flapper." This was in startling contrast to her appearance when she was first brought before Magistrate Coward. Then, according to the *Record,* "Violet was slovenly, dressed in a yellow sweater and short, tight, black skirt. She was full of wisecracks."

Chippy radiated confidence, even though he was cognizant of the law which holds "all participants equally guilty when death occurs during the commission of a felony." Kelley, despite Hirsch's death-bed statement, did not expect a jury of 12 men to send a nineteen-year-old girl mother to the chair. But he anticipated no difficulty in convincing the panel of Violet's guilt. While he hoped for a conviction of murder in the first degree with a probable recommendation of mercy, he would have been satisfied with a verdict of murder in the second degree.

Chippy lost the first round when the Court rejected his motion for a continuance on the ground his client must nurse her baby.

Part of the first, all of the second, and some of the third day was devoted to the selection of a panel. "During the examination of jurors," said the *Inquirer,* "Prosecutor Kelley was met with almost continual declaration by the jurors that they were opposed to capital punishment. It was the opinion of observers that the panelists were grasping at legal excuses to avoid serving as jurors to try the woman defendant."

At one time Judge McDevitt had to declare a recess until a special panel of 100 jurors could be drawn and the talesmen summoned into court. By mid-afternoon of the second day, only three jurors had been selected.

From time to time Chippy attempted to re-unite the baby and his mother in full view of the jurors, but His Honor put a stop to these histrionics. The best counsel for the defense could do was to hold open a door leading from the courtroom to a small chamber which had been set up as a temporary nursery. There, by craning their eager necks, the panel, during one brief recess, saw a touching picture of mother and child in loving embrace. McDevitt, too, saw the stirring pantomime. A large, black screen was all that met jurors' eyes when next the door was ajar.

The fourth day of the trial opened with a major triumph for Kelley. Hirsch's death-bed statement, accusing Violet of shooting him, was admitted in evidence.

Chippy had two major points to get across to the panel, the first that the girl was hopelessly in Oeffinger's power, and the second that Oeffinger, beyond any shadow of doubt, fired the shot that killed Hirsch. For his first premise Patterson developed testimony of a Commonwealth witness and Violet herself, and for the second he used two prosecution witnesses and produced his own "surprise" witness.

Under cross-examination Chippy asked Detective Tyson, who interrogated the pair immediately following the girl's arrest, if he knew how the two had met.

"Yes," answered Tyson. "Oeffinger said Violet was working as a soda-fountain girl in a drug store, where he overheard a telephone conversation in which she was telling some of her troubles to the man who is the father of her baby. After she hung up the receiver, Oeffinger walked over to her and began talking to her."

"Did he promise that he would help her?" Chippy asked.

"Yes," was the detective's reply. "I believe he said something like that. Anyway, he took her to his room and she lived there."

According to the *Inquirer,* "Patterson developed his client's testimony by means of skillful questioning. In her direct testimony Violet stated it was only because Oeffinger had learned her secret of approaching motherhood and had threatened to expose her that she consented to live with him. She declared that she had been held a prisoner by him and was kept in constant fear by him telling her she was being watched and followed, and that he would 'plug' her if she attempted to leave him."

In response to a question Chippy asked, Violet said, "The days I lived with Oeffinger were filled with fear. He struck me in the face and tried to choke me and would not let me go."

Two Commonwealth witnesses offered their own version of the shooting. They were Mrs. Hilda A. Gilbert and her mother-in-law, Mrs. Eva Gilbert.

"On the night of November 8, about seven forty-five P.M., we were on our way to the Stanton Theatre to see Pola Negri," said Mrs. Gilbert, and her mother-in-law concurred in every detail. "But we got to talking and rode past our stop to Twentieth Street. We were walking back on the north side of the street (the shooting took place on the south side) when my attention was attracted by two men inside a doorway, apparently wrestling.

"The door opened and the shorter man ran west on

Market Street. He stopped and turned around and fired a shot."

Since the two were on the far side of Market Street, which is wide enough for double car tracks and four lanes of motor traffic and the view usually at that hour of the evening is limited by throngs of pedestrians, Chippy was fortunate enough to be able to provide an eyewitness closer to the scene of the murder. She was Miss Jennie Mathias, whose testimony ruffled Mr. Kelley's usual aplomb.

"I was within two feet of Oeffinger," she declared, "when he shot Hirsch. I did not see Miss Dickerson at all."

The district attorney, outraged, jumped to his feet.

"Why didn't you come to me with that story?" he shouted.

"I did, Mr. Kelley," was Miss Mathias' calm reply. "But you sent word out to your reception room that you were too busy to see me. So I went to Mr. Patterson instead."

Violet was subjected to 45 minutes of cross-examination, during which the prosecution attempted to develop three major points.

"Isn't it a fact that what Oeffinger heard during that first telephone conversation with your other lover was your attempt to blackmail him as the father of your child?" asked Kelley.

"No. I was asking him to help me."

"Weren't you asking him for money?"

"I was asking him to come and help me."

Kelley next attacked Violet's story of her "imprisonment." He asked her why she didn't leave Oeffinger when he was out at work.

"Because he would go out of the house and keep coming back," the girl replied.

"Why didn't you leave him when you went out to eat?" Kelley probed further.

"Because he always took me out," was Violet's answer.

Kelley got the witness to admit that on the day of the

shooting she was alone in center city, where she met a friend.

"Why didn't you leave then?"

"Because I was afraid."

"Why didn't you tell your friend you were being held prisoner and being abused?"

"That is the reason I was meeting her that afternoon, but she didn't have the time to talk to me, so I didn't tell her."

The prosecution dwelt on the prisoner's previous friendship with the Hirsch family and her knowledge of their finances.

"You knew Mr. Hirsch, didn't you?" Kelley asked.

"I did," Violet admitted. "He was my next-door neighbor."

"Didn't you say in your statement you told Bates he had money?"

Violet thought for a moment and then answered, "Perhaps I did."

Prosecution and defense rested on the afternoon of the fourth day of the trial. Chippy's summation, which was surprisingly brief, stressed the "abuse" of his client at Oeffinger's hands and the latter's ability to "force this child to do his will in every way." It was an effective speech, and the jury was obviously stirred. "Some of the panel," said the *Evening Ledger,* "shed tears as Mr. Patterson concluded."

Kelley, who was bitterly sarcastic, spoke much longer. He ripped the prisoner's story of her dependency to shreds. He also pointed out that in the eyes of the law it made no difference who pulled the trigger. "Both," he said, "are equally guilty."

Courtroom observers felt Judge McDevitt, in his charge to the jury, gave unusually strong support to the prosecution and a number of times re-affirmed the district attorney's contention of "equal guilt." Immediately upon the conclusion of His Honor's lengthy summation, which ended about 6 P. M., the jury filed out of the courtroom and was locked up for the night.

At ten o'clock the following morning the panel informed the Court it was ready to report its verdict. Violet, looking even paler than usual, took a seat next to Chippy's. "No intimation of the verdict could be read from the faces of the jury," said the *Inquirer*. "The court crier called the roll of the jury then turned to the foreman.

" 'Gentlemen of the jury, have you reached a verdict?' he asked in a solemn voice.

" 'We have,' replied the foreman.

"The jurors arose, and at a motion from the court officer, the girl also stood.

" 'Jurors,' commanded the crier, 'look upon the prisoner; prisoner, look upon the jury.'

"Mr. Patterson bent over to reassure the ashen defendant, who was trembling perceptibly.

" 'Gentlemen of the jury, do you find the defendant guilty of murder wherein she stands indicted, or not guilty?' asked Beaston.

"The foreman looked straight into the eyes of the court officer and answered, in a low voice, 'Not guilty.'

"The girl made no sound, but she crumpled in her chair, her limbs too weak to support her slight weight. She wept, her head bowed and partially hidden by the collar of her coat. . . . Judge McDevitt appeared stunned by the verdict. Benjamin Hirsch also was stunned.

" 'My father is dead, yet she goes free,' he said. 'There is no justice.'

"The defendant's father leaned forward in his seat as the verdict was given. Then he stood erect and his eyes filled with tears.

" 'I'm certainly happy,' he whispered. 'God was good.' (He made no reference to the not inconsiderable assist given the Lord by C. Stuart Patterson, Jr.)

"But the happiest moment for the girl was yet to come, when her baby was placed in her arms by the sheriff's matron, who had mothered it while the girl was fighting for her life. As she took the child she realized that now she was free to nurse it to her heart's content (assuming nature would co-operate). With no court or jail attendants to interfere, she hugged the chubby youngster close to her breast and her eyes again filled with tears."

One can only hope the bereaved family of the late Louis Hirsch was similarly moved.

It took eight hours of deliberation for the jury to reach a verdict, it was learned later. The first ballot showed the panel divided evenly, six for acquittal and six for conviction. One by one the former won over the latter, and the fifth and final vote, as Ben Zion phrased it, "put Violet Dickerson on the bricks again."

CHAPTER 42

C. STUART PATTERSON, SR. died shortly before midnight, Saturday, November 8, 1924. George and Eleanor were at his bedside; Francis was in Cuba, a delegate to the Pan American Sanitary Conference; and Christopher Stuart Patterson, Jr. was in Trenton, New Jersey, spending the weekend with a cabaret singer he had met recently. Although Eleanor tried to reach Chippy early Sunday morning, he first learned of his father's death Monday about 6 A.M. when he bought a Philadelphia newspaper in the P.R.R. station at Trenton.

Despite the fact that he shunned publicity and only rarely permitted the use of his name in print, Patterson, Sr. would have been proud of his obituaries. All four morning papers carried laudatory stories of him, each a column or more in length, plus pictures on their front pages. The two evening papers did almost as much, and the *Public Ledger* ran a glowing editorial.

"He was," said this paper, "a prime advocate of the return of railroads to private ownership under government regulations and inspection and declared that most of the post-war labor unrest was due to the radical increases in wages with which the Government favored railroad labor. He was particularly outspoken in his condemnation of Postmaster General Burleson's system of communication which, he said, 'developed one of the most inefficient systems in the world and showed the dangers to which government control could lead.' "

Chippy attended his father's funeral, wandering into the church at the last moment and standing, cap in hand, on the fringe of the small family group which came to pay its last respects to a patriarch who had never lost his dignity. Of the immediate family only Eleanor, seated in a front pew and watching the door from the corner of her eye, saw him enter hesitatingly. She smiled faintly and nodded her head. Mary Tyson, his childhood sweetheart, also saw but did not recognize him. Before the final chords of the organ and choir faded, Chippy slipped out to Chestnut Hill Avenue. He did not accompany the hearse to the cemetery in Whitemarsh Township, where the ashes of C. Stuart Patterson, Sr. were placed in an urn by the side of those of his wife, Ellen, his daughter Jane, and son Joseph.

Some time later, after the will was probated and the press discovered that Christopher Stuart Patterson, Jr. had been disinherited, reporters asked Chippy if he had any comment to make.

"My father," he replied, "left me his good name. No son could ask for more."

Compared to another funeral, which in the broadest sense might be indirectly attributed to C. Stuart Patterson, Jr., the last rites for his father was indeed a modest affair. National publicity for it ran into stiff competition from Chicago, where, according to an AP dispatch in the *Bulletin,* "Thousands paid final tribute to Dion O'Banion, the florist, gunman, rumrunner and highjacker, slain Monday in his flower shop by three gunmen, who called him from his task of trimming chrysanthemums. His funeral was looked upon as the greatest in this city's underworld history."

One of the executioners of the many-sided Chicago horticulturist was Harry Burton, a Philadelphia big-league professional killer. Burton, theoretically at least, should not have been available for hire. Two years before he had been acquitted of a murder he undoubtedly committed. C. Stuart Patterson, Jr. was counsel for the defense.

Late in 1924 Chippy moved out of Pine Street into a two-story brick row house on Walnut Street, in the middle of a typical lower-middle-class West Philadelphia block. Among his many visitors there were Harry Burton and a friend, Kitty O'Connor. Their presence together one night as Chippy's guests, Ben Zion recalls, gave C. S. Patterson, Jr. a chance to demonstrate whether or not he had courage outside of a courtroom.

"Almost every City Hall frequenter, during the days Chippy practiced law," Ben said, "knew he had plenty of guts in front of a judge. You never thought much about whether or not he was brave elsewhere. He was the kind of man who didn't ever seem to have to prove himself. The toughest monkeys you ever saw respected him and probably would have been embarrassed if anybody had insulted Mr. Patterson in their presence. Things like that didn't happen to him.

"Well, what I'm getting at is what happened once when Harry Burton, Kitty O'Connor, Joe Curry, Aggie Allen, and a half-dozen other mobsters and their girl friends dropped in late one night. They were all sitting around in the upstairs back parlor talking about old crimes that would make your hair stand up on end. I felt rather like Jim Hawkins, scrounged up in the bottom of the apple barrel, listening with both ears wide open and no one noticing I was there at all. Nobody was making any noise above the level of conversation because the family that lived next door had a couple of small children and Chippy didn't want them awakened.

"Burton was a vicious, cold-blooded killer with a foul tongue. He could hardly complete a sentence without using several four-letter words. I'm sure he was a paranoiac, which made him painful company. He was insulted every five minutes by somebody's casual remark not at all meant to offend him, and constantly had to be placated. He was tolerated because he was quite good at his work, which was murder. He wasn't a bad-looking guy, not stupid, but I never heard him laugh, and he was insanely jealous. You never could kid him. Not at all like Joe Curry, who had a wonderful sense of humor.

"Joe had a quirk about neatness. He laughed at himself for it. He couldn't stand anything not in perfect order. He used to go around the room rearranging chairs or straightening pictures on the wall. Chippy was always dropping cigarette ashes everywhere, and it was funny to see Joe following him with an ash tray or getting one ready for him when there'd be a long ash still clinging to his lit cigarette; Joe practically put a tray underneath Mr. Patterson's chin.

"You just had to like Joe unless you happened to be on the other side of his gun. Joe was intelligent, rarely used profanity, and never took a drink. As a matter of fact he belonged to the Total Abstinence Brotherhood, which is a Catholic temperance society. If there could be such a thing in his line of work, Joe was a gentleman. Harry, on the other hand, was always having to prove himself.

"The night I'm talking about Kitty was making a play for Chippy, maybe to tease Harry and maybe not. Each time she put a cigarette in her mouth she'd bend low over the table we were sitting around and put her face near Mr. Patterson's so he could give her a light from the Rameses Number Two he always had lit. Burton was getting redder and redder with anger, and his eyes were positively glassy with hate. The rest probably knew what was going on, and they might even have helped along with the needling.

"Finally, Harry couldn't stand it any longer. The next time Kitty stuck a cigarette in her mouth and started to bend over toward Chippy, Burton jumped up, pulled his gun out of a shoulder holster, pointed it at Chippy, and screamed, 'Mr. Patterson (he *still* said "Mr."), you —— son of a bitch. Light Kitty's cigarette and I'll blow your god-damned brains out!' "

Ben paused and stared into space before going on.

"When Burton stopped speaking there was absolute silence and no motion at all. He just stood there, pointing that gun, waiting to see what Chippy'd do. Nobody else reached for their guns although I have a feeling Joe Curry would have drawn pretty quick to try to protect Mr. Patterson, but by then it would have been too late and there would have been slaughter. These men weren't Boy Scouts.

"Chippy didn't bat an eyelash and neither did Kitty. He took the cigarette from his mouth, lit Kitty's cigarette with it, got out of his chair, and walked over to Harry, who all the time had his revolver pointed right at Chippy's stomach.

" 'Harry,' Mr. Patterson said without raising his voice, 'put your gun away and either apologize to everyone here or get out and never come back.'

The strangest thing happened. Burton dropped his gun to the floor like he was hypnotized. It was a miracle it didn't go off. He slumped over the table and started to sob, no tears or anything, just dry heaves, but so powerful you could almost feel the room vibrate. Then he stood up, looked at Chippy, and tried to speak, but he couldn't. He turned around and walked out of the room, and Kitty followed him.

"When we heard the front door close, Chippy turned to Curry. I think he was afraid Curry, who was leader of the mob, would try to punish Burton.

" 'Let him alone, Joe,' he said. 'Burton's a sick man. Don't get involved with him. He's unpredictable.' "

What did Chippy's prosaic neighbors think about the activities in the house next door? Did they know who the tenant was, and were they ever upset by the strange characters who used to come in and out at all hours of the night?

"To tell you the truth," answered Anthony Pagano, an insurance man who used to live next door, "we hadn't any idea who Mr. Patterson was until we saw his picture in the papers after the Olney Bank case. He must have been living next door for over a year then. Sure, we used to see lots of taxis parked outside day and night, and men and women walk in and out of the house. I figured maybe he was a big time 'policy' man, not the kind I sell, you know, or maybe an important bootlegger. But then again he dressed so poorly we let those ideas go. I don't really know what we thought he did. I do know this. He was the best neighbor we ever had, and the kids were crazy about him.

"My little girl, Marie, was nuts about Mr. Patterson.

She was about five when he moved next door, and he never walked in or out of his house without stopping to bend down and talk to Marie and any of the other kids she'd be playing with. He bought her candy and a big doll she kept for years. One time when Hunt's Circus was in town, he asked if he could take Marie and her two brothers, Joe and Tony, to see it. We said 'yes,' and he piled them in a cab one Saturday afternoon and gave them a time none of them ever forgot. He must have spent fifty bucks. They had fifty bucks' worth of bellyaches, too. Everything they asked for he bought them—popcorn, hot dogs, lemonade, ice cream, hamburgers, cotton candy. You know kids aren't shy, at least mine weren't.

"Sometimes, like on a hot summer night, he'd come home early, always in the same cab, and bring a gallon of ice cream with him from Bassett's in the Reading Terminal; that's the best ice cream in Philly. We'd be sitting on the front porch and he'd get out of the cab, say 'Good evening' to us, walk in the house, and come out a couple minutes later with a huge glob of ice cream, at least two quarts, on a plate. He'd hand it to me over the rail which separated our porches and maybe stay outside for a minute and say something about the weather and then go back to his own place.

"On my wife's birthday we had a little party, nothing much, you understand, a few friends and relatives for supper. About eight o'clock the door bell rings, and there's a uniformed delivery boy from the best florist in town. He's got a big box for my wife. When she opened it, there's a dozen of the most beautiful roses I ever saw. There was a card inside that said 'Happy Birthday from your neighbor,' and it was signed in some scrawl we couldn't make out.

"My wife knocked on his door to thank him and ask him to come over and have some cake and wine. He ate a piece of cake, but he wouldn't drink the wine, just touched the glass to his lips and wished my wife good luck. Then he went right back. I don't know how he knew it was Mrs. Pagano's birthday unless Marie must have told him.

"I was at one of his birthdays, too. It was a month after my wife's which is in August. It was around eleven o'clock in the evening, and I had just wound up calling on a prospect. I was walking up to our house right at the same time Mr. Patterson's cab let him and a woman out. He said, 'Good evening, sir,' to me and I answered. My family were all in bed. It was pretty warm, so I sat on a rocker on our front porch to cool off with a bottle of beer, nibbling on a pretzel, before I went upstairs.

"Mr. Patterson and the lady with him were sitting outside, too, talking in low voices. I said, 'Won't you and the lady come over to my porch and have a bottle of beer?' and he said, 'No, thanks, but please join us.' I climbed over, and he introduced me to the woman as his sister. She was a real lady. You could tell that the moment she started talking. There was a bottle of wine on the table in the parlor inside, and she poured just me a drink and one for herself, none for Mr. Patterson.

" 'It's my brother's birthday,' she told me, and she smiled and seemed sort of sad, I thought. 'I try to spend it with him if he's available, but I haven't been too lucky these past years. I made a special effort to get to this one. It's his fiftieth.'

"I was only in his house a couple of times in all the five years he lived next door, but that doesn't mean he wasn't a good neighbor. The best kind to have. You minded your own business and he minded his, but you knew if you needed him for anything he was there. Like the time Joseph got sick in the middle of the night and we had to rush him to the hospital with appendicitis. I didn't have a car then, but Mr. Patterson's cab was parked outside as usual. I rang his doorbell. He answered in a second and I told him what the matter was and what I wanted.

"There must have been a lot of people upstairs, although they were pretty quiet. He called out to one of them and said, 'Joe, please take Buck's cab and run the next-door neighbor's kid to the hospital.' A nice-looking polite young fellow came downstairs, and him and a girl named Agnes helped Mrs. Pagano and me get little Joey in the cab. They both came into the hospital with us and asked if we wanted them to stay or if they could do anything. We said it wasn't necessary, so they went away. Afterwards I saw both their pictures in the paper with Mr. Patterson's. It was Joe Curry and his girl friend or wife, Agnes. But you'd never know from the kind way they acted toward us what they did for a living."

CHAPTER 43

FOR RESIDENTS of a decent well-populated working-class area of North Philadelphia known as Feltonville, May 4, 1926, began in a pleasant, orderly fashion. The forecast was "fair with a predicted high of 70," and in those unscientific days people could be sure the weatherman was right at least half the time. Wage earners who left their homes about 7 A.M. to work in city factories or Frankford mills were inclined to pause briefly and admire plants budding in small front gardens, or even to lay down their shiny, worn lunch cans on wooden stoops for just a moment so they could pull up a weed or two. An hour or so later children, usually at least three from each house, bounded down the steps on their way to public and parochial schools.

Then came a brief respite when housewives gossiped with neighbors over back fences before beginning their day-long chores. In a few homes, and their number was limited because this was a workingman's neighborhood, wives sat with "white collar" husbands, privileged to enjoy an unmolested second cup of coffee before walking to their places of employment in nearby shops or in the branch office of the Olney Bank and Trust Company, where Rising Sun Avenue, Mascher Street, and Wyoming Avenue form a triangle.

This last category included others who would be involved, before this cheerful spring morning ended, in an experience new to most of them. There was Horace Walker, a pharmacist, Walter Miller, a poultry salesman, and William O. Miller, a bank messenger not due at the Olney's main office, Fifth Street and Tabor Road, until 9 A.M. Patrolman Louis Pizzo, of the Front and Westmoreland Station, and Patrolman Joseph Kaelin, of the 35th District on York Road near Champlost Avenue, were on day duty that week and consequently did not have to report until the 8 A.M. roll call. Patrolman Cooper, on the other hand, had come off his tour at midnight and was due again at noon on a special assignment, circus duty at the big top, Barnum and Bailey, set up on Erie Avenue between Tenth and Eleventh Streets.

Actually several Feltonville men and residents of adjoining North Philadelphia areas had already put in several hours of labor by the time even the earliest departing factory worker had left his house. George Stark, who at only nineteen was a skilled automobile mechanic, punched the time clock in his shop at 5:45. Fred Loscamp opened his nearby garage, on Courtland Street near Front, at 6 A.M. Ralph Benkert, a driver for Supplee-Wills-Jones Dairy, had been on the go since 4 A.M., when he drove his loaded wagon out of the company stable to make his daily deliveries. His boss, William Hittle, a route foreman, was on the street ready to check his men a half hour before that. United Gas Improvement engineers Charles McCready and Howard Jane had been on duty since 3 A.M., while David M. Rittenhouse, a night watchman in an Olney factory, completed his day's work a few hours after sunrise.

Since the events of that morning were to cover several square miles of North Philadelphia, there were still others destined to participate directly or indirectly in the drama on which the curtain was to rise shortly after 9 A.M. Critics, all 48 of them, whose future assignment would be to render a review of the play and its cast, were at this time only names on a jury wheel not to be spun for another week.

Sound asleep in his modest row house on Jasper Street and as yet unconcerned with the actions of the supporting cast and supernumeraries of the play in which he was the star, Joseph Curry was awakened about 8 A.M. by his wife, Agnes.

"Get up, Joe," Agnes called. "It's time to go to work."

Curry, the breadwinner, arose, ate a modest breakfast, checked his costume (street clothes and a long black silk stocking), his props (a shiny black, well-oiled .38), kissed his wife goodbye, and was off. He was calm, and if he had any of those queasy feelings that traditionally disturb an actor at the moment he goes on stage, he concealed them well. He was familiar with the theater; he and all the players, Frank "Tenderloin Frankie" Doris, Harry Bentley, William Juliano, Harry Burton, and the "mystery man," knew their lines. The actions had been rehearsed well.

Shortly after 9 A.M., Miller, the messenger, entered the main office of the Olney Bank, where Leroy Stevenson, paying teller, handed him a sack of bills which totaled $80,000 and a pouch containing $317 in silver. Both were to be delivered to the Federal Reserve with other moneys collected at the Wyoming Avenue branch office. Miller was out of the building in less than four minutes. On the sidewalk he was met by Patrolman Kaelin, whose assignment that morning, as it had been on a number of previous occasions, was to act as guard. After greeting each other and their driver, William J. Lee, whose car was parked directly in front of the bank entrance, Kaelin and Miller climbed into the back seat, the money between them, and Lee drove off. Their destination was the Wyoming Avenue branch.

They arrived at 9:16, and Lee parked the car, facing south, on the Mascher Street side of the building, which had three fronts. Miller got out, strode into the branch office, and emerged three minutes later carrying a Federal Reserve sack containing $18,000 more. The runner walked toward Lee's car.

Just as Kaelin got ready to open the door for Miller, a blue Buick sedan bore down on the bank car and stopped short, blocking the former vehicle completely. Five men, their faces grotesquely masked behind silk stockings, and carrying revolvers, jumped out. One fired at Kaelin, and although his shot missed, it was close enough to stun the policeman. Another thug reached in and grabbed the bag containing $80,000. At this moment Patrolman Pizzo got into action, firing from behind a telegraph pole on the sidewalk.

Then, as Miller declared the following morning, "It looked as if there was a war going on in Olney." Joe Curry's beautifully conceived plans that worked perfectly during the first 30 seconds when the $80,000 was transferred from Lee's car into the stolen Buick were blasted by two unanticipated factors. The first was a chance shot from Pizzo's steadily barking police positive which plowed through the heavy metal radiator cover and smashed into the Buick's distributor, rendering that vehicle immobile. The second was the incredible defection of the sixth bandit, whose sole job was to stay out of sight unless something happened to the getaway car and only then to pull up quickly to offer a secondary escape device. But Harry Burton, who police always believed was the sixth man, fled when he heard the firing, speeding off in the opposite direction.

Pizzo's entrance into the act was almost purely accidental. He'd just finished morning traffic duty at a school crossing four blocks away and, for some unknown reason, was approaching his regular beat three minutes later than usual. Under ordinary circumstances, as Curry had carefully checked, he should have already "made his pull" from the police box in front of the bank and have been several hundred yards away, well out of effective firing range.

"I started to cross the street," Pizzo told a reporter from the *Bulletin,* "when I saw Kaelin, whom I knew, sitting in the bank car with Lee at the wheel.

"I waved to Kaelin and then I heard the screech of brakes, and then I saw the automobile containing the gang of men. A little fellow got out, sneaked around to the open door of the bank sedan, and took out the money and transferred it to the big car. In a few seconds shots rang out.

"I stepped back, thirty feet away, and fired. My first shot struck a rear fender but the second hit inside the engine and stalled the motor.

"The man at the wheel got excited and started to shoot. And another man in the machine stood up and with a sawed-off shotgun fired directly into Kaelin's car. Thinking they would kill him I tried to draw their attention to me, and fired three shots as I was running to a telegraph pole.

"The men ran over to the car and tried to push it across the tracks, but couldn't get it started."

At this point, Walker, the pharmacist, entered the scene and provided a brief bit of comic relief, although at the time it didn't seem funny to him.

"I had just stepped off a trolley car at Wyoming and Rising Sun Avenue," said Walker, "when I saw some men trying to push an automobile. So I walked over to help them. When I got within a couple of feet of them I suddenly saw they were all masked and carried large revolvers.

"Somebody in back of me yelled, 'Look out! They're bandits!' Just then two of them started firing at me. One of the bullets passed close to my head and struck a telegraph pole. There was nothing I could do, I thought, but keep running. So I ran."

Curry and his mob, momentarily expecting Burton to appear and to provide them with their reserve escape means, kept fighting a delaying action and at the same time attempting to get the Buick to move under its own power.

Finally Curry realized the situation was hopeless and much in the manner of a captain abandoning ship yelled, "Let's scram!" From that moment on it was each man for himself. One of the bandits dropped his revolver, scurried west on Wyoming Avenue toward Roosevelt Boulevard, and disappeared forever. Juliano, gun in hand, tried to double back on Mascher Street, but as he did he ran smack into Pizzo. The little policeman, who just about made the minimum height standard of five feet seven inches, had fired his last round of ammunition. Before

Juliano could shoot, Pizzo leaped on him and smashed his jaw with the empty gun, taking all the fight out of the bank robber. Although it was not known until later, Pizzo was responsible for still another casualty. He had shot Bentley through the leg.

Curry, Bentley, and Doris, still masked and now armed with sawed-off shotguns, which they had kept on the floorboards of the Buick, left their car in the middle of Wyoming Avenue and dashed south on Mascher on foot. They turned right into Tiber, a one-way street, just about wide enough for a single lane of traffic, and then right again on to Palethorpe, another narrow street. In the middle of the block they spotted a milk wagon, a single horse in the shafts. It was empty. Benkert, the driver, was standing on the sidewalk a few feet away, talking to Hittle, his foreman.

Both men looked up in astonishment to see three bandits, still masked, and with guns in their hands, emerge from around the corner. The tall one, Bentley, pushed the two milk company employees aside and the thugs hopped aboard the wagon. Hardly able to believe the events which were transforming a routine morning into high adventure, Benkert and Hittle watched two of the bank robbers climb over empty bottles, boxes of butter, and crates of eggs to get to the front of the wagon. Doris, who remained in the rear of the vehicle, fired a shot at Hittle. He missed. One of the pair in front seized the reins, while the third bandit smacked the horse on its rump with the flat side of his shotgun, which he then brandished in a half circle from the open side of the wagon while he jumped aboard.

The beast, used to gentle treatment and a leisurely pace, must have been as startled as Benkert. The animal leaped forward and dashed south on Palethorpe, the wagon rounding the corner on two wheels. The horse was the only one of the four who knew Palethorpe offered no escape route but merely wound its way back to Rising Sun Avenue, right where the whole thing had started.

In the meanwhile, normally peace-loving citizens of Feltonville and others who had business there that morning got angry at the uneven battle between Pizzo and the bandits and decided to help. McCready and Jane of the U.G.I., ready to park their truck in front of a job they were supervising on Rising Sun Avenue, saw the robbers turn off Wyoming Avenue.

"As Jane sent his truck lurching after the fugitives," wrote Weir in the *Inquirer,* "Horace Walker, a druggist, snatched a shotgun from the floor of the Buick and handed it to McCready. Swinging his truck into Tiber Street, Jane was first in pursuit of the fleeing badmen, with McCready leaning through the open door, hoping for a clear shot. One thug slipped at the corner. . . . McCready dived from his truck, tackled the fallen outlaw and twisted the pistol from his grip.

"As he did so, an icewagon driver ran up, lugging the heavy axe with which he split 300-pound chunks of ice. The sight of the axe, ugly as a war weapon of the Middle Ages, took the fight out of the bandit, tough 'Tenderloin Frankie.' "

Cooper, the forty-five-year-old off-duty policeman, seated in the first floor of his home, perked up at the sound of gunfire. Sadie, his wife, who was to become a widow in two more minutes, told what happened then.

"Harry was in the dining room. While he was getting ready for work, he was giving the baby, Harry, Jr., his bottle. He heard the shots. I thought it was backfire, but he knew different. So he ran for his gun and out he went. He said, 'Stay in the house with the baby, honey. I'll be right back.'

"As he left the front porch someone called to him, 'They're in the milk wagon.' So he followed the milk wagon, and I watched him until he went over the bridge, at the lower end of Rising Sun Avenue, and that is the last I heard of him until he was shot."

Cooper hopped on the running board of the half-ton U.G.I. truck and he and the thugs exchanged shots. One shot felled him, and he crashed to the ground. Passers-by took him to Episcopal Hospital, but he was dead on arrival. A slug from a .38 "special," ballistic experts later said, had been fired from Curry's gun and struck the patrolman's left temple. He died instantly.

Another citizen, Loscamp, told how he joined the chase.

"I'd left the bank that was held up," he said, "when I heard some shots and looked back. I seen Officer Pizzo running in front of the street approaching the triangle between Mascher and Rising Sun Avenue. Taking notice his gun was empty, I walked up within about ten feet of him and called his attention to the fact. I immediately turned and went back across the street and asked for a gun. Nobody seemed to have one."

Loscamp was apparently surprised and even annoyed by this discovery. He was about to walk away, disgusted, when a woman retrieved the situation.

"I got one around the corner," she told Loscamp, and the garageman followed her. But he never got that far.

"While I was going after this first lady," Loscamp continued, "some other lady leaned out of her second-story window, spoke up, and said, 'I have a gun.' I said, 'Let's have it.' She threw a little automatic out of the window with a clip of cartridges. I was loading the gun when one of the robbers took a shot at me. A Hudson touring car was starting up behind me, and I jumped on the running board. Just before we caught up with the milk wagon this U.G.I. truck pulled up. We were all firing, and they were firing back. Then I seen this party (Cooper) tumble to the ground.

"The U.G.I. truck stopped on Rising Sun Avenue near Fifth Street (where McCready and Jane spied Doris), but we kept on going, me shooting and them shooting back from the milk wagon, which was really rolling. We got as far as Seventh and Erie when the two bandits (Curry and Juliano) jumped off and ran."

Stark, the driver of the Hudson, jammed his brakes and, although unarmed, leaped out of the car with Loscamp and followed. They lost sight of the bandits on Percy Street close to Sixth Street and Erie Avenue until a housewife, standing on her front porch, screamed out in fright that the bandits had run through the front door of her neighbor's home. Loscamp and Stark, close on their heels, followed. The bandits, almost scaring the wits out of the house owners, who were seated in the kitchen, dashed through their first floor and out the kitchen door. Juliano turned right and, limping badly, entered a garage on Erie Avenue near Seventh Street, where he stepped into the arms of a half-dozen policemen who were beginning to fan out.

"I seen Curry on the corner of Eighth and Erie," Loscamp went on. "He recognized me about the same time I reached the corner. He got his gun up half way, and I had the automatic in my hand and shoved it under his chin and told him to drop it. The expression made by him was, 'You have me. Take your hand off my arm. I'll go along.' "

Loscamp was unconvinced. He kept a tight grip on Curry and left the gun jammed into the bandit's throat. A moment or two later, Stark flagged down Patrolman William Booth who was driving by. Booth, in uniform, hopped out of his car, disarmed Curry, and placed him under arrest.

Less than 15 suspenseful minutes had elapsed from the time Miller walked out of the branch bank until Curry, the last of the bandits to be captured, was in custody. One policeman was dead, one seriously wounded (he recovered), and quite a few normally peaceful Philadelphia citizens had proved that given sufficient provocation they would shoot right back at gangsters. A considerably larger number of Philadelphians who read about Cooper's murder were determined justice would be done and quickly. Even the most optimistic of these must have been surprised at the speed with which authorities cooperated.

Curry and his mob had the $80,000 in their possession for fewer than 20 seconds. All the cash was returned to the officers and stockholders of the Olney Bank and Trust Company, who hung on to it until sometime before the national bank holiday of 1932. Then the bank closed forever. Depositors received only a 15% better return on their money than Curry and his mob would have given them.

CHAPTER 44

FOR PHILADELPHIA, which usually took its time about bringing murderers to justice, and for C. Stuart Patterson, Jr., whose many clients benefited by "cooling off" periods normally lasting from six months to a year, the case of the People vs. the Olney Bank bandits proceeded with awesome speed. On the afternoon of May 5, a little more than 24 hours after the unsuccessful holdup, Magistrate Coward, sitting in Central Police Station, held all four bandits without bail for the court and the coroner.

After listening to District Attorney Charles Edwin Fox and five witnesses, a grand jury returned 30 true bills charging the Olney Bank bandits with highway robbery and other crimes. Murder indictments were held in abeyance until after the inquest into the death of Patrolman Cooper. Entrance to the jury room was heavily guarded following a tip to Police Superintendant Mills that the underworld would make an attempt to "spring" the defendants by force.

On Friday, May 7, the coroner's jury not only met but bettered a schedule the public imposed, and the four defendants were indicted for murder. Mr. Fox announced that the trial would begin Monday, May 10, in Oyer and Terminer; that Assistant District Attorney Maurice J. Speiser would act in behalf of the People; and that Judge Horace Stern (later Chief Justice of the Pennsylvania State Supreme Court) would preside. This did not allow Chippy and Lou McCabe, counsel for the defense, much time either to prepare their cases or soften the public.

Whatever salutary effect the swift course of justice was supposed to have on other evil-doers apparently was lost on friends acting in behalf of Messrs. Curry, Bentley, Juliano, and Doris, specifically, and of all other double-crossed bandits, generally. On Sunday, May 8, Harry Burton was shot to death. The police knew at once the sixth Olney bandit had been "taken care of" in gangland's own fashion.

At 9:30 A.M. Monday, May 10, when Judge Stern stepped to the bench, the courtroom was jammed. A large number of seats were filled by employees of the Department of Public Safety, ready for any emergency, while a dozen uniformed policemen stood near the door or walked ominously up and down the sixth-floor corridors. The prisoners themselves, in the custody of the sheriff during their trips between Moko and City Hall, were given additional protection.

"Three roadsters, motors running," said the *Ledger*, "rested near the sheriff's van. Beside the driver of each was a policeman with a sawed-off shotgun, and outside, near Broad Street Station, waited another roadster, similarly equipped.

"The police were taking no chances."

Chippy's first move was to ask for a severance. It was granted. The district attorney elected to try Curry first.

"Outwardly Curry is complacent," the *Inquirer* said. "He is only 28 and appears much younger, a thin, young man. Big brown eyes surveyed the judge, jurors, attorneys and spectators sullenly. Occasionally he smiled, a faint twist on the lips, a smile that did not reach his eyes.

"Mr. Patterson, a checked cap stuffed in his right-side coat pocket moved over to confer with Mr. Fox, Mr. Speiser, and Judge Stern for a moment. Mr. Patterson, backed by his assistant, Louis F. McCabe, leaned on the railing of the bar, jaw firmly thrust forward, face slightly red.

" 'I move that the case be continued on the ground that the defense has been unable, in the week at its disposal, to prepare the case,' he said."

Judge Stern promptly denied Chippy's motion. Following this, Chippy asked that the indictment against Curry be quashed on the ground that he had not been given his legal rights to challenge the arraignment of the grand jury, which, he claimed, returned the indictment within an hour after the coroner's jury had acted.

Judge Stern denied this motion, too, and the trial was on.

Before the first day ended ten jurors had been chosen from four panels totaling 116 men. Women, by mutual agreement, were not called.

Curry grinned as one prospective juror, Joseph de Mayo, was excused from service.

"I'm a milk wagon driver," said de Mayo, "and I was one of the men held up some months ago. I have a fixed opinion all right. I believe this gang is the same gang that held me up. Yes, sir, I can say I've got a fixed opinion."

"He's an egotist," Curry whispered to Chippy. "Does he think it would take six of us to stick up a milk wagon?"

By 4 P.M., May 11, the panel was completed. At 4:25 Speiser began his opening address to the jury, most of whom were married men with children.

Speiser spoke for about a half hour. Members of the jury hardly moved a muscle as he methodically outlined the crime. He demanded the death penalty and scarcely raised his voice even when he turned toward Curry.

"We will show you," he said, "how this man seated before you, with murder in his heart, took deadly aim and deliberately and willfully shot the officer in his left temple."

Then began the march of witnesses for the Commonwealth. One by one they stepped to the stand—Miller, Lee, Pizzo, Walker, Benkert, Hittle, McCready, Jane, Loscamp (who thumbed his nose at the underworld's telephone warnings to stay out of the box), Stark, Booth, the Bakers, Dr. Wadsworth, ballistic experts, etc., and 41 other men, women, and children who saw some part of the holdup and murder.

Curry, who'd been regarding the continuous stream up and down the witness' box with amazement, said to the assistant counsel, "Mr. McCabe, you ought to remind Speiser he forgot the horse."

With the trial following so swiftly on the heels of the crime, leaving no chance for time to cool inflamed public opinion, the best Patterson and McCabe could hope for was the addition of a recommendation for mercy to the jury's inevitable verdict. To achieve this the defense attempted to confuse the panel by raising a series of objections the *Record* called captious. Chippy readily admitted Curry's participation in the holdup. In cross-examination he attempted to show that bullets were flying around so thickly any one of a score of .38s could have killed Cooper. But the Commonwealth's ballistic experts negated that theory.

Chippy's face was grim as the second day of the trial drew to a close. When reporters asked him how Curry felt, he answered, "He's cool enough, but he's not speculating on the results. And that's not for publication," he added.

"At the end of the day the prisoner rose with the white-haired guard who sat beside him," commented the *Ledger*. "He walked over to the door at the right, reached it, and turning, jerked his head in a nod to his wife. She had sat through the session all day. She smiled. Curry turned and went through the door."

There were no smiles on Curry's face when Cooper's widow took the stand late Wednesday afternoon.

The district attorney attempted to portray to the jury a picture of Cooper giving the baby his bottle while holding the infant in his arms just before dashing out of the house. Chippy, who handled Mrs. Cooper with great respect, objected instantly and was sustained by the Court.

"Emotionally," the *Ledger* went on, "the effect of Mrs. Cooper's appearance, the black garments, her grief, her delicate attractive face, her whole manner were dangerous to the future of the four defendants. One could sense that in the silence of the courtroom.

"Mr. Patterson seemed keenly aware of the effect of Mrs. Cooper's appearance. Curry drooped in his chair, eyes sullen, regarding the widow with interest. He appears immune from the probings of any emotion. Never a flicker of an eyelash, never a trace of vexation, or fear or regret. Always calm, alert, nimbly jumping to his feet and standing quietly erect when Mr. Speiser wants a witness to identify him."

The garageman who captured Curry was almost the last to take the stand.

"Fred Loscamp," said the *Ledger,* "thin, brown-shirted, quiet, the star witness, clipping his words crisply, calmly related how he saw Curry on the milkwagon, how the youth fired and how Patrolman Cooper dropped over against the shoulder of Jane, the engineer, on the running board of whose truck the policeman was riding."

The jury was impressed, and even the prisoner seemed to regard him with admiration.

"There's a guy I could have used," Curry told McCabe. "Too bad he's honest."

Curry did not take the stand.

Chippy began his final plea to the jury on the afternoon of the fourth day of the trial. He spoke for only 45 minutes and referred to Curry as "a boy on the threshold of youth whom you men can send to a shameful death in the chair."

Speiser spoke for a little more than an hour. He told of Cooper's courage, of his happy home life, and of the widow he left behind.

"This officer," he declared, "was cruelly, foully murdered at the hands of a man with brutality in his heart. A man who lacked all human compassion—a viper in human form—a beast of prey."

His conclusion "moved the jury to anger," the *Record* commented.

"I sometimes feel," Speiser declared, "I must hold my head in shame because I live in a community where it is possible for men in broad daylight to terrorize communities that are living in quiet and peace of God."

Judge Stern's charge was completely dispassionate and, although short, covered every point raised by prosecution and defense. He gave the jury little choice of verdict.

"You must convict Curry of murder in the first degree or acquit him!" His Honor explained.

"There is no room for doubt. No uncertainty that Cooper met his death from a bullet fired from the milk wagon in which the bandits sought to flee after the frustrated holdup of the Olney Bank and Trust Company."

The jury retired at 9:10 P.M. Grim-faced, the 12 men returned to the courtroom an hour and 38 minutes later and told the crier they had reached a verdict.

"Guilty as charged." There was no recommendation for mercy.

"Curry's mouth," said the *Ledger*, "lifted at the corners in a wry grin when he heard the words. He was as unconcerned as he has been since his arrest."

The prisoner's reaction, according to Weir of the *Inquirer*, "was that of a man who might have been conceding a setback in the opening match of an office bowling tournament.

" 'Well,' said Curry cheerfully as he slapped the table, 'we lost the first round. But we'll beat them in the long run.' "

Two other men accused of homicide committed during the commission of armed robbery received an adverse decision that week. On May 11, the Massachusetts Supreme Court handed down an opinion confirming the judgment of a lower court which decreed Nicola Sacco and Bartolomeo Vanzetti must die for the double murder of a paymaster and guard.

CHAPTER 45

BENTLEY was next. His trial, before Judge Joseph A. Taulane, began May 22. Before the panel was completed Charles Dockman, a loom fixer and juror No. 2, to the utter discomfiture of his associates in the box, began to scratch himself violently all over. His face broke out in spots, and in a few moments the courtroom grapevine had it that Dockman was a victim of smallpox. A quick exodus of all those not in custody began at once. Curry, sitting with other witnesses under heavy guard, asked a deputy sheriff for permission to speak to Chippy. It was granted.

"Mr. Patterson," he whispered in his attorney's ear. "Please ask Mr. Speiser if I can go home, too. Tell him I was never vaccinated."

A court physician examined Dockman and diagnosed his ailment as chicken pox, fortunately beyond the infectious stage. Judge Taulane excused Dockman from duty, another juror was chosen to replace him, and the other members of the panel stayed on, slightly worried about their own physical condition throughout the trial.

Bentley was the only one of the quartet who took the stand. He had an alibi. "Mom," he told the jury, "sent me on an errand." When the holdup occurred, he testified, he was on his way to Sears, Roebuck with 20 dollars to buy a kitchen cabinet. His presence several blocks from the scene of the crime, he swore, was purely accidental. His mother, Mrs. Anna Bentley, corroborated her son's testimony, but nobody believed either of them.

The same procession of witnesses that marched before Judge Stern repeated the parade in front of Judge Taulane, and with the same results: "Guilty of murder as charged."

Juliano's trial began June 1. Taulane again presided. Chippy and McCabe offered no real defense for Juliano. Chippy told Bob Comber, who was covering all the trials for the *Bulletin,* that he hoped with the convictions of Curry and Bentley "there'd been sufficient bloodletting to appease the public" and Juliano's life would be spared. That he almost succeeded was evidenced two hours after the jury retired. Then the foreman sent a message to Judge Taulane asking the jurist whether the panel must fix the penalty at death or life imprisonment if the verdict was "guilty." His Honor answered that the decision was the jury's, not the Court's. An hour later the 12 returned to the box and the foreman made his announcement "Guilty as charged."

"Tenderloin Frankie" Doris, last of the quartet, appeared before Judge Howard A. Davis on June 14. Reporters gave him a better chance than the others and believed Doris would have at least slight hope for a recommendation of mercy. They based their opinion on the fact that he was actually in the custody of police when Cooper was shot.

"Doris," pleaded Chippy, "surely should not be held responsible for a homicide that took place while the defendant was in custody."

But Judge Davis, said the *Inquirer*, "considered the argument and then replied, 'It was immaterial that the defendant did not actually fire the shot that killed Patrolman Cooper, as it is the law that if a murder is committed by any one of a number of persons in perpetration of a robbery, then anything said or done in furtherance of the common purpose is said and done by all.'

"Paterson," the *Inquirer* went on, "then tried a new tack. The law, he agreed, held that a murder committed during the commission of a felony was the responsibility of all who took part in the felony. But Patrolman Cooper, he argued, had not been slain during the robbery of . . . bank funds—the only felony Doris could be blamed for . . . was the theft of a milkwagon."

The panel listened attentively to each argument and, disregarding both, brought in a verdict of guilty, thus fulfilling a prediction made ten years before when Judge James E. Gorman, sitting in Juvenile Court, told fourteen-year-old Doris he had "a good chance of winding up in the chair."

In their cells at Moko the four bandits must have damned their luck on May 4, when Pizzo, dodging bullets himself, and firing from the hip, managed to hit a target two inches wide 30 feet away, and protected by a quarter of an inch of steel plate. But for the damage to the Buick's distributor, it's more than likely Curry and his mob would have made their escape just as they had done on previous occasions, which police say were too numerous to mention.

Only 44 days and about nine hours had elapsed from the moment when Lee saw the bandit's car bear down on Kaelin and Miller to Doris' conviction. Justice was never before served so quickly in Philadelphia.

Patterson and McCabe had not given up. Their first appeal, made to the Pennsylvania Supreme Court, was for Doris' life. It was based on the same argument they had advanced to the jury. But the highest court in the Commonwealth upheld Doris' conviction.

Doris, "Tenderloin Frankie," the only one of the four who did not bear up well, took the news badly. Patterson and McCabe made another try. Frankie, unlike the others, possessed strictly limited intelligence. Defense counsel petitioned the lower court to appoint a lunacy commission to examine him, averring he was in desperate need of psychiatric treatment. Judge James Gay Gordon agreed and chose three distinguished Philadelphians to explore Doris' mental condition and to report their findings to Quarter Sessions Court. The trio, whose combined knowledge of forensic medicine was great, met with and examined "Tenderloin Frankie," then advised the Court that he was sane well within the meaning of the law.

On February 16, Chippy appeared before the Pardon Board at Harrisburg to plead for commutation of sentence from death to life imprisonment for all four clients. His appeal was rejected two hours after it was made.

On March 2 the prisoners were moved from Moyamensing to Western Penitentiary. Informed that gangland would make an attempt to rescue the bandits, the four, on their 190-mile journey, were heavily guarded by members of the Philadelphia Police Department, aided by two automobile loads of state troopers, armed with machine guns, one car in front and one bringing up the rear of the procession.

At Western Penitentiary the quartet was turned over to prison authorities. Guards, carrying rifles, removed the four to a small concrete building which houses the death cells and is separate from the rest of the huge prison. Up a circular stairway, with bars on both sides, the Olney Bank bandits walked to the second floor and their final earthly dwelling place.

Chippy met Governor Fisher in the latter's Harrisburg office, March 3, to plead for executive clemency. The governor's answer, telegraphed to Chippy in Philadelphia the following morning, was "No." On the afternoon of March 5, Chippy visited his clients for the last time and broke the news.

Doris was the first to be escorted from his cell to the thickly screened cage where condemned men speak to visitors. Chippy was unable to communicate with him. "Tenderloin Frankie" was in a state of stupor and beyond comprehension. Bentley was next brought out of his cell and placed in the cage. For several minutes he stood there silently. Then he began to speak.

"Juliano and I have something we think you ought to know, counselor," he said. "We pulled the Westmont Bank job last April. That was a month before the Olney Bank. The cops blamed Mat Overnack. But he wasn't in on it. He wasn't even there."

"You're not conning me, Harry, are you?" Chippy asked. "It won't get you any more time, you know."

"We're not conning you, Mr. Patterson. We can prove it."

Chippy believed him. Overnack had been convicted of complicity in the robbery of the Westmont, New Jersey, State Bank, and sentenced to a term of from ten to twenty years in the State Prison at Trenton. From his arrest to his conviction he had protested his innocence, but the only one who believed him was his attorney, Frank Voigt, of Camden.

At Patterson's request, Sergeant May summoned Deputy Warden McFarland. McFarland, used to "death-bed" admissions, at first was not impressed, but after listening to both Bentley and Juliano for about a half hour, he, too, was convinced their story was true.

But Overnack served nearly six years in the penitentiary before his attorney was able to convince the New Jersey State Board of Pardons Bentley was telling the truth. And then they only half believed him, placing Overnack on parole for three years instead of granting him the pardon he expected. On July 3, 1932, Overnack, a former stevedore, who had always maintained his innocence, was set free.

Chippy saw Curry last. There was a forced grin on Joe's face.

"I feel fine, Mr. Patterson," he said. "Don't worry about me. If you think I'm afraid of what's coming, ask Bucky to tell you what I asked him for."

Chippy smiled, said, "Goodbye, Joe," and turned away.

"Mr. Patterson's eyes were filled with tears," Art May recollected. "And you could have heard a pin drop it was so quiet. There was a couple of Pittsburgh murderers talking to each other in hog Latin and they shut up, too. Right before he was about to go down the steps Mr. Patterson stopped for a second. The bandits called out, 'So long, Mr. Patterson,' and he answered, 'So long, boys,' and walked out."

Bucky Johnson escorted Chippy to the gate.

"Did Curry tell you what his last request was?" Johnson asked.

"No, he didn't."

"He said he wanted me to get him a pair of roller skates."

CHAPTER 46

DURING CHIPPY'S almost total absorption with the Olney Bank trials and subsequent appeals, many of his other important cases were handled by his friends, brilliant, successful members of the bar, delighted to be associated with Chippy as long as they could afford it.

Ben Zion was given a lift by Sam King, a Temple University senior, who chose Chippy for his preceptor.

"Why," King admitted, "I could never figure out. I lived in a dream world for the years I was with Mr. Patterson in the Ludlow Building and when we were kicked out of there and moved to a ghastly place on Arch Street sometime in 1928. I never saw so many gangsters in my life. The office was crawling with them, and Mr.

Patterson's regular clients from Skid Row were beginning to be annoyed.

"I used to get sent out on all kinds of errands and assignments, most of which had no connection with the law. I thought I had my chance one day when Mr. Patterson told me to go out to see a Mr. Eddie Regan at his home on Norris Street and handle a case for him.

" 'It's some kind of a civil suit Mr. Regan has in mind,' Chippy told me. 'You find out what he wants and draw up the papers and I'll process them. I don't know much about civil law.'

"I knew who Regan was, a real big-shot mobster and bootlegger, but the funny part was he started out in life as a stenographer and he once won a state-wide typing contest Underwood ran. Believe it or not, he worked as George Patterson's secretary for three months after he finished Peirce Business School.

"When I got up to Regan's house he was boiling mad. I figured the least that could have happened to him was that he was shot at, but I couldn't understand how that would lead to a civil suit.

" 'Come outside, chum,' he said, 'and look at what some son of a bitch did to my car.'

"We stepped to the curb and there was his big, new, beautiful twelve-cylinder Packard. The body was a special job, heavy armor plating. The wheels had metal protectors so the tires couldn't get punctured by slugs; the glass all around was bulletproof and there was a turret on top of the back seat where he could mount a retractable machine gun. On the other side from the curb the car had a jagged scratch on one of the fenders, about five feet long and maybe three quarters of an inch deep.

"In utter fury, Regan pointed this out to me.

" 'It's a shame,' I said. 'Do you know who did it?'

" 'Sure,' he answered. 'It was one of Max Hassel's trucks.' (Hassel was a Reading, Pennsylvania, beer baron.) 'I think the guy should be taught a lesson so he'll be more careful in the future.'

"I winced when he said 'taught a lesson.' Lessons Regan taught usually eliminated the future. 'Did you talk to Mr. Hassel?' I asked.

" 'I did and what do you think he said?'

" 'What did he say?'

" 'He said, "Sue me!" So that's what I want to do. The car cost twenty-five thousand bucks, and now I'm ashamed to ride in it.'

"I told Mr. Regan I'd take it up with Mr. Patterson, but when I told Chippy I thought he'd pass out laughing.

" 'Good Lord!' he said. 'Regan better forget all about it. The newspapers would love this one. Can you imagine what they'd do with a picture of Regan's car?'

"What Mr. Patterson did was to send up Jean Barrett and a *Bulletin* photographer to Regan's house. When the gangster saw them he got cold feet right away and realized how silly the whole thing was.

" 'How'd you get the scraped fender?' Jean, who understood the situation, asked.

" 'To tell you the truth, Jeannie,' Regan said, 'Mickey Duffy scratched a kitchen match on it and he scraped too hard.' "

It was during the Olney Bank trials and therefore unnoticed by Chippy that Philadelphia's sadly begotten Sesqui-Centennial Exhibition opened June 2, 1926, in the swamps of South Philadelphia where the odor of burning garbage and discarded rubber tires, blending with stench pouring from chimneys of a busy fertilizer factory, was almost enough to deter all but the hardiest of patriots. An occasional summer breeze, sweeping several miles up Broad Street, sometimes carried the smell as far north as City Hall.

On a lazy July afternoon that summer, an ancient Indian pitchman set up shop in a little alley on Walnut Street, just off Broad, near the side entrance of the Ritz Carlton Hotel. The Redskin and the unwashed dog which slept fitfully at his master's feet were contributing factors to the general aroma, much of which was wafted into the elegant lobby of the hotel itself.

Strung carelessly between two bedraggled feathers dangling limply from the Chief's tarnished headdress was his peddler's license. For that privilege to hawk rattlesnake oil on the Sesqui grounds or elsewhere in Philadelphia, he had paid $10 to the city fathers. Business at the gates to the Exhibition where he first set up shop was so bad he decided to move to another site. He may or may not have known why he chose this particular spot, which for a hundred years or more has been a favorite location for mendicants, street hawkers, and Indian pitchmen, who usually were allowed to peddle their wares unmolested by the police department.

Occasionally the Indian would glance down lovingly at the animal who was not merely his best but his only friend. Then the pitchman would look about him in utter disgust, gazing from unfriendly passers-by who ignored him to the haughty hotel doorman who was staring at him viciously.

The Indian might have been dreaming of the happier world of his youth, a "high pitch" with girl entertainers, live reptiles, and a drummer, when he took the next dramatic step. Tossing discretion aside, he picked up a bottle of rattlesnake oil and emptied it in one enormous swallow. Since the liquid was 65% alcohol by volume, the effect on the aged Chief was instantaneous.

He let out an enormous whoop which startled the doorman into reaching, subconsciously, for his scalp. It pulled heads out of opened windows not only in the Ritz above but the Bellevue across the street, and it halted pedestrians dead in their tracks. The only one within earshot not impressed was Traffic Policeman Jack Gahagan, father of 11 children, all boys; for him Indian war cries were accepted as daily routine.

Gahagan left his post and walked over to the Indian.

"All right, Red Feather," he said. "What's eating you?"

The Indian wisely refrained from answering and merely hung his head. The dog uttered a low growl, tugged gently at Gahagan's trousers with toothless gums, then curled up and went back to sleep. The fumes from the rattlesnake oil reached the policeman's nostrils. He sniffed them significantly.

"Okay, Chief. You better go home," he advised.

Gahagan, anxious to return to his job and unsnarl traffic beginning to jam the intersection, turned to the crowd assembled around the Indian.

"Come on," he pleaded good-naturedly. "Break it up! If you want to see Indians, go on down to the Sesqui. They got a million there. More than they got customers."

In another moment it would have been all over. The crowd was laughing. The Chief, after casting an envious eye at the "tip," was packing his bag sadly when out of the Ritz rushed an officious assistant manager. He minced his way to Gahagan.

"You there," he said. "Get this disgusting fellow away from here! He's disturbing our guests."

Gahagan, six feet six, looked down on him while he slowly stroked his chin, still keeping his temper.

"Well, well. Now ain't that just too bad? May I ask who you are? I never seen you before."

"I'm in the manager's office at the Ritz Carlton Hotel. And I'm telling you to get that fakir off our sidewalk. He's been here all morning with his stinking dog messing up our pavement. It's about time you did something."

"Off *your* sidewalk! Off *your* pavement! Mister," said the policeman who despite wonderful self-control was beginning to lose patience, "who the hell ever said it was yours? God dammit, get the hell out of here yourself or I'll run you in, you miserable little fairy!"

The greatly expanded crowd, its sympathies switched to the Indian and Gahagan, began jeering the hotel man, who, nevertheless, stood his ground.

"Go ahead, officer," he warned, arms akimbo, "I defy you to. And if you don't arrest that Indian I'll file charges against him and you, too."

"You'll file charges against me?" Gahagan gasped. "Now I *will* run you both in."

Lifting the hotel man under one arm and the unprotesting Indian under the other, Gahagan strode to the corner, where, to the utter distaste of the assistant manager, he handcuffed his prisoners together. Then he opened the green metal police box, took out the phone, and called for a wagon.

Strolling out of Rubens' Restaurant a few yards south of the Broad Street entrance to the Ritz was Chippy, in time to catch the end of the scene. With Patterson were Ben Lemisch, who in those days was the best-dressed member of the Philadelphia Bar, and City Solicitor Abraham Wernick. The three edged their way through the crowd. Lemisch took one look at the bedraggled Indian standing dejectedly, with the whimpering dog in his free arm, and turned smilingly to Chippy.

"A typical Patterson client. No money, no friends, and in trouble with the law. Why don't you offer your services, Chippy?"

"I will, Ben. Providing, of course, you'll do me the honor of being co-counsel."

"All right, partner," agreed Lemisch. "What can I lose? You take your fee out of Hiawatha's headgear—it looks better than the cap you're wearing—and I'll take mine in rattlesnake oil. I imagine it'll taste better than the bathtub gin your clients have been selling me. Go on, Chippy! Talk to our client."

Patterson first approached the perspiring Gahagan.

"What's up, Jack? These gentlemen giving you trouble?"

"Hello, Mr. Patterson," the policeman answered. "It was nothing at all until this queer butted in. Now I got to lock 'em both up."

Gahagan looked down disgustedly at his prisoners. The tight-lipped hotel man said nothing. The Indian glanced hopefully at Chippy, who, despite his tattered clothing, appeared to be on equal footing with the law.

Patterson cleared his throat.

"This Indian is my client, Jack. Will you release him in my custody?"

"I'd sure like to, Mr. Patterson. I'd like to release them both, but I've sent for the wagon already and if it don't come soon I'll have traffic fouled all the way down to the Sesqui."

"Do you mind if I speak with him?" asked Chippy.

"Go right ahead, counselor. But don't let him get away. I'll hang on to *this* fresh bastard myself."

Gahagan uncuffed the Indian and Chippy took him near the curb, where he was able to shield him from the crowd growing denser by the minute.

"What's the matter, Chief? You don't want to make trouble, do you?"

The Indian shook his head.

"I'm a lawyer, Chief. I'll represent you."

The red man continued to shake his head from side to side.

"Why not? You don't want to go to jail, do you? What would become of your dog then? Come on, old man," Chippy pleaded. "Let me take care of you."

Patterson sensed the reason for the Indian's reluctance.

"I don't want any money. I got plenty." (At the moment he didn't have a dime. Lemisch had paid for his lunch and Wernick left the tip.)

"Don't want no money?" The Chief looked incredulous.

"Don't want no money," answered Chippy.

"Okay, Boss. You're my lawyer."

Then he pulled his counselor close to him and whispered, "Honest to God, Mister, I didn't do nothin', but I got a fin stashed away. Do you think the fuzz'll take?"

"Not this fuzz, Chief. You'll get in worse. Now listen to me. If your peddler's license is all right they won't do anything to you. Whatever the judge hands you he'll have to hand to the hotel man, and he won't give him a thing but maybe a little hell. We'll get a hearing right away."

Just then several sharp clangs of a bell, heard above the din of honking automobile horns, announced the arrival of the patrol wagon. The aged Indian, although still fearful despite the comforting presence of C. Stuart Patterson, Jr., managed to give a nasty leer at the hotel man being led up the steps of the police van.

"You momser! You goniff!" he hissed.

"*What* did you say?" questioned Chippy.

"That momser! That goniff! That nogoodnick bastard! It's all his fault," repeated the Indian.

"That's what I thought you said." Then, over the heads of the crowd, Patterson spoke out loudly to Lemisch.

"Come on, Ben. We'll all go up to the Hall together. And bring Abe with you. He speaks our client's mother tongue."

Into the wagon climbed the prisoners, Patterson, the elegantly dressed Lemisch, Abe Wernick, and Gahagan. The crowd followed on foot directly behind the slowly moving police van, which was hampered by heavy traffic. Jamming City Hall elevators, they poured out onto the sixth floor and into Central Police Court.

On the bench in 625 sat "Judge" Ferd Zweig, one of the few bright spots among Philadelphia's 28 magistrates. Zweig conducted his court with intelligence and humor if not with enthusiasm. Except for a policeman dozing contentedly in a corner near the bench, the "judge" had been alone when the quiet was shattered by the entrance of Gahagan, Patterson, and all the rest.

"Well, gentlemen," asked Zweig. "What's all this about?"

Gahagan answered.

"Your Honor," he said, leading the hotel man and the Indian to the front. "I have charges to make against these two."

"And you, Mr. Patterson?" questioned Zweig, looking at Chippy.

"I represent this gentleman," Chippy replied, standing in back of the Indian.

"What about you, Mr. Lemisch?" continued the magistrate. "We're not often honored by your presence. Do you represent the other defendant?"

"No, Your Honor," replied Lemisch. "I'm acting as co-counsel with my distinguished colleague, Mr. C. Stuart Patterson, Jr., in the defense of Chief Tuchas."

"Oh, yes," said Zweig. Then, turning to Wernick, "Isn't

this out of your territory, Abe? The city solicitor's not involved, or is he?"

"As a matter of fact, Your Honor," replied Wernick, "from what Mr. Patterson tells me, he may very well be, although I actually came here to act as interpreter for the Indian. However, Judge, now that I see you my presence may be superfluous."

"What about you?" asked Magistrate Zweig, casting his eyes at the silent, tight-lipped hotel man. "Aren't you represented by counsel?"

"No!" he answered scornfully. "I'm well able to represent myself."

"In that event," Zweig said, "we might as well begin."

Gahagan made his complaint first against the hotel man. The charge was disorderly conduct.

"What have you to say?" asked the magistrate.

"Nothing," replied the hotel man. "I'll waive a hearing and ask for my release on reasonable bail."

"As you wish," agreed Zweig, knowing only too well that the Ritz-Carlton would quash the case long before it reached trial. "I'll release you on your own recognizance."

"No! No!" growled the crowd, which filled half the seats in the hot courtroom and hungered for blood.

"Yes! Yes!" smiled Zweig. "Don't argue. Besides, you people are making too much noise. I'll clear the court if you do it again."

The little hotel man walked down the aisle and out the rear door. Then the magistrate turned to Gahagan.

"Now, Jack," he asked, "what's the complaint against the Chief?"

The policeman related the facts briefly. He intimated he would be happy to drop the whole thing.

"Has counsel for the defense any reply to the charge?" asked Zweig.

"Your Honor," answered Chippy, "my distinguished colleague and I admit everything."

The Chief looked utterly crestfallen, the policeman disappointed, and the audience depressed. Magistrate Zweig appeared puzzled.

"You don't leave me much of an alternative. Do you want me to fine the Chief or send him to jail?"

"On the contrary, Your Honor," Chippy replied. "The Indian was within his legal rights to give that whoop."

"Come, come, Mr. Patterson. That would constitute disorderly conduct on a public thoroughfare."

"But, Your Honor, *this* Indian was *not* on a public thoroughfare."

"Not on a public thoroughfare, Mr. Patterson?" queried the magistrate. "Where did you make the arrest, Jack?"

"Near the southeast corner of Broad and Walnut Streets where Watts cuts into Marble Court," Gahagan answered. "Now if that ain't city property why I'll . . . I'll . . ."

"Your Honor," Chippy went on, "the spot where the Chief gave his war cry is *not* city property. It is an Indian reservation."

"Wait a minute, counselor," remonstrated the startled magistrate. "You're not going to hand me that old fairy tale about Penn's Marble Court Indian Reservation back of the Ritz, are you? I've heard that one ever since I was a kid."

"It *is* no fairy tale, Your Honor. We'll prove it to you. I've asked Mr. Wernick to have the city solicitor's office prepare a certified copy of the original deed, and you'll see that our client acted entirely within his legal rights. It will take a few hours to prepare, Your Honor. In the meantime, I'd appreciate it if you would continue the case until tomorrow morning."

"All right," said Zweig. "I'd be an ingrate if I didn't do something for you gentlemen in return for enlivening a dull afternoon. By the way, what is the Chief's pitch?"

"Firewater," answered Chippy, "sixty-five per cent alcohol in each bottle. It sells for a buck, eight ounces. You wouldn't care for a sample, would you, Your Honor?"

"Heaven forbid!" returned Zweig. "I've too many dependents. Seriously, Chippy, you realize that if I let the Indian out in his own recognizance and he gives any more whoops you'll get us all in trouble. The hotel has some rights, you know. Frankly, despite you and your learned associates, I still don't have too much faith in that reservation tale. What do you want me to do?"

"Release him in our custody. We'll take him back to the Ritz. Ben will see the manager and we'll set the Chief up in Marble Court. Let him make a few bucks and tomorrow I'll guarantee his appearance."

The magistrate shook his head and laughed softly. "I suppose it can't hurt much if his peddler's license is in order. Okay, Chief. I wouldn't spoil it for the world."

He turned to the courtroom and called out:

"Case continued until tomorrow morning at ten o'clock. Court adjourned!"

With these words the crowd broke into cheers and pushed forward. A half-dozen men seized Chief Tuchas and swept him along the corridor to the elevator. When they reached the first floor they placed him on their shoulders and, surrounded by scores of others, carried him back to the Ritz, his dog clutched tightly in his arms. Lemisch and Patterson brought up the rear, carrying the Indian's pack between them.

Squeezing its way through a narrow corridor, 10 feet wide and 98 feet long, which fronted on Walnut Street between Juniper and Broad, the mob surged into Marble Court, a wide, blind alley the hotel used for deliveries. This was the "reservation." While the pitchman set up shop deep inside the "reservation," Lemisch slipped into the hotel, apprised the manager of the last half hour's events, and got his promise that the Indian would be unmolested.

When Magistrate Zweig convened court the following morning, the room was jammed to capacity. A smiling Indian, pockets lined with yesterday's unexpected take, sat between his two lawyers. The magistrate turned to Patterson and Lemisch.

"Gentlemen," he said, barely concealing a smile on his cherubic face, "how does your client plead?"

"Not guilty," replied Lemisch.

"Go ahead, then."

"Your Honor," Chippy said, "in order to save time we are prepared to admit the Chief gave out with a whoop. However, we would like to call Jack Gahagan to the stand to establish the position where our client was arrested."

Zweig nodded his head and the policeman took the stand.

"Exactly where was the Chief when you arrested him?" Patterson asked.

"He was standing on Walnut Street just off the sidewalk in a little alley called Watts Street, about thirty feet from the southeast corner."

"Now, Jack, Mr. Wernick has a map showing the area surrounding Broad and Walnut Streets. Will you mark an X on the spot where the Chief was standing?"

The chief clerk unfolded a large piece of parchment, which he put in front of the policeman. The policeman gazed at it for a moment or two, then placed the X as Patterson requested.

"Your Honor," Chippy said to Magistrate Zweig, "this map was made by the Bureau of Engineering and Surveys under the direction of the city solicitor. It is drawn to scale. If you will note the spot marked X, you'll see it was placed on Lots eleven eighteen to eleven twenty-one inclusive."

"I see," nodded Zweig.

"These lots are *not* on the city plan because they are not city property. They were part of a tract of land originally owned by the Penns and set aside by them in sixteen eighty-two as a reservation for visiting Indians, to be held in fee simple."

"This is all very interesting, gentlemen," Zweig said, "and I've done a bit of research myself since last we met. You've dug up some fascinating history, but unfortunately for your client it is not legally sound."

"Why do you say that?" asked Patterson.

"Because, counselor, this and other so-called reservations and grants of the Penns were adequately disposed of in the Divesting Act of November twenty-seventh, seventeen seventy-nine under which the Commonwealth became the owner of as much of the soil of Pennsylvania as was still held by the Penns. That ought to take care of Lots eleven eighteen to eleven twenty-one even if they aren't on the city plan."

"But it doesn't, Judge," remonstrated Patterson.

"Go ahead," Zweig said.

"At the time the Divesting Act was passed, the Revolution was still in progress. The purpose of the Act was to get funds for the Army. Thousands of acres of land, including Lots eleven eighteen to eleven twenty-one, were pledged as security and funds borrowed upon them. They were still not permitted to be sold until a subsequent Act of the Legislature granted the Commonwealth the right to dispose of them at public auction. The first buyer was Joseph Ogden, who paid one hundred and sixty-four pounds for them October eleventh, seventeen eighty-one."

Chippy paused and looked up at the magistrate, who nodded his head. Then Chippy continued.

"On June fourteenth, seventeen eighty-two, a patent was issued conveying these lots to Ogden. We won't bore you with their history except to say they've changed hands many times since seventeen eighty-two."

"What's the point of your argument, Mr. Patterson?" Zweig asked. "You and your colleague have proven the Commonwealth had a right to acquire lands and subsequently sell them to Ogden."

"That's true, Your Honor. The *sale* to Ogden was perfectly legal, but Ogden's heirs and executors had no right to dispose of them."

"Why?"

"Because, Judge, when the patent was issued to Ogden there was an additional stipulation—that Ogden pay to the Treasury of the Commonwealth of Pennsylvania on the first day of September, and in every year thereafter, a rental of one acorn. That rental was never paid."

"Can you prove this?"

"At the moment, Your Honor, my evidence is hearsay, but if I may call Mr. Wernick to the stand I think he will give us some enlightening information."

The magistrate looked questioningly at Wernick. "Is

this true, Abe?" he asked. "Don't bother taking the stand, because at this point I believe my humble court is being called upon to perform functions not granted it by the Legislature."

"So help me, Ferd," Abe answered. "The story is true. I verified it a couple of years ago."

The magistrate leaned back and paused for a moment. Then he went on.

"Gentlemen," he said, "you've put me in a spot. I don't want to blockade the rear end of the Ritz. After all, we're here to try one lone Indian on a charge of disorderly conduct. I think maybe we've had enough legal jurisprudence for one day. I suppose, at least I hope, Mr. Patterson and Mr. Lemisch, you have no desire to confound this Court and all you want is to have your prisoner freed. If that's true I shall be very happy to dismiss the charges against the Chief with one proviso."

"What is that, Your Honor?" asked Chippy.

"If I let him go I'm going to request that you and your distinguished associate make yourselves responsible for the Chief's immediate departure from Philadelphia, reservation or no reservation."

"But, Your Honor, would that be morally right or legally correct?"

"I think so, gentlemen, if you'll agree with me that the Penns were thinking of American Indians when they created the reservations and that your client has no right to use Marble Court if he is not an American Indian."

"We'll go along with you there, Judge," agreed Lemisch.

"Stand up, Redskin," ordered the magistrate.

The Indian arose and faced the Court.

"Noble Chief," asked Zweig, "what's your tribe?"

"My tribe?" The Indian frowned and scratched his head.

"Yes," said Zweig. "Your tribe?"

The Chief stood there looking at the magistrate for several seconds before understanding reached him.

"Oh," he answered. "You mean where do I come from? I'm a Litvak, Judge."

"A Litvak, eh? I thought so. A *landsmann* of mine. This is an Indian, Mr. Patterson?"

Chippy and Lemisch burst into laughter as the Court continued.

"I'm afraid, Counselors, Chief Tuchas has disqualified himself. He will not be able to pitch his wigwam on the Marble Court Reservation.

"Gentlemen," the magistrate said, winking at the Chief's counselors, "I think that takes care of everything. Court's adjourned."

CHAPTER 47

THOSE WHO KNEW Chippy well and were with him frequently—Zion, McCabe, Minnick, Joe Sims, Tom McBride—say Chippy's physical deterioration began with the execution of the Olney Bank bandits. He took it very hard. All hasten to add, however, that his mind was just as sharp as it always had been and his courtroom victories as impressive as ever. There's continuing evidence of this in the district attorney's docket books, which reveal that in 1927, despite the time-consuming appeals for Doris and the other three, he defended nine additional clients charged with homicide, and in 1928, 21 more. He kept his record of successes by winning acquittals for most. None went to the chair, even though the majority of these clients facing murder charges were gangsters and professional killers for whom the citizens of Philadelphia were beginning to develop great loathing. The effrontery displayed by mobsters, who were using city streets for internecine warfare and whose leaders bought or rented police openly, was getting under the skins of residents of the Quaker City.

Unfortunately only humble citizens and not members of the power structure of the community became aroused. Those men and women who ardently wished to break up the evil partnership between the Organization and the underworld lacked the strength to do so. The others did nothing. Although referring to a grand-jury probe which occurred ten years later, Marquis W. Childs and John Coburn Turner might have been speaking of the much publicized 1928 disclosures when they told "The Real Philadelphia Story" in the *Forum* and *Century*.

"The Philadelphia machine," said Childs and Turner, "is and has been the property of the 'best' people, the trust-funded and well-to-do, the questionable benefits derived from it have directly or indirectly gratified not so much the ambitious politician as the established property holder whose primary interest is the preservation of the status quo . . . the particular brand of petty conservatism espoused by the G.O.P. in Philadelphia is undeniably based on ownership of longer and somewhat more patrician standing. Translated into terms of Philadelphia politics, this does not mean that the ward heeler in the City of Brotherly Loot is any more resolutely proletarian than his Tammany counterpart but rather that his ultimate bosses exist in a social stratum to which he has no hope of obtaining.

"In addition, the past three or four decades have seen the migration of almost all these best people to the handsome suburbs that ring the city—Radnor, Wynnewood, Bryn Mawr, Elkins Park, Germantown, Chestnut Hill. . . . This hegira has led to an even greater civic atrophy, on the part of the rich and influential, than existed before. The most loyal upper-class Philadelphian will generally admit, freely and with a sort of perverse pride, that the city is only a necessary evil, incident to the main pursuit of the more gracious life. . . . A clear field is thus left open for municipal corruption."

Meanwhile, mobsters went about their affairs, private as well as public.

"After searching for months for Edward J. Regan, notorious gangster, to arrest him in connection with the shooting of a beer truck driver, City Hall detectives found him playing bridge with two other underworld characters in a home in Marvine Street," said the *Bulletin*.

"Regan, with Mrs. Aggie Curry who is waiting trial under $5,000 bail for her part in the shooting, Cappie

Hoffman, another gangster, and Michael Brabazon, 54, were in the midst of a bridge game when detectives came in.

"Regan and Aggie Curry, with a third man known as 'Jew Ernie' broke into the home of Leroy Lynch and shot him when he came downstairs to talk to them, it is charged, and Mrs. Curry beat him with a milk bottle. Regan and Ernie escaped. Lynch, shot through the abdomen, is recovering. Mrs. Lynch identified Mrs. Curry and Regan."

It was the *Bulletin* again which on May 12, 1928 reported further progress and an informal announcement of a betrothal.

"Sought on a hold-up charge," declared this newspaper, "a man and woman slipped into the marriage license bureau in City Hall and out again while detectives searched for them throughout the city. The couple who complied with pre-nuptial formalities one floor below Detective Headquarters, are Agnes Curry and Edward J. Regan."

The bride-to-be gave her occupation as a "domestic" but Lieutenant Charles Beckman of the Homicide Bureau said, "The only domestic work she ever did was to shine and polish guns." The prospective groom claimed he was a "secretary." To this Beckman replied, "All the secretarial work Eddie Regan did was sign confessions.

"I only wish I could have been an usher," he said wistfully after the wedding.

Chippy not only was the marriage entrepreneur but also gave the bride away. On Saturday, the same day the license was issued, the ceremony was performed by Father Hoey in the Cardinal's Chapel in the Rectory at Eighteenth and Race Streets. Cappy Hoffman was best man. City detectives, who first learned of the coming event by reading the *Bulletin*, unromantically combed the city in a desperate last-minute search for the couple whose marriage they would have liked to prevent.

Providing Eddie and Agnes could elude the police, the wedding was scheduled to take place at 10 P.M. It went off exactly on time, and a half hour later Agnes Curry became Mrs. Edward J. Regan. The groom was late for the reception held after the ceremony, but not because police had succeeded in separating the newlyweds.

"It was simply Eddie's intense devotion to business," Ben Zion recollected, "which caused him to get there so late. This is what happened.

"After the wedding all of us except Father Hoey piled into Regan's armored car. Somebody else drove Father Hoey back to Cherry Hill. We went east on Race and then north on Sixteenth, a sort of roundabout way in case the cops were still looking, although I really don't think they believed Eddie and Agnes would have the nerve to get married in Philly.

"This was a Saturday night, remember, and it was during prohibition, so lots of alky trucks were around. When we got near Thompson Street, Regan, who was sitting up front next to the driver, looked out the window and pointed to a huge Mack.

" 'Look at that one,' he said. 'I'll bet she's carrying a thousand gallons. It's Max Hassel's, and I owe him something.'

"Regan turned around to Mr. Patterson. 'Excuse me,' he said, 'would you and Ben mind getting out here and taking Agnes to your house? I'll join you later. I've got some work to do.' We left and hopped a cab. Eddie, Cappie, and three others stayed. They never told us what they did in the meantime, but it was obvious. They had knocked off that load of alky."

Death once more broke up one of Agnes's marriages. On June 30, 1932, Eddie Regan was ambushed and shot down with machine-gun bullets.

On August 17, 1928, a grand-jury probe of crime began. It had two distinct purposes: to find out the strength, width, and depth of the link binding organized crime and the Organization-controlled police department, and to destroy this chain and punish those who forged it. The first objective was a huge success; the second a dismal failure.

Seven months of exploration revealed, among other significant facts, that there were 13,000 speakeasies and saloons in operation within city limits; a police inspector "saved" $193,533.22 in one year out of an annual salary of $2,800; five captains amassed wealth from ten to 25 times their yearly pay; a lieutenant could be bought for as low as $200 a month and sergeants and patrolmen correspondingly cheaper; one bank had on deposit $10,000,000 in "alky ring" funds; one whiskey manufacturer paid $8,000 a month to the "cops" and showed its distribution in open entries on the company's books; one distillery alone shipped out 87 freight cars of illicit liquor in three months; and one small-time munitions magnate sold, within ten months, 450 Vickers and Thompson machine guns and a countless number of shotguns, revolvers, and silencers. The last was of particular significance to Chippy, who defended many of the purchasers.

After all this corruption was revealed, what happened? Not very much, declared the Philadelphia *Evening Bulletin.*

"The results of that investigation," commented this newspaper, "are a part of the history of the city. Not one gangster, known or unknown, was indicted by the Grand Jury in its 34 weeks of service, or went to jail as a result of its activity.

"Police who chose to fight made rather feeble efforts to explain sudden wealth. . . . One made many thousands raising canaries. Another made $7,000 in two years playing craps in the Navy.

"It was all a colorful and intriguing drama while it lasted, but it simply didn't bring results consistent with expectations reasonably entertained by citizens shocked by gang warfare."

The trigger which set the probe in motion and started the march of witnesses (including Christopher Stuart Patterson, Jr.) before the grand jury was the murder of a friendly little man who enjoyed hobnobbing with mobsters but learned too much about them for his own health.

"Gangsters armed with sawed-off shotguns killed Hughie McLoon, 26-year-old former mascot of the Athletics Baseball Club at 1:30 A.M. today," said the *Bulletin* of August 9, 1928.

"McLoon, a hunchback known to thousands of Shibe

Park fans ten years ago, died a short time after admission to Jefferson Hospital. . . . One of the first to reach McLoon's bedside was Magistrate Carney for whom McLoon worked for three years.

"Carney said Max Hoff had volunteered to pay for McLoon's funeral."

Four days later, Monday, August 13, McLoon was buried. Among the mountains of flowers heaped high on the casket, the largest wreath of all, 200 magnificent white lilies shaped into a huge heart, was sent by Max "Boo Boo" Hoff. It carried his card, which read simply, "We miss you already, little fellow." Those moved to tears by Mr. Hoff's touching display of sentimentality would not have been pleased to hear the caustic observation of Lieutenant William Belshaw (an honest cop). "Hoff," said this officer, "ordered the execution."

Two days after they buried McLoon, Daniel O'Leary, one of two brothers Belshaw was certain did the actual killing, was himself murdered, and during the next 72 hours a total of 14 slain gangsters cluttered Philadelphia's streets. On August 17, Judge Edwin O. Lewis ordered the August grand jury to investigate the whole sordid mess and empowered it to call anybody it wished to. The jury went to work forthwith. The former judge John Monaghan, elected district attorney under the aegis of Big Bill Vare but now eager to break away from him and set up his own organization, was in charge of the prosecution. Monaghan was able, ambitious, and knew the score. His assistant was Major Lemuel B. Schofield, Director of Public Safety, who was to die nearly 30 years later owing the government a half million dollars in unpaid taxes.

Another Vare man, Mayor Mackey, after first giving the investigation his lukewarm approval, soon became frightened to death as the lid of Pandora's box began to open and, as the city's chief executive, made every possible attempt to close it. One by one, subpoenaed and volunteer witnesses walked into City Hall, there to be interrogated before the grand jury during its 179 sessions.

On November 10, C. Stuart Patterson, Jr. was asked to

explain his "association" with known gangsters. He was *not* subpoenaed. Nobody will ever know what he said, but after three hours of questioning he walked out with clean hands. The only statement released came from Rupert Raezor, one of the stenographers, who said the jury found "Mr. Patterson's contact with mobsters to be maintained strictly on the basis of a lawyer-client relationship," and furthermore, "thanked Mr. Patterson for his voluntary appearance before it," although the jury was troubled by "Patterson's consistent and continuous victories in the courts, making additional murders more than likely."

CHAPTER 48

CHIPPY had his first heart attack in the spring of 1929. It occurred in court a few minutes after the jury brought in a verdict on a case of Chippy's. Ben Zion remembers the day very well.

"Mr. Patterson hadn't seemed like himself for more than a year before that," he said. "I suppose you could go back further to the Olney Bank executions. I don't think he blamed himself for losing the case—I'm sure he felt nobody could have won—but nothing was ever quite the same after that. He didn't laugh as much as he used to, and it looked to me as though he was tired a lot of the time. 'I'm slowing up, Ben,' he'd say to me once in a while, although he never stopped working and he still wasn't getting more than three or four hours' sleep a night.

"He even acquired a new girl friend, a beautiful Polish kid, a nightclub singer. She was the last one, too, by the way. At any rate, Mr. Patterson started to look awfully bad. He wasn't eating much either. All these years, at least he'd been having a good breakfast at the Bellevue, where John Wickas or Andy Christolas would see to it he had his juice, eggs, kippers, muffins, and coffee served just the way he liked them. Then he stopped that, and many a morning all he'd have would be a glass of aromatic spirits in a drug store, to hold him through four or five hours in court. That, coffee and those Rameses Number Twos. He must have smoked four or five packs a day. He never stopped."

Lou McCabe and Benny Lemisch, who were associated with Chippy in many of his homicide cases, also kept urging Patterson to "take it easy," but as Zion pointed out, this was not the way C. Stuart Patterson, Jr. operated.

"Both Benny and Lou used to tell Chippy all Mr. Patterson had to do was to give the orders and that they would follow through. Not Chippy. He had to interview witnesses himself, visit the scenes of the crime, talk to the prisoner, and everything else that Lemisch and McCabe, who were damned good lawyers, could have done. And Mr. Patterson continued going to magistrates' courts to try petty cases any law clerk could have handled, but he used to say, 'My clients want me. That's what they're paying for (and *that* was really a joke), and that's what they'll get.' "

Among the 16 homicides C. Stuart Patterson, Jr. handled in 1929 (nine with McCabe as co-counsel), the most difficult to defend was Andrew Caulfield, who with his fifteen-year-old nephew was indicted for murder during an $18 holdup.

Twice during cross-examination Chippy faltered, paused in the middle of questions, and leaned against the bench, rubbing his forehead with his hand. Although Kelley, the assistant district attorney prosecuting the case, was a bitter opponent, he knew Chippy would never pretend to be ill to gain the jury's sympathy. He looked up at Judge Gordon the second time Patterson appeared stricken and suggested that perhaps a brief recess would be helpful to counsel for the defense. Chippy shook his head, Kelley shrugged his shoulders, and the trial went on. Patterson's plea to the jury, during which he stressed the fact that his client had been drinking heavily prior to the holdup, lasted nearly two hours. After the judge's charge, which followed Kelley's summation, the jury left the box at 4:30 P.M. to decide on a verdict. Chippy looked very tired.

"He seemed terribly weary," McCabe recalled, "when he sat down at counsel's table. He'd been on his feet since early that morning. I asked him if I could get him anything or call a doctor, but he said 'No,' he'd be all right. I went out for something to eat, and Ben brought him back a sandwich and coffee, which he didn't touch. The jury came back about eight o'clock with a recommendation for mercy, which was the best we could have hoped for. Gordon told Caulfield he was lucky to have escaped the chair, and I *know* he was.

"When the courtroom cleared and Chippy started to walk out, he suddenly collapsed and Ben and I had to hold him up. Gordon hadn't left yet, and we carried him into chambers and laid him on a couch there. He had a hard time catching his breath, although he was conscious the whole time. He managed to smile weakly and kept telling us he'd be okay if we just got him home.

"Luckily Dr. Drayton, court psychiatrist and Chippy's cousin, was working late in his office a couple doors down the corridor, and Rupert Raezor ran to fetch him. He took one look at Chippy, felt his pulse, gave him a shot of adrenalin, and said we ought to get him to the hospital. But Chippy refused to go, and we couldn't force him. 'Call Norrie Vaux!' he said.

"Judge Gordon—he was related to Chippy, too, somehow—reached Dr. Vaux. He was *another* cousin. Norrie rushed right over from his house and Joe Sims came with him. That made four Patterson cousins. It was like a convention. Norrie insisted Chippy go to Jefferson Hospital and wouldn't take no for an answer, and Sims backed him. Dr. Vaux called for the ambulance himself, and he and Joe Sims rode along.

" 'It'll be only for a couple of days,' I heard Dr. Vaux tell Chip. 'Just for observation,' he said."

But Chippy didn't stay even that long. Early the following morning he managed to get his clothes and leave. He was back in the office at eight o'clock and in court by ten.

"I didn't get much of a chance to examine Chiffy," Dr. Vaux said later, "but I knew he was completely exhausted, physically and mentally. Fortunately he had only a mild attack this time. He had a wonderful physique to start with, but he'd been burning himself up for years, and at the rate he was going I don't see how he lasted as long as he did.

"I went to his home someplace in West Philadelphia a few days afterward. He was stretched out on a couch, and I insisted he let me examine him. He'd made a fast comeback and actually didn't look too bad, although I knew he was a sick man and I didn't like the way his heart sounded. I advised him to get away for a couple of months for a rest, but he only laughed and said he couldn't spare the time.

" 'What can I do, Norrie?' he asked. 'The law would be putting too many of my clients away if I weren't around.'

"He introduced me to the woman he was living with. She was hardly more than a girl. 'My nurse,' he said with a smile. She was lovely. Very gentle and sweet. Before I left I called her aside and told her she ought to see that Mr. Patterson got more sleep and regular food. She said she'd do her best but couldn't promise he'd listen to her. The girl didn't look so good herself. She was too thin and her cheeks were flushed. I suspected t.b. Hardly the type to take care of a sick man, but there wasn't anything I could do about it."

That year Chippy, at the age of fifty-four, became a property owner for the first time in his life. He bought, or at least made the down payment on, a cottage near Corson's Inlet, where he loved to fish. It was on a slight promontory, and the nearest house was a half mile to the west. The cottage was surrounded by sand dunes, and the master bedroom on the second floor of the two-and-one-half-story frame building faced the sea with the waves breaking on the beach less than 25 yards away.

Whatever time he could spare from his practice, and this meant only weekends or court holidays and not all of these, he spent at the cottage with Genevieve Kirk (nee

Kirkowski), who had always wanted to sing at the Met but wound up in a third-rate cabaret. The couple were usually joined on Saturdays by Tom McBride, who had a small cottage nearby, and half a dozen or more members of Philadelphia's working press. Shooey Malone and William "Bill" Connelly, chief of county detectives, frequently were there, spending the days fishing for "blues" and tuna and most of the nights talking. Except for his own illness and his worry about Genevieve's deteriorating health, Chippy was happier than he had been in years.

October 26, that bleak autumn day when the market crashed and a new era was begun, passed almost unnoticed by Chippy, who had no reason to be affected by the rise and fall of stocks.

Even though he was evicted next year from both his office and his Walnut Street home, and his health was failing rapidly, Chippy still managed to defend 11 men and women accused of homicide before 1930 ended, winning acquittals for six and manslaughter and second-degree verdicts for four others. The eleventh defendant, Pete Valenti, provided Patterson with a chance for an incredible courtroom victory over enormous odds and gave him the opportunity to prove (posthumously) his theory that capital punishment is not the answer and that it was possible for a murderer to become completely rehabilitated.

On April 9, 1930, Valenti and a companion, Vincent Minotti, unmasked and carrying guns, walked into a grocery store on South Street. The owner and his brother were behind a counter. Told by the bandits to "Stick 'em up!" one of them complied at once, but the other protested, saying "Please don't do this, fellows. Go to work instead."

At this and without warning, one of the bandits, later identified as Valenti, fired twice. The storekeeper fell to the floor, mortally wounded, but somehow able to drag himself into the street, calling, "Stop thief!" before he collapsed. He died shortly afterward in Pennsylvania Hospital.

The pair of holdup men were captured April 27 and

were positively identified. In addition, both bandits admitted participating in the holdup, which, incidentally, netted them nothing. Each claimed the other had fired the fatal shot. Minotti turned state's evidence, and Judge McDevitt appointed Chippy and McCabe to represent Valenti. The case was tried before McDevitt June 18, 1930. Assistant District Attorney Curtis Bok (later Associate Justice Bok of the Pennsylvania Supreme Court) represented the Commonwealth.

According to rules of evidence, the past record of a prisoner may not be brought out unless, of course, the defendant attempts to prove his own good character. There was little chance that Valenti, a convicted dope peddler and burglar, who only a short while before had been acquitted of murder, would try this line of defense. The Court, however, did permit Mr. Bok to elicit what looked like a damning fact, that when the murder took place, Valenti was a paroled prisoner, released by Judge Howard O. Davis after serving only two years of a ten- to 20-year term for armed robbery.

To the surprise of the prisoner, who winced visibly when this testimony was introduced, Patterson raised no objection. In fact, as McCabe said, "he rolled with the punch," and, nodding his head, whispered loud enough for the jury to hear, "Good, Mr. Bok! That's exactly what I wanted you to do."

Just how this would be of value to the defense was not brought out until Chippy's final plea to the jury. Then audaciously he placed the responsibility for the murder right in the lap of the Commonwealth. This was his reasoning:

"Valenti is no good. His record proves it. If Society releases this type of man it deserves just what it gets. Damn the law for this, but don't damn the prisoner."

It was the only argument that saved Valenti's life, the foreman of the jury said later.

"We took twelve ballots," he recalled. "At first we stood eight to four for the death penalty, but we reasoned that Mr. Patterson was right. If Judge Davis hadn't paroled Valenti in nineteen twenty-six, he wouldn't have had the chance to commit murder. He should have been in jail."

McDevitt was livid with rage.

"An indignant jurist, a bewildered jury, and a smiling, grateful prisoner—condemned to prison for life" was the *Bulletin's* lead after a verdict had been reached.

"After Court Crier Harry Beaston elicited the verdict from the foreman, Judge McDevitt plainly showing his indignation, ordered Walter Townsend, the record clerk, to read a list of Valenti's offenses.

"The clerk began, but C. Stuart Patterson, Valenti's lawyer, interjected: 'Your Honor will pardon me a minute, but I wish to make it clear in view of the extreme fairness of this jury, and the equally fair manner in which the Court handled the case, I move that sentence be imposed immediately as I shall make no motion for a new trial.'

"Judge McDevitt made no reply and Townsend went on reading.

"The list, with fifteen arrests, included what might very well serve as an encyclopedia of criminal offenses, including a charge of murder in 1924, *nolle prossed* when a witness failed to appear.

"'It sounds,' said Judge McDevitt as Townsend concluded, 'like the biography of a man who is a credit to the community, doesn't it?' The jurors appeared nonplussed.

"Then turning to the prisoner, Judge McDevitt said, 'If you had your just deserts, instead of being a burden to the Commonwealth for the rest of your life, you would be on your way to the electric chair. . . . The sentence of this Court is that you undergo separate and solitary confinement in the Eastern Penitentiary for the rest of your natural life.'

"Then, as he eyed the prisoner, Judge McDevitt raised his voice and said, 'On your way!' "

Valenti was pardoned a dozen years ago, last of the Patterson clients to be released from prison. He had become a devoted husband, father of three children, a property owner, and the foreman of a small printing shop. His employer, familiar with Valenti's past, says Pete is the most reliable, trustworthy and dependable employee he ever had.

CHAPTER 49

CHIPPY was practicing out of Broad Street Station during most of 1931. Both McCabe and McBride asked him to share their own offices with him, but he refused. Even Ira Jewell Williams, his classmate at Penn, whose firm handled only the best in corporation law, offered Patterson a room, a telephone, and as much stenographic help as he needed, if he'd move into Williams' elegant suite in the Land Title Building.

"I was always fond of Chiff," Mr. Williams said. "Sometime late in 1931 I ran into him on Walnut Street. I hardly recognized him. He was so thin, almost emaciated, and I truly believe he was hungry. I asked him if he'd join me at lunch, and he said he'd be delighted. We walked into the Bellevue. I hardly ever bother with food at midday, milk and crackers at the most, but I thought that if I ate something substantial Chiff would, too, and God knows he looked as though he needed a square meal.

"I was sure he didn't have a cent in his pockets. I ordered a steak, and so did Chiff. I ate mine, but he only nibbled at his. While we were sitting there, I suggested that perhaps he might like to move his office to our suite. I told him we'd been contemplating bringing in a man with experience in criminal practice and my associates and I would be grateful if he'd consider joining us.

"He smiled—you know that sweet, sad smile of his—and said, 'No thanks.' He did appreciate my offer and understood the spirit in which it was made, but he thought that his clients might be afraid of elevators and desert him if he moved to the twentieth floor. 'You probably don't even have a rear exit where a man might make a fast getaway,' he said with a laugh.

"When I went to pay the lunch check, I discovered Chiffy had already signed it. And I was wrong about his not having a cent in his pockets. I noticed he'd left a five-dollar bill for the waiter. That I'm sure was his last."

Even the year when he was beginning to fail rapidly and was stretching his weekends at Corson's Inlet into four days, Chippy still had income enough to provide for a decent office and a modest apartment in town instead of practicing out of the station and sleeping in third-rate furnished rooms. The nine homicide cases he handled in 1931 would have been enough to support most other members of the bar more than adequately. Two or three of the clients involved each voluntarily paid him fees of several hundred dollars, and friends of an alleged murderer he defended successfully raised a defense fund of $1,500, which was turned over to him.

Chippy's big problem until his death was Genevieve's health. His own he neglected completely. In November of 1931, Dr. Vaux, who drove down to the Inlet to examine the girl, told Chippy he should bring her to Philadelphia at once for a chest X-ray. A few days later Chippy took Genevieve to Dr. Solis-Cohen, the famous roentgenologist, who advised Patterson to send Genevieve to a tuberculosis sanitarium immediately. The girl, he said, was febrile; one lung was seriously infected and probably should be removed. Dr. Vaux and Chippy took the much-protesting Genevieve to Eagleville Sanitorium, where she was to remain for at least a year. Chippy went back to Corson's Inlet alone. Except for bare living expenses and Ben's salary, he sent whatever funds he had to Genevieve. This was a period of great loneliness for Chippy.

"On Christmas Eve of nineteen thirty-one," Joe Sims recalled, "my wife and I had just returned from church when there was a knock on our door. It was Chiff, wet, cold, hungry and pretty sick, too, I think, and I believe he was lonesome. Said he thought he'd drop in to wish us 'Merry Christmas' and was embarrassed that he had no gifts for us. He'd been to Gracehill—this must have been the first time in twenty years—to see if Eleanor was there, but no one answered the bell. We knew Nora was spending the holidays with George and his family.

"His clothes were pitiful. He had no overcoat, and it was bitter cold. He was wearing those old fishing boots of his, and he looked as though he'd been trudging through snow up over his knees. We got him into dry clothing—he used to be a much bigger man than I, but the suit I insisted he put on was far too large for him. I don't believe he would have tipped the scales at more than a hundred and twenty-five pounds then. My wife heated some soup for him, and we sat in front of the open fire.

"He told us he'd spent the day up in the wilds of Perry County getting a visiting judge to sign a writ of habeas corpus for a prisoner so the man could be home for Christmas."

Chippy stayed with the Simses for a week. While he was there, Eleanor visited him and brought both Dr. Vaux and Dr. McCloskey with her. The two physicians examined Patterson. Afterward they told Nora that unless her brother took it easy and remained in bed for a year, he wouldn't last six months.

"Even then," Dr. Vaux said, "I don't know if anything can be done. Chiff's just about burned out."

Chippy returned to active duty, although his practice, the last year of his life, had dwindled to almost nothing. Since he no longer had any semblance of an office and was spending only a day or two a week in Philadelphia, his regular clients drifted elsewhere. He even forced the protesting Ben Zion to leave, although Zion was on hand to help any time he was called. Incredibly enough, between February 5 and July 6, 1932, Chippy, without any office or staff and in wretched physical condition, managed to defend four men charged with homicide, winning an acquittal for one and second-degree verdicts for the rest. He made his last courtroom appearance July 6.

He hadn't been to City Hall for more than a month. Except for his weekly visit to Eagleville, he spent most of his time at Corson's Inlet, resting. He wasn't strong enough to go out in a boat, so whatever fishing he did was from one of the piers. On July 3, he grew restless and came into Philadelphia. Since he had only a few coins in his pocket it's likely he hitched a ride. He went directly to the Tenderloin and checked in at the Phillips Hotel, a 25-cent house on Ninth Street near Race. The next morning he tried to reach Ben Zion, who was spending that holiday with friends and didn't receive Chippy's message until late in the evening. Ben hurried down to the Phillips, but by the time he arrived Chippy had already left. Ben doesn't know where Patterson spent that night, but, since he was flat broke, thinks it was in one of the missions or even on a park bench in Franklin Square.

"He wouldn't have been the only one in either place that night," Ben said. "That was the beginning of the depression, and the busiest 'restaurants' and hotels in town were the Bowery missions. (According to the Philadelphia *Record,* during the winter of 1932, more than 15,000 men were sleeping each night in cheap lodging houses with rooms for five cents and meals for ten.)

"I caught up with Chippy the morning of July 5 in the sixth-floor corridor of City Hall. He looked so bad I could have wept. I hadn't seen him for about five weeks, and the deterioration was terrible. His cheeks were sunken in, and he had a couple days' growth of beard. He was painfully thin and could hardly walk. Yet he smiled and shook hands with me and talked as though everything was, as he put it, 'Simply wonderful, son. Simply wonderful.'

"We saw Tom Minnick. I think he actually had trouble recognizing Chip, but he put on an act.

" 'Chip,' he said, 'I'm glad to see you! McDevitt just asked me to represent a couple of colored boys and said to find out if you'd help. How about it?'

" 'An honor,' Mr. Patterson answered. 'Let's see our clients.' "

When that case came to trial, Chippy saved the prisoners' lives. The jury turned in verdicts of voluntary manslaughter. And C. Stuart Patterson, Jr. walked out of City Hall for the last time. He sent almost all of his share of the $500 fee to Genevieve, then went directly to his cottage. He remained there alone most of the time until Genevieve joined him, against her doctor's orders, late in October. Patterson had another heart attack early in November, and the doctor who treated him did not understand how Chippy could remain alive. He weighed less than 120 pounds.

Chippy managed to get up once more, although he was extremely weak. He fished a bit from the pier but spent most of his time on the porch with Genevieve, looking out at the sea. Whatever funds Ben could collect from clients who owed Patterson money, he sent on, but as Zion pointed out, it amounted to very little. Chippy made his final visit to Philadelphia in February. There was no food, very little oil left for the burner, and Genevieve needed medical help desperately. He was anxious to send her back to Eagleville. He tossed aside whatever pride he had and borrowed funds wherever he could. Everyone he approached, and there were quite a few, Ben recalls, came through.

"If they hadn't," Ben said, "I'm sure Mr. Patterson would have accepted money from George or Dr. Francis, and God knows neither of them was stingy. They'd have given him whatever he needed, I'm sure. His sister, Eleanor, was away then or he might have approached her."

Ada, also, has a clear recollection of that last trip to the city.

"I hadn't heard directly from Chiffy for fifteen years or more. We'd drifted far apart. Of course I knew some of the things he was doing. You couldn't look at a newspaper without reading about him, but somehow or other I never saw him. I'd remarried, and our paths just didn't happen to cross.

"One day Gally, he's my youngest son, was visiting me with his little girl. The telephone rang and he answered it. I was playing with my granddaughter, and I suppose I wasn't paying much attention until I heard him say, 'She's right here, Chiff, I know she'll be glad to talk to you.' I picked up the phone and said, 'Hello, Chiff,' and he answered in a voice so soft I could hardly recognize it. He tried to keep the tone light and kid me, but I think the effort was almost too much for him. He said he'd like to see me if I could make it, and when I said I would, he told me he had a room at the Hotel Philadelphian.

"I said to Gally I thought Chiff was going to make a touch, and I asked him to come along with me. We dropped my little grandchild at home, then went to the hotel. We walked to the door of the room where Chiff was staying, knocked, and Chiff said 'Come in.' The room was dark and dreary, and the narrow window faced a blank wall. The room must have been the cheapest in the place. Chiff looked simply dreadful. He was dressed in old tattered clothes, and he had a week's growth of beard on his face. His hair was snow white. He seemed very tired, but when I entered the room he struggled off the bed, stood up straight, then bent down and kissed my hand. I couldn't hold back the tears. We stayed for a half hour or so and just talked about old times and had a couple of good laughs. If Chiff intended to ask me for money, he never got around to it, or maybe all he wanted to do was to say goodbye. He knew he was dying, I'm sure. He never fooled himself about anything."

Ada sighed deeply. "I didn't know it until a little later, but Gally said he'd left a hundred dollars on the dresser. Gally was always crazy about Chiff."

A few days after his return to Corson's Inlet with enough money to last the rest of the winter and to send Genevieve back to Eagleville, had she been willing to go, Chippy collapsed.

Bob Comber and Zeke Hackney, who'd driven down to the cottage with Lou McCabe and Ben Zion, called the doctor. After examining Patterson, who was in a coma, the doctor suggested summoning whatever family Chippy had.

"I don't think he'll last more than a couple of hours," the physician predicted. But Chippy stayed alive and rallied enough to greet his brother, Francis, who arrived that afternoon. Chippy lasted that night and most of the next day. He was conscious much of the time and thought he was alone with Genevieve, but Francis remained within call. Eleanor reached her brother's bedside about 6 P.M. An hour and a half after that, Chippy breathed his last.

"C. Stuart Patterson is dead," said Dorothy Ann Harrison in the *Record* of February 18, 1933.

"In the legal world his passing means the death of a brilliant attorney, who could and would defend anyone at the bar of justice, regardless of their financial circumstances.

"In the underworld, his passing means the departure of a friend, who never turned its denizens down, but who strove with the best that was in him to help them 'beat a rap.'

" 'Chiffy,' as he was known to his intimates, but 'Chippy' in the demi-world in which he labored, died facing the ocean . . . he loved.

"To the Society in which he was born he was an outcast . . . But to the . . . underworld he was the man who stood between them and the law, who made their cause his own, who fought their battles for them. . . .

" 'Chippy' Patterson was a romanticist. About the figures of the underworld he wove a cloak of dare-deviltry and honor. . . . His manner with the women of the underworld was one of his most conspicuous qualities. He had cut himself off from his family but he could never discard his good manners, born of his breeding.

"He spoke to the gang molls as though they were social leaders. A girl with blonde hair and a tough stare was a 'little light-haired, baby-faced child' to 'Chippy.'

". . . Members of the family said the funeral will be held in Philadelphia and will be private."

All other Philadelphia papers carried the obituary of C. Stuart Patterson, Jr. on their front pages. The *Inquirer* summed it up in the final two paragraphs of its column-and-a-half story.

"Last night, as he drew his last breath," said the *Inquirer,* "there was some question among his friends—and they are legion—as to whether his own estate would be large enough to bury him. But that will be taken care of. A telegram carried news of the death to his brother,

George Stuart Patterson . . . until recently President of the Union League.

"And 'Chippy' was at last on his way back to the family that so long ago he forsook."

The funeral, with only members of the immediate family present, was held February 19. After brief services, Chippy's ashes were placed near those of his mother, father, sister, and brother in Whitemarsh Cemetery.

His real mourners were on the bench, at counsels' tables or in 619 City Hall, at Cherry Hill and Moko, in gang hideouts in the Gold Coast, in Skid Row flophouses, in doorways and gutters of the Tenderloin, in half a hundred houses of prostitution, and on windy street corners, selling apples. Who knows, there might even have been a few within the sacred confines of the Union League, the Philadelphia Club, and the State in Schuylkill.